THE
CALIFORNIA
WINE BOOK

Frontispiece: The old Edge Hill property in the Napa Valley is the residence of Louis P. Martini. The small cellar in the foreground still stands, but is idle.

THE CALIFORNIA WINE BOOK

Bob Thompson & Hugh Johnson

WILLIAM MORROW AND COMPANY, INC.
New York 1976

Printed in the United States of America.

1 2 3 4 5 6 7 8 9 10

MAPS BY HAROLYN THOMPSON

BOOK DESIGNED BY SALLIE BALDWIN

Library of Congress Cataloging in Publication Data
Thompson, Bob.   The California wine book.
1.   Wine and wine making—California.   I.   Johnson, Hugh, joint
author.   II.   Title.
TP557.T48   641.2'2'09794   76-21353
ISBN 0-688-03087-4

Contents

LIST OF MAPS

*Remember, the book you are reading
is one man's opinion of moonlight.*
— DONOVAN

In the Paul Masson finishing cellars at Saratoga, the ovals are oak, the upright tanks of redwood. (WINE INSTITUTE)

Foreword

"The discovery of a new vineyard*
does more for the happiness of mankind
than the discovery of a new star."

To any wine-lover with unatrophied taste buds and an open mind, California's wine is the most important development, the best news, since the Romans planted the vine on the slopes of Burgundy and in the sand and gravel around Bordeaux. Quite simply, the vine has found a new home in California comparable with the places in Europe (above all in France) where its best products have evolved over two thousand years of cultivation.

This sounds perhaps as though it were just a matter of location: a simple change of address. It is much more. The elements which produce a Bordeaux or a Burgundy or a Rhineland comprise first and foremost the soil and the climate (which together dictate the essential character of the wine), but parallel and just as important are the social conditions—in marketing terms, the demand.

It is no coincidence that California is among the intellectual and cultural centers of the world today, and also the place that has revolutionized wine. Californians believe in present pleasure, and they welcome new ideas. The time, the energy, and the resources many Californians are prepared to spend on refining their

*Brillat-Savarin wrote "dish"—but who in France in 1825 could have dreamed of such new vineyards as California?

pleasures can only be compared, historically, with the ways of a tiny class of aristocrats in old monarchical Europe.

In Europe the great growths developed to answer the demands of the aristocracy. In an English nobleman's cellar a hundred years ago, you would find only first-growths: it was logical that the first stratum of society should drink the first stratum of wine. But more important for us, the first stratum of society had very few members; the demand for first-growths was therefore known and the supply limited accordingly. It is not (saving their graces) that Lafite, Haut-Brion, Latour, and the rest were the only fields in France capable of making wine of that quality. Rather, it was an historical accident that they were discovered and developed ahead of their neighbors or of any other of the hundreds of acres which probably, but unprovably, could make wine as good—though, of course, marginally different.

France's wine system modeled itself on the social system, congealed around it, and was sanctified in its unfluid state by a theologically complicated Koran of laws, which attempted to say, once and for all, which field produced better wine than which. Masterly though these classifications are, there is one kind of change they cannot resist, and that is the kind that shaped them: the demand. The aristocracy has gone. Its place has been taken by the affluent society. It is asking too much of France's old vineyards to supply the world's affluent society with the precise wine that was developed for a tiny European aristocracy. Inevitably prices have risen, and just as inevitably standards have fallen. To a point compromise has worked, but if the new world (in its broadest sense) was to use wine as freely and naturally as the old one did, it had to develop its own wine idiom: to reinvent wine in its own terms.

Here not only geography, but history was kind to California. A century ago it was fully realized by the few French winemakers who knew California that her climate was the grapevine's elysium. By the early years of this century she was on the way to building an industry which, had it grown unchecked, would by now be one of the world's biggest. But Prohibition stood in its path. California was forcibly retired from the race. By the time wine making really got under way again in the early fifties, there was little in the way of active tradition to hinder a totally new back-to-square-one approach to making wine. That clean slate was the one good gift of Prohibition. It has allowed California to look for quality by scientific means.

This is not to say that winemakers in California don't constantly refer back to the European originals of the wines they make. They cannot avoid comparisons—if only because most of their vines come from France. It is a truism that a California (or for that matter a French) wine should be judged on its own merits and not on its likeness to something else. There is nonetheless an irresistible fascination in making the appropriate comparisons, and a lot to learn from them.

So what sort of wine does California make? And how does it compare with French?—above all in the vital matter of value.

To attempt an impossible generalization, one might say that California's wines combine strength with gentleness and a clean, straightforward, uncomplicated taste. By strength I don't mean alcoholic wallop or excessive headiness, but warm wineyness: the character of wine made from fully ripe grapes. What other characteristics they have depends on their grape varieties and on whether they were made for immediate drinking or for maturing. But as between any pair of similar wines, the one Californian and the other European, it is its gentleness (softness is too strong a word in the case of a well-made wine) which marks the Californian, the result of lower acidity at harvest time. From this distinction it should be clear that there is no way of saying if the California wine is "better" than the French, or the other way around. There is a built-in difference in style which makes each "better" to the person who is looking for what it has to offer.

But, both from the point of view of ripeness and of clean, memorable, repeatable flavors, California wines are designed precisely for American life. They match American cooking, which is generous with good ingredients, well seasoned and not overly subtle. If God had set about creating the ideal mealtime drink for America (which, I suppose, is pretty much what He did), California wine, the sort bottled in gallon and half-gallon jugs for national distribution, is the best answer you could expect even Him to come up with.

At this level there is scarcely a comparison to make: Europe (alas!) has nothing to match California's jug wines for quality and value. Where comparisons become significant is among premium wines selling for relatively high prices. Here some of California's winemakers, including very good ones, have overplayed their hands. Good as their wines are, they have been anxious to have them valued as highly, and therefore priced as high, as first-class French wines with generations of reputation behind them. The rarity value of the tiny production of a "boutique" has been an artificial aid to high prices. Time will tell what their level should be, but for the moment the consumer must be wary, start near the bottom and work on up only as far as he feels he is getting more for his extra dollars.

This advice, be it said, is just as applicable to European wines as it is to Californian. But with European wine, the consumer has the advantage of a vast body of both lore and laws, the conventional wisdom (occasionally misleading, but usually sound) which places, let us say, Muscadet below Chablis in quality but above it in value for money, and the regulations under which, for example, a Beaujolais-Villages is almost bound to be a better wine than a simple Beaujolais.

In contrast, California wine is a free-for-all. There simply has not been time for such patterns to emerge, and neither time nor much inclination for the law-giver to get to work. No quality classification has ever been attempted or even suggested. The industry has grown so fast that it scarcely knows itself. Its imagery and terminology are immature, barely coherent.

All hopes for future coherence center around California's distinctive emphasis on the grape variety. The naming of "varietal," as opposed to "generic," wines was the first intimation that California had progressed from imitation to invention.

Varietal names have already become the customary way to refer to the better categories and styles of table wine; in themselves they have a "premium" connotation—which they may or may not deserve.

While the jungle is the most exciting place to walk, it holds no guarantee against pitfalls. In these circumstances, the one refuge is the brand name, yet brand names have sprung up and changed hands so fast that no one has been able to keep pace with them all.

California wine is, in fact, at that fascinating stage of its development where the basic grammar has yet to be written and is probably still unwritable. The urge to work on it, however, has hit many people. At this moment who knows how many contributors to its future syntax are tasting and thinking their way through its components, establishing the grounds for discussion?

Bob Thompson and I have been among them, he for the last twenty years, I (though mainly from the safe distance of Europe) for the last ten. Five years ago we decided to make a joint contribution: to build our discussions into a book that might help get the eventual grammar under way. The giddy lurchings of an industry booming out of control made sure that nothing permanently useful would emerge for four of those years. At last, in a year of uneasy calm, it has held still long enough for us to get it in focus.

Bob's involvement with his subject is easier for me to talk about than for him. He lives near San Francisco. His ties with the wine industry, professional and amateur, go back through most of its modern (i.e., post-1950) history, yet he has never been involved in any one facet of it. The winemakers are his friends, their products his constant study and delight. Above all he is a thoughtful master of the difficult passage of understanding from palate to prose. No one excites my professional admiration more than he for his ability to pinpoint tastes in simple phrases which convey a clear idea.

This book, then, is our report on a formative stage in the early life of one of the world's great vineyards and on an industry that has already started to give America as much harmless pleasure as any from Maine to Mexico.

HUGH JOHNSON
Gt. Saling, Essex, England
August 1975

PART ONE

THE
WINERIES
and
VINEYARDS

The Scene

Now is not the easiest time to begin looking into the subtleties of California wine. The easiest time was in the early 1960s when a collector could buy four Cabernet Sauvignons and know all he needed to know about that type, when three Chardonnays were enough, when Zinfandel was the most intriguing wine of the lot, if only because the greatest number of people were making it.

But now is a more engrossing time. Two dozen Cabernet Sauvignons demand consideration. Distinctive Chardonnays are present in equal numbers. Half a dozen other wine types have developed age-worthy qualities, and Zinfandels are more diversely rewarding than ever.

The pain and pleasure of the moment is that no one can be sure from month to month which two dozen of any type are the essential ones. Cellars with fewer than ten years behind them are winning first places in comparative blind tastings against the venerable best. Counties which had fewer than 500 acres of wine vineyards a decade ago now have 35,000 acres in grapes. Old truths disappear beneath an almost daily onslaught of new wines.

On the face of it such rapid change would seem to be anarchy. I think it is not. To be sure, California wine is not in a state of stability, but it is not in the midst of anarchy, either. The winemakers are hewing to an old and remarkably consistent line. They are just hewing fast.

A student of wines has to master only three generalities to make sense of the subject no matter how volatile its details. I. The slings and arrows of an outrageously short history have kept the community of winemakers small enough for a little change to go a long way. II. Steady change is an acceptable part of a highly trained technological society, which, in California, includes both the winemakers and their prime customers. III. California terrain and climate interact far differently than do their counterparts in Europe. Although this condition is unchangeable, it requires an altered state of mind in all who learned their basics elsewhere, but wish to study California as it now is.

I

California soil began yielding wine in the late 1770s when Franciscan missionaries planted a coarse grape, later known as the mission, at each of the way stations on their colonizing march from San Diego northward to Sonoma.

Although the geographic scope was large, the audience was minute, the production of twenty missions together measured in mere thousands of gallons.

The Gold Rush of 1849 brought population, wealth, and a number of European immigrants who were able winemakers. Through the end of the nineteenth century these Europeans imported cuttings of the finest traditional grape varieties from their homelands. With the broadened spectrum of grapes they produced the good wines of a mildly glorious but all too brief era. And still the industry was small. At the crest, 90 million gallons was a year's production.

In the late 1880s the vine louse phylloxera began to lay waste to the recent achievements in the coastal vineyards. What phylloxera missed, Prohibition did not. After it began in 1919 fine grapes gave way increasingly to poor varieties or to no grapes at all. At the same time, equipment in idled wineries fell apart through disuse and the community of winemakers dissolved for lack of work.

In 1934 repeal of Prohibition made commerce in wine legal again. Immediately the academic viticulturists and enologists at the University of California began pushing the commercial industry to upgrade vineyards with finer varieties, to train its grapes with California sunshine in mind, and to make the wines as California fruit demanded rather than as European experience suggested.

Though the response of the industry was anything but quick in the first few decades, critics will do well to remember that as late as 1961 the great American public was not eager to pay $2.50 for Cabernet Sauvignons from the excellent vintage of 1958. When people did begin to prize the outstanding wines of later vintages, the rate of improvements in vineyard and cellar quickened into the wine boom of the past few years.

And still the industry is a small one. The presence of two gigantic companies, E. & J. Gallo and United Vintners, sometimes causes casual observers to think otherwise. All California, giants included, was making only 200 million gallons of wine per year through the mid-1960s, less than Bordeaux. It is making approximately 300 million gallons per year in the mid-1970s, somewhat more than Bordeaux, but far less than the French total of 1,500 million gallons annually.

II

In the joint and much appreciated absences of an obdurate peasantry and five millennia of empirical evidence, California vineyardists and winemakers have accepted in their stead the shifting support of technology.

Pickers work through rain-soaked vineyards of cabernet sauvignon at Mt. Eden, in the west hills of the Santa Clara Valley.　(TED STRESHINSKY)

Old cabernet sauvignon vines at Inglenook yield small, intensely flavored crops.   (HAROLYN THOMPSON)

Stainless steel, neutral in flavor and easy to clean, is used for receiving hoppers such as these and through the final fermentation process in most California wineries. (HAROLYN THOMPSON)

California Cabernet Sauvignons of 1935, 1945, 1955, and 1965 are all in mature good health. A lab sample of 1975 promises to live in the great tradition.   (HAROLYN THOMPSON)

Academic knowledge of vine-growing and winemaking began to be developed at the University of California in 1875 by the legendary Eugene Waldemar Hilgard. Through all the thicks and thins of later history, the university has been a center of research, a repository of wisdom, and a training school for people in all of the state's wine districts. Since the 1940s the school's graduates have come to dominate commercial vineyards and cellars, always in contact with the fatherly figures of a faculty that seemed ageless until several members retired after 1972.

In this fraternity of reasoning men, assumptions are required to stand up again and again to close scrutiny. Verities survive while they remain veritable. Outworn truths have a very hard time getting out of the library and back into daily use.

As old as the use of new oak barrels is, for example, barrels add inimitable grace notes to the flavors of age-worthy wines. The use of barrels in California increases each year. On the other hand, open fermentors made of wood are becoming as rare as steam locomotives because temperature-controlled stainless steel tanks can retain fruit flavors that are lost in the wood tanks.

For similar reasons, low-growing, head-trained vineyards are giving way to man-high, trellised ones. The fruit ripens more evenly to make finer wine.

Such changes come rapidly, but not as anarchy. The push, always, is toward adapting materials to place.

III

It is only a small oversimplification to say that each of the classic *Vitis vinifera* varieties in European vineyards is an acclimated descendant of some muscat-like grape that a Roman colonizer hauled home from the ancestral home of all true wine grapes, the Mediterranean Basin's eastern end. The struggle to bear fruit in harsher weathers changed the muscatish characters one way in Bordeaux, another in Burgundy, yet another along the Rhine.

Wherever a grape grows, to make fine wine it must ripen to a precarious balance of sugar and acidity. Sugar yields alcohol. Acidity carries the aromatics that make wine worth tasting. If the heat is not adequate for the grape, not enough sugar develops, resulting in a thin, weak wine. With too much heat, the acidity declines too soon, and all the fine aromatic qualities bake out of the grapes before they can ferment.

California does a fine job of ripening the classic European grape varieties, but California climate and geography do not bear conventional comparison with Europe as an environment for vines.

European terrain substantially lines up with the movements of Atlantic air as it sweeps eastward. The Alps are the first real barrier. Up to their flanks, no matter how unpredictable the weather might be from day to day, it affects broad expanses of terrain quite evenly.

Should the sky be overcast in Pauillac, for example, it is very likely to be overcast in Margaux and the rest of the Médoc as well. That is to say, Médoc is an expression of climate rather than politics. (Gironde is the political name of the place, which covers a lot of nongrape-growing ground beyond the Médoc.) Similarly, Côte d'Or and Rheingau describe regions of climate rather than politics.

In the grand scheme, the climate variations from north to south are the important ones. The west to east variations are much more subtle. One can grow the true riesling* grape in the Mosel, the Rhine, in Alsace, and on into Switzerland, but one abandons all hope of growing riesling without going very far south of the Rhine River.

Contrary to the European condition, the place names of all California winegrowing are more political than climatological, and north-south means very little except when it leads to wrong impressions. The real consideration is east-west, but even that is not as orderly as the north-south progression in Europe.

Two of San Francisco's most dramatic tourist attractions, earthquakes and fog, play the vital roles.

Old earthquakes buckled and folded the California coast into a series of closely spaced rows of high, steep-sided hills called The Coast Ranges. The ridge lines run north and south from the Oregon border down to Santa Barbara. All along, valleys tuck themselves between 1,500- to 2,500-foot-high walls. These coastal valleys range between twenty and a hundred miles in length and from a few hundred yards to ten miles wide. Typically, they line up two or three abreast.

When The Coast Ranges play out, thirty to forty miles inland from the Pacific, they do so abruptly, giving way to the huge bowl of The Great Central Valley. The grape-growing southern half is specifically known as the San Joaquin Valley. The San Joaquin is four hundred eighty miles long, and occasionally as wide as seventy miles. Its eastern boundary is the start of the towering Sierra Nevada mountain range.

Cool Pacific air blows across the first hills of The Coast Ranges without warming, but it cannot keep a biting edge long enough to get into the San Joaquin. This is enough to set up the broad distinction between cool coast to the west and warm interior to the east, but not enough to produce the amazing variations within the coast region. These come from the combined effects of The Coast Ranges and the 2,000-foot thick blanket of everlasting coastal fog, the one that chills July and August visitors to San Francisco so deeply.

The permanent fog bank extends along the coast from Mendocino County south to San Luis Obispo. It is caused by an interaction between cooler and warmer masses of air, which in turn are produced by the warm waters of the Japanese current and the cold waters that well up between it and the shore. The fog is permanent because the oceanic currents are, and it tends to move inland whenever The Great Central Valley heats into the 90° range or higher.

The depth of the fog's invasion depends on how hot the interior has become since dense, cold air can push in only beneath hot, light air. The exact invasion routes depend on gaps in The Coast Ranges, because the average height of the hills equals the average thickness of the fog layer. San Francisco's Golden Gate is the most dramatic gap, but a dozen others affect vineyards by allowing cold air, and sometimes fog, to slip over the vines.

The Napa Valley, though it is smaller than the Médoc, can, perhaps must, grow a dozen varieties of grapes from scattered origins in Europe. Cabernet sauvignon, the great red grape of the Médoc, does not ripen at the often foggy San Francisco Bay

*Throughout this book, the grape variety is referred to with lower case, the varietal wine with capitals, as a means of distinguishing each from the other.

California

end of Napa, but the same variety is at its best in all California just eleven miles to the north. The Burgundian pinot noir, unaccountably, ripens well in both places.

The whole coastal network of valleys is shot full of contradictions between place names and vineyard climates because the terrain is at steady cross-purposes with the movements of Pacific air. Although the weather is much more reliable than Europe's from day to day, it is far less steady from mile to mile.

To make sense of California geography as it relates to European grape varieties, scientists at the University of California began in the 1930s to develop a system of five climate zones that correspond in rough outline with the climates of major European wine districts. The purpose was to provide practical planting guides. The system is about to be replaced by a far more sophisticated one, but it is worth noting here because it has in great degree governed vines now in the ground.

The five climate Regions are defined by a basic unit of measure called the degree day, which summarizes daily sun heat above 50° Fahrenheit, then cumulative heat during the growing season from April 1 through October 31. 50° is the base temperature because plants actively grow at temperatures that warm and warmer.

A concrete example: The high temperature on a certain day is 86°, the low 54°. The mean temperature is 70° (86 + 54 = 140 ÷ 2 = 70). The daily total is 20 degree days (70 − 50 = 20). The accumulation of daily totals for the growing season determines the climate Region.

Region I is anywhere having fewer than 2,500 degree days.
Region II ranges from 2,501 to 3,000 degree days.
Region III from 3,001 to 3,500.
Region IV from 3,501 to 4,000.
Region V from 4,001 upward.
An accumulation of annual totals validates the regional summary.

In general the coast falls within the coolest regions, I through III, while the San Joaquin Valley ranges from III through the hottest zone, V. The Southern California vineyards east of Los Angeles tend to be IV or V.

In closer perspective, Region I is a collection of freckles on the maps of Mendocino, Sonoma, Napa, Santa Clara, Santa Cruz, and Monterey counties, all of them coastal. The regions looking directly toward tidal water are the most likely candidates. The cumulative heat of the growing season is close to that of Burgundy.

Region II occurs in the same roster of California counties as Region I, although there is more of it. The cumulative sun heat approximates that of Bordeaux.

Region III is to be found in each of the counties noted for Region I, plus those of Alameda (especially the Livermore Valley) and San Joaquin (a county as well as a valley, where the Lodi district is located). The Rhône approaches Region III. Much of central Italy typifies it.

Region IV corresponds to much of the San Joaquin Valley from Modesto south to Madera, and to parts of Southern California. The heat summaries are somewhat equivalent to conditions for Port grown in the Douro River Valley's warmest reaches.

Region V is to be found in the San Joaquin Valley south of Fresno, and in Southern California. The hottest parts of the Mediterranean basin, especially Algeria, correspond.

These summaries deal only with heat, not with sun hours or moisture patterns or a dozen other variables. They come close enough to allow useful selection of grape varieties, but keep enough difference to sustain fascinating variations in the tastes of wines made from one grape variety grown on opposite sides of the earth.

The Napa Valley

The Napa Valley is the place in California, the keeper of the flame, the pinnacle.

It starts alongside the bay across from San Francisco and runs thirty-four miles north and west, straight and narrow between high hills, until Mount St. Helena closes it off just beyond the town of Calistoga. The Sonoma Valley flanks it on the west side. Lake Berryessa runs parallel to it on the other.

Without wine, it would be just one more handsome coastal valley. A dozen others look a good deal like it. But there is wine in the Napa Valley and the long carpet of vines unrolling along the floor and into the hills is full of mystical messages for initiates. Napa's most prized landmarks are not the obvious knolls and creeks, but rather the boundaries of superior vineyards. And only in this of all California valleys do the majority of residents remember 1958, or 1946, or 1935 not because some war started or ended, but because the wine was good.

Why such a thing starts is impossible to know. In the case of the Napa Valley, a trapper named George Yount planted the first grapes, coarse missions, in the 1830s so he could make a little wine for his own table. Two decades later, in 1858, a German named Charles Krug decided to put Napa wine onto a business footing for the first time, still using mission grapes. Two years in Krug's wake came a medical doctor named George Belden Crane. It was Crane who decided that German grapes were a better idea than the gross missions.

From Crane's time on, the magnet has drawn people who wish to do something extraordinary. Even today, the best evidence says that Napa's greatest resource is human rather than some magic superiority of sun and soil. Napa's tightly knit fraternity of winemakers takes craftsmanlike pride in turning small advantage to large account. Among their wines nice points of style set out the differences between best and next, even when, as they sometimes do, some Sonoma or Mendocino grapes come into play.

It is eerie to think how much will has been required of Napa winemakers to keep the tradition alive. The start in the 1880s and 1890s was strong. The elegant old buildings at Inglenook and Greystone and Château Chevalier attest to that. However, from the end of Prohibition until the last half of the 1960s a mere handful of cellars produced the memorable varietals, the vintage-dated wines upon which Napa's prestige grew. Of the more than fifty new starters at repeal in 1933, only Louis M. Martini, the Cesare Mondavi family at Charles Krug, the Catholic teachers known as The Christian Brothers, and one extremely local winery, Nichelini, have stayed the course until now. Beaulieu Vineyard, Beringer, and Inglenook Vineyard made comebacks under their original owning families after 1934, but have changed proprietors in recent years. At one point, in 1960, the number of companies making wine in the valley was down to twenty-five. Only a dozen bottled enough to sell outside the county, let alone outside the state. Vineyard acreage had been eroding little by little since 1947, some of the loss in plantings of fine varieties. Even the weather turned sour in several vintages during the 1950s.

With all these limitations the valley still made more fine wine than the audience would absorb. Visitors to Beaulieu or Louis M. Martini in 1962 and 1963 could pick up perfectly cellared Cabernet Sauvignons ranging back to the vintage of 1952 for prices hardly greater than those of the current vintage.

However, the tiny cadre continued to rebuild the reputation of their valley

The Napa Valley

1	Beaulieu Vineyard		
2	Beringer Wines	20	J. Mathews Napa Valley Winery
3	Burgess Cellars		
4	Carneros Creek Vineyards	21	Mayacamas Vineyards
5	Caymus Vineyards	22	Robert Mondavi Winery
6	Chappellet Winery	23	M & H Vineyards
7	Chateau Chevalier Winery	24	Mt. Veeder Vineyards
8	Chateau Montelena Winery	25	Nichelini Vineyards
9	Clos du Val Wine Company	26	Oakville Vineyards
10	Cuvaison	27	Joseph Phelps Vineyards
11	The Christian Brothers	28	Raymond Vineyard & Cellar
11A	The Christian Brothers-Mont La Salle	29	Schramsberg Vineyards
		30	Souverain of Rutherford
12	Diamond Creek Vineyards	31	Spring Mountain Vineyards
13	Franciscan Vineyards	32	Stag's Leap Wine Cellars
14	Freemark Abbey Winery	33	Sterling Vineyards
15	Heitz Wine Cellars	34	Stonegate Winery
16	Inglenook Vineyards	35	Stony Hill Vineyard
17	Hanns Kornell Champagne Cellars	36	Sutter Home Winery
		37	Trefethen Vineyards
18	Charles Krug Winery	38	Villa Mt. Eden Winery
19	Louis M. Martini	39	Yverdon Vineyards

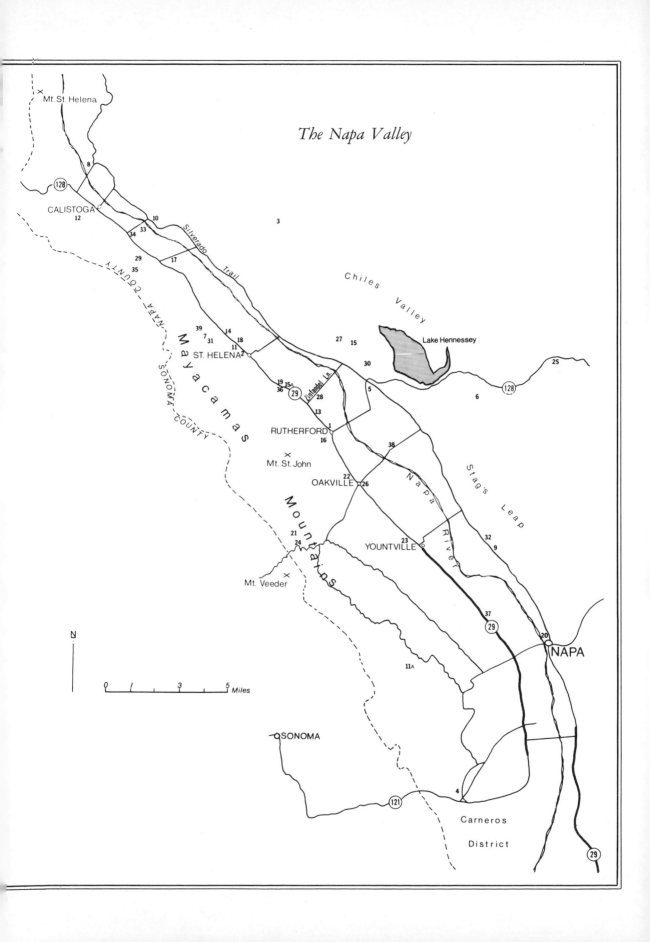

The Napa Valley

× Mt. St. Helena

⑧

(128)

CALISTOGA
12

10

34 33

29

35

17

Silverado Trail

Chiles Valley

Lake Hennessey

3

39   14
7 31   18
11
ST. HELENA

27   15

30

25

25

(128)

19 15A
36   28
(29)

Zinfandel Ln.

5

6

13

RUTHERFORD
16   1

× Mt. St. John

38

Napa River

Stag's Leap

OAKVILLE 26
22

21

24

YOUNTVILLE 23

32
9

× Mt. Veeder

37
(29)

20
NAPA

11A

N

Mayacamas

Mountains

SONOMA COUNTY

NAPA COUNTY

0   1   3   5 Miles

○ SONOMA

4

(121)

Carneros

District

(29)

with the small but growing circle of people who knew first-rate wine when they tasted it.

Finally the turnaround came, hesitantly at first, then in a rush. Heitz Cellars opened in 1961, the first new label in the Napa Valley in more than a decade. Robert Mondavi launched his winery in 1966 in the first new building of any size since the 1930s. From 1967 on, the newcomers formed a parade until, in 1974 the number of wineries peaked at forty-five.

While the wineries were in turbulent growth, vineyardists were uprooting walnut and prune orchards to plant big new vineyards, and plowing up backyard vegetable gardens to plant small ones. From the ebb, 10,200 acres in 1961, Napa Valley vineyards grew to 22,000 acres in 1974. In proper Californian form, expansion has produced a narrowing focus. No matter how many more winemakers, more and more of what they make is Cabernet Sauvignon, Chardonnay, Johannisberg Riesling, and Pinot Noir. Generic wines with Napa appellations are dwindling in volume and number as the coarse grape varieties that make them disappear from the vineyards.

In the old days, the principal distinction in the Napa Valley was between bulk wineries and the ones with their own labels. Since the wine boom of the 1960s, the prime distinction is between the sizable wineries which pioneered with labels and the new, small, estate-like cellars.

Middle-Sized Cellars

Harvests of recent years in the valley have been divided among seven major proprietors and thirty to thirty-five small ones. The Big Seven are Beaulieu Vineyard, Beringer/Los Hermanos, The Christian Brothers, Inglenook Vineyards, Charles Krug, Louis M. Martini, and Robert Mondavi. With the exception of Mondavi, they have arrived at their present sizes by diverse roads, but mainly because they were in business during the hard times when to survive meant to sell large amounts of wine for small prices.

In 1975 the ownerships were miscellaneous, but dominated by conglomerate corporations. That is less important than the fact that each was built by an old-timer in wine, a man who knew how to get himself and several independent vineyardists over the tough spots.

Definitions of size do not come easily in the world of wine. As a basic notion, a small winery is any one making 40,000 cases of wine or less per year. A middle-sized one produces somewhere between 100,000 and 500,000 cases. A big winery turns out a million cases or more per year. These divisions may seem overly broad, but in fact the equipment and manpower needs are fairly similar for all cellars operating within each division. With these arbitrary limits in mind, the largest of the Napa Valley wineries are either large or middle-sized. As businesses, The Christian Brothers, Inglenook Vineyards, and Charles Krug all are large. As Napa wineries, all are middle-sized. The definitions cannot be resolved tidily, but the main point is that each company has interests outside the Napa Valley that boost it into the realm of large, without changing the nature of the ways they go about things in the valley. The better explanations of these and their four smaller mates are individual.

Beaulieu Vineyard

For a long time Beaulieu Vineyard was the royal house of the Napa Valley, or the noblest one at least. Several factors contributed to the position. The home property in the village of Rutherford belonged to the family of Georges de Latour, who founded Beaulieu in 1900 and launched its comeback in 1934, and who was enough of a purist to set high standards for a low market. After his death in 1940, first his widow and then his daughter and son-in-law, the Marquise and Marquis de Pins, kept intact the tradition of concentrating on a few varietal wines and charging lofty prices for them. Lastly, the winemaker after 1937 was André Tchelistcheff, Russian-born, French-trained, and hand-picked by de Latour to make wines with style equal to the family standards. Tchelistcheff served well. When veteran critics of California reds look back beyond 1960, they look most often to Beaulieu.

Beaulieu no longer is the royal house of the valley. No longer does the regal family have it. The De Pins and their daughter inherited a much larger property than old Georges founded. They expanded the inheritance in their turn until it was too great for one family to sustain and so sold Beaulieu in 1969 to Heublein, Inc., the Connecticut-based food, wine, and spirits conglomerate that already owned a controlling interest in United Vintners. Tchelistcheff retired in 1973, definitively ending the old regime. Already other cellars had taken the mantle of royalty with costlier wines of greater exclusivity.

Beaulieu still has the capacity to make the kind of wines that made its reputation. The new owners have the vineyards, the cellars, and Tchelistcheff's old right-hand man to go on.

Georges de Latour had chosen some of the finest land in the valley for his first vineyards and planted them to the correct variety, cabernet sauvignon. De Latour Private Reserve Cabernet Sauvignon from that vineyard, directly across the state highway from the winery, has done as much as any single wine to restore the prestige of Napa in the years since 1937 when it had to go under the name of Burgundy to appeal to an innocent audience. As well as Tchelistcheff made this wine, he retained his soul of a Burgundian. From the outset he pressed his employers to develop vineyards better suited to chardonnay and pinot noir. His restless hunt for a Côte d'Or in California did much to identify several of the climate regions within the Napa Valley. When he finally found his best hope, in the Carneros region at the south end of Napa County, Beaulieu Vineyards made a patchwork on either side of State Route 29 from Rutherford south to Yountville. In all, the family owned 745 acres, supplementing its own crop with small purchases from friends on properties near the winery.

Heublein now owns all but the original de Latour vineyard, retained by the family, which sells the grapes to Beaulieu under contract. Newer Heublein-owned or managed vineyards feed a winery roughly doubled in size since the family days.

Tchelistcheff's contributions in the winery were as many and varied as those among the vines. The one that stands out in retrospect is his insistence early in the 1940s on aging red wines in small oak barrels at a time when almost nobody else in California was doing so. In the same era he was helping to establish cold fermentations for whites and malolactic fermentations for reds, paths now widely accepted as desirable. He had the strength of mind not to be satisfied thirty years later. From 1969 until his retirement he insisted on fermenting his Chardonnays in barrels rather than tanks, a return to ancient tradition based, he said, in the enzymatic requirements of a good fermentation of chardonnay grapes. Before 1969 he had accepted tank fermentation. (Since 1973 his successors have gone back to tanks.)

The major change at Beaulieu since Heublein, other than a doubling of the winery size, has been the replacement of old redwood fermentors with steel ones, a move Tchelistcheff helped to engineer.

The man in charge now is Theo Rosenbrand, a Hollander by birth, who served as Tchelistcheff's cellarmaster for almost two decades. University of California at Davis-trained enologists back up Rosenbrand's practical experience.

Beaulieu continues to be measured by its Cabernet Sauvignon, Pinot Noir, and Chardonnay which, although they no longer automatically rank at the head of their class, still contend for that honor each vintage.

Beringer/ Los Hermanos

Beringer/ Los Hermanos is another old-timer, like Beaulieu, that recently passed from family to corporate ownership. The brothers Jacob and Frederick Beringer founded the winery in 1870. Their descendants sold it to Nestlé, of the Swiss chocolate Nestlés, in 1971.

In this case change seems clearly for the better. The family no longer had the romantic fires that led the founders to have Chinese laborers hand hew hundreds of yards of criss-crossing tunnels into a sandstone hill for aging cellars, or to erect a shamelessly overdone Rhenish estate house on the north edge of a casual little California farm town such as St. Helena. In truth, the later Beringers had rather abandoned the effort to make anything more than honorable commercial wine. Beginning in the 1950s they ceased to produce vintage-dated wines, and blended their varietals to standards of taste that put them outside the game, this in spite of the fact that their vintage-dated wines of the 1940s ranked with the best of that era in the valley.

The Nestlé ownership began steering toward a middle course with blinding speed. Vintage-dated wines appeared on the market wearing brand new labels within what seemed mere weeks of the sale. The new owners were so quick, in fact, that critics began talking of the purchase as another corporate take-the-money-and-run operation. The signs were wrong. After some shuffling in the corporate chairs, premature wines were hauled back off the market shelves for proper aging. Since then progress has been measured, though not exactly stately.

Although the market for Beringer wines had diminished during the final decade of family ownership, vineyards and winery were sizable. There were 800 acres of vines in all, a small portion across State Route 29 from the winery, a larger piece some miles north in a Sonoma County district called Knights Valley, and, finally, slightly more than half the total in the Carneros district to the south of Napa city. A fermenting facility at Carneros supplemented the main winery at St. Helena. Their combined storage capacity was 2.24 million gallons, much of it outworn redwood and oak cooperage.

Along with some judicious renovating, Nestlé has made substantial additions to both vineyards and winery.

The total acreage owned by Beringer now approaches 2,500. Divided among twenty-eight separate parcels, the vines fall into every microclimate the valley has to offer. Far the greatest proportion is in the southern half of the valley, from Rutherford down to Napa city and in the separate Carneros district. However, sizable blocks are north of Rutherford. Also, the old holding in Knights Valley, in Sonoma County, has been enlarged. Each parcel is planted in conformance with the U.C. climate recommendations, or almost so.

In addition the company buys grapes and wine for its secondary label, Los Hermanos. These materials come from as far away as Santa Barbara County.

To accommodate the enlarged vineyards, the company has built a sizable installation across the highway from the original Beringer winery. It is to do all of the crushing and fermenting and some of the aging. The new installation is all in stainless steel tanks, leaving the old winery as the wood-aging cellar. In time there will be a wood-aging cellar adjacent to the new winery to supplement the original cellars.

In the old tunnels, the new proprietors have replaced all of the outworn barrels and tanks with new cooperage, much of it oak puncheons from Europe.

The man in charge of winemaking is Myron Nightingale, whose name might ring a bell for veteran observers of California wine. He is the man who developed a controlled environment for Botrytis—the Noble Mold—and used it to make a superior sweet wine called Premier Semillon for the old Cresta Blanca label in Livermore. At Beringer, he quickly demonstrated an ability to produce a wide range of agreeable wines priced in the middle range of vintage-dated varietals. As the new vineyards mature, he will have an increasing opportunity to make single-vineyard wines. The first one released, appropriately, was a well-developed *auslese*-type Johannisberg Riesling from Knights Valley, vintage of 1973.

A word about the names Beringer and Los Hermanos. The winery was originally named Beringer Brothers; its main vineyard was called Los Hermanos. The new owners retained Beringer as the name for the first-line label, and revived Los Hermanos as the name for less costly wines, mostly packaged in jugs.

The Christian Brothers

Although family ownerships have tended to disappear among the larger Napa Valley wineries, The Christian Brothers run very little risk of running out of family, being a teaching order of the Roman Catholic Church.

From very limited beginnings as sacramental winemakers, the Brothers have grown in all directions until they now have 2,400 acres of vines divided between the Napa and San Joaquin valleys, three major winery buildings in the Napa Valley and two more near Fresno, a grand total of 24 million gallons of fermenting and storage capacity, and annual sales estimated at 2 million cases in recent years.

The Brothers first came to the Napa Valley toward the end of Prohibition, when they bought the vineyards and stone cellars of the old Theodore Gier estate and renamed the property Mont LaSalle. On this site, carved into a redwood forest several hundred feet above the valley floor in the Mayacamas Mountains west of

Napa city, they established their novitiate and a small wine business. (The novitiate, tucked into one corner of a rolling expanse of vines, is so handsome that it always gets into photographs in lieu of the far plainer wine cellar.)

The showcase cellar among The Christian Brothers' holdings is in the main valley, on the outskirts of St. Helena. Its neighbor on one side is Beringer/Los Hermanos. Straight across State Route 29 is Charles Krug. Both are dwarfed by the enormous stone fortress of a building called, appropriately, Greystone. A wealthy man named William Bowers Bourne built it in 1888–1889 with the announced goal of making the greatest wine in the world in the largest stone winery in the world. He was too early. The existing demand for Napa wine was such as to make Greystone an instant white elephant. It stayed one, too big for a whole succession of owners, until The Christian Brothers came to its rescue in 1950.

Both Mont LaSalle and Greystone serve only as aging facilities these days. All crushing and fermenting of Napa table wines is done at a severely functional property on the south side of St. Helena, next door to Louis M. Martini. Bottling and cased goods storage is at the same site.

The Brothers theatrically refer to their new-in-1973 installation as a fermentor-in-the-round. It has a central control tower, thoroughly automated systems for crushing the grapes and moving the wine, and a radial design that lets the boss see every tank in the complex from one point. All is temperature-controlled stainless steel, a far cry from the old days at Martinez when one of the brothers would dump some grapes into a horse trough and mash them with a wooden club. That was before Napa. Quite possibly the results helped push the Brothers northward across the bay to Mont LaSalle during the 1920s.

After the wizard technology of the fermenting operation, the Brothers revert to tradition. The aging cellars are full of old upright tanks of redwood and oak, and newer oak barrels.

(The dessert wine cellars and brandy distillery of The Christian Brothers are where they should be, in the San Joaquin Valley towns of Reedley and Fresno, with specialist crews to preside over them.)

Although challenged recently by Inglenook, the Brothers' table wine production has been the largest within the Napa Valley. More than 1,500 of the order's 2,400 acres of vines are in the Napa Valley, in a series of blocks ranging from Mont LaSalle northward thirty miles to the edge of Calistoga. The Brothers buy prodigiously from independent growers in both Napa and Sonoma counties to fill their needs for varietal wine. Other counties, including some in the San Joaquin Valley, contribute to the generics.

For all of that, the order makes wine much as the other major wineries in the valley do. Their fermenting tanks are of the same sizes, and so are their aging vessels. They just have more of them. The one major difference is that The Christian Brothers refuse to vintage date.

Long ago the Brothers opted to produce consistently reliable wines and to make them available to a large share of the wine-drinking public at reasonable prices, somewhat in the way of big French shipping firms such as B&G, or Sichel. It takes considerable agility to survive in the middle ground of anything, as the people who used to make Nashes and Studebakers know so well. The Brothers obviously have

The radial design of The Christian Brothers fermenting facility at St. Helena allows one man to watch every stainless steel tank from a central point. (TED STRESHINSKY)

the agility, much of it in the long, lean form of Brother Timothy. Tim, as he is known to other winemakers but not to novices, became a part of the winery staff in the 1930s. He has been the cellarmaster through all the expansion years since 1940.

Those advertising photographs of Tim with his tasting tools do not distort the truth very much. He does not wear his churchly robes to work in the winery, and he does not have to go from cask to cask to get his own samples, as the pictures pretend, but tasting is the essence of skillful blending. Tim's palate is the ultimate arbiter of style and quality in The Christian Brothers table wines, after John Hoffman has made them and Leonard Berg has shepherded them through aging and blending.

The usual technique for assembling nonvintage and generic wines in California and the only technique at The Christian Brothers is fractional blending, which is worth an explanatory digression. It revolves around miniature samples and it gets (pardon me, Brother Tim) hellishly complicated. The goal is to assemble a certain volume of wine for bottling and to have it identical to its predecessor lot.

One lot of The Christian Brothers Gamay Noir that went onto the market early in the summer of 1973, was a fairly typical exercise. The call was for 12,000 gallons. The winemakers gathered samples—about a half-bottle of each—of twenty-two lots of wine from four different vintages, three grape varieties, and several different vineyards. After a round of preliminary assessments, the field was trimmed by half, and four blends were assembled on the scale of one cubic centimeter to one hundred gallons of available wine. (One of the limits is that all sample blends have to be practical fractions of the amounts of available wine. A cask of 2,000 gallons, for example, could not be represented by more than 20 cubic centimeters in a 120 cc model for a 12,000-gallon lot, though it could be represented by less.) None of the original four blends met the standard set by a bottle from the preceding blend, but one came close. It served as a basis for a second generation of four more blends. One of the latter four was what the winemaker wanted. It was mostly of Napa Gamay, with a little Grand Noir thrown in for fat and a dash of Pinot Noir for finesse. The recipe used seven lots of the amounts of 2,000 : 2,000 : 2,000 : 2,000 : 1,100 : 520 : 2,000 gallons.

Matters can become far more troublesome than that. The staff still talks about one bottling of Cabernet Sauvignon that evolved out of 120 lots of wine and a round dozen generations of trial blends.

As much as the Brothers blend, some of their wines have distinct pedigrees. The Special Cuvée bottlings of Pinot St. George and Pineau de la Loire come only from vineyards at Mont LaSalle. The Brother Timothy Selection red wines of Cabernet Sauvignon, Pinot Noir, Gamay Noir, and Zinfandel come from the winery's own vineyards. A good many others bear Napa Valley as their appellation of origin. It is not at all a rare occurrence for one of them to win a public blind tasting against costly competition.

Inglenook Vineyards

Of the three old-line family firms—Beaulieu, Beringer, and Inglenook—that have passed into the hands of conglomerate corporations, the Inglenook of now is least like the winery it used to be.

Gustave Niebaum, the old Finnish sea captain, bought an existing ranch called Inglenook at the town of Rutherford and began making wine on it in 1881. Within the decade he caused to be built on the property a cellar that impressively imitated a grand Médoc château. Until his grandnephew, John Daniel, Jr., sold the property in 1964, that was Inglenook.

It is hard to think of a place where change came harder. Niebaum filled the building with 1,500-gallon oak casks from Germany in which to age his wines. Daniel still was using the same casks when he sold. The ancient redwood fermentors were on the top floor going into 1964. The crew still shoveled stems into a horse-drawn cart during that vintage, or at least the one before. The only visible change I can remember in the Daniel era came with the addition of a Willmes air-bag press. A shockingly modern replacement for the old basket type, it was.

The only addition to the vineyard surrounding the winery was a small parcel near Oakville, the two together totaling 200 acres. They yielded all the Inglenook wine there was, an annual 40,000 cases of a surprisingly wide range of vintage-dated varietals for general sale, and a jug generic called IVY available only at the cellar door.

After the original sale, to the rambling empire of wineries called United Vintners,* change came more and more rapidly to Inglenook. UV quickly moved the fermenting out of the old building to an anonymous winery it owned in Oakville, a mile south, leaving the original cellars as no more than an aging facility. The

---

* See pages 129 and 130 for other aspects of United Vintners.

Oak casks imported from Germany by Gustave Niebaum still hold Inglenook Cask Cabernet Sauvignons. (WINE INSTITUTE)

The Charles Krug property as it looked in the 1880s. (WINE INSTITUTE)

vineyards jumped from their original 200 acres to 450 acres in 1966, then to 700 in 1967. After that year UV stopped showing a separate acreage for Inglenook because the limits no longer were definable. Members of Allied Growers, the vineyardists' companion organization to United Vintners, were putting their Napa Valley grapes into Inglenook's prime varietal wines more or less as proprietors. In addition, the new management introduced a less costly set of wines under the Inglenook Vintage label, drawing upon Allied Growers vineyards both in and out of Napa County.

When control of United Vintners was sold by Allied Growers to Heublein, Inc., Inglenook took still more turns. The Heublein management tacked on yet a third line of wines, called Inglenook Navalle. By this time the traditional varietals were being fermented in the winery at Oakville and aged and bottled at the original Inglenook. Wines under the Inglenook Vintage label were being made and bottled at the original Italian Swiss Colony winery at Asti in Sonoma County. Wines called Inglenook Navalle were being made partly there and partly in the San Joaquin Valley, then aged and bottled at Asti. In 1975 that is essentially how matters stood. However, Heublein has built an enormous new cellar for small oak directly in front of Niebaum's classic original. Within the next year or two a fermenting winery is to be built alongside the addition. When the production facility is in operation, the

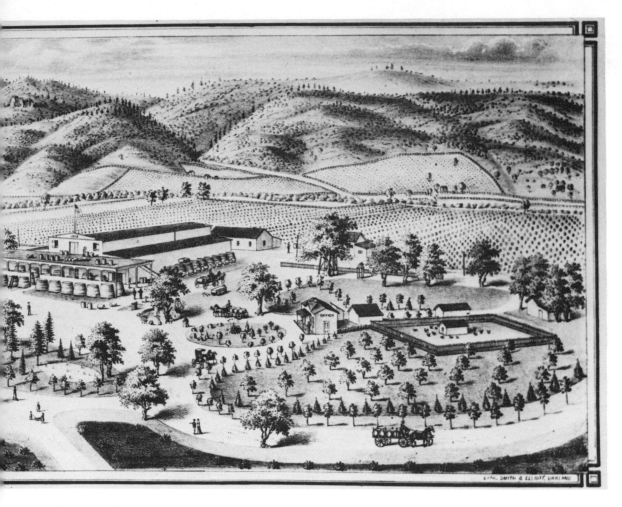

plan is for both the estate line and the vintage line to be made and bottled at the original property. Navalle wines will continue to come from Asti and Madera, competing with San Joaquin Valley wines by price and style.

One gross irony occurred during these changes. Heublein lost ownership of the old Niebaum house and part of the traditional vineyard. The situation came about because, in selling the winery, John Daniel, Jr., kept title to the classic country house and 100 acres of vineyard surrounding it. Daniel died in 1969. His widow put the house and vineyard up for sale in 1972, to the winning bid of a consortium headed by W. E. van Löben Sels of Oakville Vineyards. That group has since re-sold, but for a time sold the grapes to Oakville, to be made into wine, irony of ironies, only a few dozen feet from the current Inglenook fermenting winery, the next-door neighbor.

In the old days, Daniel and his winemaker, George Deuer, used to run an elegantly understated competition with the neighboring de Latours of Beaulieu to see who could get the most of cabernet sauvignon grown on adjoining ranches at Rutherford. Now that Heublein owns both of the wineries that particular contest has ended, but there remains a certain competitive feeling between the two winemaking staffs, at least in those wines with Napa Valley appellations of origin.

Under the regime of Daniel and the crusty Deuer (who made all of the wines from 1935 until his retirement in 1964), Cabernet Sauvignon was the pride of the house and Special Cask bottlings were the pride of the Cabernets. All of the reds came up dry, austere, and long-lived. So did the whites, which never were as good. After 1964, a new crew maundered through several vintages in search of a style. Tom Ferrell, a young graduate of U.C.-Davis, joined Inglenook in 1972, and seems aimed on a particular track. The Special Cask Cabernet Sauvignons have reverted to type. All other wines are softer than in the old regime. The reds show marks of aging in small, new barrels rather than the ancient 1,500 gallon ovals. The whites are clean and fresh after careers in steel, except that the Chardonnays have a tinge of oak. In short, the Inglenook wines have gained the middle of the road along with those of several other sizable producers of classic varietal types.

Charles Krug Winery

Charles Krug, the Prussian immigrant who launched wine as a commercial product in the Napa Valley, in 1861 bought the property just north of St. Helena that still bears his name. A fierce competitor, he quickly built his winery into one of the largest and most prestigious in the valley. The place faltered before Prohibition, and was idle throughout it. After the family firm of C. Mondavi & Sons purchased the Krug ranch in 1943 from an interim owner, they restored both the size and the prestige.

The C. of C. Mondavi & Sons was Cesare, a great bear of a man who came to the valley in 1935 after a Prohibition-induced career as a fresh grape-shipper in Lodi. He first bought the Sunny St. Helena winery, a bulk cellar on the south edge of St. Helena. When the opportunity arose to acquire the long-idle Krug label and the old ranch, Cesare jumped at the chance. He spent sixteen years rehabilitating the ranch before he died at the age of seventy-six in 1959, leaving his widow, Rosa, and their sons, Peter and Robert, to continue the business. Since Robert's departure in 1966 to open his own winery, Rosa and Peter have managed the enterprise. Peter oversees the winemaking, his principal role since his college days at Stanford then at U.C.-Davis.

Krug, when he was through, left two large stone buildings of highly individual style in the middle of the old ranch, which reaches almost across the valley floor. One had been his winery, the other his coach house and stable. Both of these buildings now house wine. So do two functional new buildings behind the original winery. Taken altogether, the place is an eclectic collection of architecture and equipment ranging from battered archaic to shiny contemporary. The balance favors old. The red wine fermentors, to cite the prime instance of battered archaic, consist of two long rows of open-topped redwood tanks in a lean-to of sketchy construction, with, at one point, an oak tree growing through the roof. The one strikingly modern part of the winery is forty paces east in one of the new buildings. There several galleries of glass-lined, refrigeratable steel tanks hold Krug wines waiting to be bottled. All the tanks tie into a pressure system that uses inert gas rather than pumps to move wine from tank to bottle. This is a particular legacy of Robert Mondavi, who transferred the enthusiasm for avant garde gadgetry to his own winery when he left Krug.

The fermenting apparatus is scheduled for replacement with stainless steel, but the rest of the property is likely to go along in its traditional forms for as long as Peter Mondavi uses it. The old coach house houses a pampered few reds and the

Chardonnay as they age in French oak barrels. The second of the newer buildings is an enormous cellar of American oak for the majority of red wines. The old winery building has miscellaneous wood cooperage, most of it sizable redwood tanks for fermenting and initial aging.

Like the other old-line firms, C. Mondavi & Sons has acquired vineyard properties in several parts of the valley to take advantage of its microclimates. In addition to sizable blocks surrounding the winery property, there is a big ranch at Oakville, and two are in the Carneros district. All told, the operating company and its officers own some 1,100 acres of vineyard for Charles Krug. The Mondavis also buy from independent growers for their Charles Krug wines.

In addition to the Krug label, the firm has a jug label called CK. It uses both Napa and San Joaquin grapes. (Earlier there were other secondary labels called Napa Vista and Mondavi Select, but these have been phased out.) CK helps explain a winery capacity nearing 4 million gallons. In fact there is more CK than Charles Krug.

In the 1950s and 1960s when there were only a few sources of fine varietal wines to choose among, it was commonly held that the basis of a good cellar could be had using Krug whites and Louis M. Martini reds. The idea was not all bad. Krug whites ranged in character from the sweet and flowery charms of Chenin Blanc—a Mondavi invention—to a consistently powerful Chardonnay. They still do. Since the heyday of the generality, though, the Mondavis have begun making Cesare Mondavi Selection Cabernet Sauvignon from their Oakville vines. The one wine is reason enough to look into Krug reds as well as whites.

Louis M. Martini

There is a curious thing about Louis M. Martini red wines. Englishmen like them, sometimes above all else California has to offer. Nothing in their pedigree suggests this possibility. Old Louis came from Pietra Ligure in the northwest corner of Italy. His son, Louis P., was born in Kingsburg, Fresno County, during national Prohibition while his father was biding time in the sweet wine business. The father studied enology in Italy, the son at U.C.-Davis. Their methods do not follow French ideas. Nonetheless, their wines, especially the reds, are deft and balanced and have a way of haunting the memory that appeals to the certified claret drinkers of England.

Louis M., Old Louis, bore the unofficial but unchallenged title, Dean of California Winemakers, from sometime in the 1950s until he died at the age of eighty-seven, in June 1974. He began laying claim to the honorary office in 1907 in a backyard winery he ran with his father in San Francisco. Subsequently he studied in Italy, then came back to work for several commercial firms in California until 1923, when he launched the business that would become his dessert winery in Kingsburg. He bought property and made his first wine in the Napa Valley in 1934, selling the Kingsburg operation in 1940. In 1957, as a mark of his seventieth birthday, Old Louis turned over the winemaking to Young Louis, Louis P., his son, a mere boy of forty-two at the time, but bulwarked by a degree in enology from the U.C.-Davis and the apprenticeship at his father's elbow.

Between the two men they have established a continuity of style unequalled anywhere else in the valley, and they have been laudable mavericks throughout their careers.

The Martini winery, in this valley full of architectural gems, does not have a frill on it. Louis M. built straight walls out of brick blocks in 1934, when a penny saved was a smart transaction. Recent additions, four buildings in all, are as plain. Probably the Martinis figured furbelows would look out of place at this late hour.

The main building, which flanks State Route 29 at the south city limit of St. Helena, has its main floor filled with bottling equipment and stacked cased goods. In a back corner is a working souvenir of the early Martini attention to technology. It is a big refrigerated room full of redwood tanks in which white wines ferment at the slowest of paces. Before temperature-controlled stainless steel tanks came along, this was the way of cold fermentation. In a narrow cellar beneath the center of the main floor the Martinis keep four rows of oak ovals ranging in size from 700 to 1,500 gallons. Although two of the newer buildings are full of oak barrels, the father thought and the son still thinks that good-sized, well-seasoned oak ovals are the perfect aging vessel for fine red wines because they lack oaky flavor. A good many of the greatest Martini reds have received their final aging in this cellar, which also contains prized lots binned in the old-fashioned way.

In addition to the oak ovals and barrels, there is a considerable amount of redwood in this 2-million-gallon winery. Like the oak ovals, redwood of size allows reds to develop slowly, which is an essential in the Martini style.

The fermentors are mostly temperature-controlled stainless steel now, but the old refrigerated redwood still is used for some whites, and the open-topped concrete tanks hold working reds each vintage.

The Martinis own vineyard acreage in amounts typical of the major old-line firms. The winery owns close to 800 acres. The family of Louis P. owns about 300 acres more. The winery purchases relatively small amounts of grapes from independent growers. What makes the Martinis mavericks in this regard is that they pay no attention to county lines, only to microclimates and soils. One block of vines is near the winery. Two ranches are in the Carneros district. The famous Monte Rosso vineyard is in Sonoma County, in the Valley of the Moon, or, rather, on a flat-topped mountain overlooking it. One of the ranches owned by Louis P. is in the Russian River region of Sonoma County near Healdsburg, another in Chiles Valley, in the hills east of the main Napa Valley. In the early years after Prohibition, before his own vineyards were mature, Louis M. scoured the state for grapes of fine quality, including folle blanche from Almadén and cabernet sauvignon from the famous old E. H. Rixford estate on the San Francisco peninsula.

At the beginning and ever since, "California" has been the appellation for Martini wines, though the fine print on the label sometimes points out the precise origins. Some of the origins are single vineyards.

Speaking of single vineyards, one of the ploys that drives outlanders daft is the Martini habit of selling special wines only at the cellar door. Louis P. Martini has the restless kind of mind that keeps tinkering with blends, or aging times, or anything else that gives flavor to a finished bottle. For example, the genuinely interested in 1975 could buy five distinct lots of 1968 Cabernet Sauvignon in addition to the regular bottling. Some used varying amounts of merlot. Some tested pure cabernet sauvignon of varying origins and varying lengths of aging in wood. Not all of the special wines are experiments. Some are just outstanding lots from outstanding vintages.

Down through the years the Martinis' greatest contributions to the literature of California wine have been reds: Barbera, Cabernet Sauvignon, Pinot Noir, and Zinfandel have been specially fine. The white Gewürztraminer of Martini also has been a pace-setting example of its type.

Like André Tchelistcheff and George Deuer and the brothers Mondavi, the two Louis Martinis observed the harvests for three decades and more, all in a straight line. They more than any of the other winemakers in the coastal counties have defined what nature does and what the human element does in California wine.

Robert Mondavi Winery

Robert Mondavi, the man, has the knack of causing things to happen. Given that gift, nothing makes him so happy as novelty. As a result the Robert Mondavi winery is one of the most startling enterprises in the Napa Valley, and has been so on an almost daily basis since its founding in 1966.

Robert broke away from the C. Mondavi & Sons family business at Charles Krug after thirty years in order to make his own mark. He hired a designer named Cliff May to work out a traditional building patterned on California's Franciscan missions. It was the first and last old-fashioned idea he had about the place, which looms out of vineyards alongside State Route 29 at Oakville, the middle village between Yountville to the south and Rutherford to the north.

Since the original building with its churchly tower and central arch was erected during the summer and harvest seasons of 1966, Mondavi has sold a majority interest in the firm to Sick's Rainier Brewing Company of Seattle, Washington, and stayed on as manager to double then redouble the capacity for wine. Two buildings, each larger than the original, hold the augmented supplies of stainless steel fermentors, oak tanks and oak barrels, plus all manner of strange and wondrous other machines to help in the work.

Mondavi's fermenting equipment for red wine tells the story of his unquenchable enthusiasm for new kinds of gear. In 1974 he used conventional steel tanks. In 1973, however, he used horizontal tanks hooked to powerful motors that kept them rotating steadily so that caps did not have to be punched down. (They did not work very well, which is why they now hang disused in the rafters.)

Another innovation is a computer that keeps hour-by-hour track of every steel fermenting and storage tank in the winery. If something not programmed occurs, bells go off in the winemaker's office and he hustles out to the offending tank to see what is happening.

Between fermentation and bottling, Mondavi wines age in oak, but not just any old oak. The Mondavis have scoured the cooperages of the world to identify every sort made, brought back samples for experiment, and settled on very specific kinds for each wine. The whites go into rather good-sized tanks or ovals from Yugoslav and German sources. The reds and Chardonnay acquire their polish in barrels from France or Yugoslavia.

The crew gathered by the Mondavis to assemble all of the purchases of cooperage became so skillful that its members formed a coopering firm on their own with the winery's blessing. It was the first new one in the Napa Valley since Prohibition.

The storage capacity for wine at Mondavi had reached a million gallons by 1972 from an original 100,000 gallons. The vineyard acreage has increased from 10 to 600, the winery-owned supply being augmented by substantial purchases from independent growers.

The winery's own vines are concentrated in the half of the valley from Oakville south to the limits of Napa city. The plantings generally correspond to climate summaries.

For several years all wines sold under the Robert Mondavi label were vintage-dated varietals. In 1975 the winery added a generic red and white at modest prices.

Robert Mondavi is, among other things, a superb promoter of California wine in general and Napa Valley wine in particular. He even has a strong track record as an inventor of new names for wines that had not sold well. At Krug he introduced Chenin Blanc as a varietal white wine in the style of Vouvray, as against a plainer wine under the plainer (and erroneous) name of White Pinot, and has seen Chenin Blanc become a runaway success in the marketplace. Under his own name he coined Fumé Blanc in order to rescue Sauvignon Blanc from undeserved obscurity. The model in this case is Pouilly Fumé, which French district has done much better by the grape variety sauvignon blanc than has Graves, but no better than the best Californian wines of the type.

Robert's eldest son, Michael, is in charge of winemaking. He has his father's optimism and his capacity to innovate. Neither man is satisfied yet that the Napa Valley has reached its potential. Among other evidence in support of this view is a seemingly endless collection of bottles and demijohns and small casks tucked here and there throughout the winery, each one filled with some experimental batch of wine or another, probing at such diverse variables as vine-training techniques, variety location, fermentation temperatures, press pressures, cooperage sizes, and, unless no question remains, phases of the moon at harvest time.

Whatever the character of the wines now available, no Mondavi wine is a careless result, but rather the upshot of the greatest application of skill and knowledge the proprietors could muster. The wines will alter in character as soon as a Mondavi thinks he has found an improvement of technique or philosophy.

The Small Cellars

At least a score of Napa Valley cellars now make wine in the romantic tradition of the great estates of Bordeaux, and on the same scale of a few hundred to a few thousand cases per year.

The remarkable fact is that nearly all of them date from the past dozen years. Between the end of World War II and the great grape rush of the mid-1960s, only John Daniel's original Inglenook and Lee Stewart's original Souverain pursued the difficult but rewarding path of trying to make great wine in more than minuscule quantity. Fred McCrea at Stony Hill worked at making great wine in minuscule quantity. The three of them constituted pretty much the whole field of estate-style wineries.

Stewart and McCrea presaged something that has become a major theme, which is the domesticity of the cellar staffs from winemaker down. In all of the earlier periods of California wine the cellarmasters were, typically, new arrivals from Europe. Even after 1934 the names were Martini and Mondavi and Tchelistcheff and the tongues spoke English with accents. The newest wave of vineyardists and winemakers bear such family names as Forman and Baxter. Even names that seem to lead back to Europe instead trace to origins on this continent. Joe Heitz is Alsatian if one goes back far enough, but he was an Illinois farm boy before army service in World War II took him to California. Donn Chappellet, for all that his name is French, comes from a pioneer aviation family in Los Angeles. Implicit in this native roster is the acceptance that wine is part of the Yankee weave now, and not just an appliqué from Europe. That, I think, is a very hopeful sign. So is the fact that some winemakers still come fresh from Europe, and are made welcome. But, in their case, what bodes best for the durability of a silvering age of California wine is the fact that they come as peers rather than mentors.

If any one man in the new wave is a watershed figure it is Joe Heitz. His was the first of the small new wineries in 1961. More important, he started out knowing that Beaulieu's Georges de Latour Cabernet Sauvignon was worth more than $3.50 a bottle because he helped make it for a number of years before starting his own business. As soon as Heitz had a wine of comparable quality, he pegged it at $6. Also, he was first to put the name of an individual vineyard on his label, to identify the source of a wine as closely as possible, and also to give recognition to superior independent growers.

Others in the valley, both new and old timers, learned the lessons quickly. Napa has not been a bargain hunter's paradise since, but in compensation has grown a long way toward its potential on the proceeds of higher prices.

Although some of the results have been curious, the flowering in numbers also has been a flowering in excellence. Newcomers have done a great part of the work in expanding the reputation of the valley, which has its groundwork in so pitifully few names.

Burgess Cellars

Burgess Cellars occupies the original site of Souverain Cellars, the gloriously scenic hill that plummets from the village of Angwin 600 feet down to a lake almost on the east edge of the valley floor. The current proprietor, Tom Burgess, a one-time jet pilot, has spruced up the cellars since he bought the winery and its twenty acres of vines just in time to crush the vintage of 1972.

With some modest additions to the collection of stainless steel fermentors and oak cooperage, the winery capacity is 40,000 gallons. The home vineyard, planted mostly to petite sirah and zinfandel, provides only a fraction of the annual requirement. Burgess, like a good many others among the small cellars, has embarked on a search for especially fine grapes from independent growers. (The previous owner, Lee Stewart, did something of the same nature, purchasing many of his grapes from the vineyard of Jerome Draper directly across the valley on Spring Mountain.) Burgess, as of 1975, had not settled on his final lineup.

Wines from the early vintages, made by a U.C.-Davis-trained young enologist named Bill Sorenson, were sound, cautiously conservative in style, though tending to be husky. There was one stylistic legacy from Stewart, who insisted on fermenting whites in oak tanks to soften them. Whites fermented in steel have a characteristic sharp finish on the palate, a good quality, but not as good to Stewart as the rounder aftertaste of wood-fermented whites. The rounded style fit Stewart, himself short and round, almost a kewpie figure. Burgess thus far suggests that morphologies are not reliable. He is tall, lean, hewn from hickory, but fond of soft, rounded whites, too.

Carneros Creek Winery

Carneros Creek Winery belongs to three partners who founded it in time to participate in the vintage of 1973 in a building with half of its walls and none of its roof.

Nearly every winery in California has begun in this way since Robert Mondavi did it in 1966. Somehow roofless inaugurals caught the gaudy spirit of the past decade, but I suspect that if Robert Mondavi marked the beginning of feverish growth, Carneros Creek may signal its end. Even as the winery began its career signs were showing up on all sides that California's wine industry had reached a time to slow down and digest all it has wrought during these past few years.

The partners in Carneros Creek are Balfour and Anita Gibson, husband and wife, and winemaker Francis Mahoney. They built a solid, compact cellar of concrete block with the thought in mind that Mahoney should be able to run it single-handed. It is located in Carneros in order to give chardonnay and pinot noir a fair trial, on grounds that the two varieties grow especially well there, but the owners agree unanimously that the future of California wine lies with cabernet sauvignon and zinfandel, and that the future of Carneros Creek Winery lies with Napa Valley Cabernet Sauvignon and Shenandoah Valley Zinfandel. Shenandoah Valley is well up in the Sierra Nevada foothills, in the heart of the Gold Rush Country of 1849.

The first wine went to market under the label early in 1975. It was a well received Pinot Noir.

The winery is designed to make 15,000 to 20,000 gallons of wine each year, nearly all of it from grapes purchased from independent vineyardists. Fermentors are stainless steel. Cooperage is all oak, most of it American white oak barrels.

Chappellet Winery

In the form of a triangular pyramid, the Chappellet Winery is one of the Napa Valley's most elegant demonstrations that form can follow function in architecture without looking as if it had been forced to.

The exterior is sheet metal oxidized to a rich red that blends into the iron-rich soils of Pritchard Hill, a 1,500-foot peak rising above the east side of the valley floor at Rutherford. The building nestles into one of the few level spots on the northwest slope, facing out over Lake Hennessy. It is surrounded by an immaculately kept 100 acres of vines.

Inside, it is one of the first work-core designs, built in 1969, almost simultaneously with a similar but larger cellar at Sonoma Vineyards, in Sonoma County.* Stainless steel fermentors fill one angle of the triangle. French oak barrels, the sole type of cooperage, fill the second angle, while the third holds cases of bottled wines. Wines going from one step in their production pass through a central work area on their way to the next phase.

The emphasis in vineyards and winery alike, for this is a genuine estate winery, is on Johannisberg Riesling and Cabernet Sauvignon, with supplementary amounts of Chardonnay and Chenin Blanc.

Owner Donn Chappellet oversees the operation of the ranch and winery as a business. A background in the automatic food vending business in Los Angeles honed his entrepreneurial skills to a fine point. The winemaking from 1969 through 1974 was done by Philip Togni, English-born, French-schooled, and a veteran of a great many other California winemaking jobs at cellars ranging in size from the gigantic E. & J. Gallo to the minuscule Chalone Vineyard in Monterey County. Togni, who seems to prefer pioneering to tenure, moved on shortly after the vintage of 1974. The new winemaker is Joe Cafaro, a young graduate of California State University at Fresno.

The eventual goal is wines of enormous substance. To date the Cabernet Sauvignon of 1969 most closely approaches the owner's best hopes, though the bone dry Chenin Blanc has drawn considerable critical attention in its best vintages.

The vineyard from which the wines come is not an old one in its present form, but the first vines on the property go back to the 1880s, when most of the vines in this frost-prone valley clung to slopes too steep for cold air to settle.

Chateau Montelena

Technically Chateau Montelena dates from 1969, when a window-shade manufacturer named Lee Paschich bought the nineteenth-century winery building of the Alfred Tubbs family in Calistoga. However, the place did not get into commercial operation until 1972 when Paschich took in James J. Barrett and Ernest W. Hahn and the three of them brought in Miljenko (Mike) Grgich as a fourth partner and the winemaker.

The winery proper restores to use a fine stone building dating from 1882, an era when this valley was full of first-rate stonemasons. An alleged resemblance to Château Lafite escapes me after close scrutiny of both places, but the main façade does have an encrustation of turrets and other Bordeauxish furbelows in support of its status as a château.

Montelena's present proprietors had the winery in operation for the vintage of 1972, and completely filled with new cooperage in time for the harvest of 1973. One gallery has two rows of temperature-controlled stainless steel fermentors, plus a row of Yugoslav oak tanks. The opposite gallery has a single row of German oak ovals, then ten rows of French oak barrels stacked head high. The total capacity is about 100,000 gallons. A separate cellar holds the bottled wines.

The plan is to make just four wines: Johannisberg Riesling for fresh, young

* The engineering principle is described in more detail in the Sonoma County chapter. See page
73

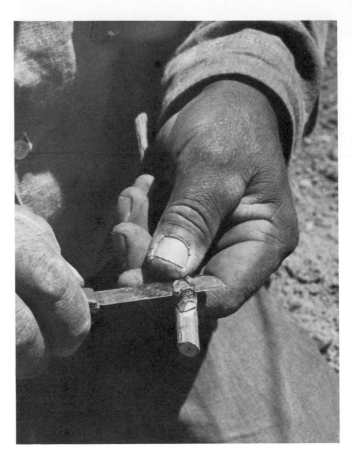

The tiny chip bud on the knife blade will grow into a whole fruiting vine—in this case grignolino. The rootstock foliage is trimmed away after the bud "takes." (HAROLYN THOMPSON)

drinking; Chardonnay for use as a long-aged white; Zinfandel as a frisky young red, and, finally, Cabernet Sauvignon as the age-worthy red.

Grgich, an enology graduate of the university in his native Yugoslavia, learned his California winemaking first with Lee Stewart at Souverain, then with Robert Mondavi. Somehow Grgich developed a harmonious sense of style out of his diverse education. His Chateau Montelena whites won instant praise as being sound and distinctive. The first reds, released in 1976, followed suit.

The winery-owned vineyards grow in the last few hundred feet of Napa Valley floor before the slopes of Mount St. Helena start their steep climb toward a 4,300-foot summit just to the north. Most of the 100-acre block is in the red varieties, especially cabernet sauvignon. These vines are supplemented with outside purchases, most of them, as the labels indicate, from a grower in the Alexander Valley, due north of Calistoga in Sonoma County.

Clos du Val Wine Company

It is axiomatic in the wine trade that small wineries survive the world over by offering distinctive wines to a loyal clientele. In part the distinction may come from a vineyard of uncommon quality, but in California a great proportion of it comes from a winemaker with an individual sense of style.

The coming of Clos du Val and Bernard Portet to the Napa Valley is a convincing demonstration, if one still is needed, that such is the case.

A rubber band holds chip bud in place on rootstock until it takes hold. (HAROLYN THOMPSON)

The only curious aspect of a winery building erected in 1973–1974 is that it nestles into one corner of a golf course east of Yountville, near the great rocky wall called Stag's Leap. Gracefully proportioned masonry walls shelter two rows of temperature-controlled stainless steel fermentors, a number of 3,000-gallon oak upright tanks for intermediate aging, and a growing collection of oak barrels coopered in Bordeaux. In short, the cellar looks much like its neighbors in the valley.

Clos du Val's own 120 acres of vineyards, adjoining the winery just to the north, were planted to cabernet sauvignon and zinfandel after 1973, in a sub-region which long has grown both varieties in volume.

While these vines are too young to have yielded fruit through the vintage of 1975, the winery has bought the same two varieties from independent growers near its own property, and coaxed from their grapes wines with pronounced French accents. One must assume that Portet is responsible, since the same vineyards in other seasons have yielded wines typical of the Napa Valley.

Portet came to the Napa Valley with an untrammeled Bordeaux palate to make Cabernet Sauvignon and Zinfandel, beginning in leased cellars in the vintage of 1972. The eldest son of the long-time winemaker at Château Lafite, he comes of a family with old roots in the Médoc. He was schooled in winemaking at the universities of Toulouse and Montpellier. What seems more important, somehow, is the fact that he grew up drinking French wines with food cooked for a French table.

The first results, reinforced by the 1973s and 1974s, were a full-bodied, tannically austere Zinfandel, and a surprisingly delicate, even feminine Cabernet Sauvignon. Each opens a new stylistic avenue for the Napa Valley.

The two reds are the only ones planned for the Clos du Val label, whose principal owner is M. Jean Goelet, a countryman of Portet's with agricultural properties in France, South America, and Australia as well as the Napa Valley. The eventual maximum capacity of the winery is 40,000 gallons.

Cuvaison

Cuvaison had its beginnings in 1970 when Thomas Cottrell and Thomas Parkhill abandoned scientific careers in Santa Clara County in order to make wine in the Napa Valley. The partnership lasted little more than a year before Parkhill withdrew. Cottrell continued alone until 1973, when a New York corporation called CT bought the property.

In 1974 the new owners began construction of a Spanish colonial-style winery building scaled to hold an eventual production of 35,000 to 40,000 gallons per year. In 1975 the corporate proprietors hired the much traveled Philip Togni as winemaker, replacing Cottrell.

In the first years Cottrell made wine outdoors in a quartet of steel fermentors set into a hillside niche above the Silverado Trail, south and east of Calistoga. The aging cellars were a handful of barrels in a rustic wood frame building. The several varietal wines did not challenge valley standards. A few of the first efforts, to be blunt about it, barely reached commercial acceptability. However, with experience and improved equipment, Cottrell got Cuvaison up to respectability before he departed.

Togni inherits a well-designed fermenting facility and a cellarful of new oak along with an inventory of plausible wines.

The winery owns a small vineyard. Most of the grapes are purchased from independent growers in the Napa Valley.

Franciscan Vineyards

Founded in 1973, Franciscan in fact got itself going only in the last months of 1975. The original proprietors, wild optimists, failed twice. The current proprietors, operating on more cautious assumptions, have a sound chance to stay in operation for years.

In brief chronology: The winery was founded by a San Francisco-based investment group, which erected and equipped a winery, and made almost 300,000 gallons of wine in its first vintage. The group sold no wine before it had to be reorganized. Some of the original proprietors participated in the second go-around, along with an infusion of Canadian hopefuls, with much the same results. The principal differences were that the second incarnation managed to sell a few bottles, and that it went flat broke. Finally, in November 1975, the present proprietors bought the name, inventory, and other assets of the business, leased the square concrete cellar building, and began operations with more cautious hopes.

The present proprietors are Raymond Duncan, a Colorado businessman, and

Justin Meyer, a veteran hand in Napa Valley winemaking, mostly with The Christian Brothers.

The basic source of grapes is 1,200 acres of vineyards in Napa, Sonoma, and Lake counties, owned by the same men as a separate venture.

They plan to crush only part of their crop for Franciscan during the next few seasons, selling the rest. In addition, they plan to sell as much of their wine production at the cellar door as they can while getting the business onto an even, if modest, footing.

Meantime, they have blended some of the old inventories into a line of moderately priced, agreeable wines, most of them varietals. The better ones go under the Franciscan label. The rest are sold as jug wines under the secondary Friars Table label.

Freemark Abbey

Freemark Abbey is the 1968 restoration by a new partnership of a defunct post-Prohibition label.

A smack of French oak pervades all of the varietal wines of Freemark Abbey, with the possible exception of the Johannisberg Riesling. This comes as no great surprise to veteran observers of California winemaking. Brad Webb sets the style of these wines. He was the enologist who helped James D. Zellerbach start California's French Oak Revolution at Hanzell Vineyards in Sonoma during the late 1950s.

Webb is one of seven partners in the winery. Three of his associates are vineyardists in the valley. One, Charles Carpy, is of pioneer Napa stock. Another, Laurie Wood, has been a lifelong resident. The third, William Jaeger, Jr., is a recent arrival. Their independently owned grapes, all from vineyards between the towns of St. Helena and Rutherford, go to the winery as the foundation of its crush. Freemark Abbey does buy small lots of special character, of which John Bosche's cabernet sauvignon from Rutherford is the prime example, and the only one with a special label to identify it.

Until 1973 the cellars were in the literal cellar of the original Freemark Abbey, alongside State Route 29 four miles north of St. Helena. The top floor of the two-story stone building had been preempted by a group of specialty shops before the partners in the new Freemark Abbey got together. Since 1973 the winery has expanded into a second building behind the original. It was newly constructed to hold the bottling room, cased goods storage, offices, and such.

The cellar proper holds about 50,000 gallons of wine when it is full. The fermentors are temperature-controlled stainless steel. Nearly all of the cooperage is European oak barrels.

After a lumbering start with too much flavor from a winery full of brand new barrels, the Chardonnay, Cabernet Sauvignon, and Pinot Noir began to place at or near the top in competitive tastings. In 1973 the winery produced a memorable botrytised Johannisberg Riesling named Edelwein.

Incidentally, there never was a religious connection in the name, Freemark Abbey. It was coined around the names of the original partners, taking the Free from Charles Freeman, the Mark from Mark Foster and the Abbey from Albert Ahern's nickname. Their winery was founded in 1939. Ahern bought out the other partners two years later, and flourished briefly. The enterprise foundered in 1962 after years of only minor activity.

Heitz Cellars

As befits a watershed enterprise, the physical aspects of Heitz Cellars reflect equally the Napa Valley's past and present.

Heitz has two winery buildings in a sheltered little fold in the hills east of St. Helena. One is a classic two-story stone barn fitted into a hillside by one Anton Rossi in pre-electric 1898 in such a way that grapes could arrive at the uphill side by the wagon load, then gravity could do most of the work of moving the wine thereafter. Face to face with the old cellar is a 1972 addition, a masonry octagon set up with a work core at its hub, so that the wine and winemaker must move only a minimal distance when the wine is racked or bottled even though electric pumps do much of the work.

A graduate of the University of California at Davis, a founder of the department of enology at California's other university wine school at Fresno, and a winemaker in other cellars before he launched his own, Heitz is able to feel at home with both old and new. His fermentors are temperature-controlled stainless steel, but both cellars are full of the fat barrels that have typified Burgundian cellars for several centuries.

The current buildings were not the beginning of Heitz Cellars. That took place in 1961 in a house-sized frame structure on State Route 29, one door south of Louis M. Martini in south St. Helena. The property had been Leon Brendel's Only One winery, a local enterprise so named because Brendel made wine from only one grape variety, an Italian red called grignolino.

Heitz acquired the grignolino vines along with the cellar, and has continued to make Grignolino and Grignolino Rosé as specialty wines, but he branched out immediately. I still remember him in the vintage of 1963 when he crushed a ton of pinot noir into five fifty-gallon barrels in one corner of the tiny cellar, and went around purple to his elbows for two weeks from punching down the caps bare-handed. However, in the first years Heitz grew not so much with the wine he crushed himself as with wise purchases of wine made by others. The classic example was his purchase of stocks from the Hanzell estate, the Chardonnays and Pinot Noirs he used to break the price line on California wine from the $3 range up to $6.

After the purchase in 1964 of what is now the main property, Heitz began to crush and ferment more and more of his own wine. In recent years he has bought very little bulk wine for finishing and blending.

Heitz does not own much vineyard except for his original grignolinos and a newer block of the same variety on the main winery property, plus a share in a vineyard on Zinfandel Lane. Rather he prefers to buy grapes from independent growers with highly distinctive properties. The best of these he identifies on his labels—McCrea, Mt. Eden, and, most important of them all, Martha's Vineyard.

This pattern has become so widely used among the small cellars of the Napa Valley that the relationships between vineyards and wineries have begun to resemble Burgundy much more than Bordeaux, however much cabernet sauvignon dominates Napa.

Within this framework of buying grapes, one variety from one vineyard, another from another, Heitz has made wines that consistently rank among the finest in California and the world at large in one critical tasting after another. The aim, especially in Chardonnays and Cabernet Sauvignons, is bone dry wine of huge proportions. Heitz's own word is, in his blunt Illinois way of speaking, guts. In addition to guts, most wines from Heitz carry a calculated reminder of their aging in wood, appropriately so in view of Heitz's role in making the Hanzell wines available to a broad audience.

The plan is for the winery to be about the same size as John Daniel's original Inglenook after several more years of slow growth. It was about half way to the goal in 1975.

Mayacamas Vineyards

An English petroleum engineer named Jack Taylor launched Mayacamas as a small winery in 1948. He sold it in 1968 before students of the game could figure out whether he was running a business or a hobby. The new proprietor, a genial young escapee from stockbroking, Bob Travers, has put the enterprise on a solid business footing without disturbing its scale. Even his long-range plan to double the capacity from 7,500 to 15,000 gallons will not alter the visible size of the carefully constructed old stone cellar or its newer concrete block companion.

Mayacamas clings to an upper ridge of an extinct volcano called Mt. Veeder, in the Mayacamas Mountains. The winery buildings nestle down into a kind of bowl where the cabernet sauvignon vines grow. In spite of a 1,500-foot elevation, the bowl makes the place secluded, its scale intimate. The chardonnays, however, are in another patch of thin soil clear up on top of the ridge where the view takes in large parts of Napa and Sonoma counties, the bay, and, on a wind-washed day, the distance-dimmed skyline of San Francisco. On all sides typical scrub forests of pine, oak, and madrone offer sanctuary to the relentlessly hungry birds with which Travers reluctantly shares his small crop.

Times change. In the early days of Napa wine most of the vineyards were well up into the hills, in part because the only frost protection was a steady slope. In that era most of the valley floor was planted to hay, because vines would not yield a paying crop. Now mist sprinklers and/or wind machines protect the vine-covered valley floor from frost while birds have become a tremendous economic threat up in the hills.

Travers is trying to make Mayacamas go with no more than four wines, perhaps only three. The three are Chardonnay, a bit of Chenin Blanc, and Cabernet Sauvignon from his own vines. The optional fourth is Zinfandel, either as a rosé or as a high-alcohol sweet wine made naturally rather than with fortifying brandy.

The vineyards at Mayacamas proved themselves during the Taylor regime, although the critical reputation of the wines became spotty after Taylor became an absentee owner and his staff began to forget to wash down the cooperage thoroughly. With renewed emphasis on careful winemaking—though not with fancy equipment—Mayacamas Chardonnay and Cabernet Sauvignon are always near the head of the class, and often at the top among the Napans.

Nichelini Vineyards

The one small Napa Valley winery with a long and unbroken past belongs to Jim Nichelini. Its fame does not spread far beyond Napa even though three generations have made wine on the family property since 1881.

The winery is an eclectic 30,000-gallon collection of barrels and casks squeezed into a stone cellar beneath a sturdy white frame house. The building flanks State Route 128 in the remote upper reaches of Chiles Valley, just one ridge short of the basin holding Lake Berryessa, or two ridges short of the Great Central Valley. The vineyards are a short distance away on a spur road leading into the heart of Chiles Valley.

Before Prohibition, Napa County had something on the order of a hundred small, anonymous wineries in simultaneous operation. Their proprietors made a few barrels of wine from small vineyards and either sold it in bulk to big firms or directly to the person who was going to drink it. In either case the unit was the barrel. It was a matter of newly emigrated winemakers running their California businesses much in the way of the ones they had left behind in Burgundy, or Italy, or wherever.

After Prohibition the business climate changed. Very few citizens bought wine at all, and almost none of them wanted it by the barrel. The bigger wineries increasingly chose to buy grapes so they could control the fermenting.

Jim Nichelini now bottles and labels his wine, but otherwise is Napa's lone remaining holdout from the old days, and happy about it. The uncluttered business technique of selling at the cellar door agrees with his gregarious nature. The wines he makes, all table wines, most of them varietal, are as straightforward as Nichelini himself, made to be drunk with meals and without deep pondering about vintages or slopes or other such, but with great pleasure nonetheless.

Oakville Vineyards

Oakville Vineyards entered the community of Napa Valley wineries largely as an act of will by one man, Wilfred E. van Löben Sels, who patiently assembled all sorts of partnerships and corporations beginning in 1968 in order to get a vineyard and winery into operation.*

Oakville had its beginnings in the Carmel Valley, in Monterey County, or at Almadén, or both. Van Löben Sels and his wife, Jean, lived in Carmel Valley in the mid-1960s, where they became friends with Peter Becker, then a winemaker at Almadén. The van Löben Sels wished to enter the wine business. Becker wished to work on a more modest scale than the one Almadén offered. They joined forces, formed Carmel Valley Wine Associates to gather capital, and began to hunt for prime vineyard land.

While ranging all through the coast valleys they decided to lease an idled bulk winery in the Napa Valley and crush some grapes from the vintage of 1968 as a kind of gesture to the future.

As chance would have it, the winery owners, three brothers named Bartolucci,

---

* Late in 1975, the van Löben Sels partnership defaulted on obligations; ownership of the winery buildings and principal vineyards reverted to members of the Bartolucci family. As of mid-1976, the winery continued to operate as Oakville Vineyards, though the future of the enterprise was uncertain.

also owned 260 acres of proven vineyard in three parcels in and near the town of Oakville. After two years of dickering, van Löben Sels arranged to purchase both winery and vineyards, forming a new limited partnership to gather the money.

The vineyards were the crux of the deal. Mature, planted to a spectrum of desirable varieties, they offered a guaranteed cash crop while the first small lots of wine were being made and aged, and the first markets for them sought. All three parcels were in cool climate Region I.

The winery, for its part, was a squat, solid masonry box full of outmoded equipment and overaged cooperage.

Since the purchase in 1970, the proprietors bit by bit have supplemented the old concrete fermentors with temperature-controlled stainless steel ones, and weeded out old redwood tanks in favor of a mixed cellarful of sound redwood and new oak barrels.

Becker, as winemaker, has persisted in making lean, even austere wines of classical styles. Van Löben Sels, as business manager, has marketed them in soberly traditional ways. The prides of the house are Cabernet Sauvignon and Sauvignon Blanc under the van Löben Sels label, and the same two wines plus Gewürztraminer under the Oakville Vineyards label. The winery also takes great pride in calling its generic wines Our House Red and Our House White rather than Burgundy or Chablis.

The ultimate goal established by the proprietors is annual sales of 100,000 cases, or a shade more than that.

Joseph Phelps Vineyards

Joseph Phelps, a Colorado contractor, came to California wine as a builder of wineries for others and succumbed to the romance himself. His winery on a gentle slope in the first rank of hills east of St. Helena is a tribute to two arts, building and winemaking.

Erected during 1974, the wood frame winery is two pavilions connected by a closed bridge. The northerly pavilion holds the stainless steel fermentors, some upright oak tanks, and a few oak oval casks from Germany. The south pavilion holds the European and American oak barrels for the aging of reds. The closed bridge holds the offices and laboratories. Phelps gave thoughtful attention to every detail in the building from a system of rolling bins and winches for getting red pomace to the press to a three-story stairway, carpeted, with a carved and gold-trimmed handrail.

The planned maximum capacity of the winery is in the neighborhood of 50,000 gallons, or, as the proprietors usually count their totals, 20,000 cases. Against this small figure the roster of three experienced winemakers is uncommonly high. The man in charge is Walter Schug, born in Germany and trained there, but an experienced hand in the valley after several seasons of working for another winery.

Somehow it comes as no surprise that the first wine under the Joseph Phelps label was a Johannisberg Riesling 1973 (crushed and fermented by Schug in a leased cellar), nor that a sizable proportion of the 100 acres of vineyard around the winery bear white riesling. Other varieties include gewürztraminer, sauvignon blanc, cabernet sauvignon, and the French strain of petite sirah. These vines, all young, will be supplemented for some time with grapes purchased from an independent grower named John Stanton who has ranches near Rutherford and Oakville.

Souverain of Rutherford

A man named Leland Stewart founded Souverain Cellars as a small winery in 1943, on the bones of one of the most beautifully situated chicken ranches in the northern hemisphere. All has changed.

Souverain Cellars, Inc., was purchased in 1972 by The Pillsbury Company, which operàtes it as a wholly owned subsidiary.* Souverain of Rutherford is the Napa Valley winery in the company, presently housed in a new building some miles to the south of the original. The company also operates a much larger winery, Souverain of Alexander Valley, in Sonoma County. Thirdly, it owns the venerable importing and sales firm of Frank Schoonmaker, Ltd.

During Stewart's ownership, the home vineyards and winery occupied a north-facing slope in the community of Angwin, a property now owned and operated by Burgess Cellars. At the beginning Stewart knew little about winemaking. His original motivation in buying the property was to escape an executive career in big business. By 1970, however, Lee Stewart had made some memorable contributions to the definitions of Johannisberg Riesling and Zinfandel, done a good deal toward establishing Petite Sirah as a varietal wine, written off Chardonnay as a waste of time, and reached a point at which he wished to slacken his pace. In that year he sold Souverain to a foursome of partners, two of them Napa vineyardists, the other two fiscal management executives. The four soon sold a majority interest to Pillsbury, stayed on as managers of the subsidiary, and launched construction of a new wood frame winery building with four times the capacity of the original. The long-range goal was to get Souverain up to annual sales of 75,000 cases, with all production coming from purchased grapes.

The theory was that the winery could not acquire fine grapes to make more than that volume of wine. The second winery, in Sonoma County, was built to produce greater quantities, which would allow Souverain of Rutherford to remain an elitist label.

Stewart has remained in contact with his old label as a consultant. His long-standing notion that white wines should be fermented in wood rather than steel to soften them has been adopted by winemaker Philip Baxter. The reds have changed for the softer under Baxter. Stewart used to make his in an uncommonly austere style.

All Souverain of Rutherford wines are varietals, vintage dated, with Napa Valley as the appellation. (For a time, before Souverain of Alexander Valley was in operation, the Napa winery offered some wines with Sonoma appellations, but this has ceased.)

Spring Mountain Vineyards

Spring Mountain Vineyards is one of those intense efforts of will that has been

---

* In spring, 1976, Pillsbury was in process of selling the winery at Rutherford, without its name. The name, Souverain, and a producing winery in Sonoma County were being sold separately.

living up to its name a little more each year and, in 1976, promises to continue to do so.

The label dates from 1968 when a Los Angeles property management specialist named Michael Robbins bought an elegant Victorian home just north of St. Helena, bonded the basement as a wine cellar, and contracted with established wineries in the valley to crush and ferment several small lots of wine for him.

In 1970 Robbins hired as winemaker Chuck Ortman, a one-time commercial artist who had spent several years in a winemaking apprenticeship to Joe Heitz. Since then Spring Mountain has conducted its crushing and fermenting operations under Ortman's direction in leased tanks, and has aged its wines in leased cellars.

In 1975 Robbins purchased the old Tiburcio Parrott property well up one flank of the peak named Spring Mountain. Parrott was a vineyardist, winemaker, and social lion of the 1880s whose property still reflects the golden age of most crafts. In the old barn fancy wrought iron grilles separate the horse stalls. The house, for its part, has inlaid oak woodwork outside the front door as well as inside.

Two hand-hewn tunnels exist as the core of the future Spring Mountain winery. One of these already has been renovated and is serving as the main aging cellar for Robbins' wines. An elegantly designed building is under construction in front of the tunnels.

Parrott's vineyards died long ago, but they were prized in their day. The main slope lies just below a famous independent vineyard of today, that of Jerome Draper. Robbins began the replanting early in spring 1976. Meantime, he has another vineyard on the east side of the valley near Oakville. It approached maturity with the harvest of 1975. Spring Mountain has title to the grapes of yet a third vineyard. Robbins is one owner in a partnership that holds almost 100 acres slightly higher up Spring Mountain than the home property.

Ortman's Spring Mountain wines to date have been remarkably consistent considering the extemporaneous conditions surrounding their birth and aging. The Chardonnay and Sauvignon Blanc in particular have been singled out by critics. Both are aged in oak barrels, as is Cabernet Sauvignon, the lone red. Fermentation is in steel.

Stag's Leap Wine Cellars

Napa's new wave of winemakers has come from every source, but I can think of none who made a longer professional jump than Warren Winiarski. The proprietor of Stag's Leap Wine Cellars came to winemaking from an academic post at the University of Chicago.

His first stop was at Lee Stewart's old Souverain Cellars, where he learned the trade from the lowly end up.

Winiarski founded Stag's Leap Wine Cellars in 1973. The winery and a vineyard of cabernet sauvignon are on the east edge of the valley, beneath a high, steep wall of rock called Stag's Leap. Clos du Val is a near neighbor in a sub-region that begins to show signs of developing an identity of its own.

The winery, nestled into a grove of oaks on a slope just above the Silverado Trail, shows the sort of thoughtful touches one might expect from a reasoning man, but is essentially a typical small cellar in this valley. The twin rows of fermentors are temperature-controlled stainless steel, and stand outdoors behind the cellar proper. Inside is a mixture of upright oak tanks, oak oval casks, and oak barrels. The tanks are mainly for fermenting and aging whites, a legacy of Winiarski's apprenticeship with Lee Stewart who used similar vessels in the same way. Reds ferment in steel then go into the small cooperage for aging.

Winiarski grows cabernet sauvignon on his gently sloping vineyard a few hundred yards east of the winery, with a patch of merlot in one corner. He purchases gamay from one vineyard in the Napa Valley, and two separate lots of white riesling, one from high in the hills east of his winery, the other lot from a grower in Mendocino County. Thus far the label has appeared only on Johannisberg Riesling, Cabernet Sauvignon, and Gamay. Other varietals will follow as the proprietor finds grapes that meet his standards.

Sterling Vineyards

The main cellar of Sterling Vineyards, erected in 1973, was designed and built as a vinous sensorium, a trip for the eye and ear as well as the palate.

The winery occupies a lofty knoll just south of Calistoga town. Visitors get from the parking lot up to it by means of a tramway, which rises 250 vertical feet and costs $2 to ride. Once inside the snowy white building, designed by one of the proprietors to resemble the ancient churches of the Greek Isles, Sterling does indeed provide a show. More accurately, it provides two interwoven shows, one arty, the other an instructive tour of a superbly equipped wine cellar.

The arty part includes a series of tile mosaics, an interplay of pastel light filtered onto the casks and barrels by stained glass windows, a roof garden of fountains, and a collection of fine antique furniture and wall hangings. For the ear there is a carillon rescued from St. Dunstan's church in London.

The working part of the winery contains superior collections of equipment ranging from temperature-controlled stainless steel fermenting tanks to whole galleries full of oak tanks and barrels from the length and breadth of Europe. All is on view from an elevated walkway that takes visitors through the entire sequence of making and aging table wines. Capacity approaches 100,000 cases.

Sterling was designed as it is because one of the business assumptions was to sell wine only in the winery in California, though people in other parts of the nation may buy through regular retail outlets.

Sterling wines are made entirely from winery-owned vineyards or ones owned by the proprietors. Sterling's directing partners are Peter Newton and Michael Stone, who also are owners of a San Francisco-based paper company named Sterling International. (The use of the symbol for Pound Sterling on the foil capsules of their wine bottles reflects a prevalence of English ancestry in the ownership.) The winemaker is a formidably skillful young graduate of U.C.-Davis named Rick Forman.

The earliest Sterling wines came from the vintage of 1969, and were made in a small building down at the foot of the hill below what is now the winery. The vineyards from which they came were planted beginning in 1964. The prime varieties are cabernet sauvignon, zinfandel, chardonnay, gewürztraminer, and sauvignon blanc. All go into vintage-dated varietal wines with Napa Valley as the appellation of origin. Total acreage is 400, all of it in the immediate vicinity of the winery at the north end of the valley. Much was beginning to bear full crops in 1975. When the winery is at its full capacity it will rank among the middle sized rather than the small ones.

Stonegate Winery

Stonegate, founded in 1973, belongs to a middle western family named Spaulding. The proprietors acquired their small but properly equipped cellar with the firm idea of making wines only from hillside vineyards. To their credit, it took them no more than one vintage to learn that not all hills grow great vines and not all great vines grow on hills.

The Spauldings own a small vineyard in the hills west of Calistoga in which chardonnay dominates the plantings, and purchase their other grapes from independent growers.

Their winery, south of Calistoga on the same lane as Sterling, has stainless steel fermentors, then oak tanks and barrels for aging. The total capacity approaches 20,000 gallons. The family makes its own wines with technical help from Robert Stemmler, a veteran hand in the valley. Their first releases, from the vintage of 1973, were Chenin Blanc, Sauvignon Blanc, and Pinot Noir.

Stony Hill Vineyard

Stony Hill belongs to a man of great style named Fred McCrea, who makes a few hundred cases of wine each year from his thirty-seven acres of shy-bearing mountainous vineyards.

In the economics of California wine, or even Napa Valley wine, Stony Hill amounts to almost nothing. But it is one of the admirable qualities of wine that gross economics cannot always get in the way of a fine bottle. Stony Hill is one case in point.

McCrea thinks all white wines ought to be fresh and delicate. He has persisted with the notion long enough and well enough for Stony Hill to pay its way as a winery. The tiny annual restatement of his theorem disappears within weeks of its availability. For a long time, though, McCrea's vineyards, which predate the winery, subsidized his tiny production of Chardonnay, Gewürztraminer, and White Riesling. For years he sold much of his crop to Lee Stewart at Souverain, or Joe Heitz at Heitz Cellars.

In 1943 McCrea was enchanted with his first view of a property then known as Goat Hill after its principal crop. He and his wife, Eleanor, bought the place, north of St. Helena and high in the west hills, as a weekend retreat and eventual place to retire after McCrea had done all he wished to do as a vice-president of McCann-Erickson, the advertising agency. The first vines, a couple dozen of them, were set out so the new tenants would have something to do weekends. After a few seasons of dabbling, the McCreas paid a visit to Herman Wente in Livermore and came home with enough cuttings of chardonnay to get into vine growing on a commercial scale. Gewürztraminer, white riesling, and a small patch of semillon came later.

Inevitably the next phase was a barrel of homemade wine. Finally, in 1951, the

McCreas built a nicely proportioned masonry cellar in a grove of oaks and launched Stony Hill as a winery on its own.

In the years since its founding the winery capacity has grown steadily to its present size, 2,500 gallons, all of it in French oak barrels and German oak oval casks. The cellar is equipped with remarkably sophisticated equipment from its custom-designed crusher and press to its two spout bottling machine, but the scale remains so small that the extemporaneous solution is a frequent part of the winemaking. My favorite recollection is of an electric blanket draped over a reluctant barrel of Chardonnay to keep it fermenting through a cool break in the autumn weather.

Sutter Home Winery

From 1945 until 1969 Sutter Home was a kind of silent partner in the Napa Valley. Its owners, a family named Trinchero, stayed somewhat aloof from the valley's close-knit fraternity of winery owners and winemakers. They made one of every type, selling at prices one cut below prevailing figures and mainly at the cellar door.

In 1969 the pattern broke. Trinchero faces became more evident at social events in the valley. The wines, costlier than before, began to appear at wine shops throughout northern California. It was almost like the wedding after one of those long, silent, ritual Mediterranean courtships.

After all those years, the turning point did not come from Napa Valley grapes. Rather it was a Zinfandel from an ancient vineyard in the gold rush country of Amador County, in the Sierra Nevada foothills. The vintage was 1968. A special label identified the wine as Deaver Ranch Zinfandel. Wine from this vineyard became an ever greater fixture with each passing vintage until, in 1974, it was the only red made at Sutter Home. The plan is to continue with a considerable volume of it, and a small annual lot of sweet light Muscat.

As a name, Sutter Home is a revival of a pre-Prohibition Napa winery operated by a family named Sutter. They occupied the present site, across State Route 29 from Louis M. Martini, from 1906 until they went out of business in 1930. Earlier the classic wood frame, barn-style winery building had been the pioneer operation of J. Thomann.

Until the thick, dark Zinfandel from Amador took over, most of the cellar had been overaged oak oval casks, plus redwood for fermenting. Now Bob Trinchero has a battery of stainless steel fermenting tanks at one side of the winery, a few redwoods for early aging, and two sizable galleries full of oak barrels for final aging of the red. A separate set of small stainless tanks in the main cellar holds the fermenting Muscat.

Yverdon Vineyards

Yverdon, founded in 1970, is a dramatic enterprise for the main fact that the proprietors, Fred and Russell Aves, father and son, have taken an extreme Renaissance view of it.

They erected a fairly sizable stone cellar, having split their own rocks for the walls. The finishing touches, also of their own design and execution, include stained glass windows, wrought iron staircases, and cast concrete pedestals on which rest oak

The traditional picker's knife in California has a short, curved blade. The grapes are zinfandels. (WINE INSTITUTE)

casks coopered by the owners, or, at least, assembled by them. Needless to say the Aves are planting their own vines on craggy slopes around the winery high up on Spring Mountain due west of St. Helena and on gentler terrain near Calistoga.

Like many others of the new wave, Fred Aves came to wine from a completely disrelated past. He retired as a manufacturer of automobile equipment in Los Angeles in favor of the new career. Son Russell is rather an instant second generation in the family winery, serving as the winemaker.

The first wines of the Aves' own making, Chenin Blanc and Gamay, reflect the spirit of the proprietors, which is to say, tough and sturdy.

Sparkling Wine Specialists

Although several wineries in the Napa Valley make sparkling wines as part of their general operations, two firms have come to do nothing else. The names are Hanns Kornell and Schramsberg. Yet another, the French-owned M & H, was, in 1975, in the process of joining them.

Hanns Kornell Champagne Cellars

Hanns Kornell Third Generation Champagne, to give it its full name, is a one-man show run by the founder and namesake, a stocky, inexhaustible man who has built a sizable business almost entirely out of his own labor. Horatio Alger could not have written a better story.

Kornell emigrated to California from Germany in the late 1930s with a good deal of sparkling wine experience and hardly any money at all. The figure he likes to quote is $3.62 at the moment he touched shore in New York. Between then and 1952 he worked for several other wineries and a couple of gasoline stations in order to accumulate enough capital to make his own start. In 1952 he was able to open a winery in a leased building near the town of Sonoma. From then until 1958 he made wine at night and sold it during the day. In the latter year, Kornell was able to buy the fine old stone winery buildings that had been the Salmina Brothers' Larkmead Cellars for a few prestigious years in the 1930s and 1940s.

Those cellars, on Larkmead Lane just south of Calistoga, now hold 2 million bottles of maturing stocks of Kornell sparkling wines, all of them made by the true *méthode champenoise* to the point of riddling in the traditional way, and disgorging as the task was done in the 1880s.

When Kornell departs from Champagne—the original place—it is in his lingering fondness for rieslings as the dominant grape in his cuvées, especially Brut and the long-aged specialty he calls Sehr Trocken. Kornell prefers rieslings to chardonnay for the taste and for the technical balance they bring to his blends.

Kornell does not own vineyards himself, preferring to scout around among his fellow winemakers in the valley for promising young wines he can buy. The sources vary from vintage to vintage, but the character of the sparkling wines Kornell produces from his mixed bag remains uncannily consistent, even constant.

The Brut and Sehr Trocken are completely dry, a good deal drier than the American palate is used to finding under the name Brut. The Sehr Trocken, left on the yeasts for as long as eight years, has aged qualities not found in American sparkling wines from elsewhere. The other Kornell cuvées are affable in style.

Schramsberg Vineyards

Schramsberg is where Robert Louis Stevenson tasted every variety and shade of Schramsberger, red and white Schramsberger, Burgundy Schramsberger, Schramsberger Hock, Schramsberger Golden Chasselas, and the Scots writer feared in in *Silverado Squatters* to think how many more.

Stevenson would not have such a long day's work now. The old limestone caves and hilltop vineyards near Calistoga go to the making of sparkling wines and only those.

Schramsberg had a great many desolate days between the last of Jacob Schram's still wines and the first of Jack Davies' sparkling ones. But Davies has been getting along very well since he quit supervising the manufacture of pasteboard boxes in 1965 for the avowed purpose of making sparkling wines that would not have to give ground to Champagnes from that hallowed place.

The technique, like Kornell's, is classic: The longest possible time on tirage using yeasts carted back from one of the great houses of Epernay; hand riddling; a dosage compounded with Cognac when there is any dosage at all; and all the other traditional steps. Unlike his neighbor just down the hill, Davies uses chardonnay and pinot noir as the bases of his cuvées, adding small dollops of other but related grapes for complexity.

Davies wishes to beat Champagne at its own game, but not at any loss to his

California identity. In fact the word Champagne appears on the Schramsberg label only because United States law requires it to, and then in the smallest size of type permitted. In short, Davies' struggle is somewhat akin to the one James Zellerbach once staged at Hanzell using Burgundy as a model.

The results thus far have won widespread critical acclaim. Schramsberg Brut is essentially of chardonnay, most of it from Davies' own vines in vintages after 1973. The Blanc de Noir comes mainly from pinot noir, also from the home vineyard in recent vintages, and is finished dry. There are, in addition, a rosé from gamay and a sweet cremant from a U.C.-Davis hybrid called flora, related to gewürztraminer.

Although a reincarnate Stevenson would have a shorter list of Schramsberger to taste now, he would have no trouble finding or recognizing the place. The road up Mt. Diamond from State Route 29 winds through the same thickets of scrap trees and underbrush to emerge in the same clearing, in front of the great white house, as it did in Jacob Schram's day. The winemaking still is housed in the uphill set of tunnels, and the aging in the lower set. The principal change is a small board and batten building in front of the lower tunnels in which the disgorging and other sparkling wine processes take place. Davies' eventual goal is to increase his production from its current 4,000 cases annually to a figure nearer 12,000 cases. The increase will fit within the existing winery.

The two men, Kornell and Davies, have established enough reputation for Napa Valley sparkling wines to have attracted a third entry to the arena of specialists. The French firm of Moët & Hennessy purchased 800 acres of Napa land in three parcels early in 1973. The plan is to build a sparkling-wine cellar on the west side of the village of Yountville on one parcel. The other two—one straddling the Napa-Sonoma County line in Carneros, the other in the Mayacamas Mountains west of Napa City—have been planted in vineyard.

To get launched in the market, M & H has contracted to buy grapes from Trefethen Vineyards near Napa city, and to make wine in an old cellar on the Trefethen property.

The first cuvée went down in 1975, in spring, using wine from the vintage of 1974. The wine and the cuvée were made by a team of enologists from Moët headed by Edmund Maudières.

The proprietors have set themselves the interesting task of labeling and selling their wine by some name other than Champagne. What that new name will be had not been disclosed in early 1976, a few months prior to introduction of the first cuvée to the market.

On the Brink

There are several ways to be on the brink in tumultuous times, and the Napa Valley has wineries poised in each of the possible postures, plus a couple which have plunged the wrong way. They are noted very briefly in the following section, in alphabetic order.

Caymus Vineyards

The propriety of a veteran grape grower near Rutherford, Caymus is a tiny cellar selling varietals, mostly within a few miles of home.

Owner Charles Wagner selects small lots of grapes from his ninety-acre vineyard for his own wine, selling the rest of the crop elsewhere. The winery, a small plain barn behind Wagner's house, is efficiently equipped, and has room to grow. Whether it does or not depends partly on the market for expensive varietals, more on the continued interest of the founder's son in expanding the small beginnings.

Château Chevalier

A partnership owns the winery. One of the partners, James E. Fruh, also owns a newly planted adjoining vineyard that is to be the sole source of Château Chevalier wines. The other principal, Greg Bissonette, is the winemaker.

The primary wines are to be Chardonnay and Cabernet Sauvignon as soon as the vineyards bear enough mature fruit for winemaking. Through the early months of 1976, no wine had gone to market under the main label, though wines from purchased grapes have been made and sold under the secondary name, Mountainside.

The romantic old stone cellar comes by its name honestly. It was built in the 1890s by a chap named Chevalier. The building hides away in a tight fold of Spring Mountain west of St. Helena, its size a guarantee that Château Chevalier always will be a small enterprise in its current form.

Diamond Creek

A California businessman named Al Brounstein retired from commerce to develop a small vineyard near Calistoga as a source of distinctive Cabernet Sauvignons. The first wines, from the vintage of 1973, were fermented outdoors for lack of a winery. Since then the fermentations have taken place under roofs, in leased space, but the volume remains minuscule.

Lyncrest Vineyards

A financial adviser named Richard Lynn founded Lyncrest as a winery after several years as an independent vineyardist. Chenin Blanc and Johannisberg Riesling from the vintage of 1972 appeared in the California market, and were fairly well received, but not well enough to prevent the firm from going bankrupt early in 1975. The old wooden winery was emptied of wine and equipment as part of the creditors' sale.

Ironically, Lynn made a sideline of counseling would-be investors in the wine business through a series of seminars, then was the first Napa winery to go under when the investment fever in wine cooled beginning in 1974.

J. Mathews Winery

A Southern California businessman named Kenneth Nelson owns and operates the J. Mathews winery and label, principally through outlets in the Los Angeles region. The winery proper goes back to pre-Prohibition times when it was known as the Lisboa cellars and specialized in a port-type wine. More recently it had been a jug winery owned by a family named Carbone. The old stone building in downtown Napa City is only an aging facility. Nelson purchases new wines in bulk for his label.

Mt. Veeder Vineyards

The vineyard is a small one planted almost entirely to cabernet sauvignon. The winery is of a proportionate size, at one side of the vines well up in the Mayacamas Mountains, on the extinct volcano called Mt. Veeder. The operating partners are Michael Bernstein, who fled a law office in Los Angeles to grow the grapes, and Kimball Giles, a long-time winemaker for small cellars in the north coast counties. The first wine went on sale in 1976. It is a Cabernet Sauvignon from 1972.

Pope Valley Winery

An old wood frame winery building dates back to 1909 under earlier owner-ships, but did not become Pope Valley Winery until 1972, when a young electronics engineer named James Devitt bought the place.

He has courted the romance of winemaking since then with a business that is full-time after a start as a weekend avocation. The wines are available only in California. Most are varietals made from purchased grapes.

Pope Valley, incidentally, is not a part of the Napa River drainage. Rather its waters flow into Lake Berryessa just to the east, then into the Putah Creek system, which empties into the Sacramento River.

Raymond Vineyards

The Raymond vineyards and winery, new in 1974, belong to a family with a long history in the Napa Valley. Roy Raymond, Sr., had a long career with Beringer Brothers before he joined his sons in a family cellar.

The family vineyard, ninety acres, is on Zinfandel Lane just south of St. Helena. Planted to several varieties, it will be the sole source of grapes for a winery scaled to take precisely as many grapes as the acreage will grow. The equipment is typical: temperature-controlled stainless steel fermentors and small oak cooperage.

Roy, Jr., is the vineyardist, Walter, the winemaker. Both men trained at U.C.-Davis.

No wines had come to market as of early 1976.

Silveroaks Cellars

The current proprietors of Franciscan Vineyards, Raymond Duncan and Justin Meyer, founded Silveroaks in 1972, with the intent of using the label only for choice lots of Cabernet Sauvignon from vineyards they own. Since acquiring Franciscan in 1975, they have retained the separate company with the original purpose still in mind. The small cellar building near Yountville holds in oak barrels about 15,000 gallons of the proprietors' best Cabernet Sauvignon from each vintage since 1973. The debut vintage is due to appear in the market late in 1976, or early in 1977.

Stag's Leap Winery

A Los Angeles entrepreneur named Carl Doumani bought the old Stag's Leap property of pioneer days in 1970 with an eye to restoring a winery that once flourished on the property. As of 1975, part of the 100-acre vineyard had been planted, and some wine had been made in a leased cellar in nearby Rutherford.

Litigation over the proprietorship of the name Stag's Leap went against Doumani and in favor of Warren Winiarski, of Stag's Leap Wine Cellars, which is just a few hundred yards to the south.

Doumani may have to alter his label before he enters the market with new wines, unless he can reverse the original court judgment of 1975 on appeal.

Trefethen Vineyards

The family of industrial executive Gene Trefethen owns nearly 600 acres of vineyard just north of Napa city, and has begun to make small amounts of wine in a finely made wood frame winery building on the site. They will proceed slowly with their own label, however, for much of their crop and most of their winery is committed to M & H, the subsidiary of Moët & Hennessy which is making sparkling wine in the Napa Valley.*

As M & H moves into its own buildings and as its own vineyards mature, the Trefethens will enlarge their operations.

John Trefethen, Gene's son, manages the property and has made the first wines under the watchful eye of the M & H cellar staff. A 1973 Chardonnay is likely to be the first Trefethen wine marketed. The planned date was autumn, 1976.

Veedercrest Vineyards

Owned by a limited partnership and operated by A. W. Baxter, Veedercrest has young vineyards on the slopes of Mt. Veeder in the Mayacamas Mountains west of Napa City, and a young winery in the basement of Baxter's home in Berkeley.

The early wines, from grapes purchased in 1972 from several independent vineyardists, have appeared in the market.

Baxter and his partners plan to construct a winery on their 300 acres in the Napa Valley as the winery outgrows his basement. Eventual annual production is to be in the neighborhood of 15,000 cases.

Villa Mt. Eden

The James McWilliams family has owned an historic vineyard near Yountville for some years. In 1974 they bonded a premises and crushed the first wine for their own label. There are to be several varietals. The first hint at their eventual quality was a 1972 Gewürztraminer made by Heitz Cellars and identified on the label as coming from the Mt. Eden Vineyard.

The winemaker is Nils Venge, trained at U.C.-Davis and seasoned by several years of practical experience in Napa wineries.

The Vineyards

In describing Napa Valley wineries and winemaking, the emphasis has been on

* See page 57.

men rather than property for the serious reason that it is men who separate this valley from others in California.

One of the ways men have separated Napa, though, is that the winemakers long since have begun to make fine distinctions among the vineyards they use. In this respect they have worked their way onto a middle ground far ahead of the other districts of California, but a long distance short of the rigid compartmenting of Bordeaux, or Burgundy, or the Mosel.

Ironically, the current patterns of ownership and the climate may balk the logical next step, the etching of some more definitive lines within the valley. Because the climates within the valley are so diverse and so versatile, the lines will be much harder to draw than the one that separates Pauillac from St. Estèphe within the Médoc. The whole of the Médoc forms its boundaries with cabernet sauvignon. A boundary in the Napa Valley must work its way through pinot noir, chardonnay, and white riesling, too, so may have to distinguish between St. Estèphe and Bernkastel as a matter of equivalents.

Since the largest and most established of the wineries draw grapes from dozens of vineyards scattered the length of the valley, their owners may be unwilling to begin carving new lines and establishing new names. What is more, the private maps in the heads of winemakers do not all trace the same routes. André Tchelistcheff draws one line important to him along Zinfandel Lane, at the south side of St. Helena. For Louis P. Martini, a more important boundary is a wavery one running a certain distance from the Napa River. The rest of the experienced hands have other thoughts. In any one head the notions differ with each grape variety.

At least the difficult task has begun. The winery owners have formed a committee and now meet across a table full of maps.

Meanwhile, the irremediables, climate and exposure and soil have contributed greatly to a practical sorting out of grape plantings within the valley. Soils range from light, decomposed granite to heavy clay, climate from cool Region I to middling warm Region III on the University of California at Davis scale, and sun exposures run the gamut. The combined factors of environment create five roughly definable districts, three on the valley floor and one in each of the parallel ranges of hills.

The coolest and cloudiest of the lot is the one called Carneros at the southern tip of the valley next to the Bay across from San Francisco. It also is the best defined for being separated from the others by salt marshes and the city of Napa.

Vineyards came to the low, rolling, grassy hills of Carneros early, but they were Agoston Haraszthy's and Phylloxera came with them. None survived long enough to be disgraced by Prohibition. Louis M. Martini started the revival of Carneros in 1952. Beringer Brothers (the old name before Nestlé changed it to Beringer/Los Hermanos) followed a few years later. The real flowering came after 1960, the year Beaulieu Vineyards bought 300 acres on a gentle rise facing out over the Bay. Since then Inglenook, Charles Krug, M & H, and the Sonoma winery called Buena Vista have joined the company of wineries with Carneros vineyards. Several independent growers also have vines in the region.

Carneros seems to be Napa's most hospitable climate for the great grapes of Burgundy, chardonnay and pinot noir, and it is these varieties that dominate the

2,000 acres of vines planted there. Curiously, white riesling does not ripen at all well in Carneros though it does yield fragrant wines for growers who will lavish care upon the grapes for uncertain returns.

By far the largest sub-region in acreage is the long, narrow mid-section of valley floor running from the north side of Napa city to a point somewhere between Rutherford and St. Helena, or, in other formulations, just including St. Helena. This is the hardest region for which to fix absolute boundaries, the most versatile one, and thus the one with the greatest number of lines running through it on the private maps in winemakers' heads. In the University climate scale it ranges from warm Region I through warm Region II, or maybe cool Region III.

Independently owned vineyards grow more than half of the grapes within this area although most of the major wineries own one or more large parcels within it. Some of the valley's most famous individual vineyards fall within the boundaries however they are drawn. The original home vineyards of Inglenook and Beaulieu are two examples. The old ToKalon vineyards are at Oakville. Before Prohibition they belonged to H. H. Crabb, who used his property to test hundreds of grape varieties as well as to grow some of the great wines of that era. ToKalon has been divided among several owners of which Charles Krug is the principal one. Not far from ToKalon, hard against the west hills, is Martha's Vineyard, the source of grapes for the Heitz Cellars Cabernet Sauvignon that has become something of a legend over the span of just five vintages.

Cabernet Sauvignon certainly is the dramatic example of how well this region can grow grapes because so many of the finest ones have come from identified vineyards within it. Less obviously it has produced outstanding Chardonnays, Johannisberg Rieslings, and Pinot Noir. The versatility is a mixed blessing in the view of purist connoisseurs, but a salvation for growers, who always can hope for a minimum of one fine varietal vintage.

Not incidentally the independent vineyardists in this region are one group of people whose presence has made the Napa Valley more favored than its competitors in the state. Since the turn of the century the valley has been a socially correct summer address for prominent San Franciscans. The value for Napa wine is the willingness of many people of wealth to grow grapes for whatever price the wineries could pay, but to grow them as well as the fruit could be grown.

Calistoga, at the north end of the valley, is the hub of the warmest part of the floor even though it is only 200 feet above sea level, not much higher than the south end. For a long time only independent growers worked these soils, and they focussed on the coarser varieties. It does not seem an accident that the two principal wineries now there, Sterling Vineyards and Chateau Montelena, did not locate on their current sites until after the development of a climate-modifying technique called overhead mist irrigation. In effect, the system sprinkles vineyards the way people sprinkle lawns, with fine overhead sprays. The result is a very considerable modification of sun heat and sun rays, one that vines cannot seem to distinguish from the mid-season showers that sweep across Bordeaux.

To this point the two most satisfactory varieties at Calistoga have been chenin blanc and zinfandel. With the advent of mist, such as merlot, pinot noir, and chardonnay have shown great promise.

The west hills, the hills of the morning light, stretch from Napa city to Calistoga. Elevation, as all students of the Merriam Life Zones know, retards the increase in warmth to a great degree, so that it is possible to be as cool 1,500 feet above St. Helena as in Carneros. In addition the eastward exposure tempers the sun still more. Alas, there are but a few pockets of soil on these steep slopes, most of them in little dips and swales that hide what vineyards there are from the view of passersby on the valley floor. Mont LaSalle and Mayacamas are the largest and best known of those flanking Napa city and Oakville. On Spring Mountain above St. Helena are Stony Hill, and the great Spring Mountain vineyards of independent grower Jerome Draper, Sr., plus a good many smaller or newer ones of promise. White grapes seem to do particularly well on these slopes. There is a dominance of such as chardonnay, gewürztraminer, and white riesling.

The east hills are a different world altogether. In contrast to the wooded slopes on the west side of the valley, these are dry, brown, sun-beaten pitches. The west hills have but a thin covering of soil. Those on the east let ribs of rock show through for miles on end. The vineyards of Donn Chappellet show the intense limitations these craggy hills impose. His vines grow on a north-facing side of Pritchard Hill. Stand in them, and the view stretches away to the north, all desolate terrain dried to the color of lion hide, except where scrub grows at the bottoms of gullies. Chappellet and Burgess Cellars at Angwin have the only major plantings on the main slopes. Others on the east side of the main valley tuck into little pocket valleys where the vines do not have to endure the withering sun until it sets. The varieties that do well are the ones that like sun: petite sirah, zinfandel, and, if the tilt is right, cabernet sauvignon.

In the valley at large a handful of varieties dominate the plantings. Cabernet sauvignon outstrips all the others with 5,210 acres. Then come pinot noir (2,525), chardonnay (2,250), zinfandel (1,315), white riesling (1,140), petite sirah (1,135), chenin blanc (1,134), and napa gamay (1,005). These few make up 15,000 acres out of a 1974 total of 22,000.

Sonoma County

At the little town of Sonoma, in the southeastern corner of sprawling Sonoma County, Franciscan missionaries established the last and northernmost of their vineyards against a steep flank of hills in 1825. A few hundred yards away on an estate he called Buena Vista, Agoston Haraszthy set out northern California's first ranging collection of classic European wine grapes in 1862. At the turn of the century, the first incarnation of Italian Swiss Colony was making the first estimable sparkling wines from California grapes. Beginning in the 1950s, a tiny cellar called Hanzell precipitated a still-growing revolution in the style of California wines when it began using small barrels made from flavorful European oak while all others used something else.

And yet Sonoma wines have languished long and deep in the shadow of those from the Napa Valley, one row of hills to the east.

From the end of Prohibition in 1933 until the end of the 1960s, most of the growers and winemakers in the county were content to dawdle along making red, white, and pink wine to sell in bulk to prestigious names in Napa or Santa Clara, or ones with money in the San Joaquin Valley. For all practical purposes there were no vintage wines from Sonoma between 1935 and 1967. Few people made varietal wines. Fewer still used Sonoma as an appellation of origin. After Buena Vista, Italian Swiss Colony, Korbel, and Sebastiani there were almost no labels, in spite of a roster of wineries that never numbered fewer than thirty.

Perhaps size and confused topography defeated the delicate balance between the sense of community and sense of competition that seems indispensable to the making of fine wine, for Sonoma is, at a minimum, two separate winegrowing regions. The Valley of the Moon faces into San Francisco Bay while the Russian

River system looks toward the Pacific Ocean. The latter region, ill-defined, has not been any too cohesive within itself in the past.

In neither valley was the difficulty with sun and soil. These were so amenable in both districts that there always were authorities to make the annual harvest season speech to the local winemakers' association, saying that Sonoma County had tremendous potential as a region for making varietal table wines, that the county might well have greater natural gifts than the Napa Valley. Sonoma's climate zones, after all, ranged from cool Region I through warm Region III in terrain so tumbled it offered every possible orientation to the sun, and so extended it offered every kind of soil.

It would even happen, from time to time, that Sonoma wines would speak for themselves. The 1935 Cabernet Sauvignon of Simi won a state fair gold medal in 1941 (and is still around, thick and dark and aggressive as ever). The honey-gold, barbarously rich 1957 Chardonnay from Hanzell has only now begun a grudging descent from its glorious peak. Other examples belabor the point, but not enough to have made Sonoma County a mecca for bibbers.

Only with the turn into the 1970s did the force that pushes winemakers to do superior work begin pushing at Sonomans.

The sense of change came with a rush. There sticks in memory a soft afternoon in May of 1971 when Russ Green hauled me up to a grassy knoll overlooking his Alexander Valley—and it genuinely was his then—and talked for hours about the astonishing wines he was getting out of his grapes. Anybody who could get excited enough to drive a Lincoln sedan across half a mile of bumpy meadow to get the right perspective on his vineyard was on the threshold of something important. Green did it twice. He had been up earlier to put some brand new Simi whites on a bed of ice in a hollow-trunked tree so we could drink a toast.

Green's enthusiasm was contagious. In the Russian River region he soon had Geyser Peak, Sonoma Vineyards, and Souverain as larger new company, and Dry Creek as smaller. They joined Korbel, Pedroncelli, and some lesser lights. Over in the Valley of the Moon, Buena Vista and Sebastiani quickened pace while several small newcomers came to surround them.

As spring rounded into summer in 1975 it became obvious that Sonoma has some growing pains. These likely will endure for the next several years, but one can hope with good reason that the region will not fall back into its laggard habits of earlier times.

First, some fine and a few potentially great wines have come out of the new age to serve as benchmarks. Second, the fine crop of new wineries will beg to be used. Third, and doubtless most important, the vineyards have been upgraded to superior quality.

As in the Napa Valley, the soaring vineyard acreage of Sonoma County—10,600 acres in 1960; 22,500 in 1974—is accompanied by a narrowing focus in grape varieties. Because bulk winemaking remains relatively important in the Russian River region, the winnowing of such common varieties as alicante and burger has not advanced as far as in Napa. However, recent plantings are primarily of coastal California's Big Four: chardonnay and white riesling for white wines; cabernet sauvignon and pinot noir for reds.

THE RUSSIAN RIVER VALLEYS

For almost a hundred miles the Russian River nudges and darts southward through the Coast Ranges on its inevitable way to San Francisco Bay. Suddenly, at Healdsburg, the stream shifts course to the west. Instead of the Bay, the Russian empties into the Pacific Ocean at a village called Jenner, fifty-six crow-flight miles upcoast from San Francisco.

The river is not a bad analogy for the local history of winegrowing.

At one early time the region had close to a hundred wine cellars in it. Most of them were humble barns, meant to do no more than shelter new wine from open skies during the first weeks of its infancy. A sparse few stone or brick structures were there to do nobler work.

Except for a dwindling of the number of cellars, the picture changed very little during the first century of winemaking in the Russian River watershed.

Not long ago—ten years is enough—keen students of California wine knew that Korbel got most of the grapes for its sparkling wine from vineyards in the region, and there was the jug wine Italian Swiss called Napa-Sonoma-Mendocino. After these, one had to hunt hard to find a wine from Healdsburg or its surrounds. A moribund Simi sold a few bottles at the door. So did lively bulk outfits, mainly including Martini & Prati, J. Pedroncelli, and, to a lesser degree, Cambiaso and Foppiano. As for the rest, bulk was the only business. Fredson and Frei, Seghesio, and Sonoma Co-op did not bottle a drop (and still do not). From the outside, Simi's sturdy building of local stone had a touch of elegance. The rest looked pretty much like warehouses, or packer's sheds, or auction barns.

Once Russ Green bought Simi and revived its label in the marketplace, the region made its sharp turn. Geyser Peak, Sonoma Vineyards, and Souverain put up buildings astonishing for size and style, establishing labels to go with them. J. Pedroncelli and F. Korbel & Bros. launched lists of serious table wines. Cambiaso built a new cellar and joined the parade. Foppiano started making varietal wines without a new building.

The Middle-Sized Cellars

Every wine region in the world needs the kind of economic and aesthetic backbone provided by firms of considerable size and skill. They help keep prices down on supplies, and they leave crannies in rail cars so little guys can afford to ship their wines away. With their wines they take the sting, or at least some of it, out of vagaries in the climate, and they set standards for the region which push the small owners to do something excellent and not just routine.

One of the greatest sources of growing pains for the Russian River region is that its middle-sized cellars have only begun to cultivate the marketplace. Most of the labels have no history of any sort. Most of the rest have only a small local audience that knows to look for the name.

This lack of established labels, plus mounting pressure from both Napa and Monterey counties, almost guarantees that the survival rate will not be 100 percent, not even for the next four or five years.

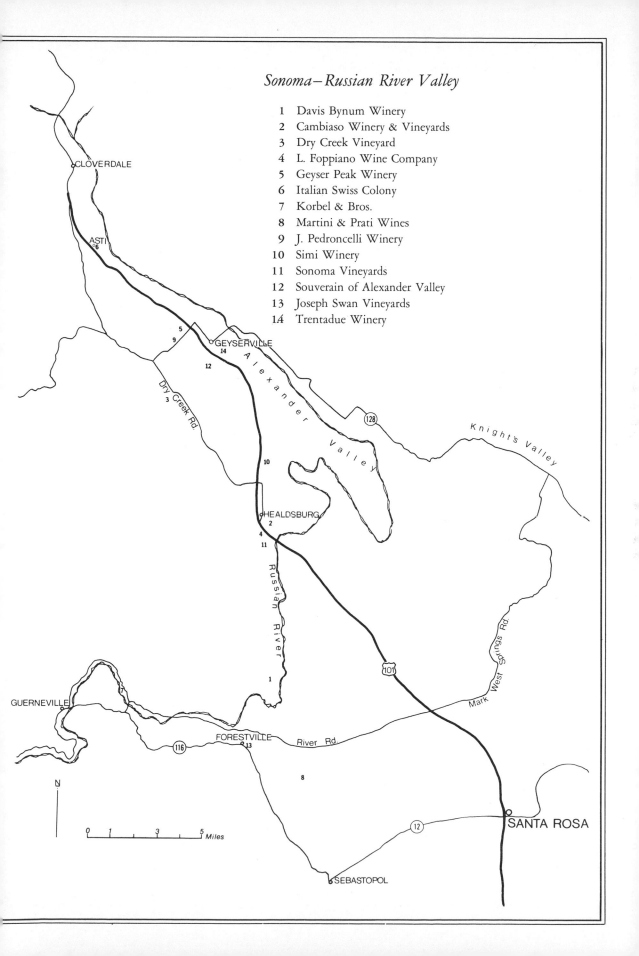

Sonoma—Russian River Valley

1 Davis Bynum Winery
2 Cambiaso Winery & Vineyards
3 Dry Creek Vineyard
4 L. Foppiano Wine Company
5 Geyser Peak Winery
6 Italian Swiss Colony
7 Korbel & Bros.
8 Martini & Prati Wines
9 J. Pedroncelli Winery
10 Simi Winery
11 Sonoma Vineyards
12 Souverain of Alexander Valley
13 Joseph Swan Vineyards
14 Trentadue Winery

Cambiaso Vineyards

Cambiaso typifies, perhaps even epitomizes, the way matters have been going in the Russian River valleys.

Giovanni Cambiaso founded the winery as a small bulk operation in 1933, well up the slope of one of the hills that helps turn the river westward. His family kept the place in the original mold until 1973, when they sold the winery and vineyard to the Four Seas Investment Company, a conglomerate corporation based, somehow, in a distillery in Thailand.

The new owners replaced a pair of old sheet iron-covered barns with a concrete fermenting cellar full of stainless steel and another concrete warehouse for the cased goods. The little old country winery became, during 1975, a modern cellar capable of producing about 100,000 cases of wine each vintage. The only building left from the old days holds Cambiaso's expanded collection of redwood aging tanks.

The original owning family remains on the property as managers for the new proprietors. Rita Ivy, daughter of Giovanni, is the general manager. Her brother, Joseph, makes the wine. Off his past record, the wines will be clean, straightforward ones. The Cabernet Sauvignon and Petite Sirah come from vineyards adjoining the winery. Others on the list come from grapes purchased from local growers.

Geyser Peak

Like Cambiaso, Geyser Peak has migrated from small country winery to major modern cellar in one swift leap. The only difference is that Geyser Peak jumped about four times farther.

Geyser Peak reaches back to 1880 as a property. It belonged for most of its subsequent career to the family Bagnani, which produced some bulk wine and a vast amount of commercial vinegar between 1937 and 1973. In the latter year the Bagnanis sold their vineyard and a pair of winery buildings to the Jos. Schlitz Brewing Company. Schlitz established Geyser Peak as a wholly owned subsidiary, and set about expanding the capacity of the old place, on a hilly site just north of the village of Geyserville, and just west of U.S. 101.

By 1975, a tilt-up concrete building housed three quarters of a million gallons worth of stainless steel fermentors. A second similar building held a similar volume of steel storage tanks. Yet a third held new supplies of redwood and oak cooperage, to supplement the by-now meager quantity in the original stone-and-redwood cellar. Cased goods rest in still another building, the one-time vinegary, on the opposite side of U.S. 101 from the rest of the installation.

To oversee the winemaking, the new proprietors hired Al Huntsinger, who had presided over Almadén's growth from a 150,000-case to a 5-million-case winery. Huntsinger brought his assistant, Armand Bussone, to serve as cellarmaster.

They have somewhat more than 600 acres of winery-owned grapes as their base supply. More than half is near the winery. Roughly 100 acres are not far away on the south side of Geyserville. About 200 acres are in the Valley of the Moon, toward its south end. Geyser Peak also buys considerable tonnage from independent growers in Sonoma and neighboring Mendocino.

Marketing of Geyser Peak wines is the province of people trained within the

At Korbel Brothers, the round brick tower is an architectural symbol of the firm, founded by a family of Czechs. (HAROLYN THOMPSON)

Schlitz organization. They overlooked or abandoned a great deal of traditional technique on their first try, and left behind still more orthodoxy the second time around.

The proprietors, while retaining Geyser Peak as the name of the producing winery on their labels, established two lines of wines. The name Summit went on less expensive generics. First-line varietals were called Voltaire. In addition, each Voltaire wine had its own distinct label, designed to evoke the character of the liquid inside the bottle.

When the debut years, 1973–1974, coincided with a tightening marketplace, the boys in marketing added varietals in half-gallon jugs to the Summit line, promising vintage dates and local appellations of origin for future editions of the Voltaire varietals. (Through spring, 1976, all Geyser Peak wines were non-vintage, with "California" the universal appellation of origin.)

F. Korbel & Bros.

There must be millions of Korbel sparkling wine corks tucked away in drawers, or Korbel bottles perched in windowsills as mementoes of weddings and birthdays. This house was for decades the premier source of bottle-fermented Champagnes of California. It continues to be a premier source, though not the only one since the advents of such as Hanns Kornell, Mirassou, and Schramsberg. Partly in response, the house has branched out into table wines and brandy in recent years under the proprietorship of its second set of brothers, the Hecks.

Korbel's red brick buildings date to 1886, when the brothers Francis, Anton, and Joseph Korbel had them erected on the last gentle slope before the Russian

River burrows between two steep redwood-forested hills at Guerneville. A pair of gingerbread porticos brings Victorian San Francisco to mind. At one end of the main building a tower advertises in a faint way the middle European origins of the founders.

Oddly, redwood forests rather than grapes brought the three Czech brothers to their property. They came in the 1870s as tobacco growers and cigar makers, not vineyardists, and redwoods made fine cigar boxes. The brothers did not switch to vines until 1881, when much of their acreage had been logged clear.

The Korbels sold their first few crops of grapes, then turned to making still wine. Only after 1896 did they make sparkling wine. Only after the arrival of another Czech, Jan Hanuska, in 1910, did the reputation of Korbel begin to grow. Hanuska had been trained in winemaking at Pilsen. Whether his genius for sparkling wines was innate or cultivated in that unlikely place, it was genius. In person he was rather a dour perfectionist but his wines had all the lilt and joy one could ask.

Hanuska continued to make superb Champagnes under the second generation of Korbels, but could not give them a taste for it. In 1954 the family sold to the brothers Heck.

Adolph, Paul, and Ben Heck, German Alsatians, had migrated to Cook's Imperial Champagnes at St. Louis, then, indirectly, to Italian Swiss Colony at Asti. They had been looking for a winery to buy while there. Korbel was it.

When the property first went to the Hecks very little changed, except that they purchased the adjoining Santa Nella vineyards, bringing the total property from 270 to 450 acres.

Slowly the evolution has come about.

The acreage in vines had increased to 1,100 in 1975, all of them flanking the Russian River, most of them just upstream from the winery. The original varieties of Hanuska's day were pinot blanc, sauvignon blanc, and french colombard for whites, and pinot noir for red sparkling wines. The Hecks have kept these, adding only chardonnay in quantity. However, the home vineyards go mostly to sparkling wine production. The Hecks buy a considerable tonnage of grapes to round out the sparkling wine supply and for a lengthening list of table wines.

Sparkling wines continue to dominate production. They never did and do not now bear Sonoma County as an appellation of origin. Neither do they carry vintage dates. The types are Natural, Brut, Extra Dry, Sec, Pink, Korbel Rouge and, oh woe, Cold Duck.

The list of table wines frequently carries Sonoma as an appellation. More and more of them are vintage-dated as the program matures.

Within the old brick walls, new equipment has replaced the gear Hanuska left for the Hecks. The changes, again, are only evolutionary, but wizard nonetheless. The most fascinating single gadget is the mechanical riddler. Pairs of horizontal latticeworks connect to an electrically powered oscillator. Bottles rest upside down in the lattices; the oscillator jostles them by the hundreds at a time. It does a gentle job, and is even more silent than Hanuska, who used to jostle bottles by hand, two at a time. Farther along, a hypnotizing set of mechanical hands does the disgorging, the business of getting the yeast out of the bottle and the permanent cork in. A raft of tireless rubber thumbs loses much less wine than the single human one that does the work in the traditional way. Other penny-saving gadgets crop up here and there, doing their tasks in ways that recall the ancient techniques, but doing them much faster.

The table wines are made separately from the sparkling wine stocks, and aged in combinations of redwood, old oak ovals, and new oak barrels.

Simi Winery

Inconsistent though its history has been, the Simi Winery has been a driving force toward excellence in the Russian River region in three eras, most especially including the present.

Giuseppe and Pietro Simi, emigrant Piedmonteses, built one of Sonoma's handsomest stone cellar buildings at the north limit of Healdsburg in 1876, and christened it Montepulciano after their home town in Italy.

They made wines of excellent reputation in the trade from the founding date until their deaths soon after the turn of the century. The brothers did not establish their own label. Few people did then. Rather the Simis sold their wine to fancy distributors at fancy prices.

Simi continued as the property of Giuseppe's daughter Isabelle and her husband, Fred Haigh. After Prohibition, the Haighs made a dramatic comeback with help from an adroit merchant named George Remington, who established Simi as one label and Hotel Del Monte Selection as an even more prestigious one. Simi wines, by either name, won gold medals at the state fair in the early 1940s when those medals were a prize worth seeking. Alas, the Haighs were not adroit at business. They caused fine wine to be made, but neglected to sell it. After Remington moved on the cellars languished, too full of old wines to admit new ones. The adjacent vineyards died by inches, some of them sold off to meet debts.

Mrs. Haigh maintained a retail room through which a thin trickle of ever-older wines passed into public hands. Through the 1960s, initiates could slip her an extra 50 or 75 cents and get 1935 Gold Medal Cabernet Sauvignon instead of the regular stuff.

In 1969, Russell Green, a former president of Signal Oil Company, bought the Simi winery to have a home for grapes from his expanding vineyards in the Alexander Valley, just over a low ridge to the east. For his money he acquired a superb stone building and an incredible mess: vinaigrous reds, sherried whites, Charmat Champagnes that had been in their tanks so long they had eaten through the linings and well into the steel walls.

The new owner weeded out the impossible wines and the irreparable equipment to begin a revival that, by 1973, was a fine aesthetic success, but a costlier one than one man could bear. Green sold Simi to Scottish & Newcastle Vintners, Inc., a subsidiary of a huge British conglomerate with its oldest roots in brewing.*

During his brief tenure Green re-equipped Simi to do the right kind of winemaking. Simi's fermentors for white wines are temperature-controlled stainless steel. For red wines Green installed brand new open-topped redwood vats on grounds that the finest reds in the world ferment in wood and he could see no reason

---

* In May, 1976, Scottish & Newcastle in turn sold the winery to Schieffelin & Co., New York-based importer of wines and spirits.

Forty years after the vintage, a long, deep bin of Simi Cabernet Sauvignon 1935 remained stacked at one side of the bottling room. (HAROLYN THOMPSON)

to ignore the challenge. He made that observation one day while his coopers still were shuffling loose staves into sequence. Four years later he still viewed the tanks with great favor.

Most of Simi's barrels were of French oak at first. Not content with the limited availability of European barrels, Green was one of the early experimenters with air-dried American oak. (The native wood had a poor reputation in the wine industry because the bourbon industry caused all of it to be kiln-dried. The advent of American light whisky left the oak folks to seek markets among the wineries because Kentucky overnight needed far fewer barrels than formerly. The air-dried barrels have turned out to be good ones for all purposes save Chardonnay.)

Green did one other good turn for the California wine industry. He hired a U.C.-Davis trained enologist named Mary Ann Graf to make Simi wines. Since she was a rookie, Green also hired the legendary André Tchelistcheff as a consultant, but his gesture did open the cellar doors to women. Several have gone on to make some outstanding wines, Mary Ann among them.

Green had time enough to fill the 300,000-gallon capacity of his cellars, but not enough time to develop an audience for that much production.

His successors inherited a much-praised inventory.

Most of the wines from 1973 and later bear Alexander Valley as their appellation of origin, another of Green's contributions. He single-handedly won legal approval of the appellation. Green retained ownership of his vines when he sold the winery to Scottish & Newcastle. He sells his grapes to Simi under long-term contract. In 1974, the entire Simi crush was from his vineyards. In future, the new proprietors assume to grow at least somewhat beyond his vineyard's capacity, but to remain an Alexander Valley winery.

Sonoma Vineyards

Sonoma Vineyards is the most recent public face of a company that has built itself from small beginnings by being aggressively unorthodox.

The beginnings were as Tiburon Vintners, a bottler and retail seller in an old frame building in the San Francisco suburb of Tiburon. The presiding figure was Rodney Strong, a one-time dancer and choreographer who then said that he could bear the thought of being an old winemaker, but not an old dancer.

As that enterprise prospered Strong incorporated it, brought in a fiscal wizard named Peter Friedman, and bought an old bulk winery in the weary little village of West Windsor, a few miles north of Santa Rosa. As Windsor Vineyards, the company launched a mail-order business built on the snobbish appeal of personalized labels, the kind that say "Selected for the 25th Wedding Anniversary of Bob and Mary Cratchit," or whomever.

When that effort was received well, the company in 1969–1970 built a dramatic new winery four miles north of Windsor, then went public, then acquired vineyard land totalling 5,000 acres, in the process changing its name to Sonoma Vineyards. As Sonoma Vineyards the firm began cultivating regular retail markets. The whole sequence of events spanned thirteen years, starting in 1961. As readers of financial pages know, the pace was too quick for peaceful financing. Sonoma Vineyards was in the news throughout 1974 and 1975 as a troubled company. During 1975 apparent salvation came in the form of Renfield Distillers, which exchanged stock for control of the winery.

A few good wines and a radically designed winery came out of the blithe years.

The best of those wines were whites. The most memorable whites included a Chardonnay 1972, a botrytised Johannisberg Riesling from the same vintage, and a Brut Champagne identified as Cuvée 102.

Each of these reflects a serious effort to grow the right varieties of grapes in the right places. The vineyards—5,000 acres at the peak, since trimmed back to 3,000— stretch from the west edge of the Santa Rosa Plain well up into Mendocino County. The Big Four varieties—chardonnay, white riesling, cabernet sauvignon and pinot noir—dominate all plantings. Most of the white riesling is out west toward Guerneville, the cabernet sauvignon upstream from Healdsburg, and the Burgundian varieties in between.

The long-range plan, launched with the harvest of 1973, was to offer the best results in lots from individual vineyards, with the sources noted on the labels. Such still is the hope.

The winery whence the aforementioned wines and a long list of lesser bottlings came is a hybrid between a cross and a pyramid in external shape. The idea, evolved by an architectural engineer named Richard Keith and executed by a disciple of Frank Lloyd Wright named Craig Roland, is functional. In California history, wineries were built into hillsides so that the grapes arrived on the uphill side and finished wine went out the opposite, downhill side. The idea was that the gravity would help wine flow through the building, electricity being absent. (The Douro Valley in Portugal is full of similar establishments for the same reason.) Keith, with an easy faith in electrical power, saw that a radial rather than linear winery could save a lot of motion. Wine could be moved easily by pumps from a perimeter to a work core, then back out to a different part of the perimeter. The winery at Windsor is the first full expression of an idea since elaborated in half a dozen other places, always isolating fermentors in one quadrant, large cooperage in another, small barrels in the third, and bottling in the fourth. Sonoma Vineyards since has pointed out the trouble with the concept, which is that it does not allow sensible expansion. In addition to the immortal original building, Sonoma Vineyards now has two additional buildings designed in the traditional flow-through pattern.

Souverain of Alexander Valley

The Sonoma cellars of Souverain made their first wines in 1972 in a borrowed corner of the same company's Napa winery under another label, Ville Fontaine. The second vintage came from the permanent home, under the name Chateau Souverain. The current name is meant to cover the wines of 1974, also made in the permanent home.

This is one way to create a lot of history in a hurry, but one doubts that the marketing boys will get any prizes for their work so far.

Souverain of Alexander Valley has been meant from the start to make distinctive wines from Sonoma and Mendocino County grapes to be sold at prices one notch lower than those of the Souverain in the Napa Valley. Both are properties of Souverain Cellars, Inc., a subsidiary of The Pillsbury Company, the Minneapolis millers.* The name Ville Fontaine dropped by the wayside when another winery showed proprietorship of the name. Chateau Souverain had to be abandoned because the public presumed it to be a costlier wine than mere Souverain when the reverse was true. Souverain of Alexander Valley is Pillsbury's best shot at a straight, explanatory name.

Through all of these identity crises, the winery building has been both efficient and an architectural wonder. In exterior form it is modelled on the hop-drying barn which is a traditional part of the Russian River scene, although its scale would allow most of the surviving hop barns in the county to fit inside. By size and shape, its two lofty towers produce a dramatic silhouette against the darkly wooded hills west of U.S. 101 and north of Healdsburg. The working winery stretches between the twin towers. It is designed to hold 2 million gallons of stainless steel, oak tanks, and oak barrels. The cooperage of all types comes in surprisingly small sizes. The thought behind the great number of small pieces is to keep wines from differing districts and

* In spring, 1976, Pillsbury was in process of selling all its winery holdings in California. A limited partnership known as North Coast Cellars was the probable purchaser of the Souverain name and the producing winery at Alexander Valley. See page 50 for notes on the Napa Valley winery.

even single vineyards separate, to learn more about the sub districts of Sonoma and Mendocino. Souverain buys all of its grapes from independent growers in the two counties.

It is this notion as much as any that attracted Bill Bonetti to the job as first winemaker at Souverain after twelve years in the Napa Valley at Charles Krug.

Bonetti is quick to agree that the Russian River region is decades behind the Napa Valley in unraveling the mysteries of microclimate, but, like the man who had the pleasure of learning that the Clos de Tart was a shade better than its neighbors, he does not mind.

Through the vintages of 1972 and 1973, the wines bore either North Coast or one of the county names as appellations, along with whichever cellar name was fashionable at the moment. The individual vineyard wines were yet to come. Bonetti, always a fine maker of whites, produced Johannisberg Rieslings and French Colombards of excellent quality. The first Zinfandel also won praise from critical tasters.

Two other sizable wineries in the region require noting.

The United Vintners plant at Asti, in the northern reaches of Sonoma County, used to be Italian Swiss Colony before Heublein, Inc., took a walk down to Madera with the name.* Now the venerable plant devotes most of its capacity to making Inglenook Vintage and Inglenook Navalle wines.

At its founding Italian Swiss was almost purely altruistic. A man named Andrea Sbarbaro established the colony in 1881 as a self-help cooperative, in effect a utopian haven for Italian Swiss immigrants to California who found themselves destitute in the Great Depression of that era. When the enterprise did not work as a utopia, Sbarbaro reorganized the winery into a conventional business firm and operated it that way until Prohibition.

The wines, then, were made by a gifted enologist named Pietro Rossi. Golden State Champagnes ranked at the very top of the California list for quality and prestige. The table wines did not lag far behind.

After Prohibition, Rossi's twin sons, Robert and Edmund, restored Italian Swiss to operation. They had been the winemakers after their father's death in 1911. Their blend of Tipo Chianti was a wine of enough style to see M. F. K. Fisher and other seasoned palates through the Great Depression of the 1930s. (Italian Swiss always seems at its best during depressions.)

During World War II the Rossis sold their Asti winery to National Distillers Products Corporation. A few years later National sold to Louis Petri, who was building his United Vintners empire toward its peak. When Heublein, Inc., acquired a majority interest in UV in 1968, ISC went along as part of the deal, to put the matter as acronymously as possible.

Nearly all of the wines now bearing the label of Italian Swiss Colony are made and bottled in the San Joaquin Valley at the UV winery near Madera. Inglenook or Lejon wines, with labels that say they were made and bottled at B.W. 1589, San Francisco, in fact come from Asti. Tipo Chianti comes from Asti.

* See page 129.

The grapes come from members of the grower cooperative called Allied, which has a minority interest in UV. The growers scatter widely across the landscapes of Mendocino, Napa, and Sonoma counties.

The winery proper has a capacity of 12 million gallons. A fair proportion of that is a new stainless steel fermentor building. A larger part is a series of three cellars full of fine old redwood tanks.

The sad irony is that ISC lost its Sonoma identity just about at the hour when the county appellation was beginning to blossom in other cellars.

Another durable family firm, Martini & Prati, has been slow to develop its own label. There is room for regret. The proprietors have made some distinctive and elegant red wine under the vague name of Burgundy. A little of it filters into public hands through delicatessens in San Francisco's Italian communities, but most of what they make goes to other wineries in bulk. Their old cellar buildings, on the plain between Santa Rosa and Forestville, date to the 1880s. The Martini family (no relation to the Louis Martinis of the Napa Valley) came in 1902. The Pratis were close behind.

The company owns a few acres of vines, but buys most of its grapes from independent growers in the region. As one measure of the enterprise, the capacity approaches 2.5 million gallons, by a wide margin the largest independent bulk winery in Sonoma.

Although the proprietors do not sell much bottled wine, they own two labels. One is Martini & Prati, the other Fountaingrove. The firm purchased Fountaingrove from what once was one of the most prestigious wineries in the state and one of the most bizarre. Originally the winery of a religious commune, Fountaingrove became a legend under the managership of Kanaye Nagasawa, an improbable but undeniable crown prince among the California winemakers of his era, from the 1880s until Prohibition. He had started out with the Brotherhood of the New Life as a journeyman printer and apprentice winemaker. Faithfully he churned out pamphlets by night and wine by day until the brotherhood fell apart. Handed title to the property on the north side of Santa Rosa, the estimable Nagasawa instantly abandoned printing to become a full-time winemaker. Fountaingrove had a brief revival after Prohibition. By 1975, all vestiges of the old winery had disappeared save for its label, used by Martini & Prati for prestigious varietals.

The Small Cellars

Small cellars making wine for their own labels are just as new a development in the Russian River region as middle-sized ones. Four of the six presently active have founding dates within the past ten years. The remaining two did not court identity for themselves until the wine boom of the 1960s was well under way.

The old family firm of J. Pedroncelli has the longest track record in the region, and the greatest one. Dry Creek, in a shorter time, has roused critical interest with its wines. The same pair have been most specific in citing vineyard sources.

Davis Bynum

A reformed newspaperman, Davis Bynum spent the better part of a decade

A handful of octagonal buildings remain from the once-vital Fountaingrove Winery near Santa Rosa. The label still exists, owned by Martini & Prati, but the old winery is now a housing-development site. (WINE INSTITUTE)

creeping up on his location on the west side of the Santa Rosa plain a mile or two upstream from Korbel.

Bynum founded his winery in 1965 on a commercial thoroughfare in the East Bay suburb called Albany. He bought grapes where he could find them. The working cellar was in a small room behind his retail store. In 1972 Bynum bought an old vineyard in the Napa Valley with some thought of moving there. Instead, he acquired the Russian River property in 1974.

The winery building was built originally as a hop barn, but underwent modifications during an interim ownership that made it easy to convert into a cellar for winemaking.

One small vineyard parcel adjoins the cellar. The rest of the grape supply comes from growers in the neighborhood who bought shares in the winery operation.

Dry Creek Vineyard

Dry Creek Vineyard is the propriety of a young Harvard graduate and one-time marketing expert named David Stare, who founded the label in 1971, built his cellars in 1972, and established Dry Creek Valley as an appellation of origin in 1974.

Stare, who can be brash, announced in advance that he was founding the Californian equivalent of a great Médoc estate. Practical problems of vineyards and inventory have kept him from fulfilling the precise goal in his first years of operation. As of 1975 his whites were Chardonnay, Chenin Blanc and, as a left-handed gesture to Bordeaux, Fumé Blanc. (Only in America would a putative Médoc estate call Sauvignon Blanc by its Loire-ish name.) The reds are Gamay and Zinfandel, with Cabernet Sauvignon on the horizon.

Though tallish vines in the foreground and a steep, wooded hill as backdrop place the estate firmly in coastal California, the winery buildings speak well of the proprietor's devotion to his ideals. An efficient stainless steel crushing and fermenting area flanks a restrained, rectangular concrete-block aging cellar full of small oak barrels. New wings to come will make the architecture quite like a Bordeaux château in outline.

While the kinships with the Médoc mature, Stare's most appreciable early wines have been Chardonnay and Chenin Blanc, both made bone dry and rich enough to age for no fewer than five years, perhaps more.

He has vines of his own, and augments the supply with purchases from neighbors in Dry Creek Valley. When the wines satisfy him, Stare identifies the source vineyard on his label.

Foppiano Wine Company

Foppiano is one of two venerable names among the small labels in the Russian River region. The original Louis Foppiano began making wine near Healdsburg in 1894. The family has persisted through all the years since, primarily in the bulk business, partly in the country jug trade, and, finally, during the past few years, as a maker of vintage-dated varietal table wines.

The family owns 200 acres next to the Russian River just downstream from the mouth of Dry Creek. The squat concrete winery at one corner of the property holds nearly a million gallons of cooperage, most of it redwood tanks. By far the greater proportion of the Foppianos' effort goes to jug wines, but the flossier varietals are a growing part of the business. Quite a few of the latter carry "Russian River" as their appellation of origin, a family contribution to the finer dividing of Sonoma County vineyard districts. Some are vintage dated.

As old-line country jug makers, the Foppianos developed a brawny sense of style, especially for their reds. Foppiano Cabernet Sauvignon and Petite Sirah from the family vines are very old-fashioned Californian reds, strong, straightforward, ready to keep company with rich, spicy country food.

J. Pedroncelli Winery

The brothers John and Jim Pedroncelli conducted a long, cautious courtship with fine winemaking before they abandoned bulk wine in favor of varietals, vintages, and the other handicaps winemakers impose upon themselves when they mean to make something rare and elegant.

The Pedroncelli winery grew out of an eighty-five-acre Prohibition-era vineyard that supplied home winemakers. In 1927 John Pedroncelli, the elder, bought his property atop the tumbling hills that separate the Alexander and Dry Creek valleys. He reactivated an old barn of a winery on the property in 1933. His sons, the present proprietors, began making small lots of wine for the family label as a side-issue during the mid-1950s.

Not long after, a San Francisco wine importer named Henry Vandervoort set the Pedroncellis on the road to vintage-dated varietals when he began to buy wines from them for sale under his own label, Importer's Choice. Although Vandervoort helped the brothers to acquire French barrels for their finest reds, and otherwise encouraged them toward finesse, they continued to hesitate between the old way and the new. They had, after all, grown up making bulk wines to sell at modest prices to unassuming palates. The family vineyards were planted mostly to zinfandel, french colombard, and similar varieties. A handful of barrels from Bordeaux did not exactly overwhelm the pioneer museum qualities that otherwise identified their cellars and equipment, nor did those barrels give the brothers a whole new sense of style.

Only when the Alexander Valley began to fill with fine grape varieties during the late 1960s did the balance begin to tip. The Pedroncellis bought grapes from Russ Green and other growers, from which Jim Pedroncelli produced some notable additions to the literature of Sonoma Chardonnay, Pinot Noir, and Zinfandel. Since then, the Pedroncellis have added stainless steel fermentors and other modern equipment to their cellars, have enlarged upon their collection of oak, and have replanted the original vineyard and a smaller, newer one to fine grape varieties.

The Pedroncelli sense of style still holds the view that the lack of flavors in a well-seasoned redwood tank makes for better wine than the overt taste of any kind of oak. Put positively, both brothers think all wines should taste more forcefully of some grape than any tree.

On balance, all Pedroncelli wines of recent vintage are much finer than any country jug. The best of them are refined enough to travel in the best of company. All have won praise, though the Chardonnays, Pinot Noirs, and Zinfandels have earned it most consistently.

Although the old redwood producing cellar and two newer concrete-block aging cellars can hold slightly more than half a million gallons, the amount of wine on sale under the family name is less than that. Californians have far and away the best chance of finding the red, black, and buff Pedroncelli label in a store. The wine does get to several major metropolitan centers across the country, always at a price which reveals the basically modest nature of the producing family.

Joseph Swan Vineyards

Joseph Swan founded his tiny winery in 1969 against his planned retirement as an airlines captain. He had his early wines fermented by friends with commercial wineries, then aged them in oak barrels in the basement of his fine old Victorian home at the edge of a village called Forestville a few miles west of Santa Rosa. Simultaneously Swan began using his off days to plant his rolling few acres to pinot noir and chardonnay.

The man, a sturdily built, frosty-eyed image of what an airlines captain should be, established a considerable reputation for thick, rich Zinfandel based on his first try. No successor has quite lived up to the original, but Swan finally retired from flying in 1974, so is free to fire his best shots. His own Burgundian varietals began to bear fruit with his retirement.

Trentadue Winery

Leo Trentadue has been beating a progressive retreat from the urban world for two decades. First he moved from the water level town of Sunnyvale, forty miles south of San Francisco, to the topmost ridges of the Coast Ranges west of that city. As the smog level climbed toward his acric he sold a considerable part of his properties to Ridge Vineyards in 1969, and bought new vineyards in the Russian River region.

The new properties, one in the Alexander Valley and one in Dry Creek Valley, are planted to 150 acres of vines of at least a dozen different varieties. Much of the production has gone straight across the freeway U.S. 101 to Souverain of Alexander Valley. Some of it goes to Ridge. A small amount Trentadue makes into wine in a pleasantly sturdy, properly equipped concrete-block cellar he built in 1972 in the middle of his principal vineyard at the north end of the Alexander Valley.

In the main Trentadue makes wine as a reliable source for himself. He likes his red wines husky enough to do battle with elk steak and his whites able to accompany shark filets. For the rest of the world the production is a hard-to-find chance to know how several vines perform in this versatile region. Trentadue makes and sells to local patrons such off-beat varietals as Carignane, Early Burgundy, and Sauvignon Vert, as well as most of the usual types.

The Vineyards

Healdsburg, because it is at the geographic and climatic hub of the region, is the easiest place from which to become oriented to the scattered vineyards within the sprawling, lightly populated Russian River watershed.

From coolest to warmest, and also from south to north, the four principal divisions are:

The *Santa Rosa Plain,* a broad, fan-shaped lowland extending from Healdsburg south to Santa Rosa and west to Guerneville, where steepening hills finally pinch it off;

Dry Creek Valley, narrow, curving, carved by a tributary with its mouth west of Healdsburg and its upper tip in the hills north and west of Geyserville;

Alexander Valley, a particularly irresolute part of the Russian River course reaching from the middle of Healdsburg east, then northward as far upstream as the Geyserville bridge, and, finally

Cloverdale-Asti, the most northerly twenty miles of the Russian River's course through Sonoma County.

In these regions, especially the Alexander Valley, have been planted most of the new vines that brought Sonoma County's acreage from 11,000 to 22,500 in the years from 1960 through 1974. Forgiving the fact that statistical reports do not show smaller than county units, one sees that cabernet sauvignon jumped from 92 acres in 1959 to 4,165 acres in 1974. Pinot noir increased from 105 to 2,520 in the same span. Chardonnay's acreage in 1959 was 16. In 1974 it was 1,810 – more than the sum of all white grapes in the county in 1959.

Where vines grow is, to be sure, more important than how many of them do.

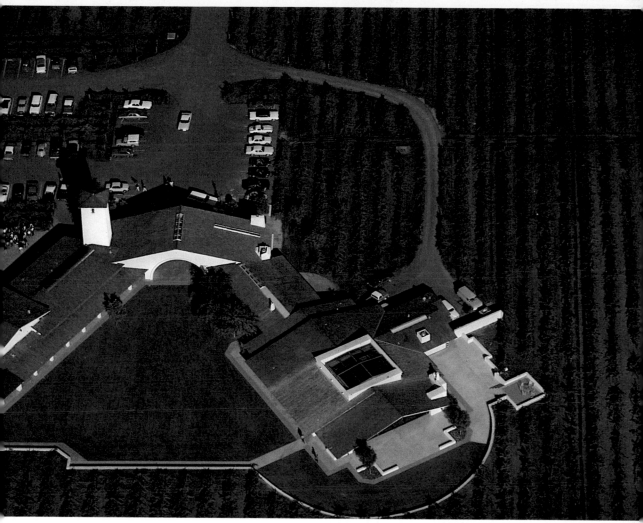

An aerial view of Robert Mondavi's ultramodern winery in the Napa
Valley.   (TED STRESHINSKY)

The first leaves of a new season swell as buds on an old grignolino vine.   (HAROLYN THOMPSON)

Steel fermenting tanks outdoors at Beringer Vineyards. (HAROLYN THOMPSON)

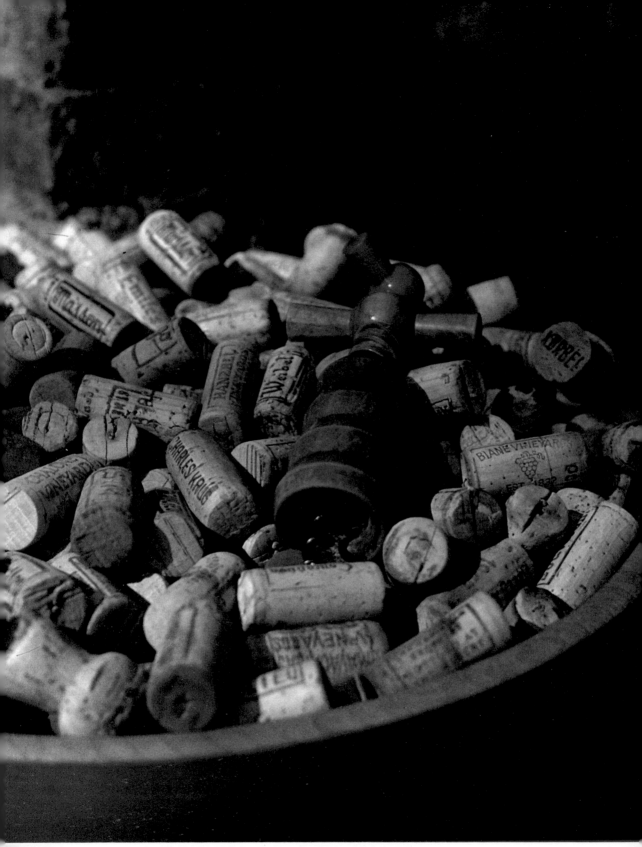

Old corks recall past pleasures.   (HAROLYN THOMPSON)

It still is much too early to know which will be the best vineyards for each variety, but the broader outlines are resolving themselves with surprising speed.

The Santa Rosa Plain, which falls almost entirely within climate Region I, has borne excellent chardonnay for the Korbel winery for two decades, and for Sonoma Vineyards since 1972. In general the plain is being planted to Burgundian and Germanic varieties. White riesling has shown a consistent tendency to develop Noble Mold at lower elevations near the river.

No formal boundary limits the plain, nor is the name used as an appellation.

The Alexander Valley seems to have the same blessing–or curse, depending on viewpoint–of versatility as the mid-section of the Napa Valley. Every variety performs well in it. How to narrow the focus of plantings will be a plaguing question for a long time to come.

Alexander Valley is a registered appellation of origin, and does have fixed boundaries: the drainage of the Russian River from the bridge at Geyserville down to the east edge of Healdsburg. Russell Green wrote the definition and won approval for it in 1972. In an older sense, the valley has two parts. The part to the north of Alexander Valley road has been in vines for years, mostly coarse varieties belonging to independent growers. The part south of that road had few or no vines before Green planted his first, cautious patch of carignanes in 1958. Now the larger and more solidly planted sector, it has a roughly even mixture of winery-owned vineyards and independent ones.

Winery proprietors include Sonoma Vineyards, Geyser Peak, the New York-based Widmers, and (in a somewhat separate area called Knights Valley) the Beringer winery. Each has property in the 300- to 500-acre range. Green retained ownership of his 500 acres when he sold the Simi winery.

If any one variety dominates the plantings it is cabernet sauvignon. Other substantial plantings are of chardonnay, white riesling, chenin blanc, gewürztraminer, and zinfandel.

On the record books, Alexander Valley is cool Region III. Green thinks much of it is somewhere in Region II. According to form, the fine performance of cabernet is predictable, but the excellent results from white varieties are harder to explain. In some primal, antiintellectual way, this pleases me, all the more because Green bought the first of his property not for vineyard land, but to recapture the swimming hole of his youth. When he followed carignane with gewürztraminer, chardonnay, and other cool region grapes, it was not at the urging of science, but because he wanted to grow wines he liked. No doubt rational behavior has given us better vineyards and better wines the world over, but I still like to see the vine surpass understanding now and again, and will always think well of this place because it did turn out better than science thought it would.

Dry Creek Valley, long a haunt of bulk winemakers, became a legally defined appellation of origin in 1974, the result of a one-man campaign by David Stare of Dry Creek Vineyard. Its past fame has been for zinfandel, slim as that fame has been. (The Pedroncelli vineyards produced most of the evidence; the labels never were more specific than "Sonoma County.") With increasing emphasis on the district, chardonnay and cabernet sauvignon seem likely to add to its reputation. Sauvignon blanc also grows well. The merlot in Louis P. Martini's Edge Hill Vineyard has yielded a pair of memorable wines in its short existence. Edge Hill is a shade too far downstream to qualify for the appellation of origin as defined, but still helps pin the valley as Region II. A vineyard well within the boundaries has a patch of ruby cabernet that will not ripen in the best of times, it being a variety hybridized to begin performing well in Region III.

The Cloverdale-Asti area, long devoted to budget varietals, lingers in that state of development. It is, as any human traveler can perceive on any summer day, the warmest part of the county. Officially it is warm Region III in the U.C.-Davis climate summaries.

Most of the vineyards in the region belong to members of grower cooperatives, especially Allied Growers.

THE VALLEY OF THE MOON

The Valley of the Moon, or, more properly, the Sonoma Valley curls between the Mayacamas Mountains in the east and the Sonomas in the west, a shorter and much skinnier echo of the Napa Valley just across the Mayacamas ridges.

Ancient Buena Vista is here. So is legendary Hanzell, the two of them making the place pivotal in the vinous history of California. More important to its present existence, Sebastiani Vineyards is here, the always solid foundation. The rest of a short list of wineries only begins to grope for places in the sun.

Most clearly defined of all the natural regions in Sonoma County, this valley had a head start on all its neighbors in grapes and wine. The Franciscan padres planted mission grapes in 1825. Agoston Haraszthy planted his great collection of cuttings from Europe in 1862. By the turn of the century cellars and vineyards virtually lined the banks of Sonoma Creek. Then three disasters came in succession. Haraszthy's cuttings had arrived infected with Phylloxera: local vineyards fell prey to the disease in increasing numbers from the 1870s onward. In 1906 the great earthquake that destroyed San Francisco also demolished a number of Sonoma cellars, Buena Vista among them. In 1919 Prohibition put an end to whatever had survived the first two calamities. Times never have been as gaudy since Prohibition as they were before it because the local boom in retirement villages preceded the boom in wine.

For all of that, vigorous hope animates both vineyardists and cellarmasters in the Sonoma Valley. The rosters of both have grown since 1970. In 1975 a majority of the wineries banded together in an association seeking legal definition of the Sonoma Valley as an appellation of origin. Buena Vista is the largest winery in the group, though not large. The other charter members are Chateau St. Jean, Grand Cru, Hacienda, Hanzell, Kenwood, Vineburg, and Z-D. Sebastiani Vineyards remains outside the association, its vineyard resources spread too wide for membership to make much sense. Still, the absence is ironic because the Sebastiani family kept vines in the valley almost single-handedly from the beginning of Prohibition until the 1960s.

Incidentally, the romantic name Valley of the Moon has an explanation. While Jack London lived near Glen Ellen, he learned that the original Indian inhabitants called the place the valley of seven moons because, in certain seasons, the moon slips

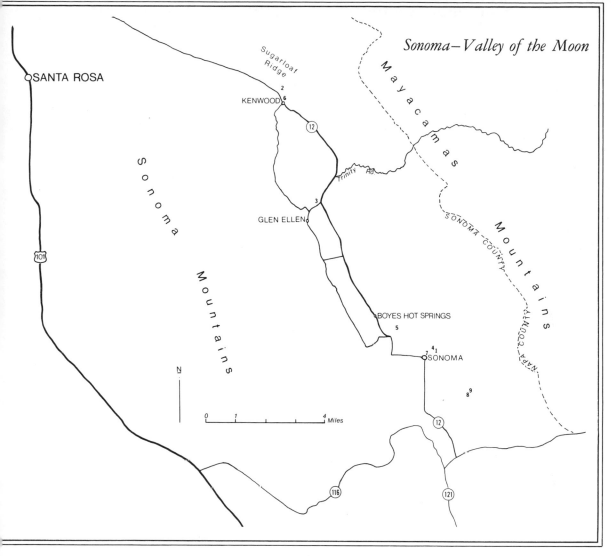

Sonoma—Valley of the Moon

1	Buena Vista Winery	6	Kenwood Vineyards
2	Chateau St. Jean	7	Sebastiani Vineyards
3	Grand Cru Vineyards	8	Vineberg Wine Company
4	Hacienda Wine Cellars	9	ZD Wines
5	Hanzell Vineyards		

behind one mountain peak after another as it rises. The author, ever a realist, left out the number in commemorating the legend.

The Wineries

Because Sebastiani alone has size, the roster of wineries in the region goes alphabetically, rather than dividing by volume of production as in other chapters.

Buena Vista

As much as Agoston Haraszthy was the father of California wine, his vineyards and cellars are its birthplace. The old Hungarian adventurer has come under severe scrutiny in recent years after a long, untroubled reign as the Father of California Wine, the man who put the industry onto the right track during the 1860s. Historians now are trying to give his mantle to Jean Louis Vignes, the pioneer at Los Angeles. Wherever the paternal responsibilities finally fix, Haraszthy did make the first large importation of vine cuttings from great European vineyards into the North Coast, and he did launch the first truly commercial wine cellars north of San Francisco Bay.

Buena Vista continues to look the part of a proper birthplace for California wine. Alongside a tiny creek in rolling terrain east of Sonoma town, Haraszthy in 1857 had Chinese laborers carve six tunnels into a sandstone hillside, then cover the mouths of the tunnels with two rectangular stone barns. His original buildings still stand. Except that towering eucalyptus trees now shade them and a parking lot now flanks them, they look very much as their founder saw them.

In spite of the timeless externals, this has not been a family history, or even a continuous one. Neither Agoston nor his sons, Arpad and Attila, seems to have been a good hand at running a business. All three drifted or were driven away from a financially troubled Buena Vista Vinicultural Society. Phylloxera in the vines contributed to the fiscal decline. In 1906 the great earthquake did enormous damage to the six tunnels and their stores of wine, and irreparable harm to the finances of the company. Buena Vista shut down as a winery while aftershocks of 1906 still rattled the countryside.

It did not reopen until after World War II. A man named Frank Bartholomew bought the property in 1941 just as he was being shipped into the Pacific Theater as a correspondent for United Press. At first he meant just to turn the place into a weekend retreat. Only after the purchase did he discover that he owned an historic winery. Bartholomew accepted the challenge of restoring Buena Vista beginning in 1945.

Under his proprietorship, vineyardists salvaged a few blocks of pre-Prohibition grapes, but mostly the old ground was planted to new vines. All but two of the original tunnels were restored. (One of the unreclaimable two, according to myth, holds whatever might be left of thousands of bottles of sparkling wine and the Chinese cellarman who was tending them when the earthquake struck.) From here and there Bartholomew rummaged up a 75,000-gallon collection of traditional 1,000- to 2,000-gallon oak oval casks, the kind that served in most of California's prestigious cellars at the turn of the century. And, not least, he acquired the services of a crusty and extremely old-fashioned winemaker named Al Brett. With these, Bartholomew restored not only the property, but the approximate style of earlier Buena Vista wines. Gewürztraminer, Cabernet Sauvignon, and Zinfandel led the list.

With the wine boom, Bartholomew became more successful than he wished to be with a retirement business. In 1968 he sold the winery to Young's Market Company of Los Angeles.*

* Bartholomew retained ownership of the vineyards, though the crop goes to Buena Vista under long-term contract.

The sandstone caves at Buena Vista are filled with oak casks. One cave houses the tasting room, too. (WINE INSTITUTE)

For a time the new owners accepted what Bartholomew had wrought, oak ovals, Al Brett, and all. In 1971 they purchased 600 acres of land on the Sonoma-Napa county line in Carneros and began planting it at the rate of 100 acres per year. In 1974 the firm acquired an additional 150 acres adjacent to the first purchase. In 1975 Brett retired as winemaker and in the same year the winery launched construction of a stainless steel fermenting facility at Carneros. The old cellars are to serve only as wood aging and bottling cellars once all the additions mature and Buena Vista has joined the ranks of middle-sized wineries.

Chateau St. Jean

In spring, 1975, Chateau St. Jean existed more as a twinkle in the eye than as accomplished fact, but a bold proposition nonetheless. By spring, 1976, it was a factor in critical assessments of its region.

Late in 1973 a trio of investors from the San Joaquin Valley, Robert Merzoian, Edward Merzoian, and W. Kenneth Sheffield bought an elegant one-time country retreat near the town of Kenwood. In 1975 they began planting 105 acres in vineyard, half of it on level terrain, the other half on some giddy slopes running up toward Sugarloaf Ridge. The partners also launched construction of a new winery, its external style borrowed from medieval France, its internal workings modern in the California sense of the word. Chateau St. Jean is scaled to produce approximately 45,000 cases per year of varietal table wines and bottle-fermented sparkling wines.

The first wines predate the cellar. The company leased equipment from another winery for the vintage of 1974, making a series of whites and reds from Sonoma and Mendocino County grapes. In the long range, Chateau St. Jean plans to grow its own white varieties and buy red grapes. Until 1978 or later, it will buy all its grapes.

Chateau St. Jean's winemaker is Richard Arrowood, tall, but rosy and round enough to be a Burgundian. His sense of style in wine owes a great deal to Burgundy and almost as much to the Rhine, but little or nothing to austere regions. The first Chardonnays and a Pinot Blanc have earned a good deal of praise.

Grand Cru Vineyards

Founded in 1970, Grand Cru immediately set itself the task of exploring the stylistic possibilities inherent in just two grape varieties, Gewürztraminer and Zinfandel.

A youthful five-man partnership led by Allen Ferrera and Robert Magnani assumed to make Gewürztraminer dry and also as a botrytised sweet wine. The plan for Zinfandel ranged wider, to include a blanc de noir, a rosé, a carbonic maceration type, and a conventional red.

The proprietors followed through on all counts between 1970 and 1975. By 1975, however, what had begun as a hybrid hobby and business was looking more like a business than a hobby. The partners decided to enlarge their production from an annual 8,000 gallons to 40,000 by 1980, and to expand the list of wines to include a Cabernet Sauvignon and a white sparkling wine from pinot noir.

Grand Cru's physical premises ingeniously adapt an outworn bulk winery to contemporary purposes. The structure was a row of open concrete fermentors and, parallel, another row of closed concrete storage tanks. Ferrera, Magnani, and company, drawing upon engineering backgrounds, put stainless steel fermentors alongside the old structure, and cut doors into the old storage tanks, transforming them into surprisingly elegant barrel-aging vaults. One of the tanks became a sterile bottling room. A prefabricated A-frame cabin built atop the barrel-aging cellar holds the offices and laboratory, plus a tasting room for visitors.

The expansion plan would add a two-story wood-frame building above the disused concrete fermentors. The upper floors would hold aging wines, cased goods, and supplies. The old concrete fermentors would become vaults for the bottle-fermented sparkling wine.

Grand Cru has 30 acres of zinfandel vineyards next to the winery. The rest of its grapes come from an Alexander Valley vineyard belonging to one of the partners.

Hacienda Vineyards

Hacienda, a one-time convalescent hospital of graceful Spanish Colonial style, belongs to the same Frank Bartholomew who brought Buena Vista back to life in the 1940s and who sold it when it became too demanding on his retirement in 1968.

The aim in the new surroundings, just a few hundred yards away from the old ones, is to make very small amounts of very fine wine, especially Chardonnay. Bartholomew's first vintage, 1972, suggests that he is clinging to both goals.

Hacienda's grapes come from the Alexander Valley. Although Bartholomew owns the old Buena Vista vineyard, and lives in a fine, summery cottage in the midst of the vines, those grapes will continue to go to the Buena Vista winery for some years under a long-term contract.

Hanzell Vineyard

However much Buena Vista might be the birthplace of California wine, Hanzell is the site of a significant rebirth in spite of a strikingly unhappy history of its own.

In the late 1940s and early 1950s North Coast vineyards were shrinking. Except for a handful of rarities sold among friends, the best of varietal wines could not bring much more than $3. A great many fine, age-worthy wines sold for less than $2. It was a hellish time for winemakers, who found themselves hanging onto old equipment and cooperage for the simple reason that the gear had been paid for.

Meantime, James D. Zellerbach, ambassador to Italy and member of a wealthy industrial family, somehow knew that California could compete far more closely with Burgundian wines than it was doing. He had the money to make practical experiments. In 1948 Zellerbach bought a secluded fold of hillside northwest of Sonoma town, planted fourteen acres of chardonnay and pinot noir, and caused to be built an impeccable jewel box of a building that would function both as a working winery and experimental laboratory.

It soon developed that barrels made from oak grown in the forest of Limoges had a great part to play in the final complex of flavors that makes up Burgundies, both red and white. The same barrels could and did move California Chardonnays a long stride in the direction of Meursaults and Montrachets, and Pinot Noirs a shorter step toward Romanée and its neighbors.

The real flowering of Zellerbach's revolution did not come until after his death in 1963. His widow, Hannah, who had lent half her name but none of her support to the winery, sold the inventory of wines at auction and closed down Hanzell to await a buyer for the property. Joe Heitz, just getting started in the Napa Valley, bought the inventory and finished aging it. He got $6 a bottle from a broader audience than Zellerbach had attempted to reach. The rest of the story can be measured by endless rows of European oak barrels and tanks in California cellars, or by a properly wide range of prices in finished bottles.

To begin at the beginning, Zellerbach had his winery building designed so its facade looked like the main elevation of the Clos de Vougeot as one looks across the main courtyard from the entry. It was, I suppose, both tribute and challenge to Burgundy, which Zellerbach admired above all other winegrowing regions in the world. He put a gifted research enologist named Bradford Webb in charge of the functional design. Webb, at present a partner in Freemark Abbey in the Napa Valley, produced a working winery that would lift most of the eyebrows in Beaune. A long row of open-topped stainless steel rectangles was scaled so that each tank holds precisely as much fermenting must as the crusher could produce in one hour. Each

On the barrel:
Back of this Wine is the Vintner,
And back through the years, his Skill,
And back of it all are the Vines in the Sun
And the Rain
And the Master's Will.

At Buena Vista, Frank
Bartholomew's appraisal of
the art of making wine.
(WINE INSTITUTE)

tank had an individual temperature control, minutely calibrated. In the lab a gas chromatograph allowed infinitely detailed studies of trace amounts of the natural chemical constituents responsible for flavor; the purpose was to pinpoint the differences between model Burgundies and trial horse Californians. At the time, the only other gas chromatographs in the industry were at U.C.-Davis and in the laboratories at E. & J. Gallo.

The cellars, at least, would have been familiar to a Beaunois. Fat Burgundian barrels filled every rack.

It was California wine's good fortune that Zellerbach had no commercial motivation. The barrel as a source of flavor was quickly identified, but domesticating other aspects of Burgundian wines took longer. The perfectionist proprietor would not confer his label on any wine until the late 1950s. When he died in 1963, the Chardonnays from 1961 on and the Pinot Noirs from 1959 on still rested in cask, and were sold in bulk, to Heitz Cellars for the most part.

After going idle through the vintages of 1963 and 1964, Hanzell came back to life under the ownership of one-time supermarket executives N. Douglas and Mary Day. They sustained but did not amplify Hanzell's reputation for the next several years until Day died in 1969, and Mrs. Day in 1973.

In 1975 Hanzell was bought from the Day estate by Easton United Securities, Ltd., of Calgary, Alberta, Canada.

Kenwood Vineyards

A retired San Francisco policeman named Martin Lee, his sons, and two other partners bought an old bulk winery called Pagani Brothers in 1970. Since then, under the new name, the new owners have been working a slow metamorphosis toward more elegant production in more elegantly equipped buildings.

The Paganis, brothers named Julius and John, had continued the operation of a winery founded by their father in 1905. They did not tinker with the inheritance, so the Lees acquired an over aged 135-acre vineyard, mostly of sauvignon vert and zinfandel, a cellarful of well-seasoned redwood tanks, and a loyal clientele of local jug red drinkers. The winery had, at least, been engineered into its hillside site by a practical-minded man. The board-and-batten buildings take physical advantage of the slope. Renovation and expansion came easily.

According to the Lees' best estimates, the supply of Pagani-made wines that came with the place should last long enough to satisfy the thirsts of all the old clients.

With new gear, including a barn full of small oak cooperage, the Lees make varietal wines, with heavy emphasis on reds.

They were, in 1976, well along in their replanting program in their own vineyard. Cabernet sauvignon and zinfandel dominate. The partners also buy grapes from independent growers, some in the immediate neighborhood, others as far away as the Ukiah Valley in Mendocino County.

The annual volume of production is in the neighborhood of 15,000 cases.

Sebastiani Vineyards

Without the iron wills of the Sebastiani family, winemaking in the Sonoma Valley long since would have been reduced to a hobby rather than a business. The sleeping giant gave a large community of independent growers a market for their grapes in those years when the wine business was lean and retirement village developers were growing fat on the charms of a small place. Before that, the Sebastianis kept a good many people going through the twin horrors of Prohibition and the Great Depression.

The extent of the civic contribution is obvious. Most of the major commercial buildings on or near the old Sonoma Plaza carry the family name. The family contribution to wine is less obvious in the landscape. The winery tucks away at the northeast corner of the town's main platte, the facade of the main cellar deceptively modest. In fact, the cellars hold some 4 million gallons of wine. The modest facade hides a series of three long buildings running back rather more than a quarter mile. What is more, the cased goods are stored in a separate building across the way from the aging cellars; it is awesomely large, too.

Samuele Sebastiani immigrated to San Francisco from Italy shortly before the turn of the century, and to Sonoma shortly after that turn. The precise date is not certain; 1902 seems likely. As did most winemakers in his era, Samuele made bulk wine for sale to merchants in the city. He did well enough to carry his business and most of his village through Prohibition and the Depression. Samuele died in 1946 when the firm was about half its present size, and when the Sonoma Valley contained only four other wineries, all tiny family affairs devoted to the jug trade.

Samuele's son August took over, and is slowly bringing the business from bulk winemaking to the production of vintage-dated varietals under the family label.

On the surface August is a different man than his father. Old Samuele loved pomp, and even would wear a suit and homburg hat into the vineyards so everybody would know he was boss. August, on the other hand, thinks bib overalls beat a suit any day. Dress code aside, he thinks of wine very much as his father did. His standards of taste are closely associated with his taste for food, and not with any abstract valuation. A good Barbera is one that tastes good with venison. The taste of oak comes best from toothpicks. A bad year of weather is no excuse to sell scrawny wine. And so on.

Furthermore, August resembles his father in being a natural survivor. He recognizes a push when it comes. In recent years Sebastiani has offered vintage-dated wines to supplement his standby blends. The style has migrated by careful stages toward such elusive qualities as the faint kiss of oak and varietal characteristics. In spite of the changes, Sebastiani wines continue to be fitted to the table of a good cook rather than the judge's bench in some competition.

August's "own" wines, Barbera and Johannisberg Riesling, remain exactly as he wants them, benchmarks for all who wish to know what he thinks.

The grapes for Sebastiani wines come partly from winery-owned vineyards south and east of town, partly from vines on leased properties in the valley, and partly from independent growers in all parts of Sonoma and Mendocino counties. The Sebastianis also have old ties in Lodi, and sometimes buy wines from there to supplement all of their generics and some of the varietals.

The winery, for all its size, is attuned to making small lots. In 1974–1975, August and his son, Sam, built a new stainless steel fermenting facility for whites in which the smallest tanks hold but 800 gallons. Between 1970 and 1974 they assembled a collection of 5,000 oak barrels in which to age reds. The cellars also have the gear to make generous lots when the grapes are ordinary.

Z-D

Z-D draws its minimal name from the initials of its founders, Gino Zepponi and Norman deLeuze.

Before Z-D, Zepponi was a systems analyst for a jet engine company, but wine came naturally as a sideline. His family has owned vineyards for some decades. Since founding Z-D in 1969 Zepponi has eased out of the defense business and set up a one-man firm that does systems analysis for wineries. The other owner, Norman de-Leuze, is an engineer of optical equipment.

The winery is no great deal bigger than its name, with a capacity of 6,500 gallons. The cellars are in an old barn-cum-warehouse in the village of Vineburg, about halfway between Sonoma town and the Carneros district, a practical location since the Zepponi vineyards are nearby and the rest of the grapes come from Carneros, just across the county line into Napa County.

The style is big wines. If they have to be a bit rough to be big, so be it, especially in the case of Pinot Noir. Z-D wines are not, however, the crude kind of stuff that comes from the organic school. The Gewürztraminer has shown disciplined scientific training and cleanliness with flavors as fresh as any from richly equipped big wineries.

The Vineyards

The Sonoma Valley runs north from the shore of the Bay directly across from San Francisco. It is shaped a good deal like an inverted comma, the broad head next to the Bay with Sonoma town at its center, the steadily narrowing tail pointed toward Santa Rosa twenty-three miles to the north.

The head of the comma is classed as Region I in the U.C.-Davis climate summaries. The tail falls in the median between Regions II and III.

Most of the famous vineyard acreage forms a tight ring around Sonoma town. The old Buena Vista vines cover rolling slopes just east. Hanzell's are north and west, on the lower slopes of Mission Ridge. Louis M. Martini's famous Monte Rosso vineyard perches on a flattened peak above Hanzell.

Chardonnay and Gewürztraminer have earned fine reputations among white varieties. Zinfandel has been a favored red variety, but, then, Zinfandel does well everywhere in Sonoma County.

Although no official statistics exist for the Sonoma Valley, it appears that total acreage within it cannot exceed 2,000 acres of vineyard.

Mendocino County

For years Mendocino County has labored along as a vinicultural appendage to Sonoma County, which is dim obscurity indeed considering that Sonoma has stayed deep in the shadow of the Napa Valley.

One scholar blames the slow development on lack of transportation–especially a railroad–to get the wines to market during the crucial last two decades of the nineteenth century. Some students blame the climate, which gives the vineyards a short but hot growing season. In any case, Parducci Wine Cellars, founded in 1931, is the oldest surviving winery in a county which seldom has had five cellars operating at once.

Times have begun to favor Mendocino more than formerly. In 1974 five wineries were producing appellation wines from Mendocino grapes; a new vineyard region near the coast was developing while the traditional district along the Russian River near Ukiah was expanding rapidly.

With Parducci, the other cellars making Mendocino appellation wines are Cresta Blanca, Edmeades, Fetzer, and Husch. In addition, Souverain of Alexander Valley and Sonoma Vineyards have made wines with Mendocino appellations at their wineries across the county line. Although Weibel has made wines entitled to the name at its fermentor facility near Ukiah, the company has yet to use Mendocino on its labels.*

Although there are almost no wines old enough to be nostalgic about, and although the capabilities of the region for several varieties are just beginning to be explored, Mendocino has made several reds and a handful of whites recognized as excellent, and distinctive to their place of origin. The Zinfandels and Cabernet Sauvignons are recognizably different from ones grown in either the Napa Valley or

* See page 108 in The Central Coast chapter for further description.

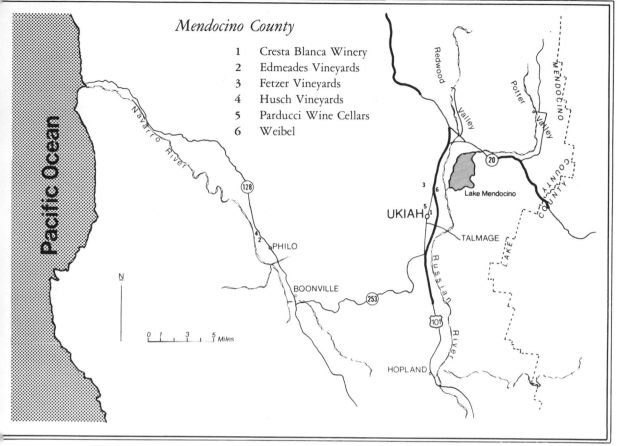

Mendocino County

1   Cresta Blanca Winery
2   Edmeades Vineyards
3   Fetzer Vineyards
4   Husch Vineyards
5   Parducci Wine Cellars
6   Weibel

Sonoma. Whites have fared less well, except for French Colombard, although new vineyards and improved equipment in the cellars have begun to force some reevaluations.

The Wineries

Although few in number, Mendocino's wineries have enough capacity to get at least some of their labels into the national market. Parducci and Cresta Blanca exceed half a million gallons storage capacity each. Fetzer approaches 100,000 gallons. Only Edmeades and Husch are tiny. They are pioneering out toward the coast.

Cresta Blanca Winery

Cresta Blanca's sudden presence in Mendocino County is only half bewildering. The long trail from the label's birthplace in the Livermore Valley has an internal coherence.

Charles Wetmore founded the original Cresta Blanca south of Livermore town in 1882, beneath the chalky cliff that inspired the name. The Wetmore family operated the winery and vineyards as an estate until 1940 when they sold it to Schenley, Inc., the distillers who already owned Roma Wine Co. of Fresno. Schenley shuffled Cresta Blanca here and there around the state until it finally wound up as one sadly tarnished corner of the Roma winery.

Guild Wineries and Distilleries of Lodi bought Roma from Schenley in 1971, acquiring Cresta Blanca as a side issue. In 1972 the proprietors of Guild decided to revive Cresta Blanca as a prestigious subsidiary, established their existing cooperative cellar in Ukiah as its new base, and, lo, the migration had reached its present point.

The co-op, incidentally, had been founded as an independent in 1946 by fifty local growers. They joined Guild some years later. The Mendocino winery makes only Cresta Blanca table wines. The dessert types come, as they have for years, from a winery at Delano. All go to Guild's Central Cellars at Lodi for bottling, at least for the present.

The Cresta Blanca producing cellars, in two utilitarian buildings, tuck between a pair of lumber mills in the northeast quarter of Ukiah, an appropriate enough site in this frontier between vineyards and commercial forests. The buildings have been substantially reequipped and modernized since becoming the home of the label.

In the first years most of the wines are identified only as "California." The Mendocino appellation has been going onto the varietals as quickly as production permits during the middle 1970s. Zinfandel and Petite Sirah were two of the first wines to win critical attention, and the first two to carry the local appellation.

Cresta Blanca was able to make an unusually quick start because Guild had been setting aside Mendocino varietals for some time before acquiring Cresta Blanca, and because the parent company could provide a competent staff from within. The style from the outset has been husky reds with pronounced bouquet from wood aging, and soft whites with at least some bouquet.

Fetzer Vineyards

Fetzer Vineyards, founded in 1968 by one-time lumberman Bernard Fetzer and his family, is one of California's few estate-like wineries, and one of the hardest to assess.

Vineyards and winery hide away in a small spur canyon several miles north of Ukiah. The vines, mostly cabernet sauvignon, sauvignon blanc, and semillon, grow on land that has been planted to grapes since the turn of the century. The Fetzers do buy some grapes each year, mostly zinfandels. When they do, the name of the source vineyard goes on the label. The winery, a graceful collection of flat-roofed buildings with some stone and some redwood walls, is at the foot of the main vineyard block. It is well equipped for making an annual 40,000 gallons of wine. Temperature-controlled stainless steel fermentors fill one cellar. Oak barrels and casks, some European and some American white, occupy the others.

To this point the short career has produced curiously inconsistent wines. The search for style betrays, I think, the absence of a seasoned palate among the staff, or at least a determined one. Every vintage yields wines to rouse new interest and new hope, but Fetzer has not yet been a label for the timid buyer in search of guaranteed pleasant drinking.

Parducci Wine Cellars

Adolph Parducci planted vines and built a winery just north of Ukiah town in 1931, thereby qualifying himself as the father of wine in post-Prohibition Mendocino County.

The family has been a major force in Mendocino winemaking since then, and sometimes the only visible one. In recent seasons the cellars have grown rapidly to keep pace with expanding vineyards in the region. In 1971 the company acquired corporate owners, but the family remains in charge of production.

The winery buildings are on the original site at the mouth of a small spur valley opening onto the Russian River course. Adolph's sons, John and George, direct its operations although the founder continues to watch over their work.

The hand of the new generation shows in a battery of temperature-controlled stainless steel fermentors installed in 1972 and in a 20,000-square-foot bottling room and binning cellar built in 1973. The traditional hand of Adolph remains visible in the main aging cellars where long rows of seasoned redwood tanks, most of them 5,000 gallons in size, hold the aging wines of Parducci. The founder did not want and taught his sons not to want any taste of wood masking the flavors of their grapes. Except for the steel tanks and a flossy new filter in the bottling room, Parducci wines are made very much in the old-fashioned way, which is to say that time does much of the work in satisfying cellarmaster Joe Monostori.

The grapes come from a thoughtfully chosen variety of locations in the Ukiah district, other parts of Mendocino County, and neighboring Lake County. The Home Vineyard adjacent to the winery has eighty acres of cabernet sauvignon, pinot noir, zinfandel, and french colombard. The Talmage Ranch, acquired in 1966, has a broader selection of whites, but most of its 100 acres in cabernet sauvignon. The Largo Ranch, not far from Talmage, was bought in 1971 and planted in 1973 almost exclusively to red grapes, although there is a bit of french colombard. In addition to these owned properties, the Parduccis have standing contracts with independent growers near Ukiah, in the Anderson Valley near Boonville, and at Kelseyville, to the east in Lake County.

The apparent emphasis on red wine varieties is real. The Parduccis, having roamed the county more thoroughly than any other student of the vine, think that Mendocino's greatest gift is for varieties that make big, husky, straightforward red wine. They keep a soft spot for french colombard, and growing hopes for some other white varieties, but reds always will be the backbone.

Anderson Valley Cellars

In the Anderson Valley, well to the west of Ukiah, two tiny wineries are engaged in the first work of establishing a new vineyard district.

Both Edmeades Vineyards and Husch Vineyards are tiny family operations only a few barrels larger than home-winemaker size. The plan in each case is to grow at least to 4,000 cases per year volume, but slowly.

Tony Husch and his wife, Gretchen, are slightly the farther along of the two. They established their first blocks of vines in 1968, and bonded the cellar in 1971. In 1973–1974 Husch built a compact, admirably well-equipped winery building to hold his Chardonnay, Gewürztraminer, and Pinot Noir. At the same time the first bottlings went to market.

Husch is learning as he goes, having dropped out of an urban business career to found the winery. While his first wines showed rough spots they also showed a consistent and generally agreeable sense of style. For those close enough to keep a watch, the label appears worth some effort.

Deron and Paula Edmeades bonded an old farm building in 1972 in which to begin making wine from vines planted in 1963 by Deron's father, Dr. Donald Edmeades. The varietal roster, includes, for now, only French Colombard and Cabernet Sauvignon.

The Vineyards

After the implausible situations in Napa and Sonoma counties, where south is cooler than north and east may be cooler than west, Mendocino's climate patterns are refreshingly regular.

Most of the 7,600 acres in the county are in the Russian River watershed, far enough inland so that sea air seldom penetrates. The climate season is Region III, verging onto Region IV in the sunniest exposures. A rough and tumbled terrain provides a considerable expanse that slopes toward the morning sun, and these slopes have been favored in the past. However, the district called Talmage, just south of Ukiah, looks west, and it has yielded some fine wines in recent vintages.

The Russian River watershed has begun to sort itself out in some detail. In addition to Talmage, much favored for cabernet sauvignon, the Redwood Valley sub district upstream from Ukiah has done well with that grape and with pinot noir and zinfandel. Potter Valley, adjoining Redwood, has yielded some chardonnay of good character. Downstream from Ukiah, vineyards around the town of Hopland are much favored for petite sirah.

The Anderson Valley is in the watershed of the Navarro River, which runs into the Pacific Ocean after a short and merry sprint through the tumbled west flank of The Coast Ranges. The new vineyards have provoked varied responses. Most of the small acreage bearing in the mid-1970s is chardonnay, gewürztraminer, and cabernet sauvignon. All hands are pleased with the uncommonly aromatic white grapes. Some think highly of the cabernet sauvignon, although John Parducci fears that the variety may ripen only every tenth year or so in the cool, often foggy valley. A late season grape, it is planted here in a place of early fall rains. A small vineyard of pinot noir has yielded excellent fruit early enough to appear a safer bet.

Because the Ukiah area is the old and still dominant district, Mendocino has far more red grape acreage than white.

The primary reds in the 1974 survey were carignane (2,367 acres), zinfandel (1,042), cabernet sauvignon (1,150), gamay beaujolais (590), and petite sirah (455). In whites, french colombard (970 acres) was trailed distantly by chardonnay (355).

Independent growers are the proprietors of most Mendocino County vineyards. The Parduccis own 330 acres. Weibel has 260 acres. Fetzer has about 100. The rest of the total belongs to growers, many of them members of Guild or Allied Growers cooperatives. (The Guild members may deliver their grapes either to Cresta Blanca or to Guild; the Allied growers deliver to United Vintners, principally for the Italian Swiss Colony winery at Asti in Sonoma County.)

The Central Coast

Old names populate the list of wineries in the coast counties south of San Francisco. Almadén, Concannon, Paul Masson, and Wente Bros. have been around since the 1880s, the steady presence of their labels on varietal table wines creating a warm vision of timelessness for Santa Clara and Livermore.

Most of the vision is illusion. No other part of vinous California has changed so much as this one, or so quickly. Since the 1950s, when urban pressure began to fill the valleys south of San Francisco with residents, old vineyards have disappeared at an astonishing rate, only to be replaced by a far greater acreage of new ones in newly developed regions farther south, above all in the Salinas Valley of Monterey County.

Nothing gives shape to this situation as well as a tour of the arithmetic.

Before the masses of people came to the San Francisco Bay area, Santa Clara County dominated vineyard acreage in the Central Coast. In the early 1950s it had 9,000 acres planted to vines. Alameda County on the east shore of San Francisco Bay was next in line with 4,000 acres. Monterey County had fewer than 100. By 1973 Santa Clara had only 2,400 acres remaining in vineyard, Alameda 1,900. Monterey County, meantime, had literally exploded from its bare 100 to 37,000 acres. Nearly all of that total came after 1969. Two of the present major growers in Monterey individually surpass in acreage the total of all of Santa Clara at its peak.

If the romance of history is lacking in Monterey County, it is more than replaced by a fiery spirit of adventure. Close to a score of the major growers in the county have banded together in an association devoted to improving knowledge of the region both in the technical sense for themselves and in the promotional sense for wine bibbers the nation over, or, if possible, the world over.

While the number of wineries in the region at large has dwindled from ninety in the years after Prohibition to thirty at present, the largest ones among the old names have led the southward migration. Almadén, Paul Masson, Mirassou Vineyards, San Martin, and Wente Bros. each live with one foot in the old counties and one in the new. Far from expiring for loss of their old original vineyards, they have grown much larger with the planting of Monterey and its neighboring counties. Several smaller neighbors, which have not planted new vines to the south, have planted new ones somewhere outside the original home counties, or else contracted with independent growers far from home. Not only do small cellars such as Concannon draw grapes from two or three counties, so do such miniatures as David Bruce and Ridge.

One result of all this motion is blurring of the traditional county appellations, and the substitution of "Central Coast" as a loose indication of where to look for the vineyards and cellars of the participants. A good many people, especially those with vines in Monterey, resist the term, fearing that it suggests greater warmth than does "North Coast," the summary term for the region north of San Francisco Bay.

In truth, the two regions are very similar in climate zones. If anything, the Central Coast is a bit cooler and less sunny than Napa and Sonoma. But it is indisputably the Central Coast of California, and deserves to be distinguished from the North Coast.

However the semantics work out, the thirty or so wine companies with bases from Alameda down to Monterey now make far more wine than ninety companies once did. For the most part they draw upon vineyards that did not exist before 1965, or, more accurately, 1969. In the early 1970s, the combined crush of the Central Coast was in the range of 40,000 tons, about equal to either Napa or Sonoma. The potential for 1977 is a shade more than double the combined total of Napa and Sonoma. One is left with no immutables and very few generalities.

The wineries of this sprawling vastness are grouped by size, as in the earlier chapters.

The Big Brands

Almadén and Paul Masson, along with The Christian Brothers in the Napa Valley, years ago elected themselves as suppliers of large volumes of reliable varietal table wines. If all California varietals were ranked vertically from most plentiful to

Alameda & Santa Clara Counties

1	Almadén Vineyards	14	Paul Masson Vineyards
2	Bertero Winery	15	Mirassou Vineyards
3	Bonesio Winery	16	Mt. Eden Vineyards
4	David Bruce Winery	17	Nepenthe Cellars
5	Concannon Vineyard	18	Novitiate Wines
6	Conrotto Winery	19	Pedrizzetti Winery
7	Filice Winery	20	Ridge Vineyards
8	Fortino Winery	21	San Martin Vineyards
9	Gemello Winery	22	Villa Armando Winery
10	Emilio Guglielmo Winery	23	Weibel
11	Hecker Pass Winery	24	Wente Bros.
12	Thomas Kruse Winery	25	Woodside
13	Live Oaks Winery		

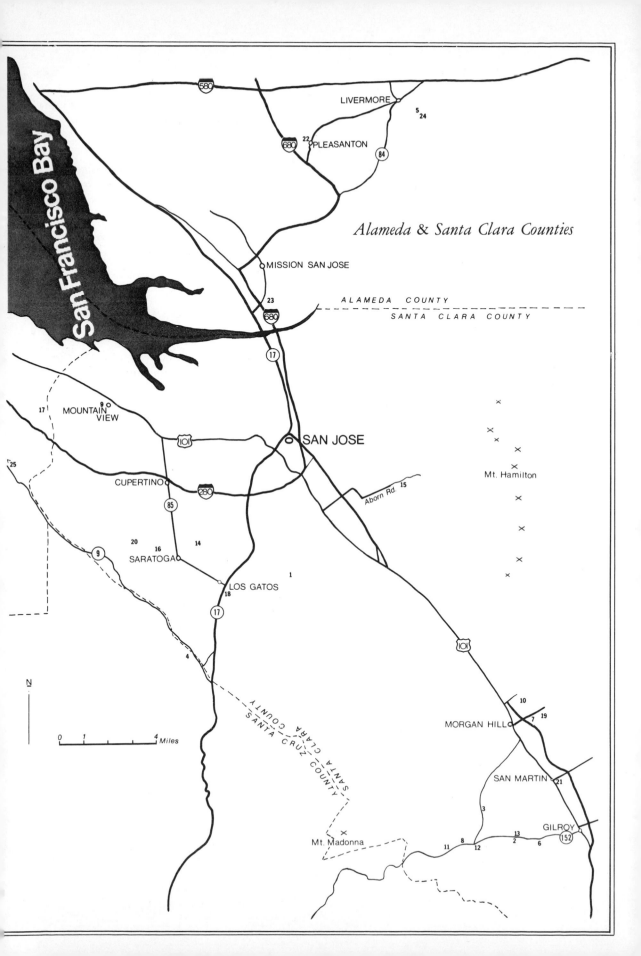

San Francisco Bay

Alameda & Santa Clara Counties

LIVERMORE

5
24

22 PLEASANTON

680

84

MISSION SAN JOSE

23

680

ALAMEDA COUNTY

SANTA CLARA COUNTY

17

×

17

9

MOUNTAIN
VIEW

×
×
×
×

101

SAN JOSE

×

Mt. Hamilton

25

CUPERTINO

280

Aborn Rd. 15

×

85

×

20   16   14

×

9

SARATOGA

1

LOS GATOS

18

17

101

4

10

7   19

MORGAN HILL

SANTA CRUZ COUNTY
SANTA CLARA COUNTY

SAN MARTIN   21

3

N

×

Mt. Madonna

13

GILROY

152

0   1   4 Miles

11   8   12   2   6

rarest, the Almadén and Paul Masson labels would appear toward the common end of the spectrum. If their production were to be matched against a similar listing of French wines, their relative position would be more or less equable with the commune wines of reliable French shippers such as B&G or Sichel.

It is curious that Almadén and Paul Masson should turn out to be matched pacers in the field, for they spring from a single ancestor. In 1852 a French emigrant named Etienne Thée settled in the Santa Clara Valley. Subsequently another Frenchman, Charles LeFranc, became his partner and the two turned to growing grapes and making wine near Los Gatos, in Santa Clara County. In time, LeFranc married Thée's daughter, eventually inheriting the business. One step farther along in the genealogy, LeFranc's daughter married the new junior partner, a rotund Burgundian expatriate named Paul Masson. After the marriage, Masson launched a vineyard and winery of his own in the hills west of Saratoga while LeFranc's son retained the original property.

The current Paul Masson company evolved out of the hilltop estate. The present Almadén organization grew out of the original Thée-LeFranc holdings. Both companies resemble their origins somewhat less than chickens resemble eggs.

Almadén Vineyards

Although the ancestry meanders back to 1852, Almadén began to take its present form a century later. In 1941 a man named Louis Benoist bought the dormant LeFranc property; in 1956 he propelled his then-small company into the first of 3,000 acres of new vineyard plantings in the lightly populated Paicines district of San Benito County, about twenty miles south of the town of Hollister, or eighty miles south of the original property.

When Benoist took his radical step, Almadén was selling about 80,000 cases of wine a year, most of it made from grapes grown on or near the original winery site, the old (and now extinct) district of Guadalupe, on rolling terrain between Los Gatos and San José.

Benoist was overwhelmed by his own audacity in 1967, when the huge acreages of new vines began to bear, demanding ever more equipment and cooperage to deal with the flood of wine. Benoist at that time sold his properties to National Distillers and Chemical Corporation, which operated Almadén as a subsidiary until 1972, then converted it to an independent public corporation.

In 1974, Almadén sold somewhat more than 5 million cases of wine, had 23 million gallons of cooperage in four wineries, owned or leased 9,000 acres of vineyard and bought grapes from that much again under long-term agreements.

The geographic range of the enterprise is as staggering as its scope. Almadén owns 3,901 acres of vineyard at Paicines, in San Benito County, and another 535 acres at LaCienega immediately to the west and still in the San Benito River Valley. In Monterey County the company owns 1,293 acres at San Lucas and 811 at King City, toward the southern end of the Salinas Valley plantings. All of its leases and many of its long-term contracts are with independent growers in these districts. Almadén also owns 257 acres of vines on a northwest-facing slope between the towns of Pleasanton and Livermore in Alameda County, and a vestigial 18 acres of vineyard at the original winery site near Los Gatos in Santa Clara County.

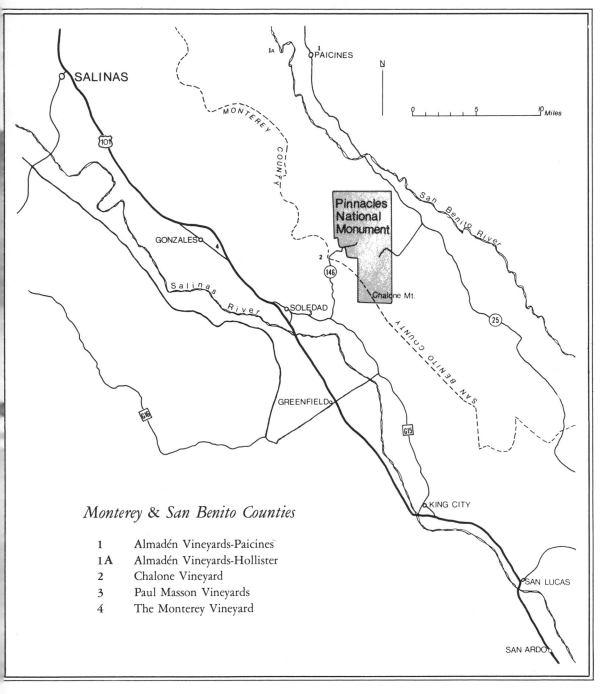

SALINAS

PAICINES

MONTEREY COUNTY

N

0   5   10 Miles

101

San Benito River

GONZALES

Pinnacles
National
Monument

Salinas

River

SOLEDAD

146

Chalone Mt.

SAN BENITO COUNTY

25

GREENFIELD

G16

G15

KING CITY

Monterey & San Benito Counties

1   Almadén Vineyards-Paicines
1A   Almadén Vineyards-Hollister
2   Chalone Vineyard
3   Paul Masson Vineyards
4   The Monterey Vineyard

SAN LUCAS

SAN ARDO

    Almadén's producing coastal wineries are in San Benito County. Varietal white wines are made in a 7 million-gallon-capacity structure of unrelievedly utilitarian outline, built at Paicines in time to hold the first crops from vines there. Varietal reds are made at LaCienega, where the storage capacity is 5 million gallons. The core of the LaCienega operation dates back to 1880. It has done prior service as the once-famous Vaillant winery. However, the core is but a small part of the contemporary whole. The old wood-frame structure is now surrounded by a series of low, warehouse-like buildings. One of the latter holds the celebrated 37,000 oak barrels in which Almadén varietal reds come to maturity, along with sherry-types.

In 1974 the company added to its roster a producing winery in the San Joaquin Valley. At Kingsburg, the winery originally was built by Louis M. Martini during Prohibition. More recently it had been a part of the Roma wineries. Almadén, on buying the old brick buildings, announced that they would be used for crushing and blending both dessert types and table wines, all from purchased grapes.

All Almadén wines are finished and bottled at the original vineyard site in Los Gatos, where the company has 4.5 million gallons of storage capacity, its sparkling wine cellars, and the bottling lines.

Bottled and cased wines are stored at yet another property, this one in San José.

Techniques for crushing and fermenting and for bottling are, predictably, modern to the minute. The aging cellars are more traditional, however surprising that may be. In addition to the 37,000 small barrels, Almadén has another 11 million gallons of wood tanks, most of them redwood, for the aging of its finer wines.

Almadén makes and sells one of nearly every kind of wine known in California. At the very top of the list, by price, is a series of vintage-dated, estate-bottled varietal table wines. Even these are of modest cost compared to the most prestigious Californian wines. The regular, undated bottlings of varietals are not at all pricey. There are generic and jug table wines, secondary sparkling wines, and dessert wines in abundance from purchased grapes and/or bulk wines.

Almadén wines are always sound, though sometimes afflicted by the flavors of overcautious handling in the cellar. The whites are made fresh and, if there is the remotest precedent, sweet. The reds almost always are marked by the flavors of wood aging, sometimes too much so. (The excesses come, I think, from their having to share cellar space with the sherry solera at LaCienega. Red wines and sherry-types rest side by side there in an environment that rather favors the making of sherry.)

Paul Masson

Paul Masson shifted in the direction of voluminous reliability sooner than did Almadén, when the Joseph Seagrams Co. bought the property in 1945.

However, the Masson organization has not grown so rapidly or so much. The proprietors do not publish figures quite so freely as their counterparts at Almadén, but most signs point to Masson being two-thirds to three-quarters the size of Almadén as of 1975, and gaining.

The label dates from the 1880s when the unquenchable original Paul Masson carved out 100 acres of vineyard in the hills west of Saratoga town, in order to make sparkling wines by perfectionist standards. Masson stayed at his task until 1938, when he sold the property to a young stockbroker named Martin Ray and retired. Ray made table wines in preference to sparkling wines, but left the scale unchanged during a brief tenure. After a gutting fire in 1941, Ray rebuilt the old stone cellar and sold the property forthwith to Seagrams. Since then the enterprise has grown without stop, always as a part of the Seagrams organization.

Paul Masson's principal vineyards now are in the Salinas Valley in three big blocks totalling slightly more than 5,000 acres. The oldest vines, planted in 1962, are on Salinas River benchland south and east of the dusty little farm village of Soledad.

Newer vines are on the opposite side of the river, part of them at the northeast corner of Greenfield, and a larger part of them west of that neighboring town to Soledad. As its base in Santa Clara County, Masson still has the original 100 acres of vineyard planted by old Paul himself, and another 330 acres in the San Ysidro district near Gilroy.

In March 1974, Paul Masson purchased 670 acres in the San Joaquin Valley near the town of Madera. Most of the land is to be planted to dessert wine grape varieties. A separate dessert wine cellar was under construction on the property in 1975.

Three wineries already existed. The principal producing one at Soledad is a sturdily handsome, ultramodern facility begun in the mid-1960s to take the first crops from Monterey vines, and episodically expanded to its 1975 scope, 12 million gallons. The big Champagne Cellars on the Santa Clara Valley floor near Saratoga were begun in 1961, and expanded in 1967, again in 1969, and yet again in 1973. It is the finishing and bottling cellar for all Masson wines as well as the production facility for all sparkling wines. Old Paul's original stone building up in the Saratoga hills is now devoted mainly to the aging of experimental lots of wine, although it doubles in brass as the scene for advertising photographs and as the backdrop to summer concerts sponsored by the proprietors.

Like Almadén, Masson uses extremely modern equipment to crush and ferment its wines, then goes back to wooden cooperage for aging its finest ones. There is less oak in general, and far fewer oak barrels in particular, than at the rival cellars. The emphasis in wood aging is on sizable redwood tanks. It is deliberate. The Masson style demands light, fresh, youthful wines.

The winery's own grapes dominate in the varietals, although the company buys substantial amounts of wine in bulk from Sonoma County vineyards to round out its supply. The generics usually contain some percentage of San Joaquin grapes, common practice among all the inexpensive to moderately priced coastal jug producers.

As the Monterey vineyards round into full production, it is probable that the Masson management will add vintage-dated, estate-bottled varietals to their roster, already long with nonvintaged wines of every type. Incidentally, Masson is a leading proponent among the coastal companies of proprietaries—trademarked bottlings. Theirs are called Emerald Dry, Baroque, and Rubion.

Middle-Sized Cellars

One of the surprising aspects of the Central Coast, in view of its scope, is the absence of middle-sized wine companies. Only four now sell in the range between 100,000 and half a million cases each year, with one more hoping to do so.

The lack of greater numbers explains itself mainly in the absence of enough vineyards before Monterey County began to develop in the early 1970s. Making wine on this scale is not overdifficult, but some years are required to develop the inventories, then the markets. Until the vineyards yield real volume, there is no chance to start the cycle. The situation rather reverses that in Sonoma County.

All five wineries in the group are greatly dependent on Monterey County grapes now, and are likely to become more so if they expand.

Mirassou Vineyards

To outsiders Mirassou Vineyards wines appeared in abundance overnight, in 1969, as if by alchemy. To insiders there was no mystery at all. Five generations of the family have made appreciable amounts of wine in the Santa Clara region, but the first four chose to do so anonymously.

The earlier Mirassous made first-quality varietal wines for sale in bulk to other producers with marketing arms, an honorable vocation and one for which the family earned a lofty reputation within the community of winemakers.

The decision to develop a family label for the family wines came when the current generation contained sales-oriented souls among its number. The fourth generation, Edmund and Norbert, sired three sons and a daughter. Young Peter Mirassou took charge of the vineyards. Son-in-law Don Alexander is in charge of production. Dan and Steve Mirassou are the sales and marketing end of the family organization.

Just as the fourth generation was beginning to pass the reins to the fifth, there coincidentally began to take place the great expansion of Mirassou vineyards beyond the Evergreen district of Santa Clara County southward into the Soledad area in Monterey County's Salinas Valley, beginning in 1962.

As a further coincidence, the arrival of mechanical harvesters in the California wine industry came simultaneously with the Mirassou move.

The result is that the youthful Fifth Generation, as it refers to itself on back labels, has pioneered all at once the family label, the vineyards in Monterey, and the notion of field-crushed wines. The latter two factors have put them under strong scrutiny both within the industry and among connoisseurs of California wines.

With their vineyards divided between Monterey and Santa Clara counties, but all of their winemaking facilities in Evergreen, the Mirassous had to become ingenious about the harvest. They crush the grapes right in the fields, into tanks that roll alongside the mechanical harvesters. The fresh juice then makes the eighty-mile trip to San José in sealed stainless steel tanks. At the old family cellars, the juice is transferred to conventional stainless fermentors in fresher condition than the must of any hand-harvested grapes.

The results are not all in hand. The first field-crushed wine, a Sylvaner, was made only in 1971. Since then other whites have been made, aged, and released. All have been sprightly in youth. How they, or age-worthy red types will fare with years in the bottle remains unanswered. After all, as people who hand harvest like to point out, a little oxidation never has done harm to Ch. Mouton-Rothschild or, closer to home, the Georges de Latour Cabernet Sauvignons of Beaulieu.

However the situation resolves, the Mirassous have done much of the recent work to establish the characters of soils and vintages in both Santa Clara and Monterey counties. They alone in this region have used counties as appellations of origin, and vintage dates, to help themselves and critics make assessments of a wide variety of wines from a long skein of years.

The vineyards at Evergreen exceed 400 acres. Those in Monterey, in two big

The original Paul Masson cellars, in the hills above Saratoga, now hold experimental lots of wine and serve as a backdrop to summer concerts. (WINE INSTITUTE)

ranches, approach 1,000 total. The main winery has a good bit more than one million gallons capacity, steel fermentors and wooden cooperage combined. A second cellar about a mile south of the original adds half a million gallons of wood cooperage. The latter building, long a bulk winery belonging to the family Cribari, was acquired in 1974 to satisfy a steadily growing need to make more Mirassou wine.

The Monterey Vineyard

The Monterey Vineyard crushed its first grapes during the harvest of 1974, about 2,400 tons of them. Even before the fact, it was the largest purely Monterey winery in the county's history, and one of the most ambitious new starts in all of California's vinous development.

The structure of the operation is unusual, and an understanding of it is essential to knowing what the proprietors hope for their venture.

At the base twenty-eight ranches in the Salinas River Valley are operated by a number of interlocking and overlapping partnerships. Most of the vineyards are on the east side of the valley at Gonzales. Some sizable chunks are to the south of Gonzales, some near Soledad, others near Greenfield. A few prized small holdings are on sharp slopes on the west side of the valley. Most of these latter are between

Gonzales and Soledad. In sum, the twenty-eight parcels come to 9,600 acres of vineyard, all of it planted to prestigious varieties.

Each of the vineyard partnerships also is a partner in the winery which is incorporated separately.

The winery is programmed to make wine for a variety of purposes. One will be single vineyard wines, or estate wines. These may go to market under individual labels. Secondly, the winery will make wine for a general label owned by all the partners as part of their proprietorship in the winery. Thirdly, the cellar will make wines for sale in bulk to other producers. The original cellar buildings will hold something on the order of 5 million gallons of wine, with space to double that figure. The diverse equipment allows the making of single-vineyard wines from ranches as small as 80 acres and as large as 1,400 acres, as well as greater volumes of wine from combined vineyards, and still greater volumes of wines intended to be sold in bulk to other wineries.

The reds and whites are made in separate buildings facing each other across a central crushing area, so that equipment in each can be tailored to the differing needs of the two different wine types.

The brothers Myron and Gerald McFarland, members of a pioneer California farm family, developed the complicated concept, and are the prime movers. Part of their concept was to form their two separate organizations along specialist grounds. Within this framework, they reserved management of the farming operations for their own company.

The winery company is under the direction of Dr. Richard Peterson, who left the established comforts of Beaulieu Vineyard in favor of adventures in a new place.

Peterson is the right sort of man for the job of developing a new winery in a new district. Trained at U.C.-Berkeley as an enologist-enological engineer, he spent several seasons as the director of research at E. & J. Gallo before moving on to Beaulieu. Having learned unflappable curiosity, he now has almost limitless opportunity to try out new thoughts, including what to do with zinfandel that does not ripen until mid-December.

White wines from the debut vintage of 1974 included Chenin Blanc, Grüner Sylvaner, Johannisberg Riesling, and a proprietary called Del Mar Ranch after the vineyard on which its grapes grew. Reds were Gamay Beaujolais and Zinfandel.

Plantings also include substantial amounts of sauvignon blanc, cabernet sauvignon, and pinot noir. Varietal wines from these were to join the roster as the vines came into bearing.

San Martin Vineyards

Under the proprietorship of the Filice family, San Martin Vineyards ambled through four decades without many cares, or much identity, either. Since its purchase by a conglomerate corporation called Southdown, San Martin has the physical chance of growing larger than The Monterey Vineyard.

The Filices made inexpensive generics on a slightly more sophisticated plane than the nearby country wineries of the Hecker Pass district, and they made varietals with somewhat less elegance than other growers in Santa Clara or Alameda. In essence, the Filices liked to grow grapes and other fruit more than they liked to make

Harvest scene at the Warm Springs vineyard of the Leland Stanford Winery in the 1880s or 1890s. The property now belongs to Weibel Champagne Cellars. (WINE INSTITUTE)

wine. As one point of evidence, they kept their 800 acres of vineyard when they sold the winery in 1972 to Southdown.

The new owners set about a rapid restructuring of priorities. They have announced their intention in a variety of ways. The first move was the release of vintage-dated red varietals from Filice vines in the San Ysidro district south and east of the winery, which is near the highway town of Morgan Hill. Secondly, as those wines went to market, the new owners were installing a sizable collection of stainless steel fermentors, new oak barrels, and other new touches in a winery which, until that point, looked like Bela Lugosi's idea of a Transylvanian cave. Thirdly, and perhaps most important, the Southdown people assigned a part of their Salinas Valley vineyards to San Martin.

Through two companies Southdown controls some 10,000 acres of vineyard near King City in the Salinas Valley's warm southern half. Most of the property operates as an independent grape-growing company called Viña Monterey. As a separate company San Martin owns 1,650 acres of vines set alongside the larger Viña

Monterey holdings. This supply of grapes is augmented by the 800 acres belonging to the Filice family. (San Martin gets those grapes until 1983. Presumably the winery will have a future choice between extending its contracts for the Filice grapes and broadening its base in Monterey County.)

Some of the young wines from the Southdown era at San Martin show promise. The winemaker, Ed Friedrich, is German by origin and temperament. Some of his early whites were crisp and clean, of a style to compete at a pricier level than the Filice-produced forerunners. The early reds show a similarly clean, fresh touch.

Weibel Champagne Cellars

Since 1939 the Swiss family Weibel has been making sparkling and table wines in old brick buildings erected near Mission San José as a pre-Prohibition winery belonging to Senator Leland Stanford. In recent years the exact status of the enterprise has grown increasingly enigmatic.

In 1972 the Weibels built the first stage of what was to become a large producing winery near Ukiah, in Mendocino County. A considerable proportion of the Weibel crush comes from their own and contract grapes grown in that area. The Mission San José cellars were to serve only for making sparkling wines.

Since 1972, the Mendocino winery has not expanded according to schedule, but has remained a bare-bones fermentor facility. At Mission San José, meantime, the stored wines show a preponderance of private or subsidiary labels. The Weibel label, whether on table or sparkling wines, is in lesser evidence. This is particularly true of sparkling wines, once the flagship of the house.

It would not be any too surprising to find that Weibel sales do not demand quick expansion, for the wines have taken a fearful beating from critics in recent years. It is not that Weibel wines are bad. They are competent enough. It is just that they never compete with other wines of the same name. Weibel Chardonnay, for example, does all right in tastings of generic Chablis, but hardly ever crawls out of last place in tastings of Chardonnays. In compensation, it must be said, the Weibel varietals usually cost a good deal less than the wines that beat them. There is little else to say.

The winery, located on a sidehill not far above San Francisco Bay, is the last survivor of a once-prosperous wine district called Mission San José. The vineyard around it also is a last survivor. On those grounds alone, it needs to be wished well.

Wente Bros.

The original Carl Wente entered the wine business in 1881, as one of the pioneers of the Livermore district, but the Wente name did not go on a bottle of wine until Prohibition had ended in 1934. Before then, the whole production had been sold out each year in bulk to other wineries in California or to San Francisco bottlers.

By 1934 the winery had become the property of two of Carl's sons, Ernest and Herman, the brothers in the company name. Herman died in 1961 having earned a secure reputation as one of the greatest winemakers in California's brief history. The family label prospered with him.

Ernest was and still is the vineyard man. His son, Karl, now manages the firm.

The stainless-steel fermentors at Wente Bros. in Livermore were among the first to be erected outdoors in the coastal regions of California. (HAROLYN THOMPSON)

Karl's aggressive, innovative stamp is on the place. Gifted with machinery, he has put it to work everywhere. Before the Wentes turned to mechanical harvesters, Karl invented a self-propelled gondola. In essence a one-ton tub on a tricycle frame, the contraption was (and still is) powered by one-cylinder engines geared to crawl alongside pickers at less than a walking pace. A number of them are still in use in old vineyard blocks not yet trained for mechanical picking. Even before these machines crept onto the scene, Wente Bros. installed a battery of temperature-controlled stainless steel fermentors outdoors. Steel was hardly known in the coast counties, and having any outdoors was a certified heresy. Now both steel and outdoor installations are common practice at boutique wineries as well as big ones.

Inside the tilt-up concrete walls, the Wente aging cellars are similarly modern, except for several galleries of ancient oak casks in which the red wines and selected whites mature, as they have since the label was founded.

Karl also was instrumental in Wente Bros. early and vigorous plunge into the Salinas Valley of Monterey County. A generous third of the Wentes' 1,400 acres of vines now grow in the Arroyo Seco vineyards west of Greenfield. It was not exactly a radical move. More of the Wente vines in Livermore scratch for a living in ground where any stone the size of a golf ball is classified as sand. Things are not very much different in the holdings at Greenfield.

The Wentes never have made anything other than table wines. It is rare among wineries of the age and size to have avoided both sparkling and dessert types, but the Wentes have.

From end to end their list of table wines tends toward a light style, and a fresh rather than overtly wood-aged one. The Chardonnay and Sauvignon Blanc long have been considered exemplary, and the Grey Riesling has legion followers. Reds have come along since the Monterey vineyards were planted, though not all of them are from there. Some of these, especially the Pinot Noir, have fared well against all challengers.

Not incidentally, the Greenfield vineyard has turned out to be one of the rare pockets where *Botrytis cinerea*—the Noble Mold—will perform its wondrous tricks in California. The Wente Bros.' Johannisberg Rieslings of 1969, 1972, and most especially 1973 have astounded German-oriented connoisseurs as *spätlese*-style wines.

The Small Cellars

If middle-sized cellars are scarce in the Central Coast, small ones are still less numerous. There are, at present, only three small enough for their wines to be rare, but large enough for bottles to be found in cities outside California.

There are, it must be said at the outset, a considerable number of miniature operations best described as semiprofessional no matter how serious their proprietors might be. The simple fact in all their cases is that the money to operate them comes at least partly from sources other than winemaking.

In this section, the three genuinely commercial companies are listed alphabetically, then the miniatures follow in a cluster.

Chalone Vineyards

Chalone Vineyards is, by every measure, a unique institution in Monterey County.

Tucked into a bench beneath a craggy basalt wall of Pinnacles National Monument, the vineyard is small now after several decades of being tiny. A new planting of a hundred acres in 1972 adjoins an original one of thirty-seven shy-bearing acres.

The history is a tenuous one, beginning in the nineteenth century when a wandering Frenchman found some quartz crystals on the site and took them to be a sign that vines would prosper there. He, or a successor, took the high bench to be Burgundian, for the old vineyards hold chardonnay, pinot blanc, and pinot noir, plus a block of chenin blanc.

The Frenchman did not prosper enough to leave his name on the place. Subsequently, after Prohibition, a man named Bill Silvear kept the vineyards going, and made enough wine to get the legend going. Almadén made some sparkling wines from his grapes, and they contributed to the luster of Chalone's reputation.

After Silvear wearied, the place went idle, enjoyed a brief restoration in the early 1960s, fell into disuse again, and finally was activated by the present owners in 1969. The present owners are a friends-and-neighbors corporation directed by a youngish amateur (in the best sense of the word) named Richard Graff.

His first vintage, 1969, suggested that he knew what he wanted to make with his grapes. The wines were dark-hued, and as full of flavor as he could get them. In 1970 and 1971 he improved on his originals, adding finesse and balance to the original strength. The character of all three years was lush and rich, Burgundian rather than sharply Rhenish as wines from the Salinas Valley floor have tended to be. After a crop failure in 1972, the subsequent wines have resumed course.

Nothing comes easy at Chalone, which is far beyond the last electric power line in the region. To grow grapes, Graff and two of his brothers have to fetch water up from the valley floor in a tank truck and irrigate through drip lines that fan out from a wooden tank at the top of the vineyard. To ferment wine in the low, white stucco building half carved into a slope near the vineyard, the Graffs have to crank the crusher by hand, and cool the cellars with loads of ice trucked in from Salinas.

Dick Graff's solace, while he waits for the wines to mature in their fat, Burgundian barrels, comes from a pedal-powered organ in a rude little house on the property. Graff arrived at Chalone by way of the music department at Yale.

The volume produced to date has been insignificant: In a typical year 2,500 bottles of Chenin Blanc is the largest fraction; 100 bottles of Pinot Noir is the small end. These sums will grow as the new vines come into bearing during the latter half of the 1970s, but the supply never will be enough to satisfy more than a handful of connoisseurs.

Concannon Vineyards

Until a battery of stainless steel fermentors went up in time for the vintage of 1974, Concannon Vineyards was in all of its visible aspects an old-fashioned sort of place.

The main cellar building has one exterior wall of brick, several of wood, and a couple made of sheet iron to match the roof. Inside, long rows of nineteenth-century upright oak tanks further emphasize a determined grip on the past.

Even before the steel tanks appeared, appearances spoke only an approximate truth. By exacting standards Joseph Concannon, Jr., is a scientific vineyardist, his brother, James II, a literate wine chemist.

The brothers are the third generation of a stubborn family. Their grandfather, James Concannon, bought forty-seven acres of rocky farm in 1883 after earlier careers as a sewing-machine salesman, hotel manager, and printer. He made the unlikely jump to winegrowing because the then archbishop of San Francisco, Bishop Joseph

S. Alemany, found himself short of altar wine at a time when the elder Concannon was casting about for a profitable investment.

After James Concannon's death in 1911, three of his sons ran the winery for a time until Joseph Concannon, Sr., bought out his brothers, Thomas and Robert. (In the era of the sons, the church paid back the debt of getting the Concannons into winemaking by keeping them in business as sacramental winemakers all through Prohibition.) When Joseph, Sr., died in 1965, his sons became the proprietors.

Family vineyard holdings have expanded from the original 47 acres to 300, of which 250 were in bearing vineyard in 1974. All of the family vines are in the Livermore Valley. Concannon wines reflect these plantings closely, although the proprietors buy some grapes from independent growers in Amador and Mendocino counties. Sauvignon blanc and semillon dominate the acreage. There also are sizable blocks of white riesling, sylvaner, cabernet sauvignon, petite sirah, and zinfandel. The grapes from outside growers have been, in the main, white riesling and zinfandel.

The day may come when the family must abandon its heritage in Livermore. The vineyards exist now only because a Green Belt ordinance lowers the taxes relative to those imposed on surrounding nonagricultural properties. Neither brother looks forward to moving. They have great allegiance to the wines from their rocky land.

Jim Concannon, a gentle, almost bashful man, produces wines after his own heart, which is to say Concannon wines are soft rather than hard. None overwhelms, but many linger in memory for being subtle, balanced, impeccably clean.

There is a school of thought in California that believes the only way to achieve a truly soft, rounded white wine is to ferment and age it in wood. Concannon Sauvignon Blanc and Johannisberg Riesling from earlier vintages would have been admissable as court evidence. The first vintage made in steel did indeed have a crisper quality, but not so much so that the essential style was lost.

Both Concannons, incidentally, have regretted Livermore's unshakable reputation as white wine country even though their grandfather did much to help establish it. For years the brothers found it difficult to sell red wine at any price. For a time in the late 1950s and early 1960s they even found themselves bringing well-aged Cabernet Sauvignons back from retail outlets for relabeling as dollar-a-bottle Claret, and they had to abandon Zinfandel altogether for a decade. More recently, the Cabernet Sauvignon has been selling well at $6, and Zinfandel made its reappearance on the list in early 1975. Now that the Concannons are the only producers of Livermore appellation wines left in the world, the worm begins to turn.

Ridge Vineyards

Ridge Vineyards was founded in 1966 by a partnership of scientists who used the hilltop winery as a weekend escape from their regular occupations down on the San Francisco Peninsula flatlands. The winery was an age-worn barn. The equipment was primitive. In essence, Ridge was a cooperative of home winemakers who financed their hobby by making enough extra to sell a bit. Having few or no commercial inhibitions, they made wines of durable but coarse character.

With time the enterprise has grown into a legitimate business, big enough to acquire a handsome old winery building and some commercial inhibitions. The wines are migrating steadily away from coarse power and toward refined strength under the direction of winemaker Paul Draper, hired in 1969 to oversee the steady expansion of the label. In addition to his academic work, Draper prepared himself for Ridge with stints in cellars in Bordeaux and Chile.

The original barn is now used only for bottling and storage of bottled wine. The producing cellars are several hundred feet higher up Montebello Ridge in a sturdy wood and stone building erected in the 1880s by a pre-Prohibition winemaker named Osea Perone. The building is tucked in a little wooded fold that looks west toward the Pacific Ocean, fifteen miles distant (rather than back across the town of Cupertino and, beyond it, San Francisco Bay).

Within, the presses are a Willmes and an equally modern Howard, the fermentors temperature-controlled stainless steel. Tidier work in the vintage season means shorter years of aging in the cellarful of American and European oak barrels and—contradictory though it might seem—smoother, more polished wines. Back in the amateur days, the wines rested as much as forty months in wood, and the proprietors advised leaving the wine to one's heirs rather than drinking it oneself. Now the barrel-aging time is down to a mortal two years, and the ruddiest of the reds are pronounced fit to drink after eight to a dozen seasons in bottle.

Only the Cabernet Sauvignon, a small lot of Zinfandel, and some minute amounts of white wine come from the small, shy-bearing vineyards around the winery. Indeed, it has reached the point where the winery location nearly is irrelevant. A very great proportion of Ridge wines come from grapes grown in Lodi, Mendocino, Napa, and Sonoma. Except for the fact that the primary partners live in the neighborhood of the cellars, the operation could more profitably be located north of San Francisco Bay. However, Dave Bennion, the prime mover, and a majority of the other owners do live on the San Francisco Peninsula and Ridge is far from moving.

Much of Ridge's value comes from its habit of keeping small lots of wine separate, and identifying the scattered source vineyards on the labels. It is, in its way, a kind of experiment station, which may offer as many as five single-vineyard Zinfandels from a single vintage. Since all of the winemaking is done to a single standard, the differences in the wines can be presumed to stem from the vines alone. Connoisseurs are delighted to presume so.

All Ridge wines are enormous in character. The reds, in particular, spend two to three weeks in the fermentors with their skins in order to wring all the stuffings out of the grapes. Filtering and fining are minimal or nonexistent. However, the proprietors and staff have an admiration for contemporary sanitation techniques, so Ridge wines tend to be much sounder of flavor than many produced by other cellars which announce that they make wine organically.

The Mountaintop Miniaturists

A man named Martin Ray was, for years, the Terrible Tempered Mr. Bang of California winemaking, a man who thought he was taking the charitable view when he wrote to his customers to say that he used grapes for his wine while the rest were leaning heavily on mixtures of sulfur and apricots; a man who, just as characteristically, told a retailer who wrote to complain of spoiled wine that Martin Ray wines were above judgment but retailers were not.

There was something to him, of course, or he would not have inspired both adulation and imitation. His legacy is a bizarre collection of wines and a school of imitators best described as Santa Cruz Mountain Primitive. The thing about a bizarre collection of wines is that a few are outstandingly good, a truth which applies to the production of Ray's imitators as much as to Ray's own works.

Ray belonged in the past tense as a winemaker for several seasons before his death in February 1976.

The label may continue, for he sold it and his property to one of his dedicated admirers not long before he died. What Ray sold is rather less than half of what he started with in 1940 after selling the Paul Masson winery to Seagrams. He lost the major part of the vineyards and his original winery in a suit brought in 1972 by disgruntled stockholders. That part of the property now is known independently as Mt. Eden Vineyards.

Some miles to the south, a dermatologist named Dr. David Bruce is making similarly styled wines in a cellar big enough to be on the brink of turning commercial. Bruce has rather more than 30 acres of vines of his own, buys from some small growers in the neighborhood, and still others as far away as Amador County in the Sierra Nevada foothills.

Some miles to the north, a chap named G. L. Burtness is making a few hundred gallons of wine each year under the Nepenthe label. His prices are somewhat more modest than the $20 to $50 a bottle top charged by Ray, Mt. Eden, and Bruce, but the wines are equally assertive.

There is one semiprofessional winemaker in the region with something like a classical sense of style. He is Robert Mullen, whose tiny Woodside winery fits beneath his two-car garage. He draws grapes from five vineyards with a total acreage of seven. A small corner of the vines are on the sainted ground of the original E. H. Rixford estate, LaQuesta. There are very few bottles of the LaQuesta Cabernet Sauvignon to be had, but of all these miniature productions, they are the ones most fairly priced and most likely worth the search.

The Hard to Classify

Wine, to its great benefit and ours, does not allow absolute categorization. Neither do wine producers. The sprawling, unstable Central Coast region supports several cellars that will not yield to generalized pigeonholes. Sometimes size balks neat placement. Sometimes the product does. However, in each case the real or potential achievements require connoisseurs to keep some kind of watch.

The listing is alphabetic.

Bargetto is a family winery founded in the 1930s at Soquel, a few hundred yards from the Pacific shore in Santa Cruz County. The old red barn two blocks east of the main street once was a producing cellar. Now, owing to a lack of nearby vineyards, it serves only to age wines the Bargettos buy from others to blend and bottle under the family label. The list includes the familiar varietal and generic table wines, and dessert wines as well. Limited in volume, Bargetto wines sell primarily in northern California.

The *Filice Winery* at Morgan Hill is both a forerunner and an outgrowth of the bigger family concern at Acampo, near Lodi.* Members of the Filice family restored a small local winery to life under their name in 1973, shortly after selling their San Martin winery to the conglomerate corporation called Southdown. When the Morgan Hill cellar and tasting proved a satisfactory trial balloon, the proprietors bought their Lodi property and retained the Morgan Hill one as an outlet for the Lodi wines.

To keep a finger in the coastal pie, the Filices bought the *Gemello Winery* in 1974. It is hard to grow lyrical over a cellar that tucks itself between a common subdivision and a bowling alley in the Santa Clara commute town of Mountain View, but the Gemello wines provoke lyrical thoughts out of all proportion to their birthplace.

Mario Gemello, who succeeded his father, John, as the proprietor, continues as the winemaker under the Filice ownership. From its beginning, in 1934, the cellar has specialized in strong, earthy reds. Until the late 1960s, they sold at the cellar door for ridiculously low prices. Then Gemello discovered that his wines were much akin to the ones from Ridge, and he brought his prices up sharply. Cabernet Sauvignon, Petite Sirah, and Zinfandel are the mainstays.

The Filices never made wine the way Mario Gemello does. It remains to be seen how they will respond as owners. The announced goal is to let the man court the muse his own way.

To date, Gemello has used locally grown grapes—mostly from vineyards on Montebello Ridge—for his most pungent red varietals. Automatically, production is limited to very small amounts.

The *Emilio Guglielmo Winery* east of Morgan Hill in Santa Clara County dates back to the mid-1930s. The founder, after whom the winery is named, built up a 500,000-gallon facility. A considerable portion of the capacity is in stainless steel. The business was and is mostly in bulk wines.

A small amount of jug wine has been going for years to San Francisco's North Beach Italian community under the Emile's Reserve label. In 1973 George Guglielmo, son of the founder, launched the Mt. Madonna label for a line of varietal table wines. The volume of these remains tiny at present for lack of a sales arm in the business. However, Guglielmo's training at Fresno State equipped him to make sound wines. Some of his red varietals have compared favorably with costlier bottles from established names. His grapes come from the immediate south Santa Clara County region.

Incidentally, the winery looks across the Santa Clara Valley to Mt. Madonna, in the west hills, hence the label name.

A transplanted Chicagoan named *Thomas Kruse* wandered in 1971 into the Hecker Pass country west of Gilroy, where he spliced some new wood into the shakiest parts of an old barn, then began making wine in it. Since then he has

* See page 135.

continued shoring up the barn and attempting wine of a sort more delicate than the usual Gilroy standards. His early attempts were at several different varietal rosés, so he could get into the marketplace quickly. He has branched out into red varietals, and such esoterics as sparkling white Zinfandel.

The small annual production goes to market under the Thomas Kruse label. The style is homemade, but refined homemade, and it is eagerly sought in the home market.

The Jesuit contribution to California wine comes from *Novitiate,* a half-million-gallon winery next to an active novitiate on a steep hill overlooking the town of Los Gatos in Santa Clara County.

Because of its churchly role, Novitiate devotes most of its storage space to sherries, ports, and the like, and sells most of what it makes for sacramental use. The list of table wines has just begun to grow in the past decade as the winery has turned slowly toward the general market.

The home vineyards adjoin the winery and school. They have shrunk away from the steepest slopes of the mountainous site in recent years, the lost acreage more than replaced on flatter terrain in the San Ysidro district between Gilroy and Hollister, in the southeast corner of Santa Clara County. Hillside vineyards are fine, according to the good fathers, until they are so steep that plow horses cannot keep their feet. Beyond that point, flat is better.

The primary plantings at San Ysidro are for varietal table wines: Pinot Blanc, Grenache Rosé, Cabernet Sauvignon, and Ruby Cabernet.

Father Ransford, the wine chemist, and Brother Williams, the cellarmaster, favor an old-fashioned, earthy approach to all their wines, which age in ancient redwood tanks and oak casks in the mazelike cellars. (The cellar buildings grew fitfully, in starts, from 1880 onward. As a result, there are no direct routes from the oldest end to the newest.)

The tasting room is the easiest place in all these United States to find the wines, though some are distributed in northern California and beyond. Not incidentally, Novitiate is one of the most friendly of all California wineries to visit.

An investment group calling itself Varietal Vintners in 1973 purchased the *Bonesio Winery* near Gilroy and the *Pedrizzetti Winery* near Morgan Hill. Bonesio, founded shortly after Prohibition ended, had made generic and varietal table wines in the time-honored style of the Hecker Pass country, using grapes from the adjoining family vineyards. Pedrizzetti, another, somewhat larger family winery launched in the same era, dealt principally in bulk wines, though the proprietors did sell some of their production in a highway tasting room.

The notion was to upgrade the styles to classical from country. In 1975 Varietal Vintners failed, and the wineries reverted to their original owners with flossier labels, but few substantial changes in the wines themselves for sheer lack of time. It remains to be seen whether the family ownerships will settle back into their old habits, or whether they have been stirred too much for that.

Villa Armando is an active cellar in the Livermore Valley without truly being a Livermore winery. Located in downtown Pleasanton, Villa Armando is owned by New Yorker Anthony Scotto, who gets most of his grapes from the San Joaquin Valley and sells most of his wine in the metropolitan New York market. For the first several years of Scotto's ownership, labels told the whole story. He called his wines

Vino Rustico, Orobianco, and the like. The aim was at New York families of Italian descent who had wearied of fermenting their own stuff in the basement, but had not wearied of the characteristic flavors. More recently the label has expanded to encompass several familiar varietals, Pinot Blanc, Pinot Noir, and Semillon among them. However, old habits persist. Villa Armando Pinot Blanc bears closer resemblance to Villa Armando White Rustico than it does to, say, Wente Bros. Pinot Blanc.

The winery goes back to 1902, when a man named Frank Garatti founded it to make bulk wine. Scotto purchased the building in 1962. In 1974 he purchased and planted a 205-acre vineyard at Sunol. In 1974 Scotto also bought the old Louis M. Martini residence in the Napa Valley. The purchase included a small stone cellar and a small vineyard.

The Livermore winery has a half-million-gallon capacity.

York Mountain Winery, last of this lot, has its origins in the 1880s. It was founded in the rugged hill country west of Paso Robles in San Luis Obispo County by a Texan named Jacob Grandstaff. Not long after it was purchased by a family named York, whence the present name. In 1972, a one-time New York sparkling winemaker named Max Goldman bought it from the last of the York family. His notion was then and still is to make first-rate sparkling wine on the property. However, in early 1975 he had just begun the serious work.

The Country Wineries

Santa Clara, venerable and diverse farming district that it is, always has had need of country wineries to serve the thirsts of its orchardists and garlic growers and the San Francisco branches of their families. Gilroy and Morgan Hill vineyards have been dedicated to that amiable purpose since 1910, when a flowering of small wineries enriched this region.

In the old days, which is to say the 1950s and before, the west hills were full of wooden barns with a few vines outside and a few barrels inside. Most of the patronage drove up to the door on Sunday afternoons to get the week's or month's supply of jug red.

Some of the old flavor lingers, especially in the Hecker Pass district west of Gilroy, but even here the prosperity of the early 1970s shook the old values, leading to cork-closed Cabernet Sauvignon where screw-capped Burgundy was once the only choice. The same general prosperity also replaced a considerable expanse of old vineyard with new tract houses as Gilroy developed into a sort of suburb of San José.

The shift from generic to varietal did not shock local palates very much, although it injured a few pocketbooks. The old styles are strong enough to overcome varietal characteristic.

Traditional Gilroy wines are built to taste good after a day in the fields. A Gilroy red, in particular, pours thick. The classic of them all is Pete Scagliotti's Live Oaks Burgundy. In addition to Scagliotti, the other old-style wineries on the rolling road west out of Gilroy include Bertero, Conrotto, Hecker Pass, and Fortino. None of these wines can be bought very far from the cellar door. Italian restaurants and delicatessens in San Francisco's North Beach are the farthest markets from home for most.

A handful of other country jug wineries survive here and there in the Central

Coast counties. One is Vincent Locatelli's little weekend winery near Boulder Creek in the Santa Cruz Mountains. Two others are Pesenti and Rotta, cheek-by-jowl neighbors in the handsome hill country west of Templeton in San Luis Obispo County.

Snobs will, I suppose, shun these places because the labels show little or nothing in the way of pedigree, and the prices are no more prestigious than the labels. Connoisseurs, however, would do well to stop by and have a look at some of the robust stuff that comes from such souls as Scagliotti's, or Angelo Bertero's, or Chick Conrotto's. They are honest men who make honest wine, of the general sort that has nourished most of the wine drinkers in history.

The Vineyards

Never has so little been known about so much vineyard land. Primarily because so many of the plantings in the Central Coast were made after 1970 there have been but a handful of wines from vineyards in Monterey County, and still fewer from ones in San Luis Obispo and Santa Barbara counties. For lack of adequate yield, not many appellation wines are being made from surviving patches of old vines in Alameda and Santa Clara counties.

As noted at the beginning of this chapter, the great tendency has been to blend. In the case of Almadén and Paul Masson, the blends encompass not only two or three counties in the Central Coast region, but are likely to have a bit of North Coast or San Joaquin fruit added in as well. The smaller wineries are more likely to stay with the Central Coast grapes, but no less likely to blend from two or more counties.

For all of the blending there are some particulars worth knowing, especially since the maturing vineyards from Monterey southward will yield ever larger volumes of local appellation wines.

The counties are noted in alphabetic order.

Alameda County

Nearly all of the vineyards in Alameda County are winery-owned ones in the Livermore Valley. A few others continue, the most visible of them is Weibel's at Mission San José.

The Livermore Valley, what is left of it, is a curiosity piece among California wine districts. It is the only one of the coastal valleys with elevation, the only one completely shielded by hills from sea air, and it has absurdly poor soil.

Southeast of Oakland, 485 feet above the east shore of San Francisco Bay, the valley has been a favored haunt of subdividers since the early 1960s. The towns of Livermore and Pleasanton sprawl formlessly across the east-west axis of a small terrain, in the spaces between two nuclear research institutions.

All of Livermore's vineyards fall within a narrow, curving band where the south edge of the valley floor begins to bend up into grassy hills. The line extends from Livermore to Pleasanton, although with long gaps in these populous times.

The location of the vineyards clearly reveals the course of an ancient arroyo, a rocky outwash that goes as deep as 600 feet in places. Around Livermore, twenty-

and thirty-pound boulders on the surface are common in both Concannon and Wente vineyards. The wear and tear on tools is appalling. A plow wears out in a few days working these properties, rather than a normal several months. Toward Pleasanton there is a sketchy pretense of topsoil, but vines work hard for nourishment there, too. Richer soils to the north do not bear vines and never have, one of the broadest hints in California that there is more to growing grapes than sunshine.

Until the 1950s there was no irrigation to Livermore in spite of its classification as climate Region III and its severe lack of rain. The arroyo's rocky bed allowed vine roots to dip well into the water table, which then stood at about 35 feet. In the 1960s reservoirs to serve the growing population depressed the water table to 120 feet and deeper, which brought out the rainbird sprinklers. Now still another shift in the water supply system is moving the water table toward its earlier levels, but still the vines are limited to the rocky bed of the arroyo. Elsewhere, the sun and soil are too rich a combination.

In the county as a whole there are but 1,800 acres of vines according to the 1974 census. Wente Bros. has 800 acres of that total in a series of connecting blocks near the winery. Concannon has close to 300 acres across county road J8 from Wente. The one-time Cresta Blanca vineyards exceed 100 acres, and are not far away.

The old Ruby Hill estate has 225 acres on a gentle slope above the back road connecting Livermore with Pleasanton. Almadén has its 200-acre block adjacent to that.

Villa Armando will add 205 acres to that total as its plantings near Sunol come into bearing.

Although both the Concannons and Wentes insist that Livermore can and should be just as famous for red wines as whites, white grapes dominate the plantings. Semillon ranks first with 340 acres. Grey riesling has 220. Then come chenin blanc, zinfandel, chardonnay, and sauvignon blanc, all in the 100-acre scale.

That the Concannons and Wentes, of all the pioneers, should be the principal survivors is at least ironic, perhaps poetic justice. At the beginning, in the 1860s, French settlers dominated Livermore. Taken with its gravelly soils, they meant to make the place into a little corner of Bordeaux. One of them, an able vineyardist named Louis Mel, had ties to Château d'Yquem. It was through him that cuttings of semillon and sauvignon blanc came from those great vineyards to Livermore, where descendants of the original plants still yield two of Livermore's finest varietal whites.

Mel, the last Frenchman of the original group, sold his vineyard to the Wente family just before World War II.

Monterey County

In the Salinas Valley, in 1961, vineyards covered fewer than 100 acres. In 1974, the valley held 37,500 acres of vines. The sum is not half so staggering as some of the individual holdings. The company called Southdown controls 10,000 acres, and The Monterey Vineyard operates 9,600. Poor old Paul Masson, with 5,000, is an also-ran, and Mirassou with a mere 1,000 is small potatoes indeed.

Cabernet sauvignon is far and away the principal variety with 4,600 acres as of 1973. Following it, in order, are zinfandel, chardonnay, white riesling, pinot noir, chenin blanc, petite sirah, napa gamay, and merlot. They range from 2,500 down to 1,000 acres each. Even grapes outside the top ten have huge acreages. Gewürztraminer, for example, covered 780 acres of the Salinas Valley in 1973. The rest of the state, together, added only another 1,100 acres.

As a vineyard valley, the Salinas superficially appears to be a sort of reversed image of the Napa Valley. It runs northwest to southeast. The cool end is at the north end and the warm one at the south, with Soledad as a rough Region I counterpart to Carneros, and King City as the Region III replacement for Calistoga. Up to that point, the comparative image is correct. However, the analogy begins to crumble under more detailed scrutiny.

The winter storms that dump twenty-five to thirty inches of rain on Napa do not sweep as far south as Soledad, where the annual rainfall seldom surpasses ten inches. The visible evidence is bare, grassy hills on the shaded west side of the valley as well as on the sun-bleached east, an unheard-of condition north of San Francisco Bay. For lack of rain Salinas Valley vineyards must be irrigated.

The Salinas River, meager as it looks on the surface, carries a great volume of water from an unexpectedly large watershed. The river rises in the hills east of San Luis Obispo town. With its tributaries it drains an area of 140 miles long and as much as 20 miles wide, carrying the flow deep down in a rocky course rather than up top in conventional river-like fashion.

Vineyards tend to run along the benchlands at the edges of the wide, shallow valley, where nothing but grass used to grow. The lean but soggy soils of the bottomland are planted to lettuce and strawberries. Grapes, needing better drainage, have filled in the marginal high ground.

However dry, the valley stays cool because of the ease with which sea fogs penetrate its northerly reaches. Monterey Bay is wide-mouthed, unlike San Francisco Bay, and the Salinas Valley is wide-mouthed, unlike Napa. As a consequence, mists cover the valley as far south as Chualar with such regularity that no grape variety ripens to that point. The mists come down as far as Soledad often enough to make whites easier to grow than reds there. Only to the south of Greenfield is the valley both dry and reliably sunny. At King City the vineyards hold a mixture of both table and dessert wine varieties.

Soledad is the crucial point at which microclimates become too complex to permit any loose generalizing. From there north, the climate summaries are mainly Region I. From there south, most vineyards are classed as Region II until King City, where there is a definite break to Region III. But, but, but and but . . .

The growers in Monterey have made much of the fact that all of the vines in the county grow on their own roots rather than on the resistant rootstock used everywhere else in California and in Europe since Phylloxera. The direct planting is possible because the Salinas Valley never had grown grapes, and thus never become infested. I am not sure it makes any difference, and will refuse to be convinced until somebody conducts some controlled experiments on the subject, but the growers insist that their vines produce more aromatic grapes because the nutrients do not have to scuffle through the scar tissues of the graft.

Only a few genuinely specific evaluations can be made at this early hour in the

Salinas Valley's vinous history. White wine has had all the best of it in critical judgings to date. The Gewürztraminer from Mirassou Vineyards west of Soledad has been one of the loveliest of its variety in the state. Chenin Blanc has done well for both Mirassou and Paul Masson from vineyards near Soledad, although with a curiously Germanic twist of character. Thrice, in 1969, 1972, and again in 1973, Wente Bros. coaxed recognizably botrytised Johannisberg Riesling from its gravelly bench above the Arroyo Seco a few miles west of Greenfield. No Monterey red has held against all comers as well as any of these white, unless one ranges high up toward the Pinnacles National Monument to include the tiny but elegant volume of Pinot Noir from Chalone.

Again, one can only say but, but, and but . . . Dick Peterson in 1974 harvested for The Monterey Vineyard some Zinfandel at high sugar and extraordinarily high acid. The date was December 11. There are other, equally mystifying hints for the future.

The varieties that seem to be drawing the greatest attention from the winemakers are gewürztraminer, johannisberg, sauvignon blanc, and semillon (all with and without Botrytis), and in reds there is a feverish hope for pinot noir.

San Benito County

Vinously, San Benito County is a veritable fiefdom of Almadén, which owns or controls all but a handful of its 4,628 acres of vineyard.

. The county adjoins Monterey County on the east, protected from the chill winds of Monterey Bay by a single line of hills. One gap in these hills allows sea air to sweep eastward across the town of San Juan Bautista to Hollister, from where it flows at a gentler pace southward, up the stream course of the San Benito River.

Most of the Almadén vineyards flank the river and State Route 25, the latter a straight-line connection between Hollister and the east gate of Pinnacles National Monument.

For Almadén the focal point is at Paicines, about midway between Hollister and The Pinnacles. The earth is not neatly folded at all around Paicines, but rather gives the impression of a rumpled bed. Almadén's vineyard blocks are square in spite of that; they wander uphill and down in impeccable rows.

The emphasis in plantings is more than faintly Burgundian, and, after that, Germanic. Chardonnay had 869 acres in 1973, and pinot noir 744. Cabernet sauvignon had 534 acres, an interloper, then came gamay beaujolais at 516, white riesling at 395, and gewürztraminer at 257.

Climate supports the choices. San Juan Bautista is rated Region I and Hollister Region II in the U.C.-Davis summaries. Paicines is only faintly warmer than Hollister.

Almadén does not use Paicines or San Benito as appellations, so there is no wine to use as a measuring stick.

San Luis Obispo County

Newcomers have taken a strong notion that San Luis Obispo County might be Bordeauxish by nature, planting 762 acres of cabernet sauvignon and another 468 of merlot in a sudden burst in the early 1970s. Historically zinfandel has dominated a small acreage of local vineyards, and thus the production of local wineries.

The old and the new do not overlap physically. The biggest concentration of old zinfandel vines is in the forested hill country west of U.S. Highway 101 at Templeton. New vineyards tend to be in the hills east of the U.S. highway, and nearer the town of Paso Robles. Most belong to independent growers and will, for lack of local wineries, go elsewhere at least for a time.

The old zinfandel vines yielded superior wines during their best days. Some won gold medals at the state fair. None of the new varieties had been in the ground long enough to make a case for itself as of 1975.

Santa Barbara County

The Santa Maria River wanders about in its wide, flat flood plain, trying to look mighty. Like most coastal rivers in California it quickly dwindles to a network of small streams once the elevation rises above 50 feet. There is, however, one difference between this river valley and the others. The Santa Maria and an extension called the Sisquoc run almost true east-west.

Most of the awesomely fast development of a 5,000-acre vineyard district has taken place on benchlands that look south, in the European tradition. Climate Regions I and II prevail in spite of the southerly latitude because the tail of the great coastal fog bank curls easily and regularly into the Santa Maria's valley.

The southerly exposure and the frequent mists have caused some skilled observers to think that this might, just might, be the place in all of California for pinot noir.

It will take some years before anyone can know. There was no local winery to take the grapes before Firestone opened in time for the 1975 harvest. Some of the early production was going to the Napa Valley, where several winemakers were running experiments to see what they might learn.

All of the vineyards are owned by independent ranching companies.

Santa Clara County

Of all the counties south of San Francisco, Santa Clara is the most fragmented vinously. It always has been a disrelated collection of subdistricts. Now that its acreage dwindles and its wineries cast about in all directions for their grapes, its dimensions are cloudier than ever.

In its day the deep, narrow Santa Clara Valley much resembled the Napa Valley for its potential subdistricts. The valley floor grows progressively warmer from Cupertino on the north to Gilroy on the south, then cools again owing to the influence of sea air from Monterey Bay. Roughly parallel ranges of hills on east and west add their dimension. In fact, their climate characteristics are magnified over those of their Napa counterparts because they are much more exposed to sea air. From the ridge line of the west hills, one looks directly down to the Pacific Ocean, only eight to ten miles distant.

At the close of the 1940s there were 8,000 acres of vines in recognized subdistricts called Cupertino, Evergreen, Saratoga, Guadalupe, and Morgan Hill-

Gilroy (the latter sometimes called Hecker Pass). By 1974, with 2,400 acres of vines remaining in the county, Cupertino and Guadalupe are gone, Evergreen and Saratoga mere shadows. Of the remaining fragments the valley floor around Gilroy is easily the largest.

In the past the south county from Morgan Hill to Gilroy has made bulk wine, most of it from ordinary grape varieties which overwhelmingly dominate the southern portion of Santa Clara. The pattern of plantings around Gilroy is changing. Paul Masson, the Filice family (for San Martin), and the Novitiate of Los Gatos all have sizable vineyards in the district now called San Ysidro, between Gilroy and Hollister, in San Benito County. These vineyards run along the bases of the east hills, and are planted to fine varieties, especially cabernet sauvignon. The old country wineries along the Hecker Pass Highway west of Gilroy continue to grow common grapes in their territory.

The area always has been thought of as Region III, at the upper limit for fine table wines. Some growers now argue that some of the territory is Region II. Except for a few bottlings by San Martin, there are no fine varietals to use as measures, and they are not ideal evidence.

The Mirassous have their winery and some 300 acres of vineyard in the old Evergreen district. This region, along the flanks of the hills east and south of San José, earned a nineteenth-century reputation for making fine claretish reds. The Mirassous, perhaps as a nod to history and certainly as a gesture to the present, replanted an old field of mixed black varieties to cabernet sauvignon in 1973. In recent years, the Mirassous have blended the wines from these vineyards with others from Monterey. As late as 1967, though, they were offering substantiation of the old claims with well-balanced reds from cabernet sauvignon and zinfandel. If there is to be any more Evergreen wine, it is up to the Mirassous to make it. They own all of the remaining vines. The climate is Region II.

In the lofty hills west of Los Gatos and Saratoga the hardy band of miniaturists struggles to keep the old promise of Santa Clara, but time has, alas, passed them and their place.

Extraordinary wines have come from the few small pockets of earth deep enough to grow a vine on the relentless slopes of the Santa Cruz Mountains, the specific name for this part of the Coast Ranges. Old Paul Masson found his hundred acres around the turn of the century, and made sparkling wines that continue to be described as legends. There are a dozen other properties in the region which, in sum, hardly double the old Masson estate. It is not only a question of soil. Sea fogs sharply limit the westerly boundary of the district. Population limits it to the east.

Romantics call the home vineyards of David Bruce, Mt. Eden, Ridge, et al. the Chain of Gold. The name describes the cost of operation as much or more than it describes the worth of the wines. The impossibilities of vineyard economics on these slopes are summed up by the fact that David Bruce and Ridge must buy grapes from other districts in order to make enough wine to stay in business. The others in the clan all have other incomes that support winemaking.

The San Joaquin Valley

Every grape-growing country with the possible exception of Germany makes most of its wines as a commodity, something to wash down ordinary dinners. The difference between California and the others is that *all* California wine is bottled and labeled for the market.

Ordinary wines in France or Italy or Spain receive neither cap nor name. They may even go home from the store in a dishpan if a bottle is lacking. The least of California's production, on the other hand, may not slip anonymously into heedless gullets. It must have some kind of pedigree for the buyer to see.

The San Joaquin Valley produces and markets most of California's modestly priced, reliable, common wines of all types. With their names out front, the producers of these wines take great pains to give good value for the money. The best of the proprietors have far more pride of product than the consuming public demands. Their effort has paid off in the long run. No other country's ordinary wines have as lofty a reputation.

Be that as it may, the San Joaquin still is no place to go in search of romance or rarity. Although a few rare, romantic valley wines exist, giving spice, the name of the main game is industrial efficiency.

Four companies—E. & J. Gallo, United Vintners, Guild Wineries & Distilleries, and Franzia Brothers—do a dominant 80 percent of the production and marketing of valley wine, which, in turn, is 80 percent of all California wine. Their wineries, and smaller ones as well, look a good deal like petroleum refineries. Long rows of lofty steel tanks exposed to the elements replace cozy cellars full of barrels. The bottled wines rest in warehouses of such size that railroad cars go through them to load rather than alongside. A million gallons is almost the basic unit for figuring size.

The San Joaquin Valley is the right place to make wine on such terms. It is reliably warm and dry. Its deep sandy loam is almost incomprehensibly fertile. And it is huge. Above all, it is huge.

From Lodi, 85 miles northeast of San Francisco, to Bakersfield, 100 miles north of Los Angeles, the valley is almost 400 miles long. Cupped between the Coast Ranges and the Sierra Nevadas, it approaches 100 miles in width at several points. Except for a lacy network of rivers it has no physical barriers. This absence of geographic limits allowed, perhaps even demanded the gigantic scale of valley agriculture. At all events, its 488,000 acres of table, raisin, and wine grape vineyards leave ample room for huge crops of cotton, hay, rice, peaches, and everything else that grows.

In spite of its size, the valley functions as one immense wine district because that is how E. & J. Gallo, United Vintners, and Guild use it. All three have winery-owned or independent contract vineyards scattered the length and breadth of it. All three have wineries at several strategic points.

Nine counties fall within the valley's scope. From north to south they are San Joaquin, Stanislaus, Merced, Madera, Fresno, Kings, Tulare, and Kern. County names almost never appear on wine labels under the California appellation laws. The major towns, also in north-to-south sequence, are Lodi, Stockton, Modesto, Fresno, and Bakersfield. The long gaps between them are filled with dozens of small towns and an infinity of worn, dusty agricultural villages, most of them forgettable, most of them forgotten. Several of the town names do appear on wine labels, in the small type at the bottom, where they offer a clue to the identity of the bottler but not to the source of the grapes.

· The regularity of climates in the valley contributes to the blurring of local geography. It is Regions IV and V in the U.C.-Davis climate classification system, all of it. Cynics call the place America's Algeria. Optimists compare it to the other side of the Mediterranean, mainly Spain. Neither image is apt. Because of the way it is farmed the valley is distinct from any other region.

Technology is the handmaiden of good table wine in the San Joaquin. New techniques have opened up new avenues of style in the coast counties of California, but they have wrought a fundamental transformation in the hot interior, where nature tends to make sweet grapes for sweet wine.

The elemental changes are in the vineyards. Most basic, Dr. H. P. Olmo of U.C.-Davis has hybridized new grape varieties tailored to produce improved table wines from vineyards in hot climates. The proven successes are Emerald Riesling and Ruby Cabernet. A new generation is on the way, with red varieties called Carnelian and Carmine already recognized as superior to all predecessors.

Along with the hybrids, the acreages planted to traditional French and Italian varieties are growing rapidly because vineyardists have learned to abate summer heat with canopies of leaves and curtains of mist. Chenin blanc, for example, had no more than twenty acres in the big valley in 1959. The 1974 figure was 14,655. French colombard, semillon, petite sirah, and barbera show similar increases.

The parallel developments in the wineries of cold fermentation, glass-lined steel for aging, and sterile filtration (as a replacement for pasteurizing) temper the taste of heat in a wine as directly as altered vineyard practice does.

The combined efforts of science and nature now permit the big valley to produce an astonishing range of wines. Nearly all of the California sherry- and port-types plus other dessert wines come from grapes grown in it now, as they traditionally have. From San Joaquin vines come a still larger percentage of the grapes that go into the premixed punches called pop wines. (The pop roster tastes all right in spots, but to call such beverages wine is a semantic misdemeanor in my book. Some of the entries are made from apples, some are perry. Even the ones with grape bases have flavor essences from Pacific Islands and jungles and other places with no connection to the world of wine. The damn language cannot endure such buffeting forever.)

Most of the table wines have been traditional generics—Burgundies, Rhines, and their mates. Since 1973, though, varietals have begun to emerge in increasing numbers as new vineyards come into bearing. There are even beginning to be a few vintage-dated wines from the valley, an implausible thought ten years ago.

Although winemaking goes back to the 1850s in the San Joaquin Valley, the pre-Prohibition legacy is close to invisible, even closer to irrelevant. For all practical purposes 1933 was a brand new start by new people in new buildings. The era was designed to set the valley on its present course.

THE MAJOR WINERIES

To survive in a land of very few wine drinkers while the United States was at the bottom of its Great Depression meant making very small amounts of wine and waiting for a buyer, or making very large amounts that could be sold soon at whatever price the market would bear. In the 1930s the San Joaquin had only the latter choice open to it. Good grapes and equipment and skill were all lacking.

Quite aside from anything to do with wine, the American public of the post-Prohibition years was becoming steadily more brand-conscious as advertising blossomed into a pervasive factor in business. A handful of people in the wine business, recognizing the trend, began to develop brand identity for wines. Out of their beginnings grew mass marketers as natural companions to large-volume producers.

The development of huge producer-marketer wine companies continues in the vast San Joaquin at the expense of its small wineries for the simple fact that reliability is a chief virtue in a consumer society. The big firms make sound wine readily available to every corner of the country.

E. & J. Gallo Winery

The ownerships of big valley wineries are mainly in the hands of public corporations, or grower cooperatives, or hybrids of the two. Most privately owned wineries in the San Joaquin are small.

Against this pattern the family-owned firm of E. & J. Gallo stands in astonishing opposition because it is the largest and most successful of them all.

Gallo, all by itself, gives implausible size to winemaking in the San Joaquin Valley. The little wine company founded in a rented Modesto warehouse in 1933 has grown into a colossus with more than 175 million gallons of fermenting and storage capacity and an annual sales volume exceeding 100 million gallons. (The exact figures are unknown and unknowable. As a family trait Gallos do not talk. However, the approximate figure is close enough to give a useful picture of the firm's size.)

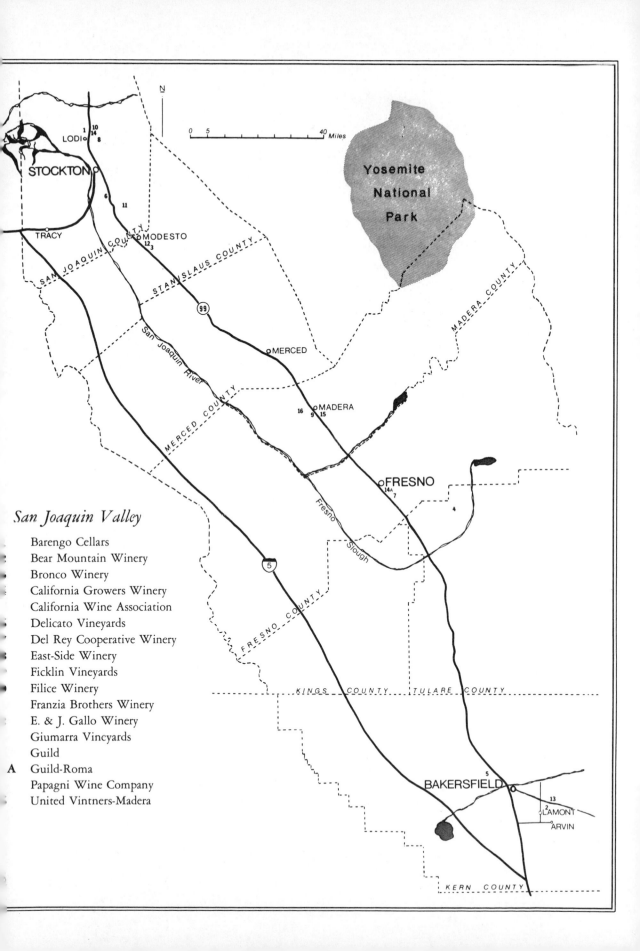

N

0 5   40 Miles

LODI

STOCKTON

TRACY

San Joaquin County

Stanislaus County

MODESTO

99

San Joaquin River

Merced County

MERCED

Yosemite
National
Park

Madera County

MADERA

FRESNO

5

Fresno County

Fresno Slough

KINGS COUNTY   TULARE COUNTY

San Joaquin Valley

   Barengo Cellars
   Bear Mountain Winery
   Bronco Winery
   California Growers Winery
   California Wine Association
   Delicato Vineyards
   Del Rey Cooperative Winery
   East-Side Winery
   Ficklin Vineyards
   Filice Winery
   Franzia Brothers Winery
   E. & J. Gallo Winery
   Giumarra Vineyards
   Guild
A   Guild-Roma
   Papagni Wine Company
   United Vintners-Madera

BAKERSFIELD

LAMONT

ARVIN

KERN COUNTY

The vast, glass-lined steel storage tanks at E. & J. Gallo in Modesto range from 200,000 to 1 million gallons in capacity each. (HAROLYN THOMPSON)

Such scope cannot be seen by mortal eyes even when they behold the physical evidence. To think that the two founders, the brothers Ernest and Julio, with their families own and manage the entire operation is even more bewildering.

The Gallo philosophy of winemaking is uninhibited by tradition and it is forthright: Make wines with flavors that appeal to huge numbers of people, and do it reliably.

As mass marketers, the Gallos play in all of the games. The craze for pop, be it wine or no, began at Gallo in 1957 with Thunderbird, and has gone on to encompass such as Spañada, Tyrolia, and Ripple in variety. There are traditional dessert types, including a sweet sherry-type called Livingston Cream that gives Harveys Bristol Cream a tough run in blind tastings but costs only one-eighth as much. Still and all, table wines are the crowning achievement. Chablis Blanc and Hearty Burgundy since the late 1950s have shown the Gallo insistence on giving remarkable quality for price paid. In 1974 the Gallos entered the varietal market with more good values for money.

The style of Gallo table wines is based in the thought that Americans do not like bitter or otherwise austere flavors in any of their foods or beverages. Thus reds and whites alike have soft, fresh characters with faintly sweet to outright sweet finishes. They are made under conditions a surgeon would admire.

All Gallo premises look the part of ultramodern, hyperefficient industrial plants and not at all like traditional wineries. The brothers Gallo barred all wood barrels and tanks from their premises early in the 1960s on grounds that wood cooperage cannot be kept clean. Every piece of their 175-million-gallon capacity is stainless steel or glass-lined carbon steel, and it is out in the open air. Foam insulation and circulating coolant systems protect the contents from inclement weather in place of roofs and walls.

All of the aging, blending, and bottling is done at Modesto, where a great delta of tanks occupies a flattened knoll in the southeast quarter of town. The main blending tank, biggest vessel in the collection, holds a million gallons. A typical tank holds 400,000 or 600,000 gallons. The storage winery is flanked on one side by a huge plant in which the Gallos make their own bottles and caps, and on the other side by a colonnaded office building. At the wide end of the deltoid storage winery is the bottling plant. At one corner of it is the production and research laboratory, an installation staffed with enough trained enologists to rival the faculty of the University of California at Davis Department of Enology and Viticulture.

The Gallo fermenting wineries, each an awesome collection of tanks in itself, are west of the town of Livingston in Merced County, and in the northeast quarter of the city of Fresno.

In addition to the properties they own, the Gallos control through long-term contracts the production of two cooperative wineries in the coast counties. One is the Napa Valley Co-op in St. Helena. The other is the Sonoma County Co-op in the little village of Windsor, in the Russian River region. In addition, the private firms of Frei Bros. and Martini & Prati steadily supply the Gallos with wine from Russian River grapes. These arrangements reflect an old dependence on coastal vineyards for table wines of quality. During the past few years, the Gallos have begun buying grapes from independent vineyard companies in Monterey County, most of them for the varietal wines introduced in 1974. Even with the addition of Monterey grapes to the mixture, the old dependence on the coast dwindles as valley vineyards improve.

It seems absurd, somehow, to say that a 6,000-acre vineyard is important out of all proportion to its size, but the main Gallo vineyards west of Livingston are that. They supply only a tiny fraction of the winery requirements. However, they have been Julio Gallo's private experiment station since the 1940s. With this property, to their eternal credit, the Gallos have learned and then pushed other growers in the big valley to follow their example. It was at Livingston, to cite a specific, that the Gallos developed vine-training techniques for chenin blanc as a valley grape.

If all of this seems to point to E. & J. Gallo as a major force in the industry at large, the impression is just. The firm pioneered mass marketing in the wine industry, is a major source of research into fermentation and aging technology, is a great source of research in vineyard management, and, because of all that, is a major influence on the taste of Americans for wine. There is so much Gallo to taste that the palates of Ernest and Julio have done much to shape those of their countrymen. As an obvious outgrowth, it is a helluva lot easier for the competition to sell fresh, soft, faintly sweet wines with a hint of spritz than it is for them to sell wine with more austere characteristics.

United Vintners

If ever an enterprise demanded a tapestry weaver to explain how it got where it is, United Vintners is it. Presently the company is in the mass market under a variety of names with pop wines, dessert wines, inexpensive generic table wines, medium priced and costly varietals, and a handful of sparkling wines, too.

In one way or another, the producer-marketer company combines elements of all the main themes of California winemaking since 1880.

UV owns wineries in all parts of the state and, with them, dozens of historic labels for its plethora of products. The most prominent names in current use are Petri, Lejon, Italian Swiss Colony, and Inglenook, but there are several others acquired in a labyrinthine past.*

The prime owner since 1971 is Heublein, Inc.,† the Hartford-based conglomerate. which also brings to market Grey Poupon mustard, Ortega chilis, Colonel Sanders chicken, Smirnoff Vodka, and only the tax man knows what else. Heublein bought an 80 percent share from the previous owner, Allied Grape Growers, a gigantic cooperative of vineyardists that retains 20 percent of UV and continues as the prime supplier of grapes to it.

A man named Louis Petri invented United Vintners in the 1940s as a marketing arm for cooperative wineries with weak or nonexistent sales organizations. A good many of the cooperatives he attracted already had evolved through mergers with still older firms going back into the 1880s. It is this fact that gives UV its amazing pool of labels.

United Vintners dominated California wine sales in the 1940s and early 1950s then began to sag toward its present position as a distant second to E. & J. Gallo. Heublein has regained some lost ground since 1971 with aggressive merchandising.

One thing Petri started to do Heublein now continues. That is to disguise as much as possible the San Joaquin Valley origins of as many table wines as possible. The company uses its Inglenook Navalle labels for several generic and varietal wines priced to compete with counterparts from Gallo. Still less expensive generics go out under the name of Italian Swiss Colony. The Inglenook Navalle wines are blends of coastal and valley grapes. The ISC wines are predominantly or entirely made of valley grapes at Madera (which location is hidden from label readers by the establishment of a post office called Italian Swiss Colony in the lobby of the office building there). ISC also is the main name for dessert wines and much of the pop stuff. Petri is disappearing as a label, along with Gambarelli & Davitto and a host of others with origins in the gloomy post-Prohibition days of the San Joaquin.

The ironic outcome of this shuffling is that tolerably skillful wine drinkers now equate the one-time Sonoma label of Italian Swiss with the standard wines of the San Joaquin, and think of Inglenook, once a pride of the Napa Valley, as a lower-middle-class coastal winery.

Whatever the label situation, some 80 million of UV's 100 million gallons of fermenting and storage capacity are in the San Joaquin at Lodi, at Escalon, at Fresno, and above all at Madera where a modernized old winery called Mission Bell is the main fermenting, aging, and bottling winery for all manner of the firm's wines. The Allied growers who supply UV with grapes are located in rough proportion to the cooperage capacities.

* For closer looks at the coastal elements of United Vintners, see the description of Inglenook on pages 30 and 32.
† A 1972 Federal Trade Commission action against Heublein alleged restraint of trade, and called for the company to divest itself of United Vintners. Court action pends as of 1976.

Guild Wineries & Distilleries   · 131 ·

The red-checkered tablecloth on the labels of Vino da Tavola endured for twenty years as a signature for the Guild, from the immediately successful introduction of the red wine in 1954.

This sort of consistency, amidst the roaring storms of change that have blown steadily since 1957, typifies the enterprise, a solid case of agrarian conservatism holding tight against the sophisticated marketers who dominate the San Joaquin Valley.

Guild is the only pure cooperative among the big four. Its 500-plus grower-members own the sales organization as well as the producing wineries. The directors, elected from the ranks, chose until 1974 to stay with traditional generic table and dessert wines, Charmat sparkling wines, and brandy. Guild's dips into the volatile world of pop punches have been hesitant and few, nor did the co-op do much with proprietary types after the original success of Vino da Tavola.

However, even conservative agrarians change. In 1974 Guild launched a list of varietal table wines under the name of Winemasters Guild. At the same time it introduced a list of imports from French, German, and Italian cooperative wineries, all to be sold under the same Winemasters Guild label. The intent is that these upgraded wines under the new label will become the new signature of the house, replacing the homey old red-checkered tablecloth, and the common wine that went with it.*

Insistence on the old values kept Guild out of the explosive growth shown by the exploiters of pop. The company runs a very distant third to E. & J. Gallo and United Vintners. This does not mean it is small, however. In 1974 the storage capacity exceeded 51 million gallons. A considerable proportion of this total came in a rush in 1971 when Guild bought the Roma and Cresta Blanca wine operations from Schenley, the distillers.

The Central Bottling Cellars in the flat expanses of vineyard east of Lodi has been the cornerstone of Guild since its founding in the 1940s. All of its wines go there for finishing, blending, and bottling. Of producing wineries, there are two near Lodi, three in Fresno (including the Roma plant), and one in the Kern County town of Delano. These San Joaquin Valley operations are supplemented by one coastal winery, Cresta Blanca, in Mendocino County.

Not one of these installations is modern in the steely 1970s sense of the word. Both Guild and Roma began as strong wineries in the post-Prohibition era when California was just beginning to catch up with the well-established European use of concrete fermentors and aging tanks. There is a growing volume of steel at Guild, and a good deal of wood aging capacity, but mainly there is concrete. Guild's cellarmaster, a soft-spoken, even shy man named Lawrence Quaccia grew up with concrete and is perfectly happy to continue using it, even though it causes most winery work to go more slowly than steel does.

Nearly all of the grapes for Guild wines come from member growers. They are

---

* Indirectly Guild entered the varietal market earlier than 1974 with its subsidiary Cresta Blanca label. See pages 93–94.

At Guild, highly automated bottling lines work at high speed. (HAROLYN THOMPSON)

in every district in California from Mendocino to Bakersfield. Before the Roma acquisition members numbered about 200. A majority of the acreage owned by them was in the Lodi district. A typical crush was 80,000 tons. Since Roma, the roster has increased to more than 500 members, the dominant acreage is at Fresno, and the crush has averaged 200,000 tons yearly.

Guild offers wine under the Winemasters Guild, Ceremony, Tavola, Alta, Famiglia Cribari, Roma, La Bohème, and J. Pierrot labels. Like United Vintners-Allied Growers, Guild has a kaleidoscopic history of property acquisitions and mergers, so has a big stable of names. Alta and Famiglia Cribari, for example, came from wineries that merged with Guild. Also like UV, Guild is paring down its roster of labels in favor of the most salable few.

Franzia Brothers

Until 1967 Franzia was the other family-owned winery of some size in the San Joaquin Valley, a vest pocket Gallo. In that year the family sold to a combine, which turned the winery into a public corporation. In 1971 Coca-Cola bought up the stock and made Franzia Brothers a wholly owned subsidiary.

While Giuseppe Franzia and his five sons owned the property they did a pretty good job of making valley table and sparkling wines to sell at the bottom of the price scale. For years they won a fat percentage of the eternal rounds of competitive tastings that go on among the winemaking staffs of the big firms selling at budget prices. In recent seasons Franzia wines have won fewer times on a faster track, but still perform creditably. As evidence of the continued good value, it can be noted that enology students at California State University-Fresno drink quite a bit of Franzia Burgundy just before the monthly checks begin arriving from home. As other evidence, the Franzias managed to double sales, from 8 million to 16 million gallons a year during the 1960s.

The winery buildings, alongside State Route 120 a few miles east of the little town of Ripon, grew piecemeal after 1933 and look as if they did. Some walls are concrete, some concrete block, and some sheet metal. The equipment reflects post-Prohibition growth in a similar series of jumps, although the 17 million gallons of storage capacity have begun to be dominated by steel since 1967.

The main label has been and still is Franzia for wines of all types. The prides of the house are Zinfandel and the bulk process sparkling wines. Since 1974, the Coca-Cola management has been moving toward more prestigious wines and higher prices.

Much of the 4,000 acres of vineyard owned by Franzia has been planted recently to grapes that presage a line of varietal table wines.

A good deal of Franzia-made wine goes into the world under other labels. There is a name to court every buyer. Old Chateau and North Mountain only begin to evoke the ethnic and geographic temptations of these subsidiary labels. The giveaway that the wine is Franzia-made, whatever its name, is the line of small type on the label reading "Made and bottled in Ripon." No other winery uses that town name, just as only Gallo uses Modesto.

THE LOCALIZED WINERIES

Aside from the dominant firms with widespread activities, a fair number of local firms operate in the San Joaquin Valley. This does not necessarily mean small. One, Bear Mountain, has 25 million gallons of storage capacity. Neither does it mean a different kind of wine. Much of the smaller or localized production is in very much the same style as wine from the big operations. However, the local cellars are—in various ways—sources of particular information.

Lodi Wineries

Of the winegrowing subdistricts in the San Joaquin Valley, Lodi is the most clearly defined and, probably for that reason, the most appealing.

Natural barriers establish the physical intimacy of the place. Town and vineyards occupy a small, flat, triangular plain bounded on the east by the Sierra Nevada foothills and on the other sides by converging streams of the San Joaquin River system. The foothills are too frost-prone for grapes, the river bottomlands too wet.

In the dry, warm middle, in the midst of a standard Valley Aggie town, some of Lodi's small wineries have established a triumphantly local character. (Small is always a relative word. In the big valley 2-million-gallon capacity is tiny.) Barengo

Cellars and East-Side/Royal Host have long histories of identifiably local winemaking. The newer Filice shows signs of joining their company. Barengo and East-Side, in addition to being pioneers of localism, are pioneer makers of varietals from U.C. hybrid grape varieties.

Barengo Cellars

Barengo Cellars has a raffish physical charm about it. Next to a railroad track in the flat vineyard country north of Lodi town, the winery first comes to notice, as Lodi wineries usually do, because the corrugated iron tower of its brandy still sticks up higher than anything else in the neighborhood. Up closer, the main cellar building is red brick with here and there a souvenir of whitewash. Inside it long rows of well-used redwood tanks are interrupted by several stacks of oak barrels.

A battery of new stainless steel fermentors outside and a new bottling line in a new warehouse building bespeak recent growth at Barengo, but the original building remains an accurate extension of the long-time owner, Dino Barengo, an affable bear of a man who wears comfortable old clothes in which to keep uncertain office hours. The absence of gloss kept some people from noticing that all was clean and orderly, qualities reflected in the wines.

Good as the wines were, few people ever saw them. Barengo hated to sell wine almost as much as he loved to make it. Most of his production went elsewhere in bulk. Dino bottled just enough to satisfy the people who would make the pilgrimage to his door and plead for some. Barengo finally solved the problem by selling the winery in 1973, to Winkler-Scheid Vineyards, Inc., and signing on as winemaker for the new owners.

Winkler-Scheid is a Los Angeles-based management company which also operates more than 2,000 acres of vineyards in Monterey County.* It immediately launched an aggressive sales campaign in Los Angeles.

Dino Barengo, the winemaker, continuously has commanded respect within the industry for his wines from Lodi vineyards, most especially for his reds. He has done a great deal for the general reputation of Ruby Cabernet, and has made Lodi Zinfandels of collectible quality. Incidentally, he also has an elegant touch with port-types and other sweet wines.

East-Side/Royal Host

Most of Barengo's local competition has come from the East-Side Winery, which sells its wines under the Royal Host, Conti Royale, and Pastene labels.

The general outline of East-Side's history does not suggest much similarity to Barengo Cellars, nor does the physical premises. East-Side was founded in 1934 as a grower-owned cooperative, and still is that. The severely functional concrete buildings alongside State Route 12 a mile east of Lodi are without architectural glamour, or even a coat of paint. The sheet metal still house and concrete sherry bakers do not add visual delight, although an impeccable cellarful of redwood and small oak does. In short, East-Side is one more demonstration that good wine evolves in somebody's head rather than inside a handsome building.

Two of the principal heads at East-Side belong to the original winemaker,

---

* Winkler-Scheid operates the Monterey properties as a farm management concern. The grapes are presently sold to Almadén Vineyards under long-term contract.

Herman Ehlers, and his long-time colleague, Reg Gianelli. Both are recently retired, but left only after firmly imprinting their style on the cellars and on the member growers whose grapes go there.

Pushed by the winemakers, the growers of East-Side formed a vanguard of progressive vineyardists in the area, planting much of the early acreage of ruby cabernet, chenin blanc, emerald riesling, semillon, and other grapes for varietal table wines.

With these grapes Ehlers and Gianelli made Emerald Rieslings that have been models for the variety, and Ruby Cabernets that run brisk races with those of Barengo. East-Side Zinfandels also rank high among Lodi reds. (It is fitting that East-Side and Barengo should contest for honors; Dino Barengo and Herman Ehlers worked together for several years in their early days as winemakers.)

Curiously, it is easier to obtain East-Side wines on the Atlantic coast than it is in California. A distributing firm called Pastene takes most of the production for New York, New Jersey, and Pennsylvania markets, selling under its own label and the name of Royal Host.

East-Side has a winery capacity of about six million gallons.

Filice Winery

With Barengo and East-Side producing solid evidence that Lodi vineyards yield distinctive table wines, a corporation called Montcalm Vintners bought an old bulk winery in 1972, gave it a pretty face and superior equipment, and embarked on a genuinely ambitious sales program. They went too fast, failed, and turned over the reins to the family Filice, the former owners of San Martin Vineyards in Santa Clara County. The announced intent of the Filices is to go ahead with the original program, but at a more modest pace.

The original program was to offer a line of Lodi varietal wines, made soft for early consumption and priced accordingly. The available labels include Filice, Montcalm, Acampo Village, and Monet. In spring 1976, the Filices were only beginning to test the market.

Their winery buildings, not far from Barengo Cellars, were erected at the end of Prohibition. Before Montcalm came, they were a plain-faced co-op bulk winery operating under the name of Cherokee Vineyard Association. Montcalm covered bare cement with creamy Spanish stucco, added grace notes of clay tile and wrought iron, and otherwise transformed the cellars into a handsome showplace.

The cosmetics announced changes of substance. The old concrete fermentors were supplanted with new ones of temperature-controlled stainless steel. Old presses disappeared in favor of new continuous types from France. The only old equipment that stayed was a 1.4-million-gallon collection of well-seasoned redwood tanks for aging. After the additions, the winery capacity was 6.5 million gallons total. The Filices have not enlarged upon that sum.

Most of the grapes crushed at Filice come from 4,900 acres of local vineyards belonging to members of the old Cherokee Co-op, as was the case during the Montcalm interlude.

Other Wineries

In addition to these wineries and the three belonging to Guild Wineries and Distilleries, Lodi has several others. One, Stockton, sells some bottled wines. It is housed in what began as the Lockeford Cooperative. The rest deal purely in bulk wines. Liberty crushes for E. & J. Gallo. United Vintners has a facility in Lodi. Woodbridge and Lodi Vintners sell in the open market.

Lodi Vineyards

In the old days when brandy and dessert wines were the lifeblood of Lodi and the rest of the valley, a grape called the flame tokay dominated the vineyards of San Joaquin County. Not only did it make a fine brandy and good sherry-types, it could be packed fresh as a table grape.

There remains a huge acreage devoted to it, 20,000 acres out of 50,000 in the county in 1974. Versatility still is no curse in the eyes of a valley vineyard owner. However, table wine varieties, once counted by tens of acres, amounted in 1974 to more than 29,000 acres. The principal reds are zinfandel (11,000 acres) and carignane (7,750). Petite sirah has 1,080. Ruby cabernet is at 277 and hanging tough. White varieties command less space. French colombard, with 1,185 acres, and chenin blanc, with 930, are followed distantly by burger and grey riesling.

Vines surround the town of Lodi. Far the greater proportion of them cut a wide swath across the slightly bumpy terrain north of town, then curve southward from the little town of Lockeford.

Nearly all of the vineyards belong to individual farmers, most of them members of one cooperative or another. Except for Dino Barengo's little patch of ruby cabernet, no vineyard is used individually.

Valley wineries pay more for Lodi grapes than those from any other part of the San Joaquin because they make finer table wines. Truth be known, the valley proprietors compete with coastal ones for some of the grapes, especially zinfandels. It is a matter of climate. Air flowing through the Sacramento-San Joaquin delta country cools Lodi off at night while the rest of the valley stays hotter, or at least warmer. Any visitor can test the theory. A midnight swim in a pool at, say, Modesto, is a luxurious act. A swim at the same hour in Lodi is chilly work.

The official classification by U.C.-Davis is Region III–IV.

Modesto Wineries

Modesto—or, to give its full name, Modesto-Ripon-Escalon—does not exist as a separate district, mainly because it is home to both E. & J. Gallo and Franzia Brothers, who leave very little to others. Two wineries of some size are located in the region, though both buy grapes and wines from afar to round out however much local supply they command.

One was new in 1973. The other dates back to repeal of Prohibition.

Bronco Wine Company is the newer one. Founded by several members of the Franzia family that sold Franzia Brothers to shareholders, it uses a 1.5-million-gallon facility near Modesto to buy and blend bulk wines for resale, mostly under the Bronco label.

The older company, Delicato Vineyards, belongs to a family named Indelicato. A few years ago it was a dusty little building beside State Route 99 at Ripon, dealing mostly in bulk wines but selling locally under the Sam-Jasper and Delicato labels. By 1974 the proprietors had assembled a modern facility with 8 million gallons of storage capacity, all stainless steel save for a small cellar of redwood. The Sam-Jasper label was being phased out and the Delicato label sold in a widening market.

One small winery rounds out the district, legitimizing the inclusion of the pleasant little town of Escalon in the process. The name of the firm is Cadlolo. Owned and operated by the brothers Raymond and Theodore Cadlolo, it sells nearly all of its wine in bulk. The capacity, half a million gallons, holds more valley red wine than any other kind.

Modesto Vineyards

The vineyards in Stanislaus and Merced counties, and the fringe of San Joaquin County that makes up part of the district are increasingly given over to first-rate wine grape varieties.

In Stanislaus County, around Modesto, the top five wine varieties (with 1974 acreages) are carignane (3,210), grenache (2,470), french colombard (2,185), ruby cabernet (2,170), and barbera and chenin blanc (1,700 each). In neighboring Merced County, where the Gallo holdings at Livingston are large enough to govern the rankings, the top five wine varieties are french colombard (2,510), chenin blanc (2,380), ruby cabernet (1,205), barbera (1,360), and grenache (915).

Incidentally, the large proportion of white wine grapes in these totals owes only partly to table-wine needs. French colombard and chenin blanc are important in valley sparkling wine blends.

In both Stanislaus and Merced counties table and raisin grape varieties are minor factors. Stanislaus has 20,100 acres of wine varieties against 4,700 nonwine acres, almost all thompson seedless. Merced has 12,300 acres of wine grapes and 3,800 acres of other types.

Fresno Wineries

For all that the Fresno district is the gigantic heart of California wine, it has no distinct identity of its own, or very little anyway.

In part, sheer physical size balks definition. As concrete example, the shortest drive from United Vintners' Mission Bell winery in northwest Madera County to California Growers' winery southeast of the corner of Fresno County is at a minimum sixty-eight relentlessly flat miles. Fresno County alone has 190,800 acres of vineyard, including all the thompson seedless used fresh or to make raisins. Madera County adds 52,500 acres to the district total, Tulare County another 73,900.

Even though the scope seems ample enough to contain any and perhaps all kinds of winemaking, most of the wineries in the region are organized to take grapes not only from the home counties, but to mix them up with wines from other parts of the state. E. & J. Gallo, United Vintners, and Guild are the dominant forces in the diffusion, but far from alone. Almadén, The Christian Brothers, Paul Masson, and other coastal counties wineries make and spirit away a great deal of Fresno dessert wine, and at least some table wine for their economical jugs.

Of twenty-six Fresno district wineries which made 208 million gallons in 1972 (out of a state gross production of 563 million *), only the sizable California Growers and the minuscule Ficklin Vineyards represented Fresno table-wine potential in more or less pure form. Since then two other wineries of some size, Del Rey Cooperative and Angelo Papagni, have joined as makers of table wines eligible for (though unlikely to receive) a district appellation.

California Growers

California Growers, a cooperative, dates to 1936 but is just beginning to make varietal table wines and to market its own production aggressively. It has been a bulk winery admired within the trade for good sherries and excellent brandy.

The driving force in the organization has been and is the family Setrakian. Robert Setrakian currently is the chief executive officer of Growers. He also buys some of its wines for marketing through his own firm under the Setrakian label. †

In early 1975 the Growers label went on generic table wines, dessert wines, and a brandy. The Setrakian label covers varietal table wines and a brandy.

The Growers winery is but a stone's throw from the first Sierra foothill on the east side of the San Joaquin Valley, four miles south of the worn little Tulare County town of Cutler. The cellar capacity in 1975 was 13 million gallons, most of the total being stainless steel. The vineyards of member growers are scattered across the nearby valley floor, interspersed with an incredible mixture of other crops.

Del Rey Winery

Del Rey, yet another post-Prohibition cooperative, limited itself to bulk winemaking until the early 1970s, at which time it developed the Rancho Del Rey label for a short list of generic table wines from members' grapes. These carry very modest prices, hesitant first steps as it were in the winery's move to develop a market for its production.

The winery, in the southeast quarter of Fresno, is a workaday building typical of the 1930s, but efficient for its task.

Ficklin Vineyards

Ficklin Vineyards is famous among consumers for the wine the proprietors call Tinta Port. Within the fraternity of vineyardists and winemakers the tiny family enterprise is known almost as favorably for its Emerald Riesling and Ruby Cabernet.

The involvement in table wine is not at all commercial, but rather one of the hundreds of cooperative ventures between commercial vineyardists and the University of California at Davis. The family planted small blocks of the U.C.-Davis hybrid varieties to see how well they would grow in a Region IV climate. Now with the experiment complete, David Ficklin, a Davis graduate, makes wines from them mainly for family use. Tiny amounts slip into the market when production exceeds the Ficklins' thirsts. Those wines have done a disproportionate share in convincing other growers in the hot parts of the San Joaquin Valley that varietal table wines from Fresno have a future in the American wine market.

---

* Gross production shrinks with distillation for beverage and fortifying brandies, and with loss to evaporation and other factors in aging wines. Thus annual sales are substantially less than production.

† Setrakian has purchased the producing wineries.

The Ficklin winery was founded near Madera town in 1948 when the late Walter S. Ficklin and his sons, David and Walter, Jr., began to make port-type wines from new importations of the premier grape varieties of the Douro River Valley. It was the first such wine in California, and still is easily the finest one. David Ficklin has been the winemaker from the beginning. His brother manages the family vineyards and other crops.

Angelo Papagni Winery

Although the Papagni family has grown grapes in the San Joaquin for 30 years, and now has 2,000 acres in vines, the Papagni winery is a new one, and a brave start.

The metal-sheathed winery building, just off freeway State Route 99 south of Madera town, is full of what hi-fi nuts would call state-of-the-art equipment: continuous presses, temperature-controlled stainless steel fermentors, centrifuges, sterile bottling, and all the rest.

The first wines came to market late in 1975. For all the modern equipment, their style is traditional. The reds are bone dry, vinous, and marked by the bouquets of small oak cooperage. Most bottlings under the Angelo Papagni label are vintaged varietals.

Fresno Vineyards

Only in Fresno County could a tremendous surge in the true acreage devoted to fine wine varieties be lost in the percentages. As of 1974, the county had 37,500 acres of wine grapes as against 139,550 acres of raisin grapes, mostly thompson seedless. The wine grape acreages are impressive for matching variety to climate and soil. The top ten are french colombard (5,835 acres), barbera (5,700), ruby cabernet (4,015), rubired (3,600), grenache (3,040), carignane (2,425), chenin blanc (2,375), alicante bouschet (2,140), petite sirah (1,360) and palomino (1,095). Rubired, incidentally, is a U.C.-Davis hybrid developed for port-types. Palomino is the classic variety of Xeres in Spain, and is used in sherry-types in California.

Vineyard locations within the county are, for all practical purposes, irrelevant. All of Fresno County is classed as Regions IV and V in the climate summary. The soils of the valley floor are uniformly rich enough to minimize distinctions from that source. For the time at least, no winery is making single vineyard wines in Fresno County.

Madera County nearly doubles the district total of wine variety grapes with a 1974 acreage of 27,610. The balance among varieties is similar to Fresno's: Carignane (5,700 acres), grenache (3,970), barbera (3,750), french colombard (3,365), ruby cabernet (2,525), rubired (2,265) and chenin blanc (1,266). The county also grows 28,180 acres of thompson seedless.

Here, because of the enormous regional acreage of it, is as good a place as any to praise thompson seedless with faint damns. Because thompson seedless is economically classed as a raisin variety by the grape-growing industry, people outside the industry have assumed that it is some sort of secondary sin to make wine from thompson. With the economic classification as groundwork, still others have removed the variety from its species, *Vitis vinifera.*

Well, confound it, thompson seedless is *Vitis vinifera,* has been exceedingly useful in wineries, is now, and will continue to be so. It has its greatest virtue and widest use as the best grape for high-proof, the concentrated brandy used to fortify port- and sherry-types. Thompson also makes both base wine and the fortifying element in much of the pop stuff, sparing other varieties for nobler use. Finally, it is a plausible blending element in table wine when grown for the purpose and harvested early enough in the season to preserve a correct sugar-acid balance. Although raisin growers have been able to impose too many poor-quality thompsons on the wineries as salvage operations ever since Prohibition, the only inherent weakness in the grape itself is a neutral, almost nonexistent flavor. A skillful valley winemaker can exploit that characteristic to his advantage, faced as he often is with overdeveloped flavors in French Colombard or Semillon. He has even done something virtuous if he lowers the price of the wine after the thompson goes into it.

Bakersfield Wineries

Bakersfield is the hub of Kern County and the next best place to Nashville for listening to country and western music. It also is becoming the center of a new table-wine district of a size to rival Monterey County, but an entirely opposite climate.

The town is at the sweltering south end of the San Joaquin Valley. The Mojave Desert is just east. Los Angeles lies a hundred miles south, on the other side of the Tehachapi Mountains, the high, dry tail of the Sierra Nevadas that curves west to the sea, making an unofficial but sharp separation between northern and southern California.

While Fresno and surrounds balance on the boundary between climate Regions IV and V, Bakersfield is a solid V.

The rationale behind planting table-wine varieties holds that growing conditions on the sloping lands east of Bakersfield do not conform to the standards underlying the U.C.-Davis system. The contention is that the vines leaf out earlier than the starting date for the summary, and that the fruit is harvested long before the heat accumulates to its Region V totals. Keith Nylander led members of the Bear Mountain Cooperative to accept the thought. Since then, a great many other growers in Kern County have followed that lead.

Although quality-wine grapes are something new since the late 1960s, fresh eating varieties have been planted around Bakersfield for forty years. Chronic surpluses of these gave early rise to several bulk wineries.

Bear Mountain Winery (M. LaMont)

The name Bear Mountain comes from the dominant peak in the landscape east of Bakersfield. The winery that borrows the name opened in 1966 when a cooperative of vineyardists bought an existing facility from the DiGiorgio Corporation, bulk winemakers in the area since the repeal of Prohibition.

Bear Mountain's principal label, M. LaMont, has its base in the village of LaMont, a mile or so from the winery. The M. LaMont marketing organization works within the larger framework of Bear Mountain, still a major supplier of bulk wines to the local industry and to bottling houses in other parts of the country.

In all, a much enlarged Bear Mountain has 25 million gallons storage capacity.

Nearly all of that total is new stainless steel and glass-lined carbon steel running in long rows alongside the suddenly dwarfed original buildings. The rest of the equipment is as modern as the storage tanks.

To date a relatively small proportion of the total wine made each year goes to market as one of the M. LaMont varietal wines. Even though the proprietors are pioneer growers of quality grapes, only a small percentage of their vines were mature enough to yield wine as of 1975. The total will grow rapidly during the next few seasons. Members of the cooperative own a substantial proportion of the 30,000 acres of wine varieties in the Bear Mountain district.

The style of M. LaMont wines follows valley traditions. The reds are freshly youthful, and dry without being quite bone dry. Tannins and other austerities are minimized. Barbera and Ruby Cabernet are the principal types. Whites are similarly fresh and youthful, and not quite as dry as the reds. Among these are Chenin Blanc, Emerald Riesling, and French Colombard. M. LaMont also has a Semillon as the driest of its whites.

Giumarra Vineyards

Giumarra Vineyards is Bear Mountain's neighbor on the tilted plain east of Bakersfield, and its principal competitor with varietal table wines from the region.

The family-owned winery goes back to 1946, but the first Giumarra wines came from the vintage of 1973, and went to market late in 1974. John Giumarra, Sr., and his family built a substantial addition to their old bulk winery to handle the new bottled wines, equipping it with stainless steel fermentors and the other familiar equipment of contemporary California winemaking.

Family vineyards surround the winery (and a phalanx of fruit-packing sheds and other buildings for other farming activities of the Giumarras). The family says. only that it owns "thousands of acres." The winery that takes the fruit holds rather more than 6 million gallons. The inaugural vintage of 1972 yielded 103,000 gallons of Petite Sirah, and 54,000 gallons of Ruby Cabernet from Giumarra vines, figures which suggest that the plantings of table-wine varieties run in the neighborhood of a hundred acres each, or less.

The Giumarra wines were, incidentally, the first vintage-dated varietals from the southern San Joaquin Valley.

A. Perelli-Minetti & Sons (California Wine Association)

A. Perelli-Minetti & Sons does not really fit the mold of a localized San Joaquin Valley winery. Neither does it fit any other familiar mold, but at least it gives heart to all who fear that conglomerate corporations are taking over the world. What used to be an octopus is now a family company.

California Wine Association was a virtual monopoly marketing organization for California wines at the turn of the century. After Prohibition ended, several principals from the original joined together to form a new giant called Fruit Industries, Ltd. Although Fruit Industries never commanded the percentage share of the market of its predecessor, it became larger in absolute gallonage at its height. In 1950 the proprietors resumed the old name of California Wine Association, establishing "Eleven Cellars" as the principal label because that many wineries belonged.

Antonio, the A. in the company name, had challenged CWA just before World War I and gone bankrupt doing so. He joined CWA with a new winery after Prohibition was repealed. After 1950, Louis Petri's United Vintners and other competition began to chip away at the power of CWA. In 1971, by which time Antonio was in his late eighties, his winery became the last survivor among the producing facilities, and he fell heir to the marketing company, along with literally hundreds of historic labels.

The A. Perelli-Minetti & Sons winery at Delano holds slightly more than 14 million gallons of wine and brandy. A high proportion is crushed and fermented on the premises, but no small amount of the wine sold by California Wine Association is made in the coast counties and shipped in bulk to Delano for finishing and bottling. By and large, the valley varietal wines sold under the Ambassador label are made from San Joaquin Valley grapes crushed at Delano. The wines sold as Eleven Cellars are made in the coast counties as classic varietals, and shipped to A. Perelli-Minetti & Sons winery. The company also uses the L&J and Greystone labels, primarily for generic table and dessert wines.

Antonio's three sons now operate the business in all its phases. Bill is the vineyard man. Fred is in charge of winery production. Both are at Delano. Mario Perelli-Minetti tends the marketing arm from a headquarters just south of San Francisco.

Antonio, however, is far from retired. Like most of the patriarchs of California wine families, he roams the empire he built nudging here, questioning there.

His primary interest throughout his long career has been the vineyard. His office at the Delano winery houses a collection of his notebooks, written in a copper-plate hand, recording literally thousands of hybridizations and other experiments among his vines. The one that pleases him most is his Perelli 101, a copyrighted black sport from a white grape vine. The grape yields a thick, strongly flavored, darkly colored red wine of versatile qualities. The family has it in mind to release a varietal table wine called Perelli 101, but cannot bring itself to remove the stocks from several successful blends long enough to acquire a supply.

Bakersfield Vineyards

The 1974 crop reports give Kern County a remarkable 44,410 acres of wine grapes. Twenty years ago there were almost no wine grapes there.

Rubired, a U.C.-Davis hybrid used for port-types, has the largest acreage of any single variety, 5,185. Following it, the major plantings are principally for table wines: french colombard (4,995 acres), chenin blanc (4,845), ruby cabernet (4,800), barbera (4,315), grenache (3,580), carignane (2,800), petite sirah (1,890), and emerald riesling (1,530). All of these are varieties well adapted to Region V climate. The county also has, against all conventional wisdom, 1,245 acres of cabernet sauvignon. The performance of cabernet in this hot part of the world may well be the ultimate test of Keith Nylander's theory that the grapes and the intense heat grow at different times, but the proof of the pudding remains some years in the future.

Most of the wine varieties are in the region between Bakersfield and the mountains to the east, close around the towns of Arvin, LaMont, and DiGiorgio. Members of the Bear Mountain Winery are calling this, logically, the Bear Mountain

District in an effort to define it as a favored part of Kern County, though not a legal appellation.

The older vineyards in raisin and fresh-eating varieties are a minor part of the region. Most of them are northwest of Bakersfield in the Delano-McFarland area.

THE FRINGES

The hills forming either side of the San Joaquin Valley and the great expanse of the Sacramento River Valley to the north of it all hold small clusters of vineyards and a sparse sprinkling of wineries. None of the districts is important commercially. Few of the wineries are of any size. However, some of the vineyards and some of the wines have charms worth remembering.

The Sierra Foothills

Vineyards have dotted the foothills of the Sierra Nevadas since Gold Rush days. Spring frosts have made most of them economic disasters for their owners.

Just east of the old Gold Rush town of Plymouth a small, remarkably frost-free fold at the 1,500-foot level is heavily planted to grapes. Two local wineries, d'Agostini and Monteviña take most of the crop, but some goes to Mayacamas and Sutter Home in the Napa Valley and some to David Bruce in Santa Clara County.

The area, in Placer County, is locally known as the Shenandoah Valley. Nearly all of the old vineyards are zinfandels, but new plantings have branched out into other varieties.

D'Agostini is the old standby for local drinkers, a family winery that has been making country red and white since the turn of the century. The vineyards go back to 1870, as does the core of the winery building. Some of the ancient oak casks in it were coopered from local wood by the founder, a Swiss named Adam Uhlinger. The casks are sources of inimitable flavors.

Monteviña, a mile and a fraction closer to Plymouth town than d'Agostini is, was founded in 1973. The propriety of a retired banker named W. F. Fields, it is directed by his young, Fresno-trained son-in-law, Cary Gott. Both think that growing conditions in the Shenandoah Valley allow the making of fine wine, partly on the basis of wines made by Sutter Home. In spite of that hope, the first wine they released was called Zinfandel Nuovo, a carbonic maceration wine after the fashion of Beaujolais Nouveau. It since has been followed by a Sauvignon Blanc. One of their great expectations is a Nebbiolo, a varietal red from the grape that dominates the wines of Italy's Piedmont.

The long-range plan for Monteviña anticipates commercial volumes of wine as Fields' 100 acres of vineyard matures.

One county to the north, at Coloma town, where John Marshall found the gold that started the rush, a couple named John and Beverly Hempt operate a miniature winery called Gold Hill, drawing on their own small vineyards and those of neighbors. Gold Hill is one of the places where cold air can slide downhill past the vines. So far there is not enough volume to sell beyond the Coloma city limits, but the proprietors think there is room around them to grow commercial acreages of grapes.

The Coast Ranges

In the low hills on the west side of the valley Frank Cadenasso runs a much different kind of winery than the Sierras support. The winery is just off freeway Interstate 80 in Fairfield, in Solano County. A gifted winemaker of the old-fashioned school, Frank Cadenasso grows 150 acres of grapes in the flat, fertile soils of the pocket valley in which his winery stands as Solano County's only producing one. For the most part he makes varietal table wines for sale in bulk to prestigious commercial labels. Some he sells under his own label, mostly at the cellar door. Favorable prices and consistent quality have made the old concrete cellar full of redwood tanks a ritual stop for hundreds of bibbers.

The family firm goes back to 1906 when the father of the current proprietor planted vines in the area.

The Sacramento Valley

Although the Sacramento Valley is almost as large as the San Joaquin and has a past history of growing large acreages of grapes, only a handful of small cellars operates in it at present.

Far up the valley, in the small city of Chico, a small winery called Butte Creek began with the vintage of 1972 to revive the large pre-Prohibition district of Viña.

Owned by a partnership of local business people and faculty members at Chico State University, Butte Creek makes only French Colombard, Gamay Rosé, and Ruby Cabernet in explicit recognition of the Region IV climate. The equipment is up to the minute, and in the charge of Dr. Marion Baldy, one of the owners, and a teacher of molecular genetics when she is not tending Butte Creek's wines. Dr. Baldy's wines from 1972 and 1973 had individual style, no easy achievement with new vines and new equipment.

There is no thought of turning Butte Creek into a huge operation on the model of Governor Leland Stanford's gigantic ranch at the original Viña. Through 1976 the wines were being marketed in the major cities of California, but not outside the state.

However, others have been attracted to the region by the success at Butte Creek. New plantings may lead to more wineries within the next decade.

Down at the bottom end of the Sacramento Valley, around the city of Sacramento, are the largest vineyard acreages (2,666 total) and the largest wineries of those on the margins of the San Joaquin Valley. The two principal firms lap over into other regions. Gibson is part of a larger winemaking company with its main producing plant in the Tulare County town of Sanger, and a second finishing and bottling winery in Covington, Kentucky. Brookside Vineyards has a local producing winery, though most of the wines are made in Cucamonga, east of Los Angeles. The cellar at Sacramento was founded as Mills Winery, and purchased by the Los Angeles company in 1968.

The small tanks at giant E. & J. Gallo hold 200,000 gallons; the largest one holds 1 million gallons.   (TED STRESHINSKY)

Preceding page: From the air, the vineyards and winery of Donn Chappellet, in the steep eastern hills of the Napa Valley.   (TED STRESHINSKY)

The Sonoma climate is so kind to grapes that seedlings will flourish in cracks on crusher-fermentor decks.   (HAROLYN THOMPSON)

The fiery red leaf is of carignane; the yellow ones are of sauvignon vert.   (HAROLYN THOMPSON)

At Sebastiani Vineyards, a stained-glass window—a traditional note in wineries everywhere.   (HAROLYN THOMPSON)

Southern California

Unless one small new glimmering hope lives up to its early promise, winemaking on the Los Angeles side of the Tehachapi Mountains is, unmistakably, a waning business, having dwindled in thirty years to half its peak acreage and a bare handful of wineries.

The glimmer of new hope comes from a place called Rancho California, in coastal hills due east of the U.S. Marine Corps training station at Camp Pendleton.

The declining region is Cucamonga. East of Los Angeles, on the road to Palm Springs, the old district must content itself with looking back upon rich history.

Not much links the two places. Rancho California's pioneer vineyardists wish to make elegant varietal table wines from grapes cooled by a wayward sea breeze. Cucamonga was and is a source of common table wines and fine dessert wines.

RANCHO CALIFORNIA

In time Rancho California may become too constricted a definition for the nascent vineyard district halfway between the cities of San Diego and Riverside.

The name covers only the 87,500-acre planned development owned by wholly owned subsidiaries of Kaiser Aluminum and Chemical, Kaiser Industries, and a Pennsylvania Railroad subsidiary called Macco Realty. Now and for the next few years, however, all vines in the region fall within the rancho boundaries, the enterprise having been planned as something of an agricultural-industrial reserve.

In 1975 the roster of vineyard owners approached a dozen. One, Eli Callaway, was operating a winery in the rancho. Another, Brookside Vineyard Company, was making special wines in Cucamonga from its Rancho California grapes.*

Callaway Vineyard & Winery

Like a good many others before him, Eli Callaway retired from the executive suite to a vineyard only to find that the move led straight to a full-time career as a winery owner.

In his case, he retired as president of the gigantic textile organization called Burlington Industries to become first an agreeably diverted grape grower and then a passionately devoted owner and director of a small winery in dry, rolling hills where no winery had ever been before.

The first blocks of vines went into the ground in 1969. Callaway caused the first small crop in 1972 to be made into experimental batches of wine at the University of California. The promise was great enough for him to ship larger volumes of grapes to a commercial winery in 1973. The resulting wines from that experiment led to his building the winery in time for the harvest of 1974.

Callaway's vineyard, some 140 acres, is planted to chenin blanc, sauvignon blanc, white riesling, cabernet sauvignon, petite sirah, and zinfandel. Average yield is less than two tons per acre as a result of severe pruning and, after that, remorseless thinning of young clusters on the vines. The winery takes all of the production from these vines, and some from the adjoining vineyard owned jointly by Callaway and a man named John Poole. The latter vineyard, 160 acres overall, is planted to the same varieties and farmed by Callaway's crew.

Both properties pitch and roll across the tops of a series of small knolls.

The winery is architecturally plain. In outline a rectangular shed, its walls are metal panels at the producing end and concrete block at the shipping end. However, the equipment is not at all plain. In spite of an original production of only 50,000 gallons, and a planned maximum capacity of only 100,000 gallons, the cellar has a specially modified Coq continuous press, a Westfalen centrifuge, and other niceties more typical of firms that deal in the millions of gallons. In addition, all of the fermentors are stainless steel and all of the oak cooperage from German forests. Incidentally, the white wines age in the cooler metal end of the building, while the reds mature in a slightly warmer, drier environment at the concrete end.

The man responsible for the choice of equipment and for the winemaking is Karl Werner, trained in Germany and in South Africa. He went to South Africa to become a specialist in wines grown in warm climates. Before joining Callaway, Werner worked several seasons in the Napa Valley.

Save for a botrytised Chenin Blanc made elsewhere in 1973, the first Callaway wines were his 1974s.

The Vineyards

The vineyards in Rancho California come within twenty-three miles of the Pacific Ocean at their closest point. The elevations range between 1,000 and 1,500

* See page 150.

Southern California

1   Brookside
2   Callaway Vineyard and Winery
3   C.M.A.
4   Louis Cherpin Winery
5   J. Filipi Vintage Company
6   Galleano Winery
7   Opici Winery
8   San Antonio Winery
9   Thomas Vineyards

feet above sea level. The climate is listed as Region III in Long Valley and the terrain leading up to it, principally because Rainbow Gap well to the west allows cool, moist sea air to flow over the region.

In 1975 the acreage devoted to vines approached 2,000. Brookside owned slightly more than 1,000 acres in what it calls the Biane Vineyard, toward the higher end of Long Valley. Eli Callaway and John Poole owned a shade less than 250 acres on the hills above the mouth of that valley. The remaining parcels were divided among several small independent growers, most of them located between Callaway and Brookside.

The vines are in this part of Rancho California partly because of the cooling effect of Rainbow Gap, and partly because of the availability of irrigation water. It never rains on these vines during the growing season for grapes unless the particular proprietor rents a shower from the water company.

The developers of Rancho California planted a test block with help from the University of California at Davis in the early 1960s. With the early results from that nursery block in hand, the university helped growers select varieties. In 1974 the leading varieties (and acreages) were white riesling (549), zinfandel (213), grenache (208), petite sirah (204), sauvignon blanc (184), and cabernet sauvignon (182). Because these figures are for the county at large, they may be distorted slightly, but not very much. Few plantings of wine varieties exist outside the rancho.

It still is much too early to choose among them. Not only have the existing vines yielded no more than two or three vintages, but the soils and exposures of the region are tumultuous enough to require further exploration for themselves.

CUCAMONGA

In 1940 the broad alluvial fan at the base of the mountains east of Los Angeles bore 25,000 acres of vineyards. Forty wine companies shared the crop in the region, called Cucamonga after an obscure crossroads at its midpoint. Now the acreage is a scant 11,000 and tumbling. Fewer than ten companies make wine. Of these several deal only in bulk.

In great degree the decline is the usual woeful response of agriculture to urban-industrial pressure. Traces of vineyards huddle in several cloverleafs of freeway Interstate 10 near Ontario, alongside the runway of the airport there, or, even more forlornly, at the back walls of graceless warehouses. Ontario International Airport and Ontario Motor Speedway between them caused the uprooting of a thousand acres of vineyard in a single year, 1970.

The much sadder fate is that the world does not have time for what Cucamonga can do exceptionally well. Memorable wines have come from vineyards at the foot of the mountains here. The first difficulty is that all of those remarkable bottlings were sweet, sherryish wines. The second, greater trouble is that they all seemed to need twenty years to compose themselves for elegant drinking. Some of the best required even more time, as the legendary 1875 Angelica of Isaiah Hellman proved when it came to full flower in 1968.* It is impossible for a winery to stay in business on such a footing. The locals, with greater or lesser reluctance, maundered into the making of tolerable but indifferent table wines to stay alive. That shift could only delay the crisis, for the San Joaquin Valley could make tolerable table wines much more cheaply and the coast counties could make them more elegantly at competitive prices.

The end result is that only one winery is producing significant amounts of local wine for markets more than a few miles away. It is Brookside. A handful of highly localized cellars fleshes out the roster to half a dozen. All their efforts leave a long half of the annual six million gallons produced to go elsewhere in bulk for blending.

---

* Isaiah Hellman was an Oakland, California, merchant who bought a Cucamonga Angelica in cask and had it delivered to northern California. Exactly who made the wine is not known.

Winter vines at the foot of the San Gabriel Mountains in the Cucamonga district. (WINE INSTITUTE)

The nostalgic ache for the glories of times gone by would be sharper if those times were not so far gone. The Franciscan missionaries planted the first vines in what is now California in the 1770s. A French immigrant named Jean Louis Vignes established the first truly commercial vineyards and winery in what is now downtown Los Angeles by 1840.* An Italian named Secundo Guasti organized the Italian Vineyard Company in Cucamonga in the 1880s, and propelled it to unheard-of size for its time. The vineyard was a single block of 5,000 acres. IVC was the crest. The route has gone downslope ever since as districts north of the Tehachapi Mountains have matured.

The Wineries

There is, to repeat a woeful point, only one winery of any size in the Cucamonga district, or any other part of Southern California, it being Brookside.

* Ironically, Vignes owned a great part of what is now Rancho California under the terms of a Spanish land grant, but never planted grapes there.

The rest are so local that one must go at least to Los Angeles to find their wines, and sometimes all the way to the cellar door.

Brookside Vineyard Co.

Brookside Vineyard embodies the past and present of Cucamonga, and the future of the place to whatever degree it has a future. It embodies the past for having occupied the historic stone cellars of Segundo Guasti's Italian Vineyard Company, and the present for having carved out a distinct niche for itself in the marketplace. As an embodiment of the future, Brookside is the prime developer of new vineyard lands at Rancho California, sixty-five miles south and east of Cucamonga.

Brookside sells its wines direct to the consumer through a chain of winery-owned retail stores that is more numerous in California than the string of Franciscan missions ever was. (A quirk in California law allows wineries to dispense free samples at bonded premises, and thus to attract a good many people who might be reluctant to invest in trial bottles.) The first stores were close to the home winery. After Brookside had saturated Southern California in the late 1960s, the proprietors bought a similar operation in northern California, the old Mills Winery, and developed a statewide operation. Now the firm is advancing into other states.

The name Brookside traces back to the 1880s when E. Vaché & Co. set about to make wine by the side of a brook in Redlands, twenty-five miles east of the Cucamonga district. The winery history since then has been governed principally by the family Biane.

A young chap named Marius Biane married a Vaché daughter during the Redlands years, and became an owner of the firm. The company and the name went idle with Prohibition. Neither Marius nor his sons, Philo and François, revived Brookside upon repeal, preferring to work within the complicated framework of Fruit Industries Ltd., a producer-marketer combine. In 1952, however, the Bianes acquired the stone buildings of Segundo Guasti's Italian Vineyard Company and revived the family legacy. Philo Biane has been the driving force, with help from his sons, Pierre and Michael, and François' son, René.

In 1972 the Bianes sold their business to Beatrice Foods, Inc., a Chicago-based food products conglomerate. The old owners have stayed on as managers.

While Bianes of three generations were building the winery they developed an implausible variety of labels. Assumption Abbey (used in cooperation with the Benedictine Order of monks) is the top mark of the house. It goes on a full range of wines, but most especially on varietal table wines from the new vineyards at Rancho California. Other labels are Brookside, E. Vaché, Biane Frères, Old Guasti, and the completely improbable Hausmarke.

The producing winery operation is almost as various as the labeling. The main aging cellar is the old Guasti winery, now squeezed between freeway Interstate 10 a quarter of a mile to one side and the main runway of Ontario International Airport a quarter of a mile to the other side. Grapes are crushed and fermented at two other locations nearby in the district, then brought to headquarters for finishing and bottling. A big underground cellar at the main winery always is full of small barrels of Angelica and all its sweet kin. Here better than anywhere else, one can stand and

Pickers work a wearying vineyard beneath the craggy San Gabriel Mountains at Cucamonga.
(HAROLYN THOMPSON)

smell the deep smell and lament the fact that Cucamonga has not found a way to prosper with the making of such wines as these.

The grapes for the sweet wines and most of the ordinary generic table wines grow in nearby vineyards. Almost all of the vines are owned by independent growers now. Included in that acreage is a sizable part of the old Segundo Guasti property. The best of the varietal table wines come from grapes grown at Rancho California and trucked up to one of the Brookside wineries for crushing and fermenting.

Students of the regional differences in table wines can learn a good deal from the Assumption Abbey varietals from Rancho California. Back labels explicitly identify which are these. Connoisseurs of sweet wines should try the Angelicas and Cream Sherries as the opportunity arises.

The Local Cellars

Of four other firms making wine in the district and selling it close to home J. Filippi is the most aggressive. The family-owned firm has several tasting rooms in the Los Angeles basin as well as the one at its winery in Mira Loma. Set amidst the Filippis' well-farmed vines on the great flat stretch between Interstate 10 and the Jurupa Hills to the south, it is a workaday structure. Within its homely walls the Filippis make generic table wines, a Zinfandel, and several Italianate sweet wines such as Marsova (Marsala with egg in it, a familiar concoction to travelers in southern Italy.)

The other local wineries are Louis Cherpin at Fontana and Galleano at Mira Loma. Both make generic table wines for local sale. In addition to these, a handful of local tasting room operations buy wine in bulk for local or broader sale. C.M.A. and Thomas are local. Opici sells both locally and in the metropolitan New York market.

A once-great Cucamonga winery began, in early 1975, the process of restoring itself to life after a long idle period. The Cucamonga Vineyard Company made famous by the family Vai and then allowed to go idle by the same family, has been purchased by a corporation which is reviving the cellars to make wine under the label of California Bonded Winery No. 1.

Finally, a bit of wine from Cucamonga grapes is made in downtown Los Angeles by the San Antonio Winery, and sold at several tasting rooms around the Los Angeles area. The owning Riboli family also buys bulk and bottled wines from other parts of the state to supply a remarkably busy sales operation.

The Vineyards

In spite of the fact that Cucamonga continues to be the best place in California to make dramatic photographs of vineyards against towering mountains, there is no way to make the real picture of vines in San Bernardino County anything but bleak.

The acreage dwindles yearly, sometimes by alarming jumps, at a time when the acreages of every other district in the state are climbing, also by alarming jumps. The place looks decadent. On every hand old vineyards are dying, some tended, most not. In the 1974 crop survey, San Bernardino had 11,400 acres of vineyard. In 1971 the total had been 12,300. As recently as 1951 it had been 25,000 acres.

Surviving varieties are appropriate to the Regions IV and V climate. Zinfandel has 3,300 acres, mission 2,300, grenache 1,500, palomino and mataro 1,000 each. All are sweet wine types save zinfandel, and it can be made amenable to port-types.

Except for a few winery-owned parcels, most of the vines are owned by independent proprietors. A few are serious about growing grapes through the next few years at least, but many are nursing superannuated vineyards through one more crop at a time while they cast about for more profitable ways to use the land.

PART TWO

THE WINES

In General

There is a wistful line somewhere in the old literature about how much fun France must have been for wine drinkers before everybody knew that the Clos de Tart was better than its neighbors.

If French wines were a well of unpredictable pleasures then, California wines are a boundless source of joy for reckless experimenters now. It is a rare month in California that does not see somebody trumpeting a newcomer of such grace, such finesse as to sweep the boards of all rivals past and present.

A considerable part of the enthusiasm is mistaken, of course, but the fact remains: A clear majority of the labels of lofty reputation have come into being since 1960, while a great many older marks of quality are drawing their wines from vineyards planted since then.

For physical and physiological reasons much of the noisy optimism is confined to the home audience.

The principal physical reason is that the home audience can absorb nearly all of the excellent wine made in California. For many years the toilsome laws of other states caused the California winemakers to take the easy course and sell within the friendly borders of their own state. Although even the smallest proprietors have been setting aside quotas for export to other states for several years now, the volumes continue to be small enough that people away from California are hard pressed to find representative samplings of all the new developments. Those outside major cities miss far more often than they hit.

The physiological difficulties arise out of the physical ones. It takes time to know California wines for themselves, and there is nothing else for it. The subtleties that give California wines their dimensions are not the ones that give Rhines or

Médocs theirs. A dyed-in-the-wool Médoc drinker, tasting his first three Napa Valley Cabernet Sauvignons,* likely will dismiss them all as tasting alike, and a bit dull. No less a personage than the Baron Philippe de Rothschild has been quoted to that effect. Reverse chauvinism makes it tempting to dismiss the remark as another *généralité de Gaul,* but, to the Baron, it was a fact. People who drink a great deal of Napa Valley wine before becoming curious about France can and do find their first few Médocs all alike, and unpalatably sharp. Just as familiarity finally allows the ear to hear the difference between Corelli and Vivaldi, so it allows the palate to recognize the fine points that separate Louis M. Martini and Charles Krug.

Labels As Literature

Through the current era of tumultuous change the only genuinely timely literature about any one wine is its own label. Federal and state laws require the bottler to print a substantial pedigree for the wine inside. One label explains much. Comparisons over a period of time sometimes reveal revolutionary changes. For example, a ten-year collection of either Cresta Blanca or Inglenook labels will reveal some fundamental shifts in production while a similar collection of Louis M. Martini labels would demonstrate uncommon stability.

The legalities of California labels are simple but strict enough to indicate a great deal about quality as well as basic facts of production. It is wisest to read from the bottom up.

Producer and Bottler

The name and location of the bottler of a wine, in small type at the bottom of the label can be more informative than the flag-bearer name in large type at the top.

The name of the firm which bottled the wine must appear along with a business location. Generally speaking, a wine that costs much money should have the same name at top and bottom of the label, and the bottling should have been done in the region of the producing winery. Less expensive wines might be moved about more freely, but in this class, too, a company with all its pride at home may offer better value than an organization which has no pride of place.

In years gone by it was an accepted practice for all firms to list the name of the town in which the bottling actually took place. This custom has eroded for one reason and another. Several companies now show the name of some prestigious city which supports nothing but a business office.

The exact wording in the small line of type legally defines the role of the bottler in the production and aging of the wine.

The words **bottled by** signify only that the firm named on the label put the wine into bottles. Legally the proprietor could buy a lot on Tuesday and bottle it on Wednesday.

The phrases **cellared and bottled by, aged and bottled by, perfected and bottled by** and all their kin indicate that the bottler also imposed some personal

---

* As noted previously, throughout this book the grape variety is referred to with lower case, the varietal wine with capitals, as a means of distinguishing each from the other.

This artist's conception of an early vintage in California probably comes close to the true scene. Certainly, grapes were trodden and presses and pumps were powered by well-muscled men. (WINE INSTITUTE)

stamp on the wine through his blending skills, his choice of cooperage for aging, and the length of time he waited before bottling, or a combination of all such options.

Now and again someone rash heaps universal scorn on the values of cellar work. This should not be done too hastily. Wine can lead a peripatetic life in California, sometimes almost a nomadic one. Often one man ferments the grapes, another buys the wine to be broken down into smaller lots for resale, and, occasionally, one of the sublots changes hands yet another time. Anything thus treated is likely to show up behind one of the less costly labels. However, the law does not distinguish between commercial considerations and nobler thoughts. It is a frequent matter that one man ferments each year for an old friend who then shepherds his adopted infant to maturity with great care. Episodically a big winery with broad distribution will make a very small lot of something very fine, and have no way to sell it unblended. A proper mixture of altruism and cash sometimes gets such wines into the hands of somebody small enough to keep them pure. Estate sales and other forced transactions can produce the same result. In all cases, the bottler can say nothing more than "perfected and bottled by," or similar words.

The phrase *made and bottled by* identifies wines from cellars which ferment 10 to 50 percent of the wine they bottle for their own label. Most medium- and low-priced wines bottled at a winery carry this designation because of the same nomadism that gives rise to "cellared" and "bottled by." There remain in California a goodly number of bulk producers who function as satellites under long-term contracts with a major producer-marketer. Other bulk wineries free-lance their production each year. In both cases the transfer of wine from one bonded winery to another one owned by someone else disqualifies the bottler from saying that he made all of the wine.

The term *produced and bottled by* can be used when the bottler ferments 51 percent or more of the wine he sells under his label. The regulation is no great shakes as a guarantee that the proprietor of the label effectively controls the fermenting of all his wine, but, in the absence of subtler gradations, it is the most widely used phrase among the prestigious varietal producers who do in fact ferment all of their wine, but buy grapes from independent growers.

Grown, produced, and bottled by is the ultimate phrase, the indication that the bottler not only did all of his own fermenting, but used his own grapes. Because of the ownership pattern of vineyards in California, it is rare. Only a handful of wine estates exists in California. Nearly all of the fine wineries buy from at least a few independent growers.

Given this circumstance a new practice is growing in use. Several wineries now name *individual vineyards* on some labels. Such a device, coupled with *produced and bottled by,* is a guarantee that the bottler fermented all of the wine from grapes grown in the single vineyard named on the label.

Estate bottled does not, alas, mean a damned thing even though several proprietors use the term honorably. Any cooperative is an "estate" in the vague interpretation of the regulation. Its members need not all have their vineyards in the same county, let alone adjacent to one another.

Alcohol by Volume

California regulations, somewhat stricter than the federal ones, require white wines to have alcohol contents between 10 and 14 percent by volume, reds to have 10.5 to 14 percent.

A majority of California table and sparkling wines show their alcohols on the label as 12 or 12.5 percent. A very few range lower, most of them from Monterey County. Quite a few edge higher.

The label must be accurate within a degree and a half, up or down, a permissiveness designed to keep the number of printed labels required down to a reasonable number. Each tank or cask of wine is likely to vary slightly in alcohol level from its neighbor, and vintages certainly do. In spite of the generous spread, most labels come much closer to a precise figure.

A good deal of sunshine is implicit in alcohols from 12 percent up, especially since California regulations prohibit chaptalization, the adding of sugar to must to achieve greater volumes of alcohol than the fruit alone could do. European wines, by way of comparison, tend to shade from 11.5 percent downward, with some from Germany showing less than 10 percent.

Incidentally, California labels showing alcohols of 7 to 9 percent, or 14 to 16 percent, cannot be found on any beverage adhering to the ancient, honorable definition of wine. Both of these alcohol ranges encompass beverages made out of whatever fruit or flavor essences you please. Grape wine may be part of the concoction, or absent altogether. The stuff can be all right as a form of premixed punch, but I wish to repeat myself and insist that it should not be called wine.

Wine Type

Two basic sets of names describe California's table wine types. Varietals make up one set, generics the other.

Varietal wines get their names from botanically specific grapes and demand criticism by name because they should conform to reasonable standards.

The regulation is straightforward enough. Varietal names for wines are authorized provided the wine derives its predominant taste, aroma, and other characteristics, and at least 51 percent of its volume from the given variety.

Direct as the statement is, no other American wine regulation is more controversial. There is growing pressure to tighten the regulation at least to 75 percent, and even to 100 percent. The 100 percenters, like all 100 percenters, assume several questionable truths; that many of the 2,000 varieties of *Vitis vinifera* are balanced well enough to make good wine all by themselves, that wide gaps make neat separations between varieties, and that regional climates and soils make little or no difference in the quality of varietal character.

A 100 percent law would be folly on the face of it. Evidence strongly suggests that 75 percent runs very close to the limits imposed by wisdom and good taste.

Accepting that a few more teeth in the regulation might be helpful, it might be better to look to Europe, which already practices the workable idea of limiting the varieties that may be used to blend in controlled-appellation wines. California vineyards already have been pared down to a relatively few varieties, about 100 in all, so regulations to limit varietal blends could be relatively simple. Even this might be premature at the moment. A good deal more experience is needed in many districts before either lawyers or winemakers will know how to make equable decisions.

Varietal character is elusive stuff at best, and still it is the basis for mastering all but a few of the treasurable wines in the world. Unbotanical connoisseurs of European wines do not always suspect this because varietal characteristic and region tend to be thoroughly integrated in Europe. For example, white Burgundy and Chardonnay are virtually synonymous in France, and Mosel and White Riesling are interchangeable thoughts in Germany.

Even though chardonnay grows in several California regions and every California region grows other whites, varietal characteristic is the distinguishing flavor of any wine that bears the name, or should be. A critic has every right to expect the specific flavor of chardonnay when it is advertised and not the equally distinct flavor of sauvignon blanc, just as he should expect to taste Royal Anne cherries rather than Bings when he has been promised the one and not the other.

The University of California's enologists at the Davis campus, needing a means of communicating the subtleties of taste to researchers in other regions, developed a list of flavor associations as a kind of index to varietal characteristics. The U.C.-Davis list and elaborations on it have become a staple part of the hobbyist's language in California. The associations are not reverent. Semillon is likened to figs, cabernet sauvignon to tea, pinot noir to peppermint. Dr. Maynard A. Amerine and Dr. Vernon Singleton, who had a great deal to do with the U.C.-Davis list, warn that its entries cannot be taken too literally. In the most pointedly distinctive of varietals the flavor associations can be apprehended only for a fleeting moment, and then mostly by tasters with enough experience to sort out a whole series of details within each sip. When the varietal characteristic is muted by blending, wood aging, and bottle bouquet even the best of tasters can go awry. (The trick is to do so shamelessly, maintaining stoutly that the wine held a legitimate source of confusion.)

The U.C.-Davis flavor associations are one of the threads in the sections of this book describing individual wine types.

California's *generic types* include burgundy, chablis, rhine, and the like. Most borrow the name of a geographic place in Europe. Some–vermouth, for example–describe a type without reference to geography, but rather to process. Others–claret and rosé–refer to color.

A subtribe of generics known as proprietaries uses registered trademark names in lieu of the more common generic names. The coinages do not allow imagination to stray far from the point. Paisano or Vino da Tavola substitute for Chianti. Rhinecastle replaces mere Rhine, and so on.

Generalizing on the wines that lie behind the generic names is impossible. Regulations impose no limits on grape varieties that may be used. Further, the limitations on residual sugar, alcohol contents, and other specifics are permissive. As Maynard Amerine once put it in formal summary, "the wine must conform to the standard of identity for the type as set up in the regulations, or, if there is no such standard, to the generally accepted trade understanding of such class or type." Trade understanding prevails, and the trade is very understanding indeed.

This is not to dismiss generic wines. Quite a few of them are better by a long chalk than some of the frailer varietals. It is just that each must be taken on its singular merits. There is no such thing as identifying and complaining about bad form in a California Burgundy because no form is inherent in it.

The use of these names goes back to the immigrants who developed commercial winemaking in California after the Gold Rush of 1849, and who used names such as Hock and Mosel and even St. Julien without restraint or guilt. The continued use is our own responsibility. As a nation we insist on a polished package and popular name for all our foodstuffs. The winemakers survive in business by obliging us. If we wish to get rid of Burgundy as a name, all we must do is buy the wines called Our House Red, or Livermore Red, or any of the other homegrown names.

Appellations of Origin

County boundaries are the basic unit in California's system of appellations of origin. Up to now they have been serviceable enough. As time goes on, however, it becomes apparent that the system will need some tuning up to keep pace with the growing maturity of the industry.

As written the law requires only 75 per cent of the grapes in a nonvintage wine to come from the state county of origin, a tougher 95 per cent in a vintage-dated bottle. A 1972 amendment, designed to allow appellations of origin for field-crushed wines, permits wines to be fermented in a different county than the one where the grapes grew. Formerly the crop had to grow and the wine be fermented in the same county.

The liberal laws are not likely to change during the current period of startling change in vineyard acreages all over the state. However, there already exists a trend toward identifying geographic regions smaller than counties, as noted in the sections on wineries and wine districts. If this progress is to persist the laws will need tightening rather than loosening. It does not seem unreasonable to think about requiring 100 percent of the grapes in any appellation wine to grow within a single county when the county itself has become an umbrella for several legally defined subdistricts.

Already there is enough structure to suggest how the system might develop.

"California" is the blanket appellation. The law now requires 100 percent of the grapes in a "California" wine to grow within the state.

"Coast Counties," "North Coast Counties," and "San Joaquin Valley" already exist as appellations for regions encompassing several counties. The two coastal appellations require 100 percent of the grapes to be grown within a specified region.* This level of appellation points toward a slight refinement that would parcel the state into four or five major zones each with a distinct geographic and climatic profile.

Individual counties are and always will be useful designations one step more specific than the regional divisions noted above, especially if the regulations are rewritten to require 100 percent of the grapes to come from the named county.

Most of the coastal counties further lend themselves to subdistricting. A number of examples are in legal and historic existence. The Livermore Valley, a small corner of Alameda County, is the prime example. In Sonoma County, the Alexander Valley and Dry Creek Valley have won recent legal status as defined subdistricts. Lodi, in San Joaquin County, is a defined appellation which has, regretably, fallen out of use on labels of some good wines made there.

Microclimates will continue to boggle anything like a European system where communal or regional appellation also is a frequent guarantee of a single varietal wine type, or no more than two.

---

* Alameda, Contra Costa, Lake, Marin, Mendocino, Monterey, Napa, San Benito, San Luis Obispo, Santa Barbara, Santa Clara, Santa Cruz, Solano, and Sonoma counties, are all within the Coast Ranges mountain system.

Vintage Dates

Although California grapes ripen with monotonous regularity season after season, the wines vary in keeping quality and all the other ways that lend depth and mystery to the contemplation of them. Three decades of evidence has disproven the old fiction that every year is a vintage year in the loftiest sense of that idea.

However, California vintages continue to be perilous territory for form players. The basic handicap is the interplanting of varieties in each region. A season that is meat for white riesling may be poison for cabernet sauvignon, or vice versa. When the vineyards are side by side and sandwiched between two blocks of pinot noir, something will have to suffer. (On the other hand, growers get something excellent out of almost every year.) In addition, there is a simple lack of wines to compare. One has hundreds of examples to use in assessing a vintage in the Médoc or Côte d'Or. In California only the Napa Valley can field as many as a dozen examples of any one varietal. No other county could scrape together as many as half a dozen as recently as 1970.

In short, vintage dates are most useful one bottle at a time. Even in the Napa Valley two lucky and two unlucky winemakers can make hash out of any generality about the quality of any one year.

For all of the disclaimers, there is comment about vintages in descriptions of individual wines in which the growing season matters even slightly.

Incidentally, the regulation requires that 95 percent of the grapes in a wine must be from the harvest of the stated year. The allowance is so that topping up of casks and barrels can be carried on legally without the nonsensical waste of keeping odd containers of every size from fifty gallons down to a pint.

The Abstract Factors

The best of laws help identify a few concrete aspects of winemaking. Otherwise they can do no more than inhibit people from making bad wine.

Everywhere in the world a wine of style begins with a man who can be bullheaded about that most abstract of standards, taste. If a great wine exists clearly in a stubborn mind, the man will find a way to get his idea fermented, aged, and bottled for other people to share.

In Europe the stubborn man may have had his idea a dozen generations ago, and caused it to be fixed with property boundaries and strict limitations on what may be grown within those boundaries. In the short run, to return to an old theme, California wine is much more the product of the current generation of individual persons than it is of any properties. If communal boundaries are embryonic, the frozen limits of individual properties do not loom on a recognizable horizon.

People whose experience is mainly with Europe sometimes criticize California winemakers for attempting too many wines. There is, granted, some justice in the contention, but not as much as its makers suppose.

There is a practical advantage in making differing wines from several grape varieties grown within a single region. Each variety has its own ripening curve and its own fermenting curve. The California harvest spreads itself out from the last days of August to as late as mid-November, which means that the number of wines fermenting at any one time is not overwhelming. Further, each variety as it ferments behaves in its own way. White riesling, for example, will dawdle along, turtlish but reliable, whereas pinot noir will play the hare, quick in bursts but apt to stop too soon. A winemaker of any intelligence at all should be able to do the right thing by each of his wines in such conditions. (For my money the winemaster of a Burgundy grower-shipper has a harder lot in life than any Californian. There he is with a dozen technically different vats of chardonnay and an equal number of pinot noir. All of the chardonnays look alike, but one wants to turn brown, so should be kept cool, while another wants to stick, which calls for a bit of warming up. His pinot noirs give him even less peace of mind.)

No, the diversity of wines under each California label does not burden a winemaker just by existing. The problem is only to limit the list to types for which the man in charge has ideas he wishes to pursue. Happily, the old notion of the full line is disappearing in favor of a select list as both wine merchants and wine drinkers grow wiser. Prohibition is dying hard, but it is dying.

The limitations on any one person are so various and so personal that the tides of commerce cannot be made compatible. The two main factors seem to be place and variety of grape. There are some first-rate winemakers in California to whom the state is a small enough set of boundaries provided they can keep a personal sense of style. Dick Peterson of The Monterey Vineyard is one of these. He has made good wine from the blend of a dozen counties, and from a single vineyard in the Napa Valley, and now he has begun to try his hand in the new vastness of Monterey County. Joe Heitz, on the other hand, has made excellent wines in more places than Peterson has, but no longer feels comfortable with any grapes that did not grow in the middle section of the Napa Valley. He cannot even be persuaded that the Carneros district is a legitimate part of the valley.

Grape varieties produce the same range of reaction. I do not think that Louis P. Martini and Lee Stewart are in close agreement on many of the fine points of style, but they wholeheartedly share a lack of fondness for chardonnay and a deep love for white riesling.

Beyond these fundamentals there exist all the questions of technique in fermenting and aging and blending and all the rest.

In the end it is much the same proposition as with painters. Some wander freely among watercolors, oils, acrylics, or anything else that will produce color on a surface. Others cannot be coaxed out of one chosen medium for any price. I guess the hip kids pinned down the limits when one wrote the motto: If it feels good, do it. That certainly is the only approach to drinking wine at table.

The Red Wines

An old article of faith among cellarmasters is that they cannot fool red wine drinkers. The assumption is that red is the most natural of wines and thereby the quickest to reveal shoddy grapes or slippery cellar practices.

Probably this is true, though, if so, a great tribute to drinkers because red wine is an overwhelmingly diverse challenge to anyone who would judge it. The selection of grape varieties is wide; a majority can make a wine dry or sweet, tart or bland, astringent or not, for drinking young or old—and in any combination of those factors.

Grape varieties are, beyond doubt, the first and richest layer of interest in California. The fifteen to twenty favored varieties that go into varietal wines have characters that rouse up such diverse flavor associations as green olive, kraut, peppermint, cigar ash, and licorice. Most of these flavor associations were developed by scholars at the University of California at Davis, though some come from hobbyists. All, farfetched as they seem, have a basis in the microscopic variations of acids and other natural flavoring compounds that make one grape variety differ from another just as the varieties of other fruits do. Most of the commonly grown ones in the state originated in France, a handful in Italy, fewer still in Spain. An increasing number are hybrids developed in California.

Cabernet sauvignon, the great red variety of the Médoc in France, is by all odds the great star in coastal California vineyards in the present.

Several other varieties trail in cabernet's wake. Merlot, another Bordeaux grape, recently re-arrived in California to become a blend grape with cabernet and stayed to become a modest success in its own right. Ruby cabernet, the gifted child of a marriage between cabernet sauvignon and carignane, is cabernet's counterpart in the interior valleys of the state. Carignane on its own is a major variety in vineyards, but a base for generic burgundies, clarets, and chiantis more than a source of varietal wine. Carignane's origins are in the extreme south of France and northern Spain.

From Burgundy, the premier grape is pinot noir, although its reputation in California lags a distance behind cabernet's. Other varieties from the region are gamay (also called napa gamay), gamay beaujolais (in fact a frail strain of pinot noir), pinot st. george (also called red pinot), early burgundy, and some varieties too obscure to make varietal wines. These grapes are inferior to pinot noir in the same degree as merlot and the others in that group are lesser than cabernet sauvignon.

The Rhône region of France has contributed three grapes under two names. The name that does double duty is petite sirah. The two varieties it shelters are sirah and a coarser cousin called duriff. No one has yet untangled the statistics to determine how much of each exist in older plantings, but new vineyards use sirah under the name of french sirah and duriff under the name of california sirah just to keep the botany straight. Both varieties go into the varietal Petite Sirah and into a great many burgundies, especially the more costly ones from coast counties producers. The other Rhônish grape with large plantings is grenache, though it is used very little for red table wine.

Four northern Italian varieties grow in California. Barbera is the most important in quantity and the most prestigious. Others are charbono, grignolino, and nebbiolo.

This leaves zinfandel, California's "mystery grape," as the other source of great amounts of varietal red wine. For decades its origins have been lost because records accompanying its importation were destroyed in transit and because the variety acquired new characteristics once here. Now there is a spreading belief that it is an acclimated form of a southern Italian variety known there as *primitivo*. The official word has yet to come down from U.C.-Davis, where Dr. H. P. Olmo and his associates have been sleuthing after zinfandel's origins for fully three decades.

Climates and other factors of regional environment produce their effects as an added layer of complication for each variety before the winemaker has his chance. The causes are explained in the opening section of the book as much as they are known.

A great many options remain to the man in the cellar after variety and environment have played their roles. The greatest demonstration of this truth is not in California, but in Burgundy, at the Clos de Vougeot, where fifty owners divide forty acres, to produce an astonishing range of character and quality in wines called Clos de Vougeot. Californians do produce their share of evidence along the same lines. The results of shared crops from single vineyards cannot be explained otherwise.

Blending plays a fundamental role, be it blending of one variety from several vineyards, several varieties from one vineyard, or several varieties from several vineyards. The 51 percent varietal regulation allows virtually endless possibilities. One might lament 51 percent just slightly, but one should not lament variations on understandable themes. That, in the end, is the main charm of wine as a hobby.

For other variations as discernible or more so, winemakers can ferment and age each wine type in dozens of different ways to impose a personal stamp. One of the fundamental devices of style is the way in which the wine is aged, in new wood, or old, or no wood at all, in large casks or small, for more time or less.

It is not even necessary to make a better/worse judgment to say that California red wine has become a great deal more interesting in the past decade because new styles of wood aging opened up during that time. The watershed moment, to repeat once again, came at Hanzell when J. D. Zellerbach used new European oak barrels in an effort to make California wines of chardonnay and pinot noir approach more closely their Burgundian counterparts. When he succeeded in measurable part, all winemakers producing varietals were obliged to think about what they were doing. They have not all agreed, which has resulted in a broader spectrum of style in each varietal type.

Wood, like grapes, is of different species, even families. Redwood, for example, imparts an aroma to wine that is highly reminiscent of the smell of a cedar chest, or a cigar box, or a freshly sharpened pencil, depending on how intense it is. Barrels made of American white oak add a curiously dry smell not unlike the smell of a brand new corrugated pasteboard box, or, in its most intense form, not unlike the apple-ish smell of bourbon whiskey, which also derives much of its aroma from new American oak barrels. European oaks contribute a sweeter, almost vanillin-like note to the nose of a wine.

These aromas are most developed in wines aged in small, new barrels. With each succeeding use the wood loses flavor. A large, old tank is very nearly flavorless.

At this point, California reds reflect every point of view about wood aging from long terms in small new wood to short terms in large old wood, to every kind of hybrid system.

Winemakers also take varying decisions on how durable wines should be in our mobile modern times. Very few customers remain who own moated castles and hereditary cellars. Some masters of small cellars cater to that stark minority with reds that ferment, juice and skins together, for weeks. The great majority run temperature-controlled fermentations in which the skins are drawn off after no more than a week, to make wines of earlier charm and shorter life. Both approaches have won comparative tastings. A handful of winemakers even are using the Beaujolais technique called carbonic maceration in which berries ferment uncrushed to achieve a frivolously light, sweet wine in a very short time.

BARBERA

Barbera, coming of peasant stock, has had difficulty acquiring social status in the United States no matter how rich and beautiful the wine might be.

In its original home in the Piedmont, in northern Italy, barbera is made into a varietal that ranks behind no fewer than six different guises of nebbiolo, and no better than even with varietal wines made from dolcetto and fresia, hence its lowly reputation.

In California barbera is, without challenge, the premier grape among all the varieties brought from the Piedmont and, in a couple of hands at least, makes one of the genuinely distinctive varietal wines in the state.

Barbera's reputation as a worthy varietal wine rests on a small acreage in Napa and Sonoma counties, where Louis M. Martini and Sebastiani Vineyards dominate its production. Most of the wine called Barbera is more modest in character and comes from the San Joaquin Valley.

The grape has broader status among growers and winemakers than the varietal wine has among drinkers. In part this popularity is practical. Barbera bears well, and retains good color and high acidity in the warmer climate regions of California. These qualities make it a desirable base for all manner of red generics as well as a useful varietal wine base. During recent trials barbera also has proven itself adapted to mechanical harvesting, no small advantage in the big vineyards of the San Joaquin Valley.

Acreage figures are a reliable indication of how well San Joaquin growers regard the grape, but not an adequate index of the affection its coast counties growers have for it. The grape is thought to be at its best in warm Region III, which means it must compete with both cabernet sauvignon and zinfandel for limited space. While collectors of Cabernet Sauvignons will pay dearly the audience for Barbera is small and dominated by clutch-pennies. Barbera from the coast counties automatically is a lamented love, for growers and admirers of the wine alike.

A good Piedmont-style wine should be flavored enough and tart enough to cut through sharply seasoned sauces, game meats, and even fatty sausages. The Barberas of Louis M. Martini and Sebastiani Vineyards and a few small coastal producers do so. The curious thing about them, for all their strength, is that a flavor association is hard to pin down. The U.C.-Davis list says very fruity and tart, and lets matters go at that. In most literature Barbera is described as vinous, which means it tastes like wine.

For a red to taste like wine is no insult. Barbera from the coast is one of the stoutly winey reds in the whole spectrum, a great deal weightier than Zinfandel, and close to Petite Sirah. It is tarter than Petite Sirah, and of roughly equal astringency from its tannins. Proper coastal Barberas need time in bottle to round off the tart edges and to diminish the astringency. The best of them are so rich in fruit character that only age can bring them to deservedly elegant maturity.

San Joaquin Valley Barberas are characteristically softer and milder. Warmer growing conditions reduce tannins in ripe grapes, and also diminish the aromatic compounds. Wise winemakers accept the nature of the fruit and adjust their styles to a softer, rounder character.

As a sheer object lesson in the influence of climate, a coastal Barbera and one from the San Joaquin Valley do very well.

Coast Counties Barberas

Louis M. Martini and Sebastiani Vineyards, between them, are responsible not only for the best of Barbera's reputation, but for the two essential styles.

Louis Martini makes Barbera in the way he prefers to make all of his reds, in large, well-seasoned casks in which he can preserve the flavors of the grape and still impose a distinct cellar style.

The heart of the wine is grapes from Martini's Monte Rosso Vineyard in the hills above Sonoma town. The climate Region is in the border area between I and II, cooler than the university advises for barbera. The advice, as always, has an economic factor weighed in. Disregarding the threat of crop failure and waiting for the grapes to ripen late allows the Martinis to make a fresher, more delicately balanced wine than anybody else who works with the variety. Delicate balance does not mean fragile wine. Martini Barberas, for many years the only vintage-dated ones in the state, last ten years with ease. The favorable vintages go longer, as witness the 1960, which was just settling into stride in 1973 as a long, complex wine of quality. The 1966s and 1968s promise similar rewards to the patient bibber.

Sebastiani Barberas taste of grapes from sunnier vineyards and of longer careers in well-seasoned wood. In short, they are a shade heavier or coarser than the Martinis. The shadings are subtle, but detectable in any head to head comparison. The point for concentration in distinguishing between the two is freshness of fruit flavor, slightly greater in the Martini. Beyond that the similarities are greater than the differences.

Small as the differences are, they make the Sebastiani a wiser choice with game meats or other strong dishes, and the Martini a more graceful companion to meals of more restrained flavors. The meeting point is crab cioppino, a seafood stew native to San Francisco and guaranteed to make a man sit ever more solidly in his chair as the evening wears on.

Sebastiani Barberas have not been vintage-dated until recent years. Older nonvintaged bottles seem indestructible, however.

Other Barberas from vineyards north of San Francisco show strong family resemblances to the two major ones. Parducci, with a small vineyard in Mendocino County, makes a most satisfactory bridge between the Martini and Sebastiani styles. Heitz Cellars Barbera approaches the Sebastiani style very closely. Neither carries a vintage date.

In the Central Coast region a veritable throng of small producers offer Barberas from a few small vineyards. The labels have included Louis Bonesio/Uvas, Pedrizzetti, Guglielmo, Conrad Viano, San Martin, Villa Armando, and Gemello. Of these Gemello has had the greatest sense of style as well as good basic character.

San Joaquin Valley Barberas

Awesome as the total acreage of barbera is in the San Joaquin, most of it is too new to have produced much wine, let alone many wines. What has emerged is consistent with the general style of the valley. The wines are clean, and almost certainly off-dry. Wood flavors or other sources of bouquet do not creep in, with a single major exception, and another minor one.

The diminished tannic astringency and lower acidities imposed by valley as opposed to coastal growing conditions mean that valley Barberas are more agreeable in youth, but less likely to bear up with age. Thus the fresher style is the right one for them.

M. LaMont and E. & J. Gallo Barberas are widely available. Giumarra and Setrakian Barberas are made in considerable volume, but are rather harder to find than the first pair. Angelo Papagni Barbera, introduced in 1975, also has potential for volume, but is scarce at present.

M. LaMont, from the Bear Mountain winery just east of Bakersfield, has been the most attractive of valley Barberas to people whose tastes lean toward coastal style. It is dry, vinous, with more than a trace of tannic bite in the finish. The excellent first edition of Papagni surpassed the M. LaMont.

Giumarra Barbera 1973 from the same region is of similar though slightly heavier character. The vintage date is rare in the valley. It was the inaugural year for the label.

The Barbera of E. & J. Gallo, introduced in 1974, is a much lighter, softer wine than either the LaMont or Giumarra. It is so light and soft, in fact, that one barely recognizes the presence of alcohol as one glass slips down after another. I prefer a shade more vinosity for my own taste, but the flavor is absolutely agreeable.

Setrakian Barbera, from a collateral label of the Grower's Cooperative, is made from grapes grown south and east of Fresno. In its early bottlings it was a wine for particular tastes. Thick, dark, tasting of the cellars in which it was made, it won most of its audience among people who like to drink country wines in family restaurants. The other, much smaller source of a bouquetish Barbera from the valley is a little family firm west of Fresno. The Barbera of A. Nonini was designed for and is prized by Basque shepherds seeking bouquet rather than fresh fruit as a main flavor.

CABERNET SAUVIGNON

One night in 1968 there appeared on a festival menu the 1951 Cabernet Sauvignons from Beaulieu Vineyard, Inglenook, Charles Krug, and Louis M. Martini.

Each of the four wines was, no surprise, a lustrous tribute to the qualities California sun and soil can put into cabernet sauvignon grapes. The shocking fact of the moment was that the four labels on the table were the keepers of the flame, the continuity of fine wine from repeal of Prohibition to that moment. They, alone, consistently offered vintage-dated, collectible red wine throughout that lean three and a half decades.

The old scarcity of Cabernet Sauvignon, and makers of Cabernet Sauvignon, was logical in its time. Everywhere in the world where they grow, cabernet sauvignon grapes can be used to make wines for Calvinists in cold places to drink without feeling any too sinful. Cabernet sauvignon's varietal character is likened to tea or herbs, to leaves and stems rather than fruit or flowers. Such flavors encourage penitential thoughts when the wine is drunk young. Post-Prohibition was no market for young Cabernet Sauvignon, and there was no other kind.

Once a taste for the wine is acquired, though, there is no substitute. The labyrinthine balancing act that is a mature wine, or even one that only promises to be mature some day, makes this the measuring stick for any region in California that can grow the variety. Every coastal county falls into that realm.

Bordeaux is the ancestral home. Because the overbearing flavor of the grape survived transplanting to the New World, there is a durable temptation to make direct comparisons of all wines made from it. That temptation should be resisted, or at least the comparisons should be oblique. Bordeaux winemakers mitigate the flavors of cabernet sauvignon in different ways than do their California counterparts.

Médocs are dominated by cabernet sauvignon, but blended in varying degree with merlot, cabernet franc, petit verdot, or all three, partly as a matter of taste, and partly as a matter of growing conditions.

The quintessential California Cabernet Sauvignon is unblended. A few wineries seeking individual style have begun to experiment with merlot blends in recent years. My own feeling is that nature softens cabernet in California the way merlot does in France, but that the potential complexities of blending ought to be an available option for Californians, too. Zinfandel and carignane have been used for the purpose longer than has merlot, although without fanfare.

The University of California at Davis allows that a Cabernet Sauvignon remains true to type with as much as 25 percent blend grapes in it, but no more.

The university also recommends a fairly generous range of climate and terrain for the variety. Not much of the coast counties region does not qualify as appropriate. Although there are some detectable differences by region, the characteristic taste is unmistakable, even when other grapes are a discreet part of the blend, until the winemaker begins to age what he has fermented.

A willful person can disguise the leaves and stalks with the spices of new barrels, or leave them unsullied by using large, well-seasoned cooperage.

Bottle age can blur a Cabernet's identity still further, to the point that even experts can be humbled in a blind tasting.

Even so, this is the best wine short of Muscats for learning how to look for varietal character, because only grapes of the cabernet family make such herbaceous flavors in red wine.

Blended or not, aged in small wood or not, California Cabernet Sauvignons mature on a very different curve from any Bordeaux. It is, I think, a matter of sunshine. In addition to the sun's other effects it preserves the fruit flavors in wine wondrously.

A genuinely ancient Médoc, when it begins breaking down, will acquire the ungracious smell of spoiling cabbage. The process may require a century, but is inevitable. Contrarily, a California Cabernet Sauvignon, when it reaches the end of its road, will taste of sun-dried fruit—not raisins, precisely, but close. Through all the years leading up to decline that basic difference is more or less discernible, more if the grapes grew in a particularly sunny vineyard, less if they came from a place often shrouded in coastal fog.

The best of California's Cabernet Sauvignons start out rough and tannic, but never quite as sharp and edgy as their more acidic French counterparts. Drinking a freshly bottled Cabernet Sauvignon from Napa or wherever is more a learning experience than a pleasure, but not all vetch because the first hint of dried fruit softens the varietal stalky flavors.

Not long after that first, fresh moment in bottle, a purebred California Cabernet Sauvignon enters a long, sullen adolescence. The freshness of youth erodes before wood, age, or the other elements of bouquet can bring mature polish. Almost all Cabernet Sauvignon between the ages of four and five is dull. In sturdy ones the condition may last until the wine is eight years past the vintage.

When elegant balance comes it is time to rejoice. Too few wait for the hour to strike. Too few know this wine in its prime.

Nobody really knows what an "old" California Cabernet Sauvignon might be, Prohibition having cut out the middle of the aging curve. The scant evidence from pre-Prohibition times, a few bottles of Gustave Niebaum's Inglenook from the 1880s, had fared at least as well as Médocs of similar age when bottles of both were opened for tasting before one of the national wine auctions a few years ago. A 1935 from Sonoma County retained its youthful vigor at twenty-nine years, suggesting that a California Cabernet Sauvignon made for all it is worth could be good with dinner at the age of forty. Further evidence is likely to be slow in coming because only three or four wines from the 1930s and 1940s are durable enough to test the probabilities.

There is one curious sidelight about vintages of Cabernet Sauvignon. Connoisseurs love the big, hard years that age forever without wearying. Winemakers, on the other hand, seem to favor the lighter seasons, even the fickle ones. Like other parents, they probably like to see their progeny responding to tutelage.

Napa Valley Cabernet Sauvignons

Cabernet Sauvignon and the Napa Valley acquired their lofty reputations in partnership while they were restoring California's name among connoisseurs of classic wines after the toils of Prohibition.

That cabernet sauvignon grapes would make world class wines in this valley was not, however, a post-Prohibition discovery. Vineyardists and cellarmasters knew what they had before 1900, when the varietal name began to appear on a widening array of prestige labels. Two of the early growers were Gustave Niebaum at Inglenook and Georges de Latour at Beaulieu Vineyard. Their adjoining properties at Rutherford were planted heavily to cabernet sauvignon, presaging the present.

Without doubt the vineyards ranged around the foot of Mt. St. John, on the west side of the valley at Rutherford, have yielded contemporary Cabernet Sauvignons of greater character than any others yet made in the state. The Martha's Vineyard Cabernet Sauvignons of Heitz Cellars come from a property near Oakville, toward the sòuth end of the subdistrict. Nearly all Cesare Mondavi Selection Cabernet Sauvignons of Charles Krug come from the famous old ToKalon Vineyard just to the north of Martha's. The famous vintages of Georges de Latour Private Reserve and of Inglenook Vineyards Special Cask came from the ancestral properties at Rutherford. Most still do, although the pedigrees are less certain under the Heublein ownership of Beaulieu and Inglenook than they were when families were the proprietors.

In other parts of the valley to north, south, and east, isolated vineyards give birth to outstanding Cabernets. Nearly all localities in the valley and on the hills around it yield fine wine of the variety in impressive volume, but nowhere else can a winemaker be so certain of making extraordinary wine vintage after vintage as in the narrow belt between the state highway and the west hills, from Rutherford down to Oakville.

Despite the sharply etched boundaries, the wines that come from within them are gratifyingly varied in style.

The traditional standard for all other Cabernet Sauvignons to measure themselves by has been Beaulieu Vineyards Georges de Latour Private Reserve, which has a consistent history as long as its name.

The de Latour's seigneurial rights stem partly from the vineyards, partly from André Tchelistcheff's sense of style. Tchelistcheff, beginning in the late 1930s, caused the wine to be fermented for deep color and intense grape flavors, then guided it through malolactic fermentation for the nuances provided by that mysterious evolution of malic to lactic acid, and, finally, aged the wine for two to three years in American white oak barrels. That program remains unchanged.

Tchelistcheff refused blend grapes and European oak, both on the grounds that they blur the lean tastes of cabernet sauvignon with soft or sweet qualities.

Newcomers to California Cabernet Sauvignon usually find themselves puzzled by a young de Latour. Both the malolactic fermentation and the long aging in small barrels diminish the freshness of flavor in the wine without making it mature. In fact, critics with a pure orientation to Médocs often prefer the regular bottling of Beaulieu Cabernet Sauvignon on grounds that the de Latour is prematurely weary and bound to fall apart before long. It does no such thing. Tchelistcheff long ago recognized that it takes a great deal of will in the cellar to overcome the towering strengths of Rutherford grapes with the stylish complications that make wine great rather than merely good.

The founder, whose name is on the bottle, had the strength to allow his winemaker a technique that demanded years of costly aging. So did old Georges' heirs, his daughter and granddaughter, until they sold Beaulieu in 1969 to Heublein, Inc. It will be some years before the true measure of the corporate owner can be taken. The vintages through Tchelistcheff's retirement in 1972 went according to the old formula, eventually to become fit company for sinfully rich dishes of lamb, or duckling, or, after enough years, sweetbreads.

The regular Cabernet Sauvignon of Beaulieu, made from vineyards of lighter character, is a fresher, fruitier wine, but still a properly austere demonstration of the flavor of cabernet sauvignon grapes grown in a favorable climate. It is fermented and aged with gentler qualities than the de Latour in mind, a six- to ten-year wine rather than a ten- to thirty-year wine.

While Tchelistcheff was following his thoughts at Beaulieu, John Daniel and his winemaker, George Deuer, were working in a different direction across the highway at Inglenook. They harvested and fermented for a leaner, more tannic wine, then aged it in big old oak ovals Daniel had somehow preserved through the Prohibition years. There is only one word for one of their Cask Cabernet Sauvignons: formidable. It was a hard wine in youth and a hard wine in age, the right thing to serve at the annual awards banquet of the sword swallowers convention, and yet a beauty no matter how steely.

At the time all Inglenook Cabernet Sauvignon came from the home vineyard and was made to the style. The Cask wines were particular favorites of the proprietor, but not made differently from the regular releases.

Now, under a young, U.C.-Davis-trained winemaker named Thomas Ferrell, Cask wines are made in the old way, or almost, and mostly from the winery's own vineyards at Rutherford. In fact, the continuing allegiance of old patrons to the old style has caused the current owners, Heublein, to start a program of replanting the remaining eighty acres of winery vineyard to cabernet sauvignon at the expense of the polyglot contents of earlier years. All of this acreage will be available for cask wine.

However, the regular releases of Inglenook Cabernet Sauvignon under the

Pickers in the Napa Valley, circa 1890. (WINE INSTITUTE)

present ownership are aged in small wood and otherwise made in a more approachable style than the one Daniel favored. The grapes for these wines come from a variety of vineyards all up and down the valley. After several lackluster vintages between 1963 and 1969, the regular bottlings began to show signs of gaining some favorable identity of their own after Ferrell's arrival. The critics of corporate Inglenook, of whom there have been many, began to relent with the release of the regular 1970.

The regular bottlings are softer, less herbaceous in varietal character than the Beaulieu regular releases, but otherwise quite similar in style.

Charles Krug joined the company of cellars with special wines from the Oakville-Rutherford region rather late, in 1963, after the owning Mondavi family bought the old ToKalon Vineyard. ToKalon originally belonged to a great experimental vineyardist named H. W. Crabb, whose deserted stone winery building broods over one corner of the great block of vines. By the time the Mondavis acquired a substantial percentage of the original property its suitability for cabernet sauvignon was well established.

As a matter of style, Cesare Mondavi Selection from Krug rather splits the difference between Georges de Latour Private Reserve and Inglenook Cask, being leaner and less ripely fruity than the former, but less tannically austere than the latter. The Mondavis age the wine for two to three years in a mixture of American and European oak barrels to soften the edges of an unblended and very intense varietal wine which always is one of the important measures of a vintage in the Napa Valley.

The Mondavis had explored such possibilities before 1963 with their regular bottlings. The 1959, for example, was an enormous precursor to what is now Mondavi Selection. (Mondavi Selection, for its part, started out as a smaller wine than it has become.)

Regular Charles Krug Cabernet Sauvignon, like the Beaulieu and Inglenook, is a much gentler kind of wine, fermented and aged to be affable from its first appearance in the market. Where a Mondavi Selection appears able to age a score of years without strain, the regulars tend to peak before they are six and start slipping downhill by the time they are twelve. Although light, they are patently Cabernet Sauvignons from the Napa Valley, and a considerable boon to apartment dwellers and others without hereditary underground cellars.

At Heitz Cellars Joe Heitz does not worry much about the woes of apartment dwellers. All of his Cabernet Sauvignons are made to last as long as the quality of the grapes will allow.

The Heitz wine that has become a legend with just four vintages is Martha's Vineyard, from the small property of Tom and Martha May. Hard against the west hills between Oakville and Rutherford, that vineyard gives Heitz the kind of enormously deep flavor he wants from cabernet grapes, and a curiously distinctive note of its own, an aroma not unlike allspice. In fainter concentrations the flavor is called Rutherford Dust in the Cabernet Sauvignons of Beaulieu and Inglenook. In light vintages, the spice nearly overpowers the varietal characteristic of cabernet

Glass-lined steel tanks hold finished wines at Charles Krug until they can be bottled. (WINE INSTITUTE)

sauvignon. But in the big years like 1966, 1968, and 1970, but above all 1968, it slips into elegant proportion with the tealike aroma of the grapes themselves.

Heitz, like his old friend and colleague André Tchelistcheff, likes very ripe grapes for the softening effect mature fruit gives, and he likes long aging in wood as a source of complication in the mature wine. The major point separating the two men is European versus American oak. Where Tchelistcheff prefers American oak, Heitz is fond of balancing his wine with some of each.

The regular bottlings of Heitz Cellars Cabernet Sauvignon differ from the

The oak-shaded facade of
Mayacamas Vineyards cellar
building. (HAROLYN THOMPSON)

Martha's Vineyard only as much as the grapes do. The fermenting and aging
practices are essentially identical, although the regular may go to bottle a bit sooner.

Martha's Vineyard goes back only to 1966, and Heitz Cellars only to 1961. The
Heitz label reaches further back in vintages, to 1954, because Joe Heitz launched his
cellar in the role the French call *éleveur,* which means he bought and blended some
wines older than his business license. Beyond that he worked for other cellars in the
Napa Valley on vintages going back to the late 1940s, so his sense of style has
developed over a longer span than one might suspect.

Louis M. Martini is with Cabernet Sauvignon as with all varietals the laudable
maverick. The late Louis M. himself went back to the eve of repeal as a maker of
vintage-dated Cabernets. Never during his career did he limit himself to the Napa
Valley, let alone to the Rutherford-Oakville belt, nor did he limit himself to
purebred Cabernet Sauvignon, or to any other hard and fast rule. Son Louis P.
Martini follows the parental wisdom. The wines made by either man or the two
working together consistently have been among the most stylish in all California.
Often the style is more claret than Cabernet, but no less savory for that.

It is almost a joke at this point that critics start out with each new vintage of
Martini grumbling about its infidelity to the ideals of Cabernet Sauvignon and then

end up eight or ten years later marveling at the elegant balance of the mature wine.

Because the Martinis blend with merlot (or zinfandel or any other grape that would compensate for the deficiencies of a particular vintage), they consistently produce a wine that is fresh and charming in youth before it dips into the dull adolescence that always precedes seductive maturity. In short, it is an extraordinarily feminine wine.

The Martinis may not insist on the leaves and stalks of pure cabernet sauvignon, but they do insist on putting the taste of fresh grapes foremost in their Cabernet Sauvignon, and it is this that gives the wine its youthful grace. The automatic implication is that they do not favor either extremely ripe grapes, which make a heavy wine, or new barrels for aging, which diminish the fruit tastes. The implications are correct.

In the end, the light, deft style is not as durable as some of the others, but it is more than durable enough. Martini Cabernet Sauvignons always go ten years, and sometimes twenty. Now and again, a big vintage will go fully three decades, always ready to do graceful duets with beef as easily as lamb or duck or sweetbreads or anything else that calls for harmonizing flavors from the wine.

The Martinis, characteristically, go the other way about on special selections from their peers in the valley. The regular bottling is what they prefer for style and substance; the Special Selection Cabernet Sauvignons are an erratic but absorbing collection of experiments. From the fine vintage of 1968, to cite the classic example, Louis P. bottled five special lots. Among them they represented possible modifications of the basic style, control lots to see the effects of miscellaneous exaggerated qualities, and tests of differing aging practices. They were offered, not as wines of special greatness, but rather as wines of unique instructiveness to serious hobbyists of wine. The labels do not give the pedigrees. Sometimes a special announcement does. Sometimes the buyer has to call in at the office to find out what particular lesson he has in hand.

Some of these Special Selection wines have been so successful as to cause minor changes in the character of the regular wine, but never such radical ones as to surprise the regular clientele. A retrospective tasting of any ten-year span of Louis M. Martini Cabernet Sauvignons always is remarkable for continuity as much as for excellence.

The grapes come principally from winery-owned or family-owned vineyards near St. Helena, in Carneros, at Monte Rosso near Sonoma town, and from the Edge Hill vineyard near Healdsburg.

These labels–Beaulieu, Inglenook, Charles Krug, Heitz, and Martini–must be the base for judging the success of any one vintage in the Napa Valley in the early 1970s because they are consistent in quality and style. Labels other than these have track records too short for sure-handed assessment. The basic quality of Napa Valley cabernet sauvignon grapes is certain, but the depth of style and the durability of individual bottlings is not. Varietals other than Cabernet Sauvignon are mature after two or three years in bottle, but an austerely styled Cabernet has not begun to round off the corners that soon. Even the softer ones have not had a chance to develop all of their charms. The final judgment on a Napa Valley Cabernet Sauvignon of quality ought not come before the wine is a dozen years old. With that as a requirement consider the rest of the cellars: Mayacamas was reborn in 1967; Souverain made a new start in 1968; Robert Mondavi can look back no further than the vintage of 1966, and so on through a roster with many entries younger than those.

Leaving last judgments until later, first judgments promise a long and joyous future for drinkers of Napa Valley Cabernet Sauvignon.

Mayacamas Cabernet Sauvignons since the vintage of 1967 have been one of the most distinctive in character of all the Napa wines. The essential herbaceous flavor of the variety is accompanied by a faintly musty note much like the one that crops up in many wines of the Médoc under the guise of *goût de terroir.* The accepted flavor association for this musty quality is French barnyard, which, for anyone who ever has reveled in the earthy aromas of a proper farmyard in summer, is an altogether attractive idea. The wine balances off these pointed qualities with an adroit hint of oak. In sunny vintages, Mayacamas Cabernet Sauvignons are dark-hued, deep-flavored wines. Tannin and alcohol seem ample enough for them to keep very well for a decade, perhaps two. The fruit character is lighter than that of the Rutherford district.

The vines, set out in a bowl high on the flanks of an extinct volcano called Mt. Veeder, go back further than 1967. However, the proprietors previous to Bob Travers kept their light wines in overaged, undercleaned barrels, and produced only curiosity pieces. Their most admirable deed was passing along a mature block of vineyard when they sold the property. Only once, in 1968, has Travers gone outside the Mayacamas property for cabernet sauvignon grapes. In that year he bought a lot from the Martin Ray property in Santa Clara County to supplement a meager crop from his fifteen acres of bearing vines.

Souverain Napa Valley Cabernet Sauvignons also have a divided history, though not so drastic a shift as Mayacamas'. Beginning with the vintage of 1968, the current corporate proprietors have leaned toward a relatively soft, fat kind of Cabernet Sauvignon. The tannins are subdued, and so are the tealike or herbaceous tastes of the variety. The round flavor of new European oak cooperage enhances the soft notion.

The grapes are purchased from several vineyards scattered throughout the valley, most of them at Rutherford or south of there.

The 1968 had tremendous charm as a young wine. So did the 1970. How these vintages and their successors will fare with time remains to be seen, but the innate balance augurs well.

In the earlier days when Lee Stewart owned the label Souverain Napa Valley Cabernet Sauvignons were unrelentingly austere wines, regal successors to the still older Cask wines by John Daniel at Inglenook. The 1963 Souverain can still mount an effective counterattack on any palate.

The overwhelming impression produced by Robert Mondavi Napa Valley Cabernet Sauvignons in the vintages since 1966 is their flawlessness, their textbook perfection. They taste clearly but not overpoweringly of the variety, have an impeccably controlled overtone of European oak on the nose and again in the aftertaste, and do not reveal the faintest sign of a human foible anywhere. The absence of an individual quality, an endearing idiosyncracy, is the only thing that can be said against the wines. They are infallibly good as a checkpoint in assessing varietal character and a safe wine to serve when the boss comes to dinner, but only time will tell whether complexities will or will not develop in the bottle that will make them wines to keep. The winery owns cabernet sauvignon vineyards in the southerly third of the valley, from Oakville down to Napa City, and buys from independent growers in the same region.

Since the first release from the vintage of 1967, Freemark Abbey has developed two distinguishing marks in its Napa Valley Cabernet Sauvignons. The winery uses a dollop of merlot for softening. Also, it moves the wine directly from the fermentors to new European oak barrels, emphasizing the woody aromatics more than most as well as further softening the blend.

The dollop of merlot usually runs in the neighborhood of 12 percent. The small oak aging period runs from twenty-two to twenty-six months, depending on the strength of the vintage. The techniques are purely Bordelais, but the wine is particularly Californian as a result of them.

Guesses about the longevity and ultimate quality of Freemark Abbey Cabernet Sauvignons run a fascinating gamut. In 1975 even the 1967 seemed relatively immature, able to develop. The grapes come primarily from two vineyards to the east of Rutherford. Both are properties of partners in the winery.

Freemark Abbey makes a tiny amount of a second Cabernet Sauvignon from a single vineyard near the original de Latour vineyard of Beaulieu. The wine is called Cabernet Bosche after John Bosche, owner of the vines. Made in the regular Freemark Abbey style, the early vintages have been strong in varietal character. Collectors seek them out each year for comparison with other wines from that favored strip of land from Rutherford down to Oakville.

Oakville Vineyards has shown an inclination to take over the role vacated partially by Inglenook and entirely by Souverain. The first Oakville Vineyards Cabernet Sauvignon, a 1968 from a variety of North Coast sources, had the lean, craggy taste of old Inglenooks both for its herbaceous varietal character and for the dusty quality imparted by old, old cooperage. The 1970, released under the winery's collateral van Löben Sels label, had a Napa Valley appellation, and was of much the same character and style as the forerunner.

With one wine, the 1969, Sterling Vineyards has tantalized connoisseurs with a fascinating amalgam of stylistic possibilities. The grapes, from vineyards around the winery at the warm Calistoga end of the valley, somehow seem lighter, make a wine quicker to mature than most others. The inclusion of some merlot in the blend does not explain the situation, because it does not diminish the tealike flavor of the cabernet as it does elsewhere. The hint of European oak is discernible in the bouquet, but subtle. Thus far, the Sterling appears to mature earlier than almost any other Napa Valley Cabernet Sauvignon of present or past, but for all of that is a complex and well-balanced wine.

The possibility of a winery establishing a distinctive style in one vintage does exist, has in fact been done. The process depends on a winemaker willful enough and confident enough to step into a new situation as a person in complete control. Bernard Portet launched Clos du Val Napa Valley Cabernet Sauvignon in the vintage of 1972 as a delicately fruity, moderately tannic, and quite tart red wine. His personal preference is to drink red wines young, by which he means within three or four years of bottling. As a result he aims for early complexity, in part through use of merlot in the blend, in part by moving the wine first into small oak tanks then into new European oak barrels. Equally as important, he makes the balance of flavors to French standards.

An eloquent contrast is immediately at hand. On the adjoining property, Warren Winiarski makes Stag's Leap Wine Cellars Napa Valley Cabernet Sauvignon with very nearly the same sequence of steps, but a palate shaped in the United States and a sense of style born in the Napa Valley. His wine has the softer, riper fruit taste that makes it much more easily identifiable as a Californian, although it differs markedly from its nearest stylistic rival, the Freemark Abbey. Winiarski's first vintage at Stag's Leap was 1972.

As much as it is possible to show a firm sense of style in one season, it also is possible to avoid that. Chappellet Vineyard offered its first wine, of 1968 but undated because of a legal technicality, as a relatively light one, but a rough-hewn rascal nonetheless. In the following vintage, the Chappellet again lacked polish, but this time had a burly enough body to get away with it. The 1970 showed the first signs of moving toward a middle ground on both counts. The wine comes from the Chappellet family vineyards, on a steep, north-facing slope in the hills east of Rutherford. The future may see yet another shift in style as Donn Chappellet explores the potential of his isolated site, and searches at the same time for the winemaker who wishes to be there.

One other small cellar has made a cautious, correct beginning with Cabernet Sauvignon. It is Burgess Cellars, which released a full-bodied, slightly heavy 1972 that hews to the old Napa Valley style of Beaulieu as closely as any other, but which does not yet have a distinctive voice of its own.

Spring Mountain Vineyards has taken a riskier approach to its early Cabernet Sauvignons. After a fine first offering blended from 1968 and 1969 grapes, and a seriously flawed 1970, the wine has begun to settle on a course that leans heavily on the tannic austerity of cabernet sauvignon and on its tealike or herbaceous flavors. As a style, it mines the same general vein as Oakville, or Inglenook Cask, or others similar. Proprietor Mike Robbins and winemaker Chuck Ortman seem to be finding a comfortable stride with that profile, and Spring Mountain is beginning to be a label to watch.

Several other small wineries released their inaugural Cabernet Sauvignons in 1975 and 1976. These include Carneros Creek, Caymus, Chateau Chevalier, Chateau Montelena, Cuvaison, Diamond Creek, Joseph Phelps, Stonegate, Veedercrest, and Yverdon. Still others are a bit further away.

Of these, Carneros Creek, Caymus, Chateau Montelena and Joseph Phelps all showed considerable early promise.

All of this leaves until last two of the largest producers.

Beringer/Los Hermanos is one, The Christian Brothers the other.

Beringer changed its stripes entirely when the Beringer family sold to a corporate ownership controlled by Nestlé, Inc., the colossal Swiss food combine. The old, highly blended wine disappeared in a trice in favor of a spanking new 1969 Napa Valley Cabernet Sauvignon. It came to market a year ahead of its time, but sound. Since then the Beringer has leveled out as a wine made and priced for early consumption, and admirable as such. It is Cabernet Sauvignon pure, but with a lot of the bite removed.

The Christian Brothers throughout their long history have taken the nonvintage approach to reliability. Their Napa Valley Cabernet Sauvignon is blended to a remarkably high standard, but a soft and agreeable one. The wine gives an excellent introduction to the varietal character of cabernet sauvignon along with a pronounced example of the bouquet that comes from long aging in well-seasoned cooperage.

These two wines between them are as good Cabernet Sauvignons as the state has to offer at modest prices for steady consumption.

Such wines aside, vintages are of greater importance with Cabernet Sauvignon than any other red varietal because age-worthiness is the heart of their value to collectors. In summary:

1965 – A light but beautifully balanced year for all hands. The wines are mature, and should be drunk at an early date.

1966 – Huge wines from one of California's richly sunny vintages. They are thick, even faintly raisiny, and likely to go on for another decade or two. There is not a failure to be had.

1967 – A thin, relatively weak year with no wines of great durability. A few are modestly charming, but there is nothing to drive miles to get.

1968 – A fine vintage, perhaps the finest of its decade for combined durability and elegance. All of the durable wines remained mute, needing more time, as of 1975. A few of the lightly rigged ones had begun to be agreeable drinking, pointing toward fine futures for their burlier mates.

1969 – A better vintage than originally touted, not huge, but a source of some very finely drawn qualities in wines that are not maturing much faster than the 1968s.

1970 – No decade since Prohibition has started out half so well. The wines have superb balance, and the promise of long life. I have yet to taste a failure.

1971 – It still is too early to know much, but there is at least fair promise.

1972 – Much too early to know much, except that the year will be extremely uneven because of early, unending fall rains. Those who harvested in time have a chance. Those who waited were washed out.

1973 – A bumper crop, and a good one. The exact character has yet to reveal itself, but the fruit came in in excellent balance. The Stag's Leap from this vintage placed first ahead of several fine Médocs in a blind tasting by French experts in Paris.

1974 – A difficult vintage because everything ripened at once in a warm autumn after a laggard growing season, but the quality is at least adequate.

This list goes back only as far as do the fairly available stocks, which is not far enough to test the ultimate character of Napa Valley Cabernet Sauvignon. While there is no commercial means of obtaining older wines, anyone who runs across an estate sale or some such would do well to look for any 1964, 1961, or 1959, any of the four 1951s noted at the opening of this chapter, or any Beaulieu Vineyards de Latour Private Reserve from the 1940s, but especially 1947 or 1941.

Sonoma County Cabernet Sauvignons

The recent history of Cabernet Sauvignon in Sonoma County is impressively dim. There was only one dated wine from the vintages of 1964 through 1966. Two showed up in 1967, three in 1968.

Times began to grow richer with 1970, which will yield no fewer than eight vintage-dated Cabernet Sauvignons from Sonoma County cellars. There may be more after all of the late bottlers have made themselves felt.

Most of the future hopes lie with the Russian River watershed, where the great preponderance of the county's new cabernet vineyards have been planted. Strong hints are in the early wines that this region will do well with cabernet sauvignon. The climate regions are II and III, very much akin in all particulars to the climate in the Napa Valley.

J. Pedroncelli got the early start in the region with its 1967 Cabernet Sauvignon from vineyards in Dry Creek and Alexander Valleys. There has been a vintage Cabernet from the winery each year since. All have smacked generously of the herbaceous character of the grape. All have been well-balanced, agreeable wines from deeply ripened fruit. The earliest bottlings had a bit too much flavor from new redwood tanks to be classic, but beginning with the 1969 this label is one to lay down for leisurely examination.

Simi, after several bottlings of composite wines from the old Haigh regime and the subsequent Russ Green proprietorship, made its first contemporary wine from the vintage of 1970 and promptly won a gold medal with it in the competition at the Los Angeles County Fair. The Los Angeles competition is not the toughest one in the world, but competent judges there put the Simi out in front of some other wines with broad-based prestige. From Alexander Valley grapes, it is clear evidence that favored parts of the Russian River region can yield the same generously agreeable kind of Cabernet Sauvignon as the middling warm stretches of the Napa Valley.

The following vintages have gone in different directions, but not out of willful change. After Green left Simi, his successors, Scottish & Newcastle, sadly found themselves saddled with two difficult vintages back to back. Winemaker Mary Ann Graf and consultant André Tchelistcheff made a 1972 Cabernet Sauvignon with 40 percent merlot because the cabernet vineyards got caught in the rains that inundated the whole North Coast. While it is not the wine they intended to make, both are proud of the complexity and balance they managed to salvage from a dismal harvest. Future editions will turn back toward the varietal character of cabernet, which will allow longer wood aging, a philosophy Tchelistcheff has kept since his retirement from Beaulieu to a career as a consultant.

F. Korbel & Bros. entered the vintage-dated arena late in 1974 after several years of providing a sound, varietally identifiable Cabernet Sauvignon at bargain prices. The first vintage is 1970; the signs are that the wine will go on being a first-rate commercial Cabernet Sauvignon meant for relatively early drinking.

Sonoma Vineyards offered a 1970 Sonoma County Cabernet Sauvignon as its first vintage-dated effort. Lighter, less varietally identifiable than any of the wines noted above, it nonetheless was a competent red and a hopeful precursor to a program designed in time to yield several single-vineyard wines from each vintage.

Foppiano Russian River Valley Cabernet Sauvignon, vintaged since 1971, is a classic old-style Sonoma Red, varietally identifiable but not refined, or self-consciously made in one style or another. It is good, sound red wine meant to be drunk, not sipped. As such it tells a great deal about the climate and soils of the Russian River region around Healdsburg. All of the grapes come from the Foppiano's own vineyards just south of that town. Cambiaso nonvintage Cabernet Sauvignon has been slightly less successful in recent bottlings for the presence of a bitter note in the finish, but it is much the same kind of wine. New equipment and cooperage may rid the wine of its recent shortcoming. Leo Trentadue makes a perfumey, full-bodied Sonoma Cabernet Sauvignon from his own grapes, ripened as fully as they can be. The first vintage, 1971, had enough spunk to cause me to lay away a few bottles to see where it goes. The suspicion is that it will go where the Foppiano goes, for they have started down the road together. The supply is minute, sold mainly at the cellar door. Martini & Prati produces and bottles a small lot of Cabernet Sauvignon for local sale under its Fountaingrove label. The wine is light, bouquetish from old casks, and priced absurdly low.

Two sizable newcomers are just entering the market. Souverain of Alexander Valley made its debut with a 1972 Cabernet Sauvignon bearing North Coast Counties as its appellation. The wine is light, correctly made, a promising beginning but not a wine by which to judge the future of an ambitious label. Geyser Peak Winery has a nonvintage Cabernet Sauvignon out under its Voltaire label. The appellation is California, but the proprietors of the Schlitz Brewing Co. subsidiary plan to shift over to vintage-dated wines with specific appellations at an early date. Meantime, the existing wine is light, pleasant, and gently evocative of its variety.

One small cellar waits impatiently in the wings for its first Cabernet Sauvignon to smooth out in barrel. It is Dry Creek Vineyards. David Stare, its owner, wishes to make something extraordinary.

The Valley of the Moon may have a greater recent history with Cabernet Sauvignon, or it may have less. That picture is not clear. In either case it has a smaller future for lack of space.

Buena Vista Cellars has offered a seldom-broken sequence of vintage-dated Sonoma Cabernet Sauvignons. However, some labels say only "Bottled by" while others say "Estate grown and bottled by." While all are from Sonoma County vines, only the estate-bottled ones guarantee that the Sonoma Valley was the lone source of the grapes.

Sources to one side, Buena Vista Cabernets of recent seasons have been erratic in quality and style. The most impressive ones have been formidable wine and formidable Cabernet Sauvignon. Dark-hued, fresh, unrelentingly herbaceous in aroma, they have been crisper than typical California reds and tannic enough to tan hides. The 1968 is the most impressive example of this sort of Buena Vista. With just a shade more polish, the Buena Vista could become a real factor among age-worthy Cabernets from all of California. Alas, the wine is just as likely to be badly oxidized and otherwise out of sorts as it is to be fine. One must buy with caution.

August Sebastiani thinks to make his wine taste first like Sebastiani red, and secondly of cabernet sauvignon. This means first that the wine is blended more often than not, and second that it is aged for as long as four years in large and small cooperage before being bottled. What emerges is a sound, traditional California red, smacking hugely of sunny vineyards and of time in wood. It is old wine from the day it first goes on the market, but slow to age more.

Until recently, the Sebastianis blended years as well as grapes, making an even older wine than they now offer in their vintage-dated series that began with 1967. The appellation is North Coast Counties.

A small vineyard called Kenwood began offering a vintage-dated California Cabernet Sauvignon with the harvest of 1970. Principally from Sonoma and Mendocino grapes, it is a soft, light wine, its cabernet aroma accompanied by a firm hint of earthy old wood and a fainter hint of new barrels. There is still some groping for style, but the wine bears watching.

Mendocino County Cabernet Sauvignons

Mendocino County is poised, tantalizingly, on the brink of a whole new career with Cabernet Sauvignon.

There has been a small acreage of cabernet in the Ukiah Valley for years, most of it made by Parducci into a good but heavy, faintly countrified wine. The Ukiah area has a climate near the tolerance of the variety for heat.

More recently, vineyardists have planted cabernet well to the west of Ukiah near a village called Philo. The climate summary there is at the low end of Region I.

In the vintage of 1969, the Parduccis made several Cabernet Sauvignons from differing vineyard districts including the Ukiah Valley and Philo, the latter also known as Anderson Valley. The fermenting techniques were identical. All the wines were aged in medium-sized, well-seasoned redwood tanks because the Parduccis share Louis M. Martini's Italianate aversion to the taste of wood in wine.

The Ukiah wine was what it always had been: heavy, almost raisiny, but so cleanly made that it is entirely enjoyable as a kind of California original. The Philo wine, on the other hand, showed some of the classic French barnyard aroma, and certainly was the product of cooler, less sunny vineyards. It was properly lean, close to a definitive example of what herbaceous means in the case of cabernet. Drinking it, one cannot help but feel it will age with grace.

The Parduccis fear that the Philo climate is so marginal for cabernet sauvignon that the variety will ripen only one year in ten, not enough for a grower to survive on. Some further vintages will appear because the vines will live out a lifespan. They will be worth an exploratory bottle at the least.

Meanwhile the other Mendocino wineries have stayed thus far with Ukiah district grapes.

Cresta Blanca offers a sound, gentle, nonvintage California Cabernet Sauvignon designed for early, easy drinking.

Fetzer has the opposite, a thick, dark-hued, uncommonly astringent wine overlaid with a curious vegetative flavor. Repeatedly, with this and a few other wineries there will be the remark that the wines have a particular bouquet of their own. These odors—called "form flavors" in the trade—come with seasoned cooperage, or, even more mysteriously, with the buildings that hold the cooperage. Some are pleasant, even welcome, especially when not too overt. Very old tanks of redwood or oak tend to develop an aroma not unlike the smell of rich black earth, the humusy stuff of damp forests. In faint concentrations it is wholly agreeable, but strong doses are less easy to like. Another "form" is reminiscent of drying vegetables, especially kindred to asparagus or cabbage in character. Again, faint concentrations can be agreeable, especially in a wine with the herbaceous aroma of cabernet, but too much is deplorable. Fetzer balances on this tightrope, with too much vegetative taste for some, and just the right amount for others.

Central Coast Cabernet Sauvignons

Of all the grape varieties, white or black, grown in the Central Coast, cabernet sauvignon has marked out the clearest paths for itself. In spite of a small roster of local producers, the most impressive differences within the region clearly stem more from sun and soil than from any acts of will in the cellars.

The handful of tiny vineyards in the hills west of the Santa Clara Valley consistently yield fruit reminiscent of the crops from the cool vineyards north of San Francisco Bay, but just a shade less lush. The newer vineyards of Monterey County produce a leaner, greener taste in the wines from their cabernet sauvignons than any other region in the state. Livermore, contrarily, grows grapes that temper cabernet sauvignon's austerity to a great degree. Varied as the styles are within the small roster of cellars, these regional differences in varietal characteristic show through year after year.

After the easy generalizations specifics come hard. In the older parts of Alameda and Santa Clara counties the vineyards are too few and too widely separated for one to know whether they occupy the most suitable land, or exist merely by the hazards of chance. Newer plantings in Monterey and San Benito counties have not yet had time to prove their basic qualities let alone any relative values.

Ridge, Gemello, and a couple of even smaller wineries take the production of vineyards in the west hills of Santa Clara, where cabernet sauvignon yields very fine wine indeed.

Ridge compounds the full, herbaceous character of cabernet from its vineyards on Montebello Ridge by fermenting and aging the wine to last forever. The new wine stays together with its skins for a week after the fermentation goes dry. The aging time is two years, mostly in new American oak barrels. Although such is the habit with every red at Ridge, no other grape variety serves the purpose so well.

The current practices came with Paul Draper when he joined the winery in 1970 and turned more in the direction of finesse than the winery had been headed earlier. The early vintages were fermented crudely, then aged in small barrels for as long as four years in hopes of developing some polish. The first Ridge Cabernet Sauvignon came from the vintage of 1962. The vintage of 1970 is far enough back to go except for those who love might for its own sake. It is a dark-hued, deeply tannic wine, and it also has a degree of acidic tartness not common in either Napa or Sonoma Cabernet Sauvignons. Some hints of a form flavor have begun to develop in Ridge reds. Connoisseurs of the house identify it with the flavor association of pickle, an unsettling thought but an excellent factor in the wine at its present concentration.

Episodically Ridge will buy grapes from the Napa Valley or another distant locale and make a separate lot of Cabernet Sauvignon, but most bottlings are from the winery's own sharply sloping vineyards, on a crest that looks west to the Pacific Ocean and east into the San Francisco Bay basin.

Gemello makes Cabernet Sauvignon from a miscellany of grapes, but mostly from a vineyard not far down Montebello Ridge from the Ridge vines. The style is similar, but tempered enough to be a useful alternative if Ridge is a shade too astringent and rugged for an individual taste. The wine is available only locally. A few miles to the north, Woodside makes a light, finely wrought Cabernet Sauvignon of classical varietal character. The vines, a scant acre and a half of them, are the last surviving piece of the old LaQuesta Vineyard, originally the property of Dr. E. H. Rixford. LaQuesta was a legend in pre-Prohibition California winemaking; Woodside labels the wine by that name in tribute to the original. There is so little of it that the supply literally goes to friends and neighbors, who share it around just enough to cause great lamentations for the disappearance of Portola Valley/ Woodside from the lists of commercial wine districts.

Some distance to the south, David Bruce makes Cabernet Sauvignon the way Ridge used to, mostly from grapes on his own property in the hills west of Los Gatos. It is big enough and rough enough to go with mastodon steak.

Across San Francisco Bay, in the dry, warm hills to the east, Livermore Valley Cabernet Sauvignon is what Concannon Vineyards elects it to be. Concannon owns all of the cabernet acreage in the valley and is the sole producer of a Livermore appellation wine of the variety.

The current ones are vintage-dated Limited Bottlings, a program that began with the harvest of 1962 and has gone forward from there with a sequence of relentlessly consistent wines. They are gentle by the standards. The herbaceous aroma of the grape is subdued by Livermore sunshine. So are the tannins. And yet each vintage produces a wine unmistakably of cabernet sauvignon for clear ruby color as well as nose and taste. Long aging in sizable old oak casks imparts fugitive hints of age without masking the essential grape. As usual for Concannon, the wines are impeccably clean, able to coax reluctant souls into the fold of admirers of Cabernet. The same qualities that cause it to appeal to newcomers sometimes will drop it into the lower ranks in comparative tastings, but even fierce critics gladly will have it at table with good food.

The wines endure time in bottle very well, but do not demand it. The 1965, to cite a specific, was on top of its form in its tenth year, but it had been on the top of its form as soon as the Concannons released it.

Incidentally, a comparison of this wine from a lean soil in Region III with a Parducci from a rich soil in Region III is an instructive exercise.

The south extreme of Santa Clara County offers some potential for other thoughts about cabernet sauvignon in warm Region III.

San Martin, after its long years of producing jug-style wine no matter what the grape varieties, began in 1973 to work toward more sophisticated styles. The announcement by new owners of serious efforts to come was a limited bottling of 1968 Cabernet Sauvignon from vineyards at San Ysidro, just to the north of the town of Hollister. A step up from the older nonvintage wines, it still left ample room for new winemaker Ed Friedrich to make improvements.

San Martin will have soon the option of producing both Santa Clara and Monterey appellation Cabernet Sauvignons; the primary vineyards of the controlling Southdown Corporation are in Monterey. But the San Ysidro properties of the Filice family, minor partners now in the winery they founded, support enough cabernet to continue a separate bottling if the proprietors wish.

The old family firm of Mirassou has a similar choice, although it has evolved in a different way. Before 1966, Mirassou Cabernet Sauvignon from a small vineyard at the winery was sold at the door as a sideline to the dominant business in bulk wine. As the winery expanded its bottled wine business with big new vineyards in Monterey County, there first were hyphenated Santa Clara-Monterey appellations, then, beginning with the 1972s, purely Monterey appellations. Earlier, small lots of Harvest Selection Cabernet Sauvignons carried Monterey as the appellation. In 1973 the family uprooted some old mixed plantings at the winery in favor of a new vineyard of cabernet sauvignon. As that matures, the regular wine is likely to be the Monterey appellation, and the special lot a Santa Clara.

The Harvest Selection Monterey Cabernet Sauvignons of Mirassou from 1966 forward taste of another world altogether than any of their peers from Alameda and Santa Clara counties. Style separates them somewhat. The Mirassous ferment lighter than Ridge, and age in new wood rather than old as opposed to the Concannon practice. The fundamental differences, however, come from the vineyards. Monterey appears to yield Cabernet Sauvignons so pungently herbaceous that they would be called stemmy if grown elsewhere, their makers accused of allowing too many leaves and stems to get into the crusher and fermentor. In addition, the misty climate at Soledad does not build as much of the sunny taste of ripe fruit into cabernet as other regions with clearer skies. The result, a curiosity for California, is a wine with intense flavors, but light body. The Mirassous by 1970 had decided to turn the lean green taste into its own virtue rather than failing in an attempt to copy the fuller-bodied, riper Cabernet Sauvignons of the Napa Valley.

As The Monterey Vineyard and others join in making Monterey Cabernet

Sauvignon, we will learn more about what is Monterey and what is Mirassou.

Santa Clara County supports a number of small cellars, most of them in the Gilroy region, and conscientious producers of country-style Cabernet Sauvignon, which is to say straightforward red without much polish, but quite likely with some bouquet from ancient cooperage. Among these: Bertero, Fortino, Hecker Pass, the Mt. Madonna of Guglielmo, and Novitiate of Los Gatos. In Alameda County, Villa Armando does a similar job with the variety.

The big wineries in the region do not limit themselves to local grapes. The labels of both Almadén and Paul Masson say only "California" as the appellation. The base of Almadén Cabernet Sauvignon is winery-owned vineyards in San Benito and Monterey counties. Similarly Paul Masson Cabernet Sauvignon has a considerable base in its vineyards in Monterey County.

Almadén nonvintage Cabernet Sauvignon is, as other Almadén reds, strongly marked by the flavors of its long aging in American oak barrels in a warmish cellar, which is to say it has a bit of a baked quality in among the fruit flavors. The herbaceous taste of cabernet sauvignon grapes is but faint. The vintage bottlings are stronger in varietal character, but the same in basic style.

Paul Masson is equally characteristic of its label style, which takes almost the reverse approach to Almadén's. All Paul Masson reds are soft, direct, and fresh rather than aged or otherwise bouquetish. The thought is less apt in Cabernet Sauvignon than in Pinot Noir or Zinfandel, but the wine is at least affable. The regular bottling, nonvintage, is assembled from several sources, so is fatter and sunnier than a pure Monterey wine. Masson offers a chance to check with an estate bottling wholly from Monterey.

Weibel is the last of the producers with headquarters in the Central Coast. Its vineyards are mostly elsewhere. The dominant source for cabernet sauvignon is around Ukiah, in Mendocino County. The varietal has been inconsistent in recent years, is not overwhelmingly characteristic of its variety, but tends to be sound red wine and not too costly.

Other Cabernet Sauvignons

A handful of producers make Cabernet Sauvignons, or offer purchased ones lacking enough pedigree to define the source. A few others work in regions where cabernet sauvignon is not typical. Of these, four are worth note. California Wine Association buys bulk Cabernet Sauvignon, mostly in the Napa Valley, for its Eleven Cellars label. The wine emerges light, clean, tending to be a bit bland, but fair value for the money. Frank Cadenasso makes a Cabernet Sauvignon from his vines at Fairfield, alongside the Sacramento River. Somehow he achieves a light-bodied, pale red with intensely herbaceous nose and a slightly sharp finish. Again, the price is right.

Winemasters Guild makes a Cabernet Sauvignon assembled from several districts, but especially Mendocino. It is a reliably sound wine, straightforward, slightly heavy, but with enough quality and varietal character to make it worth the modest price.

Finally, two wineries are making Cabernet Sauvignons from grapes grown in Rancho California, south and east of Los Angeles in the dusty hill country behind Camp Pendleton. The evidence is contradictory. Brookside makes a light, rather neutrally flavored wine under its Assumption Abbey label. The 1973 inaugural Cabernet Sauvignon of Callaway Vineyards and Winery is an opposite, a thick-bodied, dark, tannic wine with strong herbaceous character from the grapes. At least it is such in barrel. It will take some years for this vintage, and some additional vintages to show what is what in a newly developing region of at least some promise for this and other table wines.

GAMAY AND GAMAY BEAUJOLAIS

California Gamay and Gamay Beaujolais are and are not the same wine. They come from two different grape varieties, but, in most cases, tasting them does not reveal that. Both wines tend to be simple, agreeably fruity reds meant to suffice when Pinot Noir would cost too much, or taste too dry.

The grape variety called gamay beaujolais has turned out to be a frail strain of pinot noir. The one called just gamay, or, sometimes, napa gamay, is truly gamay. Presumably both varieties arrived in California as cuttings from the Beaujolais district of France although proof is lacking.

On rare occasions the wines from gamay beaujolais challenge good ones from finer clones of pinot noir, but mainly they provide affable competition to those from the true gamay.* There they rest, in the middle range of character, not quite able to match first-rate Pinot Noir for distinctiveness, which, in view of the general reputation of Pinot Noirs does not put them high on the social ladder of California reds. On the other hand the gamay beaujolais vine does not bear heavily enough for its wines to compete purely on price against either varietals or generics from more prolific varieties. As a final handicap, only climate Region I ripens the fruit in balance for its best wine. Region III seems too warm altogether. This means the grapes for a modest wine must compete with titans for an extremely limited space. It is not an easy situation for making friends among growers or winemakers. A winemaker has done a very good turn of work when he achieves the proper balance of modest charms and modest price in a Gamay Beaujolais.

The vine called gamay or napa gamay yields fuller crops in a broader climate range than does gamay beaujolais. Its characteristic flavor is fresh and sprightly, and surprisingly intense. The lack is finesse, or complexity. However, the modest price of the finished wine compensates for that. Wines called Gamay would seem better adapted not only to survival, but to proliferation than ones called Gamay Beaujolais. However, the current roster of labels does not bear out this premise. Greater numbers of Gamay Beaujolais are present in greater volume than the Gamays.

---

* Any wine from gamay beaujolais legally can be called Pinot Noir; the option is with the producer. The situation virtually guarantees that a wine named Gamay Beaujolais will be a light one.

Several styles are open to each varietal. The basic one is forthrightly simple, agreeable young red, somewhat the California counterpart to a *passe-tout-grains* Burgundy. A second is a slightly more distinctive red, a social equal to a Beaujolais Villages. Or, third, it can turn frivolous and play at being a Nouveau type.

To make a simple, unaffected red the general approach is a cool fermentation to minimize tannins or other harsh characteristics, perhaps a shade of residual sugar, then an early bottling and quick sale.

Someone thinking to achieve a bit of polish may ferment completely dry, then give the wine a short turn in wood cooperage to add grace notes of age.

A genuine Nouveau-style red requires a specialized fermentation using the technique called carbonic maceration. The grape clusters are thrown into the fermentor whole, stems and all, and the fermentation started up. Enough juice is pressed out by the berries' own weight for the yeasts to become active, but the essential idea is for fermentation to take place inside the skin of each unbroken berry. The wine is pressed at the end when the skins have become fragile. Carbonic maceration imposes its own curious flavor over the varietal characteristic of grapes. It is a volatile sort of smell, faintly reminiscent of airplane dope, fingernail polish remover, or other ethery compounds. It combines with the grape smell to produce a lively character, and a strong one. Most drinkers react with great pleasure or equal aversion the first time they taste the stuff, then do not change their minds with further exposure.

In any conventional form, Gamay and Gamay Beaujolais are not wines for which one should insist on vintage dates, or particular appellations of origin. All one should expect is a soft wine of straightforward charms, but a bit more specific in flavor characteristics than a routine generic. When blends of years or regions can help keep the character up and the price down, they should do. Carbonic maceration wines should have vintage dates, but only as a reminder to hurry up and drink the stuff before anything else can happen to it.

Napa Valley Gamays and Gamay Beaujolais

The Napa Valley has ample vineyards of both gamay and gamay beaujolais. The long list of producers divides about half and half between the two varietal types.

Beaulieu Vineyards, which launched its Napa Valley Gamay Beaujolais with the superior vintage of 1968, makes the most considerable wine of the name. It has deeper color and richer flavors than any of the others, and yet manages to be youthful and soft. The proprietor's own Burgundy, a blend of gamay and mondeuse, doubtless applies pressure on the winemaker to go forth and do good work, being one of the most convincing examples in the state that generic wine can be excellent.

The Christian Brothers' nonvintage Napa Valley Gamay Beaujolais competes favorably, although the style is less zesty and more marked by flavors of age from The Brothers' big old oak or redwood tanks. (There is not much to choose between woods after generations of wine have soaked the cask black clear to the outside.) The essence of The Brothers' Gamay Beaujolais is a subtle addition of some older wines to the new majority.

Inglenook Vineyards and Charles Krug produce vintage-dated Napa Valley Gamay Beaujolais very similar to each other. Both are pale-hued and light-bodied in most years compared to the other two.

Among the Gamays The Christian Brothers have one they call Gamay Noir which is very close kin to their Gamay Beaujolais. The touch of age is, if anything, a bit more pronounced. It is one of the least expensive and most reliable bottlings in which to find the taste of age in a soft, essentially fruity red wine. As usual there is no date.

Robert Mondavi makes his Gamay with at least some thought toward Nouveau-style wines from Beaujolais. The fruit aromas of the variety are enhanced by what seems to be a hint of sweet, but could be the untrammeled freshness of a wine fermented cool and bottled quickly. In any case there is an open invitation to take such liberties as light chilling or medium heavy chilling for summer picnics. The appellation is Napa Valley and the wine is vintage dated.

Between these, but closer in style to The Christian Brothers come Inglenook, Nichelini, and Oakville Vineyards. The Oakville works hardest at being a wine of strength and character, a latent puritan caught up among a lot of hedonists.

Some of the newer small cellars in the valley have Gamays or Gamay Beaujolais which have not been in existence long enough to show definite styles. Cuvaison, before it changed winemakers in 1975, had a Gamay Vivace fermented and aged as a fresh young red and a Gamay Nouveau in the carbonic maceration style. Stag's Leap Wine Cellars introduced a 1974 Gamay Beaujolais early in 1975. The debut wine was soft, fresh, and impeccably clean. Finally, Yverdon began with the vintage of 1972 to produce a curiously heavy, earthy Gamay Beaujolais, a coarse wine but an agreeable one.

Sonoma and Mendocino Gamays and Gamay Beaujolais

Although the acreages of both grape varieties are fairly substantial in Sonoma and Mendocino counties, only recently have Gamays and Gamay Beaujolais become prominent on wine lists in the region.

Sebastiani Vineyards leads the way in all respects with a wine the proprietor calls Gamay Beaujolais Nouveau. It is only half a Nouveau, but may be the right idea for California in any case. By French definition a Nouveau is a Beaujolais fermented by carbonic maceration and sent to market in November of the same year as the vintage. At Sebastiani, August Sebastiani will have nothing to do with the grape juicy stuff that emerges from carbonic maceration, but he will make a conventional light red and bottle it for sale as soon as it finishes fermenting. Even the lightest such Gamay Beaujolais is uncommonly rough at a month or two of age. In November a small glass to toast the vintage is enough. What happens during the next year is what interests the Sebastianis. Then their Gamay Beaujolais Nouveau smooths into a balanced red of distinct character. It is light, the fruit flavors fresh, and yet it has some of the elusive overtones that mark wines of loftier pedigree. When the wine is two to three years old it shows a mature side hard to find in inexpensive bottlings.

The first wine of the sort came from the vintage of 1972, and has been repeated annually since then.

Sebastiani supplies of their Nouveau will expand through the next several years as a sizable new vineyard on cool bay flats south of Sonoma town comes to full maturity. An adjoining older block was the prime source through 1974.

Before embarking on their particular kind of Nouveau, the Sebastianis for years made and conventionally aged a Gamay Beaujolais that was not vastly different in character.

Over in the Russian River region the proliferation of new cellars is the source of several new bottlings of Gamay Beaujolais.

Souverain of Alexander Valley has an instructive counterpart to the Sebastiani bottlings, presuming that the first attempts indicate a consistent approach. Their Gamay Beaujolais is fermented to make a light, dry wine, but is given several months of aging in small oak tanks before bottling rather than a few weeks in large redwood. The Souverain makes a gentler impression in its early months than does the Sebastiani, but does not seem to develop the nuances of bottle bouquet so swiftly or completely.

Dry Creek Vineyard offers a tiny annual volume of Gamay Beaujolais in much the same style as the Souverain, but the wine is fuller bodied and sharper. It is vintage-dated. Sonoma Vineyards, on the other hand, goes a stride lighter and blander than Souverain with its vintage-dated Gamay Beaujolais. Much the same wine can be bought in California under the company's secondary Windsor label.

Two Gamay Beaujolais come from the Mendocino County neighbors, Cresta Blanca and Parducci. The Parducci, from vineyards near the winery, is fermented to a modestly austere dryness, then aged in small redwood tanks until it smooths. The result is a straightforward, uncommonly durable wine for its type. The Cresta Blanca bottlings in the early 1970s were less robust, perhaps because the winery under the Guild ownership had some old stocks from the Schenley proprietorship to blend out.

Sonoma and Mendocino between them offer only two Gamays, one from Sonoma Vineyards and the other from Trentadue. The vineyards for both are in the Russian River district around Healdsburg. There similarities cease. The Sonoma Vineyards Gamay, made in considerable volumes, has been very light and tinged with a hint of sweet to help the fruit flavors along. The Trentadue is made bone dry, in tiny quantities, with the emphasis on husky qualities rather than soft or delicate ones. People frequently describe wines as women. This one would play pretty good third base and bat well.

Central Coast Gamays and Gamay Beaujolais

A curious split separates Gamay Beaujolais from Gamay in the Central Coast region. All of the Gamay Beaujolais come from the sizable producers in the region while the Gamays come only from tiny places.

Mirassou Vineyards has produced the most intriguing Gamay Beaujolais from the region. A blend of Monterey and Santa Clara County grapes, the wine has an atypically complex character. The Monterey contribution is sprightly fruit flavors.

The sunny Evergreen slopes in Santa Clara yield fruit with a bit of fat. Mirassou cellar flavor completes the sketch. The latter makes a precarious balance to keep. The wine has been at its best in its youngest days. Its vintage date serves as an index.

Paul Masson's nonvintage Gamay Beaujolais is a similar blend of grapes from cool Monterey with others from sunnier climes. In its case, no cellar flavors intrude. The wine is impeccably clean, a direct invitation to carefree use with casual meals.

The Monterey Vineyard offered a 1974 Gamay Beaujolais fermented and aged in stainless steel as an archetypal fresh young wine with just enough residual sugar to soften the sharp edges. Purely of Monterey County grapes, it is uncannily light and crisp, a wine for immediate drinking.

Wente Bros. has a Gamay Beaujolais blended from its Monterey and Livermore vineyards. Vintage-dated, it has been light, but tart enough to make it a better wine with warm meals than with blithe picnics.

Almadén's Gamay Beaujolais has been less than youthful, the result one presumes of aging in small oak. It has been too thin to absorb the wood bouquet with real grace. Weibel Gamay Beaujolais has been similarly indistinct in recent seasons.

Among the small producers of Gamay there is no consensus at all about style. Ridge ferments its Gamay on the skins in the characteristic effort to make something powerful and needing age. Gamay, like topical humor, does not always keep its form long enough to prove the point. However, people who like vast amounts of stuffing in every wine they drink have an appropriate choice. The source of supply can vary from vintage to vintage, but always is explained on the label. The most recent, 1971, came from a Napa Valley vineyard.

The remaining producers—Conrad Viano, Pedrizzetti, and Villa Armando—make their Gamays as country reds, with ample whiffs of bouquet from well-seasoned cooperage. The appellations are California. None is vintage dated.

Other Gamays and Gamay Beaujolais

A handful of producers in regions other than the coastal counties offer one or the other of the Gamays.

Dino Barengo in Lodi each year offers a light, soft Gamay Beaujolais, as does Frank Cadenasso. Barengo buys the grapes. Cadenasso has his own vines near the Solano County town of Fairfield. California Wine Association offers a Gamay Beaujolais each year under its Eleven Cellars label. The company purchases bulk wine, usually in the Napa Valley, for its blends. Finally, Brookside has a Gamay Beaujolais under its Assumption Abbey label. The wine is made from Brookside's vineyards at Rancho California. The style is faintly sweet, and light.

All of these wines are sound, commercial bottlings, and priced right.

GRIGNOLINO

Grignolino belongs to a tiny minority of producers and is admired by a proportionately tiny minority of bibbers.

The producers strongly suspect that they are dealing with at least two clones of the variety, perhaps even with two very similar varieties. The wines bear out the thought. Although all Grignolinos are uncommonly tart and quite astringent, they form two groups sharing almost no other flavor characteristics.

In contrast to the generous but vague charms of Barbera, the most distinctive wines called Grignolino are lean and they etch themselves on the palate. The university flavor association list calls them spicy-fruity. More specific, they have an overtone that is startlingly similar to the orangey essences of triple sec and kindred liqueurs, and which is curiously appropriate to a sharp, light, young red wine. Other Grignolinos, presumably from the other clone, do not have the orangey overtone. Its absence makes them considerably less identifiable than their counterparts though their tart, tannic qualities hardly leave them neutral wines.

The combination of tart and tannic in a dry, preferably young wine requires bibbers who seek wines for their strengths. For such souls, Grignolino is an obvious companion for well-seasoned tomato sauce dishes, for game, and for lamb or mutton.

Tart astringency is rare in a lightly colored wine of no better than modest aging ability, which Grignolino also is. The combination runs against classical red wine standards. Because of this, the university does not recommend planting grignolino in California, although its warning admits that some excellent wines have been made and sold under the name. (The scholars suspect that the best ones were blended with something else in a report written some years ago.)

No doubt the meager acreage will not grow much, but those of us who admire the grape for both its red and rosé wines should not allow any shrinkage in the vineyards, either.

Napa Valley Grignolinos

Little Heitz Cellars and big Beringer divide the small acreage of grignolino in the Napa Valley. The two of them also demonstrate the probability that grignolino is more than one thing.

Heitz Cellars Grignolino always is made young and lively, the only Heitz red not marked by the characteristic flavors of aging in small oak, the better to preserve the curious, tangy grace note of orange essence which distinguishes this from all other varietals.

The wine is made only from Joe Heitz' own grignolino vineyards, an old block on the valley floor just south of St. Helena, and a newer block on the winery property in the hills just above the Silverado Trail due east of St. Helena. It always carries the Napa Valley appellation of origin, but never is vintage dated. The inclusion of a softening dollop of older wine is an essential counterpoint to the aggressive charms of the young majority in each lot. Rarely, the soft older flavors will dominate, turning the wine into a harmonious elder statesman of Grignolinos. Finding such a one is happenstance. Careful cellaring is no guarantee of it. Even an individual case may contain one or two such bottles among others of typically coltish character. The most learned of Grignolino tasters are reduced to hoping that lamb is on the table when the cork on one is drawn.

Beringer Grignolino is of the nonorangey sort, a wine much more along the lines of a tart young Zinfandel if comparison can help define the character. Like the Heitz, it is of Napa Valley origin, not vintage dated, and not overlaid with woody bouquets. It never has, in my experience at least, become a graceful older wine, but has accompanied with great reliability tomato-sauced meats and pastas that want a brisk, cleansing red.

Central Coast Grignolinos

Central Coast, in this one case, could be more narrowly defined as Santa Clara Valley. A clear majority of the state total of grignolino grows in vineyards flanking the town of Gilroy.

The University of California at Davis scholars, in noting that grignolino was in some way or another schizoid, grumbled that identification in the vineyards was difficult. Statistics point to Santa Clara vineyards as the probable source for the statement. The wines from them are an even more tantalizing indicator. Santa Clara Grignolinos almost always have some of the essence of orange that so clearly identifies this wine from Heitz Cellars, but it also almost always is tempered, perhaps by climate, more probably by mixed plantings.

San Martin Vineyards is the most available bottling among several from the region. Others, to be had mostly at the cellar door, include Bonesio/Uvas, Guglielmo, Filice, Bertero, and Thomas Kruse. All follow the general descriptions of Grignolino: Pale red color, tart, tannic, and spicy-fruity. The essence of orange is a flickering shadow in the background, now firmer, now fainter.

The Bonesio/Uvas and Kruse bottlings of recent years were the most probable sources of the orangey essence, although the Bonesio frequently hid the quality behind a strong bouquet of ancient casks. The San Martin, on the other hand, has tended to fall into the same camp as the Beringer. The vineyards, properties of the Filice family, are in the San Ysidro district east of Gilroy. Because of this, San Martin has offered the wine on occasion as an estate selection, vintage-dated specialty at far flossier prices than Grignolino adherents are used to paying. This of all Grignolinos has been a wine of indistinct character.

Other Grignolinos

Four cellars spread as widely apart as the vinous geography of California allows offer the other available Grignolinos.

The defunct Ellena Brothers winery had a few acres of grignolino, in the

Cucamonga district east of Los Angeles. The crop has gone in recent years to Opici and San Antonio, which firms have made similarly ordinary wines from the grapes. Presumably the climate in the region is warmer than the variety will endure with grace.

Cadenasso, the lone winery of Solano County, offers a Grignolino from its vineyards near the town of Fairfield, in one of the little valleys that looks out toward the Sacramento River. Frank Cadenasso ages his wines in sizable oak oval casks for longer periods than most other producers age their Grignolinos. The results are soft, well-balanced wines, light in body and flavor by the standards of the variety.

Finally Cresta Blanca, in Mendocino County, has a Grignolino in much the same general style as Beringer's.

PETITE SIRAH

To develop a wine type of great and inimitable character takes diverse minds exploring every subtle shading of quality they can imagine.

By that standard Petite Sirah has a long way to go in California. Although the grape has been around by the thousands of acres for dozens of years, few winemakers thought of it as anything more than a useful blend grape for burgundy-types until the early 1970s.

The first days of petite sirah as a source of varietal wine were the mid-1960s when Concannon Vineyard and Souverain Cellars made almost simultaneous first efforts. After they had toiled alone for several years, interest began to grow in other quarters. The vintage of 1968 yielded half a dozen individual wines. The vintage of 1972 produced fourteen wines bearing the year. Another six wine companies were offering nonvintage bottlings as the 1972s went to market.

These producers are just beginning to add a few fine lines to the rough sketch of what Petite Sirah might be in California. They are in the happy position of working with that treasured American character, the underdog. U.C.-Davis repeatedly has said that wines from petite sirah are above average in quality, slow to mature, but not especially distinctive. The one flavor association that distinguishes a Petite Sirah from other red varietals is a faint peppery note just at the end of a sip.

As a single grape varietal the textbook Petite Sirah should be full-bodied, reasonably tart, more tannic than most other reds, and vinous in flavor, all of which sounds suspiciously like Barbera. The wines are as similar as their descriptions, although their grapes need to be grown in differing climates. The petite sirah is at its best in climate Region II. Its wines grow steadily heavier and coarser in warmer conditions. Barbera, on the other hand, prospers in Region III and warmer.

In recent years the University of California has made a distinction among plantings known as petite sirah. Some are called the California strain, others the French strain. It appears that much of what has been known as petite sirah is in fact a somewhat altered descendant of a similar Rhône grape called the duriff. Some of the California plantings, meantime, assuredly are sirah. Thus far no one has sorted all the older plantings, although new ones of the duriff descendant are identified as California strain petite sirah and those of sirah are identified as French strain. In any case, there is little likelihood of two varietals emerging from the confusion.

However the botany is handled, California Petite Sirah as a wine poses a case in which a liberal varietal law could permit legendary wines to be born out of judicious blending. Certainly the variety's (or varieties') finest performances elsewhere in the world have been as the senior partner in a consortium. In its great home, the towering slopes along the Rhône River in France, the sirah is accompanied in appellation wines by carignane, duriff, grenache, gamay noir, cinsaut, picpoule, and half a dozen more varieties. Even the Australians, who judge their shiraz infinitely superior to its California counterpart, increasingly blend the grape variety with cabernet sauvignon to make claret, or grenache or pinot noir to make burgundy.

While the Californians work toward legendary dimensions, their current Petite Sirahs are no less than sound. Some are uncommonly rich red wine by any measure.

Napa Valley Petite Sirahs

Napa Valley winemakers have a substantial acreage of vineyard on hand for exploring the possibilities of Petite Sirah as a varietal. The vineyards came into being mainly to satisfy the need for good blending wine. As a result a preponderance of the plantings are in the warmer north end of the valley where they will bear large, well-ripened crops. However, some plantings extend into the cool region south of Oakville where finer character might develop.

One way and another the handful of explorers are making uncommonly good use of the possibilities in spite of the fact that petite sirah acreage has been shrinking in face of competition from more prestigious varieties. The unifying factor is a conscientious effort to make something elegant, even classical out of the old blender's friend. The going is tough, but hopeful signs are at hand.

Souverain Cellars, the original source, continues to set the style and pace for Petite Sirahs from the Napa Valley. Lee Stewart originally made a big, tannic, full-flavored sort of wine. His successors have added a subtle shade of flavor from new oak casks and subtracted a corresponding degree of tannic astringency. The style changes have left the wine identifiable as Souverain, and yet given it an extra dimension.

Robert Mondavi produced his first Petite Sirah from the vintage of 1970, immediately serving notice that he would challenge Souverain with a wine of similar style and substance. If any difference separates the two, the note from aging in new oak cooperage is slightly more pronounced in the Mondavi.

Freemark Abbey dipped hesitantly into Petite Sirah production in 1969 with a bottling so small it never reached the public market, then resumed on an annual basis with the vintage of 1971. The vineyard is a small, old one atop a craggy knoll on Spring Mountain, on the west side of the Napa Valley. It yields intensely flavored grapes. Brad Webb and his colleagues at Freemark Abbey ferment for tannic austerity and full body, then age the wine in small, new oak. The result, at least when the wine is young, is complex, but not so smoothly harmonious as the

Souverain or Mondavi. The profile is one of a classically age-worthy red, an Hermitage style against the Châteauneuf du Pape style of the others, if a comparison helps.

Burgess Cellars introduced a husky, relatively straightforward Petite Sirah with the vintage of 1972. Much of the fruit comes from the old Lee Stewart vineyard in the east hills, and the style harks back to his original. The only other Petite Sirah from Napa County available in 1975 was Jim Nichelini's, a sturdy, earthy wine made in the old-fashioned way of California country red. Most of it sells at the cellar door.

The roster is due to expand by several labels. Among these, the Joseph Phelps will be the first made only of certified French strain Sirah.

Sonoma County Petite Sirahs

Like Napa, Sonoma has a considerable acreage of petite sirah planted for the main purpose of making solid red wine as a base for burgundy or some such. Most of it is in the Russian River watershed, in places warm enough to produce reliably ripe, sizable crops.

The steadiest wine of the lot comes from the Foppiano Wine Company vineyards and cellars at the south edge of Healdsburg right on the banks of the Russian River. Always the wine has been thick and dark, its tannins fierce enough to battle spicy stews. While vintages from 1971 forward continue to be straightforward in style, good wines in which to seek the black pepper flavor that characterizes the variety, they also have migrated away from an earlier coarse quality in favor of more subtle balance.

Cambiaso, a nearby neighbor in Healdsburg, has a Petite Sirah in the coarser, heavier style, one that even finishes slightly bitter in the old-fashioned way of California reds.

Both of these wines age in large, well-seasoned cooperage, which preserves the taste of the grape rather than obscuring it with easily perceptible notes from the wood aging.

A very small cellar, Trentadue Winery and Vineyards, makes a vintage-dated Petite Sirah in a style much like the Cambiaso.

Sonoma Vineyards Petite Sirah has been the most widely available of any of these. The early bottlings, released in 1973 and 1974, were light, soft wines by the standards of the variety and locale, shadows of the real thing albeit pleasant ones. The small winery of Davis Bynum offered a similar Petite Sirah to the Sonoma Vineyards.

Only one winery in the Valley of the Moon has a Petite Sirah. Kenwood Vineyards ages a full-bodied but soft wine in small oak to acquire complexity. In its early editions the Kenwood was agreeable but not distinctive. The volume is tiny.

Mendocino County Petite Sirahs

Mendocino, from its relatively small acreage, provides a considerable amount of Petite Sirah, and one of the most intriguing bottlings of them all.

Cresta Blanca is responsible for the intriguing entry. The original bottling released in 1973 gave only California as the appellation. Subsequent releases have said Mendocino. All have been kindred, genuine originals, fat, dark hued, with rich fruit flavors and an even richer overlay of exotic bouquet. The exotic yet appropriate note is spiritous, fugitive. Probably it comes from aging in small, new American oak, but somehow it faintly suggests brandy.

Other Petite Sirahs have been as rich and well balanced as these but not as mysterious. Enigmatic flavor is a powerful asset in wine, and, in this case, an excellent companion to meat sauces of complex harmony.

Parducci, the pioneer cellar of the Ukiah district, has produced vintage-dated Petite Sirahs from local vineyards since 1967. They are sturdy, reliably sound reds with all the correct attributes plus a faintly earthy bouquet from the well-seasoned redwood tanks in which they mature. They are similar in style and quality to the Foppiano Petite Sirahs from much farther downstream along the Russian River.

Last of the Mendocino Petite Sirahs in volume and virtue is Fetzer's, which, like the winery's other reds, is so strongly marked by the cellar taste that it must be loved or despised on that ground alone. Otherwise the wine is dark, full-bodied and tannic. It comes from the winery's own vineyards north of Ukiah.

Central Coast Petite Sirahs

The Central Coast counties with the exception of Monterey do not support large plantings of petite sirah. In theory this is all for the best since Monterey has an appropriate climate and the rest of the region is generally a bit overwarm. Facts run just slightly counter to the theory in one of two outstanding bottlings.

Concannon Vineyard Petite Sirah, working against all the best academic advice, is one of the genuinely praiseworthy achievements made with the grape variety in California. It has a Livermore Valley appellation, where the climate is certified Region III, too warm.

The wine does betray its sunny origins. It has less tannin than a typical Petite Sirah from cooler regions, and, in compensation, that silky, supple feel on the palate usually attributed to natural glycerine in a warm-climate wine. The temptation exists to put a typical Concannon Petite Sirah into two blind tastings, one against a miscellany of Rhônes and the other against some Daõs from Portugal. The assumption is that it could fit comfortably into either camp. In any case it is very much a Mediterranean kind of red wine, the sort that wears a thick velvet glove over the most malleable of iron hands. Its essentially pleasing character wins it first places in blind tastings by connoisseurs and novices alike.

The other outstanding Petite Sirah of the region comes from more predictable sources. Mirassou has been making a Petite Sirah from a blend of Monterey and Santa Clara County grapes since the vintage of 1968. Cool, misty Monterey provides the acidic, fresh fruity character. The warmer hills east of San José add meat. The result is a wine of depth and durability. In one or two vintages, but especially 1969, the overlay of cellar tastes from Mirassou became too great to be enjoyable. In other years, however, this wine has been one of the most tantalizing exhibits in favor of

Petite Sirah as a varietal of classic stature. With Concannon, Souverain, and Cresta Blanca, it has been an essential in the definition of the varietal to date, a wine that has complex balance early and still gives every indication of having the strength to age into something finer, more subtle. In contrast to most of the north coast Petite Sirahs, the color is light and the tannic astringency played down, and still the flavor is intense.

Wente Bros. also has had a Petite Sirah since the vintage of 1968, but not so successful an effort in the early going. All the promise is there of a wine much like the Mirassou. The earliest editions, however, had too great a dose of sulphur to overlook. Succeeding ones have been moving steadily in the correct direction. San Martin also has a Petite Sirah, nonvintaged to date, but made from vineyards in similar locations to the Mirassou and Wente ones, and showing some signs of developing a similar style.

Several of the small cellars in and near Gilroy in south Santa Clara County produce Petite Sirahs with much the same strong, straightforward character that marks Foppiano, Parducci, and other North Coast bottlings. Guglielmo's Mount Madonna Petite Sirah, vintage dated, with a Santa Clara appellation of origin, comes very close in style and character to the Foppiano, especially for the distinct note of black pepper that is the hallmark of the varietal. The tiny Hecker Pass winery has a Petite Sirah with all the same qualifications.

From time to time Ridge Vineyards produces a Petite Sirah, usually from Napa Valley grapes. As always, the emphasis is on huge body, dark color, and great tannic austerity, sometimes at the expense of outweighing the grape flavors.

Other Petite Sirahs

In the San Joaquin Valley, Barengo Cellars produces and sells a dark, heavy, slightly off-dry Petite Sirah that pleases as a valley red, but runs somewhat counter to the general notion of the varietal. Down at Cucamonga, Brookside grows grapes for its Assumption Abbey Petite Sirah at its cool Rancho California vineyard, producing from them a light but dry and varietally correct wine. The Callaway Vineyards and Winery Petite Sirah may be a fine one when it appears. The first vintage was 1974.

PINOT NOIR

The literary history of Pinot Noir in California has been dolorous since 1896, when the great E. W. Hilgard of the University of California told his regents he had serious doubts about the grape variety and the quality of its wine.

Against that grain can be posed a luminous list of winemakers who choose a Pinot Noir as their greatest single triumph in the cellars. Louis M. Martini and André Tchelistcheff are but two from recent history.

The dilemma for drinkers of wine is that both sides are right. In the broad sum of history California Pinot Noirs have been pale shadows of the greatest red wines from the ancestral home of the grape variety, Burgundy. However, broad sums never are the essence of wine. On their best days California Pinot Noirs have been the stuff of legends. On their merely good days they have been wines to admire.

Pinot Noir's weaknesses, to dispose of them early, are mainly in the grape, which is genetically unstable, prone to all known ailments, and severe in its requirements on sun and soil. These woeful truths apply no matter where pinot noir vines grow, even in sainted Romanée. The wine of pinot noir, for its part, ferments tempestuously then ages in a series of sulks.

Through the 1940s and 1950s California styles tended to accept the weaknesses, working around them. Typically the wines fermented dry on their skins, to about 13 percent alcohol, then aged for a year or more in large, well-seasoned cooperage. From this they emerged with a pale brick red color, obvious astringency, and a relatively indistinct varietal character. A number of cellarmasters fattened up their Pinot Noirs with blend wine from petite sirah, adding to an already Rhônish character. Wines of the sort were and are uncommonly durable. The outstanding examples of pure durability are the 1880s Inglenooks, much faded now but still alive. Wines from more recent vintages have been more than merely durable. André Tchelistcheff's 1947 from Beaulieu Vineyard continues, today, to be rich, exquisitely balanced, a flawless companion to the cheeses after a memorable dinner. It has not been anything less since 1950. A good many others have lasted fifteen years without fading.

During the 1960s Californians at last began to work toward the Burgundian strengths of pinot noir, in search of a thick, even meaty red wine. James D. Zellerbach made the first essential contribution to the new age when he used small barrels to age his wines. Zellerbach's Hanzell wines did not, however, become Burgundies. His vineyards, tipped sharply to the south and slightly to the west, were too sunny to allow that. Later growers of pinot noir have been migrating steadily toward cooler climates for new plantings. The two prime examples are the southern quarter of the Napa Valley, especially the district called Carneros, and the Salinas Valley of Monterey County from Gonzales down to Greenfield. These areas, between them, have yielded most of the richly memorable Pinot Noirs since 1968. At the same time, the U.C.-Davis and commercial nurseries have been sorting clones carefully to get rid of enfeebling virus diseases in the vines and to intensify the character of wines from the variety.

Clonal sorting is more important for pinot noir than most other grapes because the variety is notorious for its genetic changeability. Burgundy has at least fifteen recognized clones, or strains of pinot noir. California has three or four, including the one until recently identified as gamay beaujolais. Karl Wente, an able vineyardist as well as a fine winemaker, thinks that clonal blending may be the key to a greater future for California Pinot Noir. After a vine by vine tramp through the vineyards at Romanée he came away convinced that soil has less to do with the greatness of that place than a magical balance of clones, or even varieties of Burgundian grapes.

When connoisseurs talk about great red Burgundies they describe the wines as kingly, or decadently rich. Certainly California Pinot Noirs are neither kings, nor decadently rich. The best ones are ample, fleshy wines, but too soft to be kingly. Because the variety yields wines not especially tart or tannic, a fine Pinot Noir is as soft and rich on the palate as tender beef and just as subtle, which makes the meaty analogy a useful one. The U.C.-Davis flavor association uses pepperminty as the definitive grace note in Pinot Noir. André Tchelistcheff identifies a good one by the tiniest reflect of raisin in the aftertaste.

Pinot Noirs made after the Burgundian rather than Rhônish style mature quickly. Typical examples develop by their fourth year, and begin to slip before they are ten.

The jury will be out in California for a time yet, waiting to see how well the new thoughts of earlier picking, cooler climates, and small barrel aging come together in matured wines. Compared to Cabernet Sauvignon there continues a dearth of special selections, suggesting that the winemakers themselves continue to look ahead. But the frequency of good vintages is improving, and so are the releases of special lots of Pinot Noir.

Napa Valley Pinot Noirs

The Napa Valley is the center of aesthetic ferment on just what Pinot Noir ought to be in California, and thus the focal point of hope and despair.

There is an almost universal temptation to do the purist thing and make 100 percent Pinot Noir varietals, in the hope that improved vineyard location will be one enhancement and improved clonal selection another. In practice many cellars do some blending with the assorted gamays and petite sirah while the vineyard purification is in progress.

Blend grapes, incidentally, are easy to spot in a Pinot Noir. The variety's color is a light, true scarlet for lack of any violet pigmentation. Not even a faint purple tone intrudes in the wine unless it comes from a blend grape.

Blending aside there are two basic schools of thought on style in the Napa Valley. One favors overt flavors of European oak in the finished wine. The other school wishes to keep the flavor of the grape unmasked by any flavor from wood. The proponents of European oak include Beaulieu Vineyard, Heitz Cellars, Freemark Abbey, Robert Mondavi, Sterling Vineyard, and Souverain of Rutherford. The nonwood stylists are Beringer, The Christian Brothers, Inglenook Vineyard, Charles Krug, and Louis M. Martini. All but Martini use Napa Valley as the appellation of origin. Only The Christian Brothers is not vintage dated.

Beaulieu Vineyards has a long and remarkably consistent record with Pinot Noir, principally because André Tchelistcheff loved to struggle with it throughout his career there. Some evolution has occurred. Before 1965 the principal vineyards were near Rutherford; since that vintage the dominant planting has been at Carneros some miles closer to San Francisco and the Bay. Also, older BV Pinot Noirs aged in American oak casks rather than European oak. Both the new vineyards and the new oak have tended to soften or fatten the wine, to make it meatier and somewhat more Burgundian in character. However, Tchelistcheff–and now his successors–have clung to the old Rhônish reflect of very ripe grapes in the aftertaste, and the long wait that puts a hint of aged bouquet in the wine even before it goes to bottle. One does not tinker too much with legends.

Freemark Abbey has taken an approach similar to Beaulieu's since its debut with the vintage of 1968. The wines, from vineyards near Rutherford, are a bit paler in color than the BVs, an accurate reflection of a lighter body, though by no means a signal of neutral character.

Robert Mondavi Pinot Noirs have, comparatively, emphasized fresh fruity characteristics of the grape since the first vintage, 1966. Possibly the freshness comes from picking the fruit a few days earlier than the others, fermenting the wine at a slower rate by keeping it a few degrees cooler, or bottling at an earlier time. In any case, the raisiny reflect in the finish is diminished to near zero. The complication of flavor from the oak works against a different kind of foreground, resulting in a wine of tremendous but ephemeral youthful charm. In 1971 Robert Mondavi Pinot Noir made a considerable number of people think they were drinking a true Burgundy, but that wine appears to have been an unrepeatable curiosity.

Most of the grapes come from vineyards between Oakville and the little city of Napa.

Sterling Vineyards made a wine with considerable kinships to the Mondavi in 1971 although, somehow, it remained unmistakably Californian. The pedigree is amazing. The Sterling vines were planted as gamay beaujolais in the late 1960s, in the warmish Calistoga district. One of the first crops yielded a wine of surprising depth and finesse, which sold as Gamay Beaujolais. Later, when gamay beaujolais was botanically identified as a clone of pinot noir, Sterling announced that it would make the wine each year, then decide at bottling time whether it had enough power to be called Pinot Noir, or enough delicacy to merit the name Gamay Beaujolais. After several years hand running of no Gamay Beaujolais, the Sterling managers opted to aim for Pinot Noir in every vintage. The winemaker, Rick Forman, is as baffled by the wine as the authorities are, and as happy to drink it.

As a man who played the role of *éleveur* to establish a label before getting his own winery into full production, Joe Heitz managed in ten years to present an encyclopedic range of styles in Pinot Noir. The 1959, 1960, and 1961 vintages came entirely from the Zellerbach estate in Sonoma. One lot of 1962 came from there while another was made in the Napa Valley. In 1963 Heitz made a small lot of his own, and bought another from a Napa neighbor. The 1966 was another assembled Napa Valley wine. In 1968 and 1969 Heitz made all of his own wine. The Hanzell vintages smelled Burgundian and tasted Californian. The 1963 and 1966 vintages fell into the old, Rhônish style of California. In 1968 and 1969 Heitz began to draw near the Robert Mondavi style, although his wines were a shade more delicate in fruit flavor. A 1972 continued in the style set by the 1968.

The missing years hint that Heitz does not always find enough to like in pinot noir grapes. He does not. In fact, he has no assured supply of the variety. The presence of a Pinot Noir under his label is therefore something of a guarantee that the vintage was a sturdy one in the Napa Valley.

Louis M. Martini, ever reliable, makes Pinot Noir to taste first, last, and always of the grapes from which it came, and not of the barrel in which it developed. If there is any flavor other than grape, it is a faint, earthy quality imparted by the ancient 1,000-gallon oak casks Louis P. Martini favors for all classic reds as his father did before him. The result consistently is one of the most distinctive wines in the state, delicate, subtle, elegantly balanced, and thus not reminiscent of either Burgundian or Rhônish styles from either France or California. Although delicate and early to mature, a Martini Pinot Noir from a good vintage often fares better after ten years than weightier wines from elsewhere in the valley.

The first vintage-dated Martini Pinot Noir, the 1957, came entirely from the winery's vineyards at Carneros. It was Louis M. Martini's personal choice as the best wine he ever made, and he still drank it with something very close to ecstasy in 1973. The next vintage was 1962, then came 1965. Since then the parade has skipped only 1967. The Carneros vineyards provide the base for all Martini Pinot Noirs, but only the Special Selection bottlings are from that single vineyard.

The Christian Brothers' nonvintage Pinot Noir is cast somewhat in the same vein as the Martini, a light, subtle wine with the unmistakably earthy hint of old casks in its bouquet. It does not have as many layers for the palate to sort through as the Martini, but, at its modest price, is a wine to know.

The Pinot Noirs of three sizable wineries, Beringer, Inglenook, and Charles Krug, all fall in the middle realm for depth of character. Neither do they tip heavily toward any cellar style.

During the family ownership, Beringer Pinot Noirs were indistinct to say the best for them. The corporate proprietors from Nestlé have restored the essential character of the variety in a light, fresh wine. It has been steadily that since the vintage of 1969. The Inglenook Pinot Noirs of recent vintages have arrived at the same state from the opposite direction. In the days of the family ownership, Inglenook made the wine as a fascinating bridge between the soft delicacy of the Louis M. Martini's and the rich astringency of the Beaulieu's, but the last of those was the 1964. Of the three, only Charles Krug appears headed in the direction of richer character. Earlier vintages of Pinot Noir from Krug tended to be light and a bit sharp. As the winery's Carneros vineyards mature, the wines seem to be gaining in body and varietal aroma. Also, the expanding library of new oak cooperage at Krug begins to be perceptible in the nose of vintages from 1972 onward.

Several newcomers have begun to offer Pinot Noirs in recent years, but have not shown enough vintages to establish a position. Souverain of Rutherford has released two; Burgess Cellars, Carneros Creek, Caymus, and Stonegate have released one each. Two additional cellars have Pinot Noirs from 1974 aging in cask. All of these are wines of more than mere acceptability, with the Carneros Creek the most promising of them.

Although Napa Valley Pinot Noirs are not infinitely durable, vintages do make a considerable difference. In quick review:

1965—A sturdy vintage. The Louis M. Martini Special Selection was the best bet as of 1975.

1966—A drowsy summer produced high alcohols and bouquetish rather than fresh wines. Heitz Cellars, released only in 1972, remains toweringly strong.

1967—Generally a washout after early fall rains. No wines of interest survive.

1968—The glories of youth have passed, but the wines of a famous vintage retain a certain weary charm eight years after. Any 1968 is worth checking out, though individual bottles have faded too far even when properly cellared.

1969—The wines never did have the charm of the 1968s, but they plod along in healthy condition. The richer ones have aged into something modestly graceful.

1970—The vintage splits the difference between 1968 and 1969, being more durable than the former and more charming than the latter. In 1975 they provided reliably mature bottles for current consumption.

1971—In general this seems to be the finest vintage for Pinot Noir since 1968. Robert Mondavi and Sterling in particular have developed as wines of depth and complexity, but all seem successful.

1972—Early fall rains caught a few producers, but most came very close to the 1968s with wines of great youthful charm.

1973—Another difficult vintage for producers whose vineyards ripened late, but a promising one for everyone who beat the rains.

1974—This looks to be another vintage in the sunny vein of 1966, but new plantings since then may give it a different face.

Sonoma and Mendocino Pinot Noirs

As always, Sonoma County serves as a microcosm of the whole coast region, partly because its climate ranges so widely, more because its winemakers are an anarchical enough lot to pursue a variety of styles.

The Sonoma Valley is considerably more proven than the Russian River watershed. Logically the Sonoma Valley is well suited to pinot noir. Much of it is Region I, cooled by misty breezes blowing off San Francisco Bay. The hills, a mixture of steep slopes and gentle rolls, offer great expanses of the lean soils pinot noir seems to favor most. A considerable number of them turn their backs to the afternoon sun, also a benefit to the grape. Plantings in the Russian River region are too new to be judged for themselves, let alone against any other district. However, the hills west of U.S. Highway 101 seem to offer a promising combination of growing conditions. A number of people have staked a considerable acreage on the assumption.

The Pinot Noir producers in the Sonoma Valley are Buena Vista, Hanzell, Sebastiani, and Z-D, with all but the last-named having relatively long records to assess. In the Russian River, Korbel, Pedroncelli, Simi, and Sonoma Vineyards are newcomers all.

Hanzell, the fountainhead of Burgundian style in California Pinot Noir, has stuck to its original last throughout its episodic career. The founder, J. D. Zellerbach, hit a lucky streak of cool years in the late 1950s and early 1960s. His wines of that era were big, rich rascals of astonishing longevity. Only the 1957 went to market under his label. (Earlier vintages did not measure up to his expectations, and were sold privately with simple identifying tags. The 1959 and later vintages went to Heitz Cellars in bulk as part of the estate sale after Zellerbach died in 1963. All survived in pleasing health by 1975.) The late N. Douglas Day started the revival of

Hanzell with a 1965 of Hanzellian power, but not much finesse. In truth, the wine at nine remained a rough old cob. Subsequent editions from the Day years migrated slowly toward finer characteristics. The vintage of 1975 came from a Hanzell in its third ownership. Whatever else happens, California sun will shine through any Burgundian veil.

Z-D pushes power at the expense of elegance in much the same way as Hanzell. The proprietors, Norman deLeuze and Gino Zepponi, say their first vintage, 1969, was too light for their taste, and that the 1972 is the wine they envisioned making when they launched the winery in 1969. The earliest vintage is darker than California Pinot Noir tends to be, and remarkably tannic for a Pinot Noir from anywhere. The 1972 exceeds the debut bottling on both counts. The style is to ferment the wine dry on the skins, as in the olden days of Burgundy, and never to fine it during its career in small barrels.

For people who like fierce wines, all is well. Z-D Pinot Noirs are very cleanly made, not subject to spoilage. The question for the rest of us is whether the fruit flavors can outlast the hard edges of youth. The fruity characteristics of pinot noir have not shown great staying power, but, then, these grapes from a vineyard in the Napa half of the Carneros district have not behaved as pinot noir in other ways. The 1969 did not change noticeably through its first seven years.

Buena Vista Pinot Noirs bear some resemblance without being so uncompromising. They have a tart, almost austere quality in spite of being lighter in body and less intensely flavored. Perhaps this is how the grape grows in the district. It has been difficult to judge Buena Vista precisely because the firm bought much of its wine from other producers for several years while new vineyards were being planted and brought into production. Still, the appellation of origin was Sonoma, and winemaker Al Brett was able to specify the characteristics he wished to have. As new vintages are fermented at Buena Vista, the picture should clarify itself.

In any case, these are three Pinot Noirs to go with venison.

August Sebastiani is the old-fashioned Californian in the Sonoma Valley. His Pinot Noirs have the traditional casts of sun and wood aging about them, along with a discernible reinforcement from petite sirah. August would have it no other way. The petite sirah goes in because pinot noir is, in his view, too scrawny to make good wine by itself in California. The blended wine ages for three years or more in big redwood tanks then polishes up for a few months in small oak because the proprietor wishes to be sure of the harmonies before he lets anything out into the world.

Most of the appellations of origin have been California until recent times. The last few bottlings have carried North Coast Counties, or Sonoma. The older wines sometimes carried bin numbers, but no vintage dates. Since 1967's rich crop, they have borne dates.

The best of Sebastiani Pinot Noirs drive purists daft. They ignore Burgundian ideals, and are not altogether conscientious about being Pinot Noirs, but they are too enjoyable to be ignored. Their durability further recommends them. A private label bottling from 1964 was just getting into stride in 1974. There is no telling when the 1968 will reach the top of its form. In contrast, the Napans were fading before August Sebastiani moved his wine from big tanks to small barrels, let alone into bottles.

Of the producers in the Russian River Valley, only Pedroncelli has offered enough wines to be judged with any certainty. After a few undated bottlings, the brothers Pedroncelli began vintage dating with the 1968, and have continued yearly since. Like Louis P. Martini, they mistrust any overt taste of oak in their finished wines. They tend to make their wines slightly heavier, or less delicate than the Martini, but enough similarity exists so that fans of the one likely will be fans of the other.

The appellation of origin is Sonoma County. The Pedroncellis own pinot noir vines in the Dry Creek Valley, and buy some grapes from growers in the Alexander Valley.

At Simi, winemaker Mary Ann Graf has had André Tchelistcheff as a tutor through her first several vintages. The vintage-dated Pinot Noirs, with Alexander Valley as their appellation of origin, show the fine Tchelistcheffian hand. The reflect of raisin is faintly present in the finish, as is the bouquetish note of a longish career in new oak. However, the overall impression is of a wine less sturdy, less intense than the Beaulieus. In defense, 1971 was a first try, and 1972 was a gloomy vintage. It seems a wine worth watching for the next several years.

The Foppiano Pinot Noirs have been clean and very straightforward in 1971 and 1972, made husky, aged in large, well-seasoned cooperage, and bottled for the flavor of their grapes. The family vineyard at Healdsburg supplies all of the grapes; the appellation is Russian River Valley.

Korbel's nonvintage California Pinot Noirs of recent release have been among the most agreeable of the commercially assembled wines available. The style of these has leaned toward fresh, delicate balance without great complexity. A program to produce richer, vintage-dated Pinot Noirs from the winery's own vineyards is well under way.

The most promising replacement for the earlier Korbels seems to be the Pinot Noir offered by Geyser Peak under its Voltaire label.

Late in 1974 Souverain of Alexander Valley released its first Pinot Noir, from the vintage of 1972. It was sound wine from a difficult vintage, but not the one to judge the winery by.

Somebody has to bring up the rear in any grouping. Sonoma Vineyards does that job for Sonoma County, maybe even all North Coast Pinot Noirs, with a thin and somewhat sharp example.

Across the county line, Parducci Vineyards makes a dark, husky, straightforward Pinot Noir. It carries a vintage date and a Mendocino appellation. John Parducci is another of the old-line California winemakers who mistrusts small oak because too much flavor lurks in the wood. His reds age in middle-sized redwood tanks until they soften, then go to bottle with as much grape flavor as careful cellaring can preserve.

Cresta Blanca makes a nonvintage Pinot Noir with some hints of wood aging, and slightly more of the reflect of raisins that comes with letting the fruit ripen an extra few days. The wine tends to be pleasantly balanced without being intense or full bodied.

Mendocino may develop a different style for Pinot Noir as the cool, foggy Anderson Valley district develops. The tiny Husch winery had the earliest evidence aging in wood as of 1975.

Central Coast Pinot Noirs

The eventual quality of Pinot Noirs from south of San Francisco Bay remains largely hidden from view.

Except for Almadén and Paul Masson the history of the varietal is surprisingly brief. Wente Bros., for example, entered the lists only with the vintage of 1963. Mirassou Vineyards waited until 1966 to make a Pinot Noir. The roster of small producers was equally tardy to begin, and remains spasmodic as well.

The late blooming of Pinot Noir in the region means that the origins of individual bottlings are diffuse. The small acreages of older vines in Alameda and Santa Clara counties tend ever more to lose their identities in larger blends. The establishment of vineyards in Monterey and San Benito counties is too recent for great truths to be known about their grapes.

Some few bottlings have come from individual vineyards, or sharply defined districts. The volumes are tiny and the sources scattered. The evidence to date suggests that Monterey County may be the best hope because so much of it is climate Region I.

Chalone would be the single most encouraging piece of evidence in favor of Monterey Pinot Noir if the vineyard were not so remote from the others, and if one thirsty person could not drink the entire annual production between vintages. Prodigious 1969 yielded 600 bottles of an intricate, symmetrical wine with as many charms in youth as it is likely to develop with age. Later vintages have been as small or smaller.

Proprietor Dick Graff ferments and ages the Pinot Noir from his toil-worn vines in small oak barrels in an effort to achieve wine as thick and fleshy as one from some rich part of the Côte d'Or in Burgundy. He gets a paler, leaner wine, but a classic Pinot Noir for all of that, and a persuasive argument that a wine of the variety does not have to be decadently rich to be called great.

It is hard to make a case for tiny wineries doing a finer job than larger ones with most varietal wine types in California. Certainly miniature cellars have not done more with Cabernet Sauvignon or Chardonnay than wineries of considerable volume. Pinot Noir, however, may be a justification all by itself for the place that makes somewhere from three to twenty barrels a year, shepherding each through its cranky adolescence as an individual. Such as Chalone and Hanzell and Z-D have made wines with greater character than any of the larger firms, possibly excepting Robert Mondavi.

The tantalizing hope that other vineyards in Monterey County will produce wines of stature equal to Chalone's is only a hope in 1975. The larger vineyards below Chalone on the Salinas Valley floor have yielded lighter, lesser wines thus far, though the oldest vines there are only ten years old. Most proprietors have continued to blend their Monterey crops with grapes or wines from elsewhere.

Mirassou Vineyards is the consistent exception to the general practice of blending. The winery has offered vintage-dated Monterey Pinot Noirs yearly since 1966, with the lone exception of 1968. It also has produced special lots of Monterey Pinot Noir in several vintages. Consistently they have combined light body with intense fruit flavor. Fruit flavor is too general a description. People are beginning to suspect that Monterey County produces less of the sun-dried fruit flavor that marks most of California, and more of the faintly green plantlike note that identifies many French reds. The Mirassou Pinot Noirs lend credence to the notion. Small oak cooperage lends an agreeable complication to the wines.

If there is a point on which to quibble it is the imbalance between the intense aroma and the lack of body.

Paul Masson made a sort of inaugural gesture to its Monterey vineyards with a special lot of Pinot Noir called Cuvée 943, released in 1972. The near future should see the release of additional wines purely from Monterey County grapes. Meantime, the regular bottlings of Paul Masson California Pinot Noir are blends of years and places, light, soft, and straightforwardly fruity.

The other proprietor of Salinas Valley pinot noir vineyards old enough to bear crops is Wente Bros., which has not made a Monterey appellation wine. Wente owns a substantial acreage of pinot noir in the Livermore Valley, and blends the two.

Karl Wente frankly keeps an eye on Burgundy as he makes his Pinot Noir, not so much for techniques as for end results. Wente thinks California pinot noir grapes too fragile to make a legendary wine as they exist. In the absence of the diverse pinot noir clones he feels to be the heart of great Burgundies, Wente is using a country cousin of pinot noir called pinot st. george to add girth and color to his wine.

His fermenting and cellaring techniques are somewhere between the old Rhônish style and the new Burgundian one as these are understood in California. He ferments for a soft, fruity wine then ages it in well-used oak oval casks for no more than a year in order to preserve the taste of fresh fruit. Curiously, the wines are only modestly attractive in youth, but a few seasons of bottle age turn them complex, and elegantly balanced. For example, the 1967 had reached a silky, supple plateau of excellence by 1972 and still was on that plateau in 1975.

The Monterey grapes are present in large enough volume to give some of the faint green plantlike note that also identifies the Chalone and Mirassou Pinot Noirs as coming from there.

Almadén Pinot Noir, nonvintage, with a California appellation of origin, is dominated by grapes from the company's 500-plus acres of pinot noir in San Benito County. The wine is bouquetish, as all Almadén reds are, and plausibly full bodied, though not a definitive example of the grape's varietal character. A vintage-dated bottling appears from time to time, always much the same style as the nonvintage wine, though usually with a more defined flavor of pinot noir to boost it along. Both wines are among the finest of Almadén's reds, exceedingly pleasant reminders of how good an inexpensive varietal can be in California.

Santa Clara County is two separate districts. The south half of the county, from Morgan Hill down to Gilroy, is warm and sunny, Region III in the U.C.-Davis climate summaries. The west hills from San José northward are fog-beset Region I. Predictably the west hills yield the better Pinot Noirs of the two districts, but even they do not seem as promising as Monterey or several parts of the Napa-Sonoma-Mendocino region.

The proprietors of Ridge Vineyards are not much taken with pinot noir because it lacks color and astringent vitality. The single attempt, a 1971 from vineyards near the winery, came to market accompanied by a glum appraisal from the winemaker, who deplored the lack of color, of varietal character, and of regional character, but allowed the wine's drinkability.

David Bruce holds pinot noir from the Santa Cruz Mountains in higher esteem. He ferments the grapes from his two patches of vines in the old Burgundian way, with skins and juice together for at least fourteen days, sometimes more, then ages the wine in small barrels for eighteen months to two years before bottling. The result is dark, rough-hewn wine of undoubted pinot noir characteristic, but not as full-flavored a bottle as one might expect from the cool, shy-bearing vineyards or the method of vinification.

San Martin offers a limited bottling of Pinot Noir from the San Ysidro vineyards near Gilroy. First offered from the vintage of 1968, the wine bears all the marks of too much sun for the variety. It retains only faint traces of the rich flavor of pinot noir. The regular bottling has more flesh on its bones than the special one. San Martin will want reevaluation as its big holdings near King City in Monterey County come into bearing.

Weibel produces a limited quantity of vintage-dated Pinot Noir from its vineyards at Mission San José, legally in Alameda County but environmentally an extension of the Santa Clara Valley. It is a soft, lighthearted red wine, most probably the naïve little domestic Burgundy that amused with its presumption. The regular nonvintage Weibel Pinot Noirs come mainly from Mendocino County grapes. They are sound commercial reds and priced as such.

A handful of Pinot Noirs from the country wineries in the Central Coast region taste typically of country red wine more than they taste typically of the variety. The modest prices allow easy enjoyment of such as Bertero and Villa Armando provided the drinker raises the glass in a correct frame of mind.

Other Pinot Noirs

California Wine Association offers a sound, commercial Pinot Noir under its Eleven Cellars label. The wine is purchased in bulk and aged at the company's producing winery in Delano, in the southern San Joaquin Valley. Llords & Elwood Velvet Hill Pinot Noir is an assembled wine of modest charms sold by a Los Angeles firm which contracts with other producers for the fermenting and aging of its wines. Finally, Brookside makes a Pinot Noir from its Rancho California vineyards for sale under the Assumption Abbey label. Both it and the Eleven Cellars are light in character and style. The Llords & Elwood strives for weight.

RUBY CABERNET

The first commercial Ruby Cabernet in the history of the world was made from the vintage of 1946 by a Fresno winery long since disappeared.

Ruby cabernet is the grape variety developed at the University of California at Davis by Dr. H. P. Olmo for the specific goal of opening the enormous expanses of the San Joaquin Valley to distinctive table winemaking.

For the precise record, ruby cabernet is a cross of a carignane seedling with cabernet sauvignon pollen. The cross was made in 1936. Originally known as station seedling 234F2, the first vine bore its first fruit in 1940, producing one half-bottle of wine which tasted fine enough to encourage propagation of the variety. The long, hot summer of the San Joaquin needed a vine that would retain acidity until ripe, one characteristic of carignane, but it also needed one with some subtlety of flavor, the contribution of cabernet to the cross.

Made to its fullest potential as a dry, age-worthy red, Ruby Cabernet can bear a considerable resemblance to Cabernet Sauvignon. The differences are not a matter of falling short, but rather of going past the original to become an exaggeration of it. If a proper Cabernet Sauvignon's aroma is tealike, an all-out Ruby Cabernet's is the last cup in a well-steeped pot. A winemaker with a sense of style can temper Ruby Cabernet into a wine of considerable charm.

As a commercial wine Ruby Cabernet started slow. Through the 1950s there were but a handful of small lots, most of them made with at least half an eye to helping the university learn more about the variety's behavior in a spectrum of locations. The first critical splash came in 1966, as best I recall the date, when East-Side Winery of Lodi showed its Royal Host Ruby Cabernet at a major tasting of Cabernet Sauvignons in San Francisco. It was not the wine of the night, but impressive enough to send a number of social and critical lions out on a hunt for more of their new discovery. Times have grown steadily better for the varietal since then.

A few more than a dozen Ruby Cabernets are at hand at present. As the acreage figures suggest, nearly all are dominated by San Joaquin Valley grapes. The range of style is surprisingly diverse.

San Joaquin Valley Ruby Cabernets

Three masters have made Ruby Cabernet in the San Joaquin Valley. Dino Barengo of Barengo Cellars, Reg Gianelli of East-Side, and David Ficklin of Ficklin Vineyards between them have demonstrated more of the grape's potential for excellent red wine than all the rest together.

For year in, year out consistency Barengo may deserve the title of grand master. The wine has come from Dino's own small vineyard near the winery, on the north limit of Lodi town, and it has been a polished, thoughtfully balanced red that

An immaculately tended vineyard at the Ficklin cellars. (HAROLYN THOMPSON)

belonged somewhere in the upper quarter of all California reds of its season, ahead of several of the less distinctive commercial Cabernet Sauvignons. It always tempered the astringent austerity of the grape variety with a few fat flavors of ripe fruit, though never so much as to harm durability. The durability runs at least seven years according to the oldest bottle in my cellar, but three years will bring a good lot to maturity.

The current corporate proprietors of Barengo Cellars have broadened the market beyond the ability of Dino's vineyard to produce, but have retained both style and character.

In spite of the original single vineyard origin Barengo always used California as the appellation, and used bin numbers rather than vintage dates. Both of those practices remain in effect.

The Ficklin Ruby Cabernet, sold only at the winery door, is of similar character. David Ficklin makes the wine for his family table and to help university explorations into the character of its grape variety. The Ficklin family vineyard adjoining the winery at Madera is in a climate considerably warmer than Barengo's, but the senses of what a claretish red should be are so similar in both men that the wines emerge much like each other. The Ficklin is a shade softer in acidity, and a shade drier in compensation.

Collectors hang on to Ficklin Ruby Cabernets, and are required to write their own codes on the homemade labels. There is neither vintage date nor bin number.

The late Reg Gianelli at East-Side took a most austere view of Ruby Cabernet during his long tenure. His successors continue the style he set. Royal Host Ruby Cabernets are dry, unrelentingly herbaceous or tealike or whatever the exact flavor association, and, what is more, are perceptibly complicated by the bouquets of long aging in small, well-seasoned oak upright tanks. The wines are so uncompromising, in fact, that they constantly call to mind the early statement by Dr. Olmo that tasters find the aroma of Cabernet more easily in Ruby Cabernet than in Cabernet Sauvignon. They are superior bottlings to people with a taste for austere reds, and a bit toilsome to people who like wines to be cuddly.

East-Side is a cooperative. The grapes for its Ruby Cabernet come from member vineyards, nearly all of them on the plain east of Lodi town. The appellation is California; there is no vintage date or other indication of individual lots, except for the ones scrawled on the labels by people who collect this wine along with Barengo and Ficklin. Before 1974 the label was simply Royal Host. Since 1974, the premier Ruby Cabernet has been Conti Royale, produced by Royal Host.

Since 1973, several of the larger wineries in the San Joaquin have offered Ruby Cabernets in substantial volumes. They were required to wait until the acreage became large enough to support mass marketing programs.

The bigger producers compromise rather more with the old, heavy, slightly sweet style of valley reds than does Barengo. However, the Ruby Cabernets of such as E. & J. Gallo and M. LaMont lean toward classically dry red much more than Burgundies from the same labels.

M. LaMont Ruby Cabernet, made by Bear Mountain Winery from grapes grown in the Bakersfield region, came first, and has defined the center ground of style for all Ruby Cabernets. The wine is soft, a shade off-dry, but light-bodied enough to be called delicate. E. & J. Gallo and the Ambassador Ruby Cabernet from A. Perelli-Minetti & Sons have been in the same vein since their appearance in 1974. The M. LaMont remains the most distinctive of the lot, though pressed closely by Ambassador.

Giumarra Vineyards, near neighbor to Bear Mountain, calls its vintage-dated wine from ruby cabernet by the name of Cabernet Rouge. The first vintage, 1972, was thick-bodied, with some tannic bite to compensate for the intensely ripe, almost raisiny varietal character. Setrakian Ruby Cabernet, made at California Growers winery southeast of Fresno, is kindred in style to the Giumarra, but lacking the tannic austerity that helps save the Giumarra from seeming over coarse.

Other Ruby Cabernets

A few vineyards of ruby cabernet edge out into the coast counties, but nowhere near enough to supply the volumes of wine behind coastal producers' labels. Almadén, Inglenook, and Paul Masson offer budget Ruby Cabernets for the obvious commercial reason. A handful of small producers such as Heitz offer an occasional Ruby Cabernet out of more complex motivations.

Since the Ruby Cabernets of the commercial labels compete with those from San Joaquin producers, and come from vineyards there, notes on them follow directly after those on the pure valley labels.

Inglenook Navalle Ruby Cabernet has been the class of the budget-priced field since its introduction in 1973. It is a light, deft wine that shows more clearly than most of its mates the inheritance from cabernet sauvignon, and which has been reliably free of any off-note from its handling in the winery.

Almadén introduced its Ruby Cabernet at the beginning of 1975. The only one of the lot aged in oak, for the avowed purpose of making it age-worthy, the wine has nothing definable wrong with it, but fails to please. It is just plain too much of a good thing, like that Hungarian linguist in *Pygmalion,* or a friendly puppy weighing more than forty pounds.

A handful of costlier Ruby Cabernets round out the field.

Twice in its existence Heitz Cellars has purchased Ruby Cabernet for sale under its label. The first was a vintage 1962 sold in 1965. The second was a nonvintage sold in 1973 and was still to be found in a few shops in 1975. The more recent model caused Joe Heitz to be mindful of the old Olmo caveat about cabernet character in huge abundance. He tempered the basic wine with a small percentage of Grignolino, which also had the effect of making the finished product a bit more tart than Ruby Cabernet usually is. Though not a completely classical red, it is very fine, a tribute to the grape-growing capacities of the San Joaquin Valley from a man with a considerable regard for the potential of the place.

Up in the Sacramento Valley a tiny cellar called Butte Creek is expanding upon the literature of claretish wines from sun-drenched vineyards right on the spot. The first vintage, 1973, yielded a surprisingly tart, highly tannic, purplish wine of exceeding strong flavor. The wincmaker, Dr. Marion Baldy, deliberately avoided a malolactic fermentation, which both softens a wine and adds complexity, in order to keep her Ruby Cabernet fresh and potentially long-lived.

The Butte Creek winery is in the little college town of Chico. The vineyards are a few miles north, near the old vineyard property Senator Leland Stanford called Viña.

The roster of Ruby Cabernets is scheduled to expand by several labels during late 1976 and early 1977.

 ZINFANDEL

In the classic formulation of the aptitude tests is Zinfandel . . .

- The mystery wine of California
- A light, claretish red
- America's Beaujolais
- Rosé
- A rare white wine
- An even rarer white sparkling wine
- A sweet, naturally portish red
- All of the above?

The answer, as all veteran victims of multiple-choice examinations know, is all of the above, although the degrees of truth vary even more than on quizzes about politics.

The mystery wine part of the story comes from zinfandel's lost ancestry. The legendary tale has been that Agoston Haraszthy brought the cuttings around Cape Horn in 1861 for planting in Buena Vista vineyards at Sonoma. This account has it that the identifying tag was muddled en route, or that there never was one. The grape variety, depending on which fate one chose for the tag, was an obscure German variety called zierfandler, or a secret treasure from Hungary known only to Colonel Haraszthy. The more prosaic assumption has been that nobody knew who brought it or from where, and that Haraszthy's importation was only one of several if he brought any zinfandel at all. In any case, there is no grape named zinfandel in old ampelographies from Europe, and no wine of even faintly similar character was made on the continent until cuttings went back there a few years ago.

Scholarly research by Dr. H. P. Olmo and his associates at the University of California at Davis now points strongly toward a south Italian grape called *primitivo* as the ancestor, although its wine is very different in character from all contemporary California Zinfandels. The news is going to ruin a day for all those Haraszthyian romantics who could smell the volcanic soils of Hungary in every sip of Zinfandel.

The many possible variations in the wine come from the grape variety's uncommon flexibility. The vine will grow tolerably well in every climate from Region I through Region IV, bear well, and ripen readily. Once harvested, the fruit ferments without coaxing from the winemaker.

As red wine, Zinfandel has more potential tannic astringency than Pinot Noir or the other Burgundians, but less than either Cabernet Sauvignon or Petite Sirah. The berryish fruit flavors are tart, not round like Pinot Noir's, and yet a Zinfandel is not austere in the way of a Cabernet. White juice opens up all avenues of color. A good vineyard of zinfandel is, said quickly, the master of a thousand disguises.

Made true to type in the middling warmth of Regions II and III where the vine prospers best, Zinfandel is a distinctively aromatic dry red wine that can be aged for several years, but does not demand the time. Whether any one bottling is lightly claretish or an American Beaujolais depends on where the winemaker stands on the characteristic merits of cabernet sauvignon and pinot noir. The confirmed cabernet person will coax out tannins and other austerities for his Zinfandel. The pinot fancier will make his wine juicier, though the notion of a red Loire seems more apt than a Beaujolais to my palate.

In either case, the young wine should be expected to reveal its true identity through its distinctive aroma. The U.C.-Davis flavor association list keys on the tart taste of blackberries, which points accurately enough to the quality that separates Zinfandel from other varietal wines. Cabernet Sauvignon and its relatives evoke visions of herbs, trees, and other leaves and stems. Pinot Noir, for its part, rouses images of soft, meaty flavors. The tart fruit of Zinfandel stands apart from either of those, and is more distinctive than the "vinous" accorded Barbera and Petite Sirah.

The wine has been regarded with great favor since the 1880s, by winemakers for its reliability, and by foreign and domestic critics for its combination of easy companionship and distinct character.

Good as Zinfandel can be, often as it can surpass a mediocre Cabernet Sauvignon or Pinot Noir, it falls short of a titanic reputation for lack of the extra depths or infinite layers of flavor that define great wine. August Sebastiani once said it truly: Zinfandel is good to drink every day, not so great that it wears you out.

Like other red varietals of the second rank, Zinfandel has not inspired people to mark out vineyards where the variety comes to unspeakable perfection. However, there is a sort of tacit agreement among connoisseurs of Zinfandel that Sonoma County has an edge over the rest. It is not some Haraszthyian piece of romanticism; skilled tasters steadily rank Sonoma bottlings at the head of the list in blind tastings because they are more aromatic. Sonoma Zinfandels more than most others attain the claretish qualities that make some tasters use it as a sort of base level for Cabernet Sauvignon. In this scheme, any Cabernet that does not outrank a good Zinfandel is not a very good Cabernet.

Lodi, Mendocino, and Napa all can challenge the heartland with their best Zinfandels.

Experiments with white wines, sparklers, and other such mainly reflect the economics of abundance rather than natural suitability. Zinfandel does, however, make an excellent rosé.*

Napa Valley Zinfandels

One of the tributes to Zinfandel's character is that the Napa Valley community of winemakers worked as hard to improve it as any other varietal throughout the great flurries of critical interest in Cabernet Sauvignon after 1966. It is a classic case of craftsmen not losing sight of a bread-and-butter livelihood during an era of improbable glamour. Most of the producers in this valley full of cabernet sauvignon

---

* See page 299 in the section on varietal rosés.

vines aim, logically, in the general direction of claretish austerity, but a few pursue softer thoughts to estimable ends.

The sizable acreage devoted to zinfandel lies mainly on the valley floor north of Rutherford town, or within climate Regions II and III. The soils are fertile in most of the vineyards.

Louis M. Martini uses both Napa and Sonoma County vineyards to make a Zinfandel of delicate but impeccably polished character. Nothing else is as deft, or, at least, nothing else comes so close to my prejudiced view of what Zinfandel ought to be. A Louis M. Martini Zinfandel from a ripe year tastes as fine as and not unlike wild blackberries themselves when you can sit there in a shaded patch with the smell of the vines and the woods and you cannot pick fast enough to take any home.

Louis M. worked for his sense of style. He made vintage-dated wines from the variety as early as 1936 and kept at it through all the lean years after, when other producers did not pay much heed. Louis P. has kept the faith since the late 1950s. Essentially the wine is made as other Martini reds: after fermenting in open tanks it goes into large, well-seasoned redwood for a time. Later, if a particular lot has special character, it may move into 1,000-gallon oak ovals for its finishing touches. Most go to bottle about eighteen months after the harvest, and onto the market a few months after that, mostly fresh, but graced by the faint first hints of bouquet from the ancient cooperage. A few select lots stay at the winery for later release as Private Reserve or Special Selection wines.

Old Louis always said that his Zinfandel was produced to be drunk when it was four years old. He said that even when he served a bottle in its twenties and watched everybody at the table to be sure they knew what they were tasting. Still, his basic advice was and is correct. The wine is in mature balance at four, ready to cheer novices and skilled hobbyists alike. However, it is not a time to cry if a few bottles of a fine vintage such as 1968 get lost in the cellar until they are six, or ten.

In Lee Stewart's day Souverain Zinfandels were big, rough-edged rascals. The new proprietors of the label had not altered the wines very much through the vintage of 1973, except to augment the overlay of small wood aging. Souverain Zinfandels continue to be as densely flavored and tannic as young bottles of the varietal can be, which is surprisingly dense and tannic. The vintages of 1967 and 1968, the oldest Souverain Zinfandels with vintage dates, suggest that the wine never will become as highly polished as a first-rate vintage of Martini, but its burly charm is more than adequate compensation in an alternative style.

At opposite ends of the valley, Robert Mondavi and Sterling Vineyards once again—as in the case of Pinot Noir—have strikingly similar ideas about what a varietal should be. Both are more temperate about tannin than Souverain, both favor fuller body than Martini, and both polish the strongly berryish fruit flavors of their Zinfandels with aging in small barrels of new oak. Where Souverain is of a style to score high with drinkers of big Cabernet Sauvignons and Martini is mated to the tastes of those who favor lighter, more feminine Cabernets, these two cellars make Zinfandel more in a way to appeal to admirers of Pinot Noirs. Mondavi produced his first Zinfandel in 1966, but did not settle into his current stride until the 1971. Sterling has been consistent since its first vintage, 1969.

Zinfandels in the hopper, just before being crushed. (WINE INSTITUTE)

Perhaps it is too early to say that Clos du Val has brought a new dimension to Napa Valley Zinfandel after only its first wine, the 1972, but I think not. Bernard Portet, the winemaker at Clos du Val, came to the valley with the pure palate of a Bordelais. He made his first Zinfandel as a tart, aromatic, and uncommonly astringent wine in the style of a Bordeaux red. It is at least as tannic as the Souverain, but not so full-bodied or fat or sun-washed, or whatever it is that gives weight to Souverain on the palate. The 1973 and the 1974 showed the same character in cask in 1975. Portet frankly made the wine to last, using grapes from the immediate vicinity of the winery, which is to say from one of the coolest areas in the main valley. Clos du Val bears very close watching by drinkers who favor the lean astringency of wines from the Médoc.

The rest of the field echoes with dimmer voices what these five have to say.

Charles Krug Zinfandels resemble the Louis M. Martini ones for general style vintage after vintage. The differences are fine points. The Krug wines are more straightforward, simpler if you will. They lack the delicate hint of an earthy taste from old casks, and their fruit flavors leave a slightly sharper, less polished impression on the palate. These are, may I hasten to add, subtle differences, not gross ones.

Heitz Cellars offers a Zinfandel only episodically, when the proprietor finds something he likes available in bulk from another winemaker. The recent ones have tended to be blends of younger and older wines, dominated by the brisk fruit flavors of the young wines, but softened by the bouquetish older element.

Oakville Vineyards Zinfandels of 1971 and 1972 both have California as their appellation, and say only that the wines were made and bottled by the proprietors, which suggests that they, like Joe Heitz, buy much of their Zin. The Oakville style is fleshier, with, mayhap, a faintly detectable touch of sweet at the end of the sip. A hint of the raisiny taste of warm growing conditions is there, too.

Of the larger cellars, Inglenook offers two Zinfandels. The vintage-dated Napa Valley one has been a trifle shaky in recent vintages–thin, and beset by too many flavors from old cooperage–but as in the cases of Inglenook's other Napa reds it seemed to be rounding into richer shape with the 1972. The best buy still is the Inglenook Vintage Zinfandel, dated, and carrying a North Coast Counties appellation of origin. In essence it is what used to be Italian Swiss Colony Zinfandel in the 1950s, and reliably carries on the old ISC tradition of a softly fruity wine with a firm whiff of blackberry in the nose to go with a softened finish. The grapes come from Allied Growers vineyards in all the counties north of San Francisco Bay. The wine has been made and bottled at Asti, though both operations are scheduled to move to the Napa Valley when a 1975–1976 construction program at Inglenook is complete.

Beringer nonvintage Napa Valley Zinfandel, after years in the doldrums, is now a first-rate demonstration of how savory can be a wine blended to a commercial standard. It strikes for the soft, fruity side of Zinfandel's character in the same way as Inglenook Vintage does, and hits closer to the mark in a tight competition. It is the sort of wine I would have for dinner every night if I could, but which I save for the best family meal of the week as economics presently stand.

The Christian Brothers Napa Valley Zinfandel, also nonvintage, competes in the same reliability stakes as the Inglenook and Beringer bottlings. The Brothers were caught short in the early 1970s. Several bottlings in a row were paler and less rich in fruit flavor than normal. However, the sizable vintages of 1973 and 1974 replenished the cellars with wines that smack less of San Joaquin than the pale ones did, all of which proves that the best of blenders can be caught out by a sequence of poor harvests.

Several of the Napa Valley's new, small wineries have released their first Zinfandels. The names include Burgess Cellars, Chateau Montelena, Cuvaison, Stonegate, Raymond, and a few more. Thus far the Burgess Cellars and Chateau Montelena show considerable promise.

Nichelini Vineyards, Napa's small, essentially local winery, offers a Zinfandel in the same vein as its other reds, a dark, richly flavored wine with enough varietal character to hide most of its rough edges, and to make whatever lack of polish seem right and good in the context. It comes from the Nichelini family vineyards high up in the Chiles Valley hills east of the Napa Valley proper.

Last there comes a winery that makes only Zinfandel, but which is not strictly speaking a Napa Valley enterprise. Sutter Home makes Zinfandel as its only red, buying all of its grapes from a famous old vineyard, the Deaver Ranch, near

Plymouth in the Sierra foothills, some 120 miles east of the winery. And yet the wine fits into the Napa Valley framework well enough to compete with bottlings exclusively from valley grapes. Bob Trinchero gets the grapes down off the mountain in lug boxes, a truckload at a time, ferments them in temperature-controlled stainless steel tanks, then ages the wine first in redwood and then in new oak barrels. The result always is dark hued, full bodied, and austere enough to suggest great aging potential.

The development of this wine as the exclusive production of Sutter Home is a 1974 occurrence. However, Trinchero began offering Deaver Ranch Zinfandels as specially labeled lots with the 1968, and won grudging admiration from some case-hardened Napa Firsters. Through 1972 Trinchero was weeding out some overaged cooperage, which contributed a musty overtone to otherwise impeccable Zinfandel. Since 1972 all the wood has been new, the wine fresher.

Sonoma County Zinfandels

Sonoma cellarmasters have a vast supply of zinfandel at their command, much of it from mature to downright ancient vines, and they use the grapes very well indeed in a casual, salt-of-the-earth sort of way.

The ancestral home of zinfandel in California is, of course, the Sonoma Valley, from where Colonel Haraszthy—to give him his due—vigorously propagated both the vine and varietal wine in the 1860s and 1870s. In the old days hundreds of small cellars made wine from a nearby patch of zinfandel. Now the valley has but three tiny cellars and two larger ones making varietal Zinfandel. The Russian River long since has become the dominant source of Zinfandel in the county. There a dozen cellars, seven of them large enough to sell across the country, make the wine.

To begin at the beginning, Buena Vista still makes Zinfandel in much the same way as Haraszthy's crew must have made it, from vines growing in much the same ground. In fact, one small, rolling vineyard of craggy ancients is presumed to date from pre-Prohibition Buena Vista. Although their contribution is more to the legend of the wine than to its volume, Buena Vista has clung to the authorship of its Zinfandel through all the years when many of its reds were bought from other wineries for bottling. The style has been consistent: a dark red, uncommonly tart, quite tannic wine with more than a faint hint of oxidation from its aging in old wood. The Haraszthys described their techniques in such terms. Winemaker Al Brett accepted the style throughout his long career, until his retirement after the vintage of 1974.

All of Buena Vista's vines are in climate Region I, which may account both for the tartness of the wine and its intensely blackberryish aroma. All bottlings have carried Sonoma as their appellation. Most have been genuinely estate bottled. Some have been vintage dated.

Although the cellars are but a few blocks apart, Sebastiani Vineyards Zinfandels have been vastly different from the Buena Vistas even when differing greatly among themselves, and Sebastiani Zinfandels have come in diverse styles as the family has grown away from bulk winemaking, into bottled wines. Some, like the Bin 184 released in 1972, have been thick, heavy, with some of the sun-baked flavors typical of the San Joaquin Valley Zinfandels even though Bin 184's appellation was Sonoma. Others have been lightly rigged, bone dry wines. August Sebastiani's own preference seems to be for tartly berryish Zinfandel with an overlay of bouquet from long aging in large wood. The 1970 Reserve Bin bottling released early in 1974 had all of those qualities and August's complete approval. The 1972 followed the same line when released early in 1975. The drier, tarter style may seem to put the Sebastiani in league with the Buena Vista, but in fact puts him closer to major Zinfandels of the Russian River. Sebastiani knows how to soften a wine in wood without losing the fresh flavors of the grape.

Kenwood Vineyards, one of the small newcomers to the valley, offered a soft, rather light 1971 Zinfandel as its inaugural bottling, then in 1972 shifted toward a much fuller wine, fermented to get full body and some tannic astringency, then aged in small new oak until its flavor became an overt part of the whole. As a young wine, it seemed a bit clumsy, but the potential for age is in it. As Marty Lee refines his first notion, the Kenwood label will bear close watching.

The vineyards are close by the winery at the warm northern end of the Sonoma Valley.

Nearby Grand Cru went in the reverse direction. Its proprietors originally set out to make Zinfandel in every fashion from age-worthy red to white. They have retreated from that idea, and their lone red Zinfandel from 1973 on is a pale, soft one known as Zinfandel Coulant. The idea is a wine of Beaujolais-like frivolity, but only fermented light rather than by carbonic maceration. So far the result has been innocuous.

One of the surest signs that Zinfandel is on top of its form in the Russian River region is that the cellars there make it so well so consistently. J. Pedroncelli and Martini & Prati have long records. Simi and Korbel have competed favorably when they have competed at all. The old Italian Swiss Colony made some legendary Zins when it functioned independently.

Since 1967, J. Pedroncelli Sonoma County Zinfandels have been much the sort of wines that make me like Louis M. Martini's: delicate, deft, artfully balanced between blackberryish aroma and earthy bouquet. The primary vineyards are the Pedroncelli's own on the round-backed ridge separating the Dry Creek and Alexander valleys, although the family crops are supplemented from both valleys. Some years Pedroncelli Zinfandels are a shade coarser and more austere in character than the old master's, sometimes to their benefit. Always they are among the most appreciable bottlings of the varietal red in the state.

Simi Zinfandel has been several things since Russell Green launched the renaissance of the old cellar at Healdsburg in 1969. The first releases blended his own new wine with some old stuff from the previous ownership. Only with the 1972 did Simi become a vintage Alexander Valley appellation wine. The style is softer than the Pedroncelli, less tart and less tannic both, but the berryish varietal character is strikingly similar.

Foppiano Vineyards Russian River Valley Zinfandel, vintage dated since the 1970s, falls just on the other side of Pedroncelli from Simi. It is a heavier, more austere wine rather than a softer one. Again, the regional character of Zinfandel almost overrides the individual style of the cellar.

Of the broadly available labels, these three share the notion that Zinfandel should be claretish. Souverain of Alexander Valley served notice with its debut vintage, the 1972, that it will join them. A pair of miniature cellars round out the list working within the general style. Leo Trentadue ferments to achieve a strong, durable wine, aged in small oak to give it a fleshy quality somewhat along the lines of the Simi. As a young wine it does not have great finesse, but is made carefully enough to mature into something complex and harmonious. Joseph Swan Zinfandel has become something of an enigma. The debut vintage, 1969, was an enormously rich wine, but balanced. Subsequent vintages have grown increasingly coarse and increasingly marred by off-notes of the sort that rouse images of ill-kept cooperage.

Korbel first offered Zinfandel as a nonvintage wine of uncommonly soft, gentle quality. It was the one wine that first made Chinon a more apt comparison than Beaujolais. A vintage dated 1972 followed without changing the style at all. With Beringer from the Napa Valley and Paul Masson, the Korbel ranks as one of the best buys among unpretentious reds of soft, roundly fruity style, and one of the most versatile reds for early consumption. The world does not have too many reds that go well with elegant food served informally, light enough to leave a productive afternoon ahead of a superb midday meal.

The Dry Creek Vineyards Zinfandel Primeur 1973, first offering of the varietal by a small newcomer to the region, reached for the same style as the Korbel but finished up being a bit sharper or more austere. As proprietor David Stare gains experience with the grapes from a vineyard near the winery the label will bear watching.

Two other wineries offer Sonoma Zinfandels. One, Cambiaso, has just begun to turn toward bottled wines after a long career in the bulk trade. The early bottlings resembled those of Foppiano in all respects save that the finish had a tannic bitterness rather than mere astringency. Winery and vineyards were in transition in 1975. The other Sonoma label belongs to Martini & Prati, which sells a bit of Zinfandel (and a few other wines) as a sideline to their main business in the bulk trade. The wines are light, soft, and perhaps just a shade off dry. Against the gentle fruit flavors there poses an earthy note from ancient oak ovals. Sometimes the latter quality is too intrusive, but in many bottlings it is a subtle complexity in a wine lamentably easy to drink.

The wine labeled Italian Swiss Colony Zinfandel is an amalgam of Sonoma, Mendocino, and San Joaquin Valley grapes made in the soft, faintly sweet style of the San Joaquin and sold at low price for daily use. It is superior among its kind, but not akin to the true Sonomans in style or substance.

Mendocino County Zinfandels

The Ukiah Valley is an extension of the Russian River Valley to the north of Sonoma, a shade warmer perhaps, but no less suited to zinfandel. Three cellars offer varietal wines from the grape which, among them, make a convincing statement that this variety performs better than any other red grown in the district.

The veteran is Parducci Wine Cellars. The family has been making a vintage-dated wine since 1967 after a long career with undated blends. John Parducci shares the Italianate notion with Louis P. Martini, the Pedroncellis, and a few others that Zinfandel can profit from two or three seasons in large, well-seasoned cooperage, but that it should not go into barrels. The wine emerges from Parducci's medium-sized redwood tanks less than vibrantly youthful, but still a fruity bottle rather than a bouqueted old one. This thought is one of the most attractive for Zinfandel, and the Parduccis consistently express it well. Their wine may be a shade less aromatic than some of the others, but always is full and balanced in its restrained way.

Cresta Blanca released its first nonvintage Mendocino Zinfandel in 1972 and won friends. The initial offering bore a heavy bouquet of spiritous notes, even hid its fruity flavors behind them. Subsequent editions have kept some of that bouquet, but have subdued the characteristic so that the principal impression is the unmistakable berryish taste of zinfandel. The wine has the same general softness of counterparts from Beringer or Paul Masson, but also has the complicating bouquet for those who seek winey tastes rather than grapey ones in their reds.

The last of the Zinfandel producers in Mendocino poses a whole set of riddles. In recent vintages the tiny Fetzer has offered as many as five Zinfandels bottled by individual vineyards. Not only has the grape character ranged from pallid to fierce, the styles have ranged from freshly fruity to heavily oaky. The game is strictly for experimenters.

Central Coast Zinfandels

For mysterious reasons, Zinfandel never quite caught on in Alameda and Santa Clara counties, although both can produce good ones. In the mid-1960s Concannon made a fine dry Zinfandel, but had to abandon it for lack of customers. In the same era Wente Bros. made a 100 percent Zinfandel to sell in jugs at the winery under the name of claret. Mirassou sold a few bottles at its cellar door. So did Gemello. That was the lot. Neither Almadén nor Paul Masson had any Zinfandels.

In the new era of vineyards in Monterey and San Benito counties, Zinfandel has made some strides. Mirassou now produces and sells an appreciable volume. So do Almadén and Paul Masson. Nearly all of the small cellars now have Zinfandels. And yet the status of the varietal somehow seems dimmer in this region than it does north of San Francisco Bay, or in Lodi. Between the old reluctance and the new change this wine type has not been defined as precisely as some others.

Mirassou Vineyards has, as usual, produced most of the specific evidence. Even it is erratic information because both winery and vineyards have been undergoing changes throughout the past decade. In the early 1960s the wine was purely from Santa Clara and sold mainly at the cellar door as a sideline to the family bulk business. After 1967 the label business became a prime consideration, and the wine began to be a blend of Monterey and Santa Clara grapes from Mirassou vines in the two places. Some of the bottlings after 1969 have been purely from Monterey. During the Santa Clara days the wine was full-bodied and fleshy, with few or no austere notes. As Monterey fruit has played an increasing role the wine has become lighter, more tart, without losing any intensity of fruit flavor. The limited bottlings with Monterey as the appellation of origin have been, predictably, still lighter bodied and more tart than those blended of Santa Clara and Monterey grapes. All of the wines with Monterey grapes in them share a curious note that is more reminiscent of vegetative matter than of fruit, the distinction that so often separates French wine from traditional Californian bottlings. Some tasters are beginning to suspect that sunlight has as much effect on flavor as sun heat does, and that Monterey comes closer to France in hours of clear skies than any other part of California. In any case, Mirassou Zinfandels, especially the ones with Monterey on the label, are an original style in California. The Mirassous age their Zinfandels in small oak to round off the tart edges, but end up with a wine of far different dimensions than those from north of San Francisco Bay even so.

The possibility remains that some part of the vegetative note comes from the Mirassou cellars. Veteran critics of California wines long have been able to identify Mirassou wines by a persistent form flavor much like the note that occurs otherwise only in Monterey wines.

Paul Masson nonvintage California Zinfandel, introduced in 1973, is in spite of its indistinct pedigree a blend much like the Mirassou. A considerable proportion of Monterey grapes provide an intense aroma while others from warmer places give a soft, rounded quality. Because the wine is labeled only as "made and bottled," there is no way to track down the outside sources, though Sonoma and Lodi are most probable. No hint of wood or other bouquet intrudes in the finished wine. The taste is zesty and berryish to a greater degree than in other Masson reds. With Beringer, Cresta Blanca, and Korbel, the Masson Zinfandel is one of the wines that makes California's commercial production an increasingly attractive middle ground for drinkers who wish to have distinct character for a modest price.

The rest of the commercial Zinfandels from labels headquartered in the Central Coast have rather less to recommend them. Weibel Zinfandel, increasingly identified with Mendocino County, shows the most hopeful signs of gaining character as a sound, varietally true Zinfandel. Wente Bros. has made only a pale-hued, light-bodied wine under the name in its first few releases since the vintage of 1961. Almadén Zinfandels lag a lamentable distance behind even the Wentes as light, thin, sharp wines. San Martin is on the threshold of its renaissance, and should not be judged until its 1974 vintage appears in the markets.

Zinfandels from the prestigious small wineries in the region are numerous, but the grapes tend to come from afar.

Keeping track of Ridge Vineyards' Zinfandels almost requires an extra cellarbook. Every year brings a new galaxy of the wines in all styles, from any number of places. There were five separate bottlings of 1969s, two from vineyards in Lodi, two from Sonoma County, and one from their own Montebello Vineyard at the winery. The vintage of 1971 yielded another pair from Lodi, one from Sonoma, one from Mendocino, and the homegrown model. These are just the conventional reds. The rosés, whites, and natural sweets are left to later discussion.

The proprietors, as is their general wont, try to produce wines of extreme strength. There is one, the 1970 from the near-the-winery Jimsomare vineyard, which winemaker Paul Draper predicts will need thirty years to come around. Aside from the fact that I may not last another thirty years, the strong suspicion lurks in me that light-hearted zinfandel itself is an unwilling candidate for such honors. Even "light" Zinfandels from Ridge carry admonitions on the label to wait, four, five, even ten years, which is to say that the light ones are stout by general standards.

André Tchelistcheff often uses the image of a smoothly polished ball to describe a mature, elegant wine. That is how a great wine should and does feel on the palate. A young, unbalanced wine also is a ball, but it has stray flavors sticking out, like arrows, in all directions. In this image a weighty Ridge Zinfandel certainly is a purple sea urchin in youth, perhaps forever.

On the positive side, it must be said that the wines have an enormous amount of flavor, and that they are cleanly made. Draper ferments juice and skins together for as much as two weeks, then sends the wine directly to small barrels for aging.

The home vineyard, Montebello, falls in climate Region I. The wine from it is a rare example of how grapes grow in cool places, Buena Vista being the only other that comes to mind. Of all the Ridge Zinfandels, though, the ones labeled Geyserville or Lytton Springs, both from the Russian River area of Sonoma County, have the greatest natural stuffings.

Concannon Vineyard has reentered the lists with a Zinfandel after an absence of several years. The vintage-dated first offering is a 1972 carrying a Livermore Valley appellation. It comes from the warm, gravelly vineyards adjacent to the winery. The wine is light by general standards, but deftly balanced and bone dry after a longish career in ancient oak ovals that leave no flavor of their own, but do soften and polish a red to a nicety.

The once tiny Gemello winery is now the more capacious Gemello-Filice Winery, and the wine in a state of transition. Very likely it will continue to be dark, tart, and tannic wherever the grapes might come from because Mario Gemello continues as the winemaker and that is how he thinks Zinfandel should taste.

Several of the Mountaintop Miniaturists make thick, coarse Zinfandels that somehow manage to delight a lot of home winemakers. David Bruce is one. Nepenthe Cellars is another. Bruce gets his grapes from a vineyard in the Sierra foothills. G. L. Burtness at Nepenthe acquires his locally when he does not grow all of his own.

In addition to these limited editions Santa Clara and other central coastal counties offer another dozen Zinfandels from a gaggle of country wineries. The alphabetic roster is Bargetto, Bertero, Bonesio, Fortino, Filice, Hecker Pass, Guglielmo (under the Mount Madonna label), Thomas Kruse, Pedrizzetti, Pesenti, Conrad Viano, and Villa Armando. Of these the wines of Mt. Madonna and Thomas Kruse are the most distinctive in quality and the most polished in style. Hecker Pass, a newcomer in 1974, shows signs of producing a Zinfandel of some finesse.

San Joaquin Valley Zinfandels

Because zinfandel grows so willingly in California, the wine is made as a varietal in all districts and all climate regions, including the warmest part of the San Joaquin. Contrasted with Zinfandels from the coolest coast vineyards, valley Zinfandels teach excellent lessons in the effect of climate on character and quality. That they do so with sweet good humor makes the schooling agreeable as well as informative.

Heat during the growing season diminishes acidity in the grape faster than it builds sugar, which means that wines from hot country grapes tend to be heavier or coarser than their counterparts from cool vineyards. Some of the aromatics cook out, too, so that the fruity flavors can be lost in the finished wine unless the winemaker stops the fermentation while enough sugar remains to point up whatever varietal characteristics linger. The greater the heat the greater this compensation is likely to be.

In the early days of California winemaking the cellarmasters tended to exaggerate the climate by waiting until the sainted month of October to harvest. Studies at U.C.-Davis finally showed them that harvesting in August would improve the sugar-acid ratios in the grapes. This, plus temperature-controlled fermentation has allowed the valley to approach much closer to traditionally tart and tannic styles in red winemaking in recent years.

Enough differences remain that many wineries augment their valley grapes with a proportion of fruit or bulk wine purchased from the coast counties. Even in these an ineffable, inevitable valley character remains to be tasted.

Lodi maintains a distinct identity as a source of Zinfandel because Barengo Cellars and East-Side Winery/Royal Host have willed it to have one and because it has the coolest growing conditions in the San Joaquin Valley.

Barengo and East-Side, the latter under its Conti Royale label, run a stylish competition to see which one can produce the most classical Zinfandel from the northernmost vineyards in the San Joaquin.

Barengo opts for a shade sweeter finish, and, thus, a heavier wine that calls to mind lush fruit fully ripened on the vine. The tart, berryish nose dwindles to a faint ghost of itself. However, the Barengo is not a sweet wine. Rather it is a soft, generous one. Romantics would call it a veritable Reubens brunette. The East-Side approach is to allow the fruit to ripen just a shade less fully, then to finish the wine a bit sharper and drier, with, mayhap, a kiss of well-seasoned oak to go along with the varietal character. Neither wine carries a vintage date. Though both qualify for a Lodi appellation as often as not, the labels always read only "California."

Clear at the other end of the San Joaquin Valley the wineries around Bakersfield have begun to establish a local identity for wines grown in a climate generally classified as Region V. The Zinfandels of M. LaMont (from the Bear Mountain winery) and Giumarra Vineyards tend to be softer and slightly sweeter than their Lodi counterparts, but not identical. The M. LaMont impresses as a more delicate, a drier wine. The Giumarra leans more in the traditional San Joaquin direction of raisiny-ripe fruit and heavy body. Both, however, are a good deal more deft and dry than a true San Joaquin Valley Red of the old school.

Franzia Zinfandel comes closest to the ancient verities of the big valley with a truly soft, perceptibly sweet character. Setrakian Zinfandel, from grapes grown near Fresno, is much like the Franzia.

Under its recently developed Winemasters Guild label, Guild Wineries & Distilleries is assembling a nonvintage, California Zinfandel with a drier, more classic style than any of the other major commercial marketers working in the national market. The wine draws somewhat on stocks from Mendocino and other coast counties, but is dominated by valley grapes. The E. & J. Gallo Zinfandel, similarly blended from coastal and valley stocks, has been an uncommonly light, pallid red in its earliest bottlings, but it has been dry and mildly astringent, suggesting that the Gallos may be headed toward more traditional red wine styles. United Vintners' Italian Swiss Colony Zinfandel, yet another coast-valley blend, has been steadily balanced between the heavy and sweet wines of old and the light and not-quite-dry school of thought. Of these three it slips down most easily, though veteran dry wine people will prefer the Guild for its greater vinosity. The Ambassador Zinfandel from California Wine Association may be the happy compromise, for it fits neatly between the Guild on one hand and the ISC on the other.

The Curiosity Pieces

Zinfandel grapes, in ample supply, always are available for experimental winemaking. The variety's versatility has caused it to appear in every kind of guise, with every kind of success. In the interest of keeping the record straight the most visible of the recent experiments are catalogued below.

Nouveau. Carbonic maceration as a fermentation technique needs more allies than gamay to gain a foothold in California. The need is not for a specific varietal character, since carbonic maceration obliterates most of that, but for an aromatically fruity, uncommonly tart must. Zinfandel meets both standards, so has been made after the fashion of French Beaujolais by several cellars, most of them new ones seeking identity in a competitive era of growth.

The original carbonic maceration Zinfandel in California came, so far as I know, from the small Sonoma winery called Grand Cru. The vintage was 1972. In 1973 a new winery in Amador County, Monteviña, added one called Zinfandel Nuevo. (Presumably Nuevo is a nod to the Spanish name of the winery itself.) In the same year the Napa winery Sutter Home contributed a Zinfandel Nuovo. (Well, a majority of California's winemakers are of Italian descent, including the proprietors of Sutter Home.)

Early voting favored the Monteviña as being truest to a Beaujolais type. That is, it tasted very cleanly of grape and of the estery quality imparted by the fermenting, and not at all vinous.

In early 1975 the rage for carbonic maceration wines seemed to be withering. Sutter Home planned to drop out. Grand Cru had dropped carbonic maceration though it was keeping its Zinfandel extremely light and fresh through a short fermentation on the skins. Still, if an audience for Nouveau-style wines develops in this country, zinfandel is likely to do most of the work of satisfying it.

White Zinfandel. The urge to make white wines out of black grapes is one of those look-ma-no-hands challenges to technical skills that is hard to resist. The job is to separate white juice from black skins before the faintest hint of color creeps into the fermentor. To this point five California winemakers have succumbed to the basic notion, and a sixth has gone the whole route to make a white sparkling wine from zinfandel grapes.

The still wines, to be downright glum about it, have not been worth the trouble, with one fleeting moment of exception. Ridge Vineyards made a White Zinfandel in 1970 that clearly was a white wine for several months after bottling. A rich, almost viscous wine, it was a fine toy for hobbyists to use against their peers, who seldom knew whether to believe their eyes or their palates. By late 1973 the game was over; the wine had darkened and its flavors had abandoned their early harmonies to advanced tastes of age.

The other candidates, from David Bruce in Santa Clara County and Grand Cru in Sonoma, did not offer even a brief pretense of being white wine. Both started out partridge-eye pink and tanned with each passing day. Neither was either notably fresh of flavor. A tiny Napa Valley winery, Caymus, did not even advertise its pale Zinfandel as white, but started right out calling it partridge eye.

Faculty members in the Department of Enology & Viticulture at the University of California at Davis, having experimented at making white Zinfandel themselves, scoff at any and all new tries as a waste of time and good grapes, with apparent justification.

The sparkling wine from Thomas Kruse of Gilroy is a typically darkish white Zinfandel with bubbles in it.

Late Harvest Zinfandel. This is a lethal but lovely idea coined at Ridge Vineyards. Ports and other sweet wines of the sort get their 18 to 20 percent alcohol partly through natural fermentation, partly through the addition of grape brandy. The spiritous flavor is an obvious warning against intemperate consumption. Late Harvest Zinfandels, on the other hand, get their 17 percent alcohol entirely through natural fermentation. There is no warning flag, unless a faintly earthy taste from a lot of yeast does the job. One just coasts from second glass to third to incapacity. Fortunately bottle prices ranging from $15 to $25 help limit intake sharply. In addition to three from Ridge, Mayacamas in the Napa Valley has made two. Although they fall outside the scope of this book for being other than table wines, they are wines of merit. All have shared the perfumey aroma of overripe grapes nicely balanced against a sweet but not cloying finish. The first was called "essence" by Ridge. All since have been labeled "Late Harvest."

MISCELLANEOUS RED VARIETALS

Of the seventy or so black varieties of *Vitis vinifera* that remain in California after the stars have been accounted for, half a dozen are distinctive enough to appear now and again as varietal red wines.

The names of the six are Carignane, Charbono, Grenache, Merlot, Nebbiolo, and Pinot St. George.

They exist at the suffrance of the consuming public, which must be willing to learn the names of a few more grapes rather than relying on the old, familiar generic names. By and large the wines that come from these varieties disappear into generics, or else are the minority grapes in blends known by other varietal names.

Carignane

Carignane for years has ranked first among all black varieties in total acreage in California, recommended by the facts that the variety bears heavy crops, retains sprightly acid levels even in the warmer parts of the San Joaquin Valley, and is not overpowering in character. In short, it makes an excellent blend grape. As such it has been and will continue to be the base of huge volumes of burgundy, claret, and chianti. As a varietal wine, Carignane could and possibly should replace many of those generic bottlings, though without an increase in price.

Growers all over the state call the grape kerrigan. Even people with names like diBiasi think carignane is Irish. There was, in 1974, some 30,700 acres of it to mispronounce over. Eighty percent of the total forms a blanket from one end of the San Joaquin Valley to the other. The coast counties share 5,500 acres among them.

While recommending the variety for climate Regions III and IV generally, the University of California held as early as 1880 that carignane makes its best wines in the upper Russian River Valley and in the warmer parts of the Santa Clara Valley. Coastal plantings reflect that judgment. Mendocino County has 2,355 acres, Sonoma another 1,710. In addition those two Russian River counties produce the three most available commercial bottlings of Carignane, the varietal.

Simi has carried the flag for Carignane as a varietal since Prohibition was repealed. Young Simi Carignans (spelled without the final "e") from Russell Green's Alexander Valley vineyards are agreeable indeed. They have a pleasant, fruity quality and not much astringency or other austerity in them. A faint, yet coarsened similarity to the herbaceous taste of Cabernet Sauvignon explains the choice of carignane as the other parent of ruby cabernet.

That Carignane should be drunk young and without serious contemplation is borne out by earlier bottlings from the previous owners of Simi. The old Simi Carignans stayed in casks for years, then in bottles for years more. They never fell apart, but neither did they develop hidden strengths. Anyone who ever has licked the sweat from his upper lip on a hot summer's day and recorded the faint, musty taste of it has some idea of what happens to the sunny charms of Carignane with age. They fade into something acceptable, but not rare.

Trentadue, toward the north end of the Alexander Valley, makes young Carignanes very similar in character to the newer editions from Simi. If anything they are a bit heavier and coarser. The small volume is sold locally.

The Carmine Carignanes of Fetzer Vineyards, upriver in Mendocino County, share the varietal characteristics of the grape with their Russian River fellows, but are heavily overlaid with the taste of Fetzer cellars, a taste so strong it evokes strong preference or strong aversion. Again the volume is small.

From time to time John Parducci has been tempted to bottle a varietal Carignane from an outstanding vineyard near the winery, but, as of 1975, had yet to succumb to the notion.

Oakville Vineyards did set aside some wine from an exceptional vintage, releasing it as Napa Valley Grande Carignane 1973. The wine as thick and dark, but so soft as to beg immediate drinking.

Although U.C.-Davis regards the Santa Clara Valley as a favored location for carignane, and the variety is in fact the most widely planted in the region with 260 acres, little Carignane is bottled there. David Bruce and Nepenthe make a barrel or so each year, most of which sells at the cellar door. Both wineries favor thick, dark, rather coarse styles.

In Europe, incidentally, the major plantings of carignane are in the south of France and in Spain, their yield sold mostly as *vins de consommation.*

Charbono

Until the mid-1970s, only Inglenook Vineyards made a varietal Charbono in all of California. It has been a kind of house pet of the winery since the 1940s. The new boys include Davis Bynum and Angelo Papagni.

Charbono, of indistinct Italian origins, makes a wine not unlike Barbera, except that it is softer. In fact, the winemakers at Inglenook add a small percentage of Barbera at the crush each year to firm up the character of the wine.

Inglenook Charbono always is vintage-dated, always with a Napa Valley appellation. On rare occasion it has aged into an enormously complex, powerful old wine at fifteen, even twenty years. Most seasons, the wine makes an agreeable companion to spaghetti, or crab cioppino, or whatever would seem right with Barbera.

The university recommends charbono only for Region I, and then mainly as a neutrally flavored source of color in blended wines. The total acreage in the state is so small that no statistics are kept for it.

Grenache

Grenache automatically suggests rosé because that is the variety's principal identity in California and in the Tavel district of France. In addition it is a useful component in blends for tawny port-types because of its pale color and high sugar content when left on the vine for extra ripening.

Infrequently someone makes some grenache into varietal red wine. The varietal characteristic is highly distinctive. The academic flavor association key is "estery," which is to say something highly volatile such as fingernail polishes, distillates, and other substances that seem to the nose to hover between liquid and gas.

Almadén Vineyards made the original red Grenache under the coined name of Grenoir Original. The proprietors suggest it as an alternative to a fresh young Beaujolais. It is as good a suggestion as any, although the wine is too heavy and too perfumey to be taken quite so lightly as that. Several small wineries in the Gilroy district of Santa Clara County make similar wines.

In 1975 Guild launched a Grenache Nouveau under its Winemasters Guild label, thereby going as far as one can go with the notion of a fresh but estery young red. On top of the varietal character of grenache, the folk at Guild heaped the similar flavors that come from the fermentation technique called carbonic maceration.*

For some unaccountable reason, David Bruce elected to take Grenache seriously, or at least to charge $6.50 a bottle for his. Grenache is not the sort of wine one pays $6.50 a bottle to have unless one already knows himself to be an incurable addict either for Grenache or for everything Bruce makes.

Merlot

Merlot, in 1974, was on the brink of becoming a fad in California. By 1975 some of the fever had gone out of the situation, but some signs of permanence were settling in.

Mild interest developed in the late 1960s when several wineries began experimenting with the variety as a source of more claret-ish style in their Cabernet Sauvignons. Almost simultaneously, merlot started to acquire an identity of its own as a varietal red. The interest, measured in acres, jumped from 200 in 1969 to 2,800 in 1973.

The dual role of blend grape and pure varietal has logical origins. Merlot is blended into nearly all of the great wines of the Médoc, and is the only grape in some of the finest St. Emilions and Pomerols. However, if the purposes are parallel in France and California, the results are closer to perpendicular. In the Médoc, merlot ripens early and bears heavily, practical advantages where fall rains can decimate the cabernet sauvignon vineyards before they ripen fully. In St. Emilion and Pomerol, merlot makes wines of uncommonly pointed, intense character. In California, on the other hand, merlot does not yield much more than cabernet sauvignon; the latter ripens in good time in all districts in most years. As a result merlot's value in blending is mainly aesthetic, a means of tempering cabernet when the latter grows too austere or aggressive for the winemaker's taste. Alone, merlot seems to make a soft, agreeably bland cousin to a Cabernet Sauvignon. Merlot may prove more varied in the future. The evidence to date comes from just two cellars.

Louis M. Martini produces a Merlot from his Edge Hill Vineyard in Dry Creek Valley west of Healdsburg. The first one, a trial lot, blended the vintages of 1968 and 1970. Subsequently Louis P. has kept at least some Merlot out of his Cabernet Sauvignon blends in each vintage, and released a 1969 and a 1971 for sale.

* See page 189, in the section on Gamays.

Sterling Vineyards at the north end of the Napa Valley has made a Merlot in each vintage since 1969. The 1971 was in the market in 1975. All have come from the winery's own vineyards.

The wines from the two labels are strikingly similar for varietal character, and just as dissimilar for style. The Martini Merlot is aged in sizable and ancient oak ovals so that it goes to bottle tasting purely of the grape. It softens quickly into mature wine. The Sterling Merlots are treated more as Bordeaux, aging a relatively short time in small barrels of new European oak, then held in bottle for as long as two years before release. The choice between the two labels is a matter of personal preference centering around the tolerance for oaky bouquet.

The U.C.-Davis suggests that Merlot's soft qualities make it wine for early drinking. The Martini and Sterling Merlots to date bear out that thought. They have some strength to endure longer, but seem fully mature at three to four years.*

Ample vineyard exists to expand the supply of Merlots. Monterey County has the greatest acreage, 970, followed by San Luis Obispo with 470, Santa Barbara with 360, Sonoma with 350, and Napa with 340. Eleven other counties from Mendocino down to Riverside share the remaining few acres.

Not all of the plantings will do well if merlot has remained as finicky as it was in the 1880s, when it earned only scorn from University of California viticulturists. Most of the early plantings were in the warmest coastal districts and in the San Joaquin Valley. The variety failed miserably in both places. Only after World War II did the university begin to recommend further trials in climate Regions I and II.

Nebbiolo

Nebbiolo is a classic example of the way migration can upset old social orders. It is beyond question the premier variety of the Piedmont in Italy, where it makes Barolo, Barbaresco, Ghemme, Gattinara, and some smaller giants. Barbera is taken far more lightly. Alas for it, nebbiolo has been an inferior performer to barbera in any head-to-head trial in California.

The total acreage in California in 1974 was a shade less than 400, with half of that newly planted in Stanislaus County.

One winery, California Grape Products, made small lots of varietal Nebbiolo under its H. O. Lanza label, using grapes from the southern San Joaquin Valley. It was well made, perfectly agreeable, but indistinct from good generic reds. The old Cal Grape winery was sold, and the wine discontinued some years ago.

However, Nebbiolo's day as a varietal may yet come. One grower in the Shenandoah Valley, east of Plymouth town in the Gold Rush country of the Sierra Nevada foothills, thinks he has found a magical site for nebbiolo. If the early promise bears out the wine will be marketed under the Monteviña label. The early volume will not exhaust the American marketplace. Monteviña's test plot is a single acre.

---

* Sterling also has produced a frivolous Merlot in the style of a Beaujolais Nouveau, using the Beaujolais technique of carbonic maceration. It was a critical success as a Nouveau-type. For an explanation of carbonic maceration, see page 190.

Pinot St. George (or Red Pinot)

The roster of wines called Pinot St. George, or, alternatively, Red Pinot, has shrunk from three to one in recent years. The Christian Brothers have maintained their Pinot St. George as one of the most prestigious reds in their roster. Inglenook dropped its Red Pinot after the vintage of 1972 when the old vineyard ended its career. Cresta Blanca's Red Pinot had gone into eclipse some years prior to that.

The University of California at Davis does not care much for the variety. In recommending against further plantings, scholars at the school said that it was "inferior to Pinot Noir and even Pinot Pernand and Meunier in everything except production." They continued in their report with the observation that the variety would not have lasted in the state except for a lack of true pinot noir.

The same report also admitted that under highly favorable conditions the variety could yield a wine of enough quality and character to be mistaken for Pinot Noir. It is on those grounds that The Christian Brothers have hung on to their small acreage at Mont LaSalle in the hills west of Napa, using it to make an estate wine. As all of the winery's reds, this one blends a majority of brisk young wine with a dollop of suave older lots to make a light, but balanced and complex red.

Mature acreage of pinot st. george in all California amounts to 175. In most counties it is shrinking. However, somebody in Monterey County has plans for the variety. There, the total of 479 acres—all new since 1969—presages some company for The Christian Brothers' lonely bottling.

GENERIC RED WINES

Generic red wines are blends of several grape varieties made with one of two motives, or some mixture of both. First, blends can be a good deal greater than the sum of their parts, and there exist winemakers who enjoy the challenge of getting two and two to equal seven. Second, blending has corrective powers that allow unbalanced grapes or wines to be brought together in inexpensive but agreeable bottles, to the economic benefit of winery and drinker alike.

The commonest name for blended red these days is Burgundy. Chianti, Claret, and a handful of proprietary names round out the field. The names mean what the individual proprietors think they mean. It is rather safe to say that all proprietors think a generic name means a soundly made wine. It also is safe to say that the dimensions of most generics are modest, calculated to give easy pleasure. Beyond those generalities, a generic name is about as useful as the fabled report of the three blind men on the outlines of an elephant.

This does not mean an absolute lack of consensus. Generics from the houses that produce the costlier varietals in the coast regions are likely to be fairly dry to bone dry, with some tannic austerity. There is no distinction between Burgundy and Claret, but both of those likely will be a bit lighter and sharper than anything called Chianti. The country jug wineries in the coast start making Burgundy about where the varietal producers quit saying that in favor of Chianti. The producers in the San Joaquin Valley, though their wines are more refined than country jugs, make Burgundy as an off-dry wine with no austere qualities, and make Chianti as an overtly sweet one.

A few wines in each district are distinctive enough to allow individual description. The rest can only be judged on how accurately they reflect the style of a favored house, or, failing that, on price.

Napa Valley Generic Reds

Year in and year out Beaulieu Vineyards vintage-dated Napa Valley Burgundy is among the most distinctive of the state's generic reds. As the black label points out gamay is prominent in the blend, giving the wine "more than the usual claims to the name of Burgundy." The wine, soft, rounded, faintly bouquetish after aging in small barrels, lives up to the contention in blind tastings. In most vintages it is worth putting down for a year or so of bottle aging to round off the edges. In fine vintages selected lots of BV Burgundy are given a special label to set them still another notch above typical generics. The first such bottling was a 1968.

Beginning with the wine released in mid-1973, Heitz Cellars nonvintage Napa Valley Burgundy challenges the Beaulieu in character and style although it is not necessarily made from the same grape varieties. Small wood aging and well-developed grape tastes are the keys to its stylish substance and to its similarity to the Beaulieu.

Louis M. Martini nonvintage California Burgundy takes a different tack. In most if not all years it could qualify for a varietal label as a Petite Sirah. The style emphasizes the varietal character of that grape. The wine is dark-hued, dry, and noticeably tannic. It is, without compromise, a red wine for people who like red wine with edges on it.

Several Napans are struggling to abandon borrowed generic names. Oakville calls its dry, husky blend Our House Red. Robert Mondavi has a lighter, sharper wine called, even more simply, Red Table Wine. Sterling's is called Red, no more.

Two Burgundies with Napa Valley producers' names on them go off the other end of the scale from such as BV or Heitz. They are Inglenook Navalle Burgundy and the CK Burgundy of C. Mondavi & Sons, both of which are fat, off-dry wines in the San Joaquin Valley rather than the Napa Valley style, and priced accordingly. Some of the blend comes from the San Joaquin, which is how a coastal producer gets to a fat and happy style whenever it happens. Los Hermanos, the secondary label of Beringer, is rather drier and more austere than either of the other secondary label Burgundies.

The rest of the Burgundies appearing under the labels of Napa Valley producers tuck into the middle range between Beaulieu and Inglenook Navalle, shading closer to Beaulieu. A considerable number of the smaller, newer cellars do not offer generics.

Sonoma and Mendocino Generic Reds

In spite of the long tradition of making bulk red in Sonoma County few distinctive generics come from there.

Sebastiani North Coast Burgundy, like all Sebastiani reds, is aged for as much as three years in both large and small cooperage to give it the softening that comes with age rather than residual sugar as well as bouquet. It is vintage dated, and rather costly as generics go. The winery has other, less pricey Burgundies in jugs. It also has a Chianti aged in wood and dominated enough by carignane grapes for the wine to taste of the variety. (With the Louis M. Martini, it is one of few dry Chiantis in California.)

The supply of Martini & Prati Burgundy is small, local, and variable from lot to lot. However, it is worth an episodic look for the times when it is dry and deftly appealing.

The rest of the roster of Sonoma Burgundies fall within the extremes posed by Sebastiani and the pure San Joaquin Valley style of Italian Swiss Colony. Of the lot, Simi and Pedroncelli are useful benchmarks for judging any of the others.

Across the line in Mendocino County, Parducci Vineyards Burgundy, sun-kissed, husky, very cleanly made, is one of the appreciable generics of the region. As all Parducci reds, the wine ferments dry then ages in middling-sized redwood. Both factors contribute to its straightforwardness and its durability.

Italian Swiss Colony's Tipo Chianti, the nearest thing to a throwback to the old days when Italian Swiss and the winery at Asti were synonymous, also is the closest California counterpart to a true Chianti. It is dry, pale in color, and always has at least a dollop of well-aged wine to give it bouquet. The combination of pale color tinged with amber from long aging in wood, and well-defined bouquet typify Italian Chianti Classicos. The Tipo varies for being made mostly of zinfandel rather than Tuscan grapes. It is the sort of wine that wins loyal drinkers because it is so distinct in character. Also, a comparison of this with Louis M. Martini or Sebastiani Chianti gives instructive evidence in the variability of generics.

Central Coast Generic Reds

Generic wines in the Central Coast counties divide into two distinct groups: the sound, commercial ones, and the country jug winery bottlings.

The jug outfits offer the more distinctive possibilities. Peter Scagliotti's Live Oaks Premium Burgundy is an unaffected pleasure, a heavy, off-dry red made cleanly and with enough stuffings to last a few years should stray bottles get lost in the cellar. It is, in my view, a model of what a good, inexpensive country red from California has been since repeal of Prohibition.

Scagliotti's peers in the region work to keep pace. Conrad Viano in Martinez does well at it. Others include Bargetto, Bertero, Bonesio/Uvas, Fortino, Guglielmo's Mount Madonna and Emile's Reserve, Hecker Pass, Pedrizzetti, and Villa Armando.

The commercial generics from Almadén, Concannon, Paul Masson, Mirassou Vineyards, San Martin, Weibel, and Wente Bros. all are polished, competent wines. None makes as forcible an impression as the most distinctive of the generic reds from north of the Bay, but all are safe buys for daily use. The styles are at enough variance that personal preferences will fall sharply with one.

Generics all over California diminished in character during the recent shortage of bearing vineyards. As the heavy plantings of the late 1960s and early 1970s leave quality grape varieties in increasing surplus, the producers of generics in the Central Coast will have not only a greater selection of grapes, but wider choice among grapes. The vineyards of Monterey County appear to be distinctive enough to alter the wines toward a lighter, leaner and yet more aromatic character than in the past.

San Joaquin Valley Generic Reds

A few small wineries have pursued dry red generics for years. Finest of these has been East-Side/Royal Host Burgundy, aged in wood long enough to pick up a complex bouquet and dry enough to carry one well. Barengo Burgundy has been a shade less dry, a shade less bouquetish, but essentially similar. Both of these are accurate indicators to traditionalists that the valley can yield red wines with enough backbone for steady mealtime drinking.

E. & J. Gallo generic reds dominate style in the San Joaquin Valley. Gallo Hearty Burgundy is the base point for thinking about all moderately priced red wine. It is off dry, and free of any tannic or other austerity. The Gallos buy much of the material for Hearty Burgundy—either as grapes or as bulk wine—from Coast counties vineyards. Petite sirah has been a principal grape, although the characteristic roughness is honed out of it so well that its presence is hard to recognize.

Most of the major commercial labels in the San Joaquin follow the Gallo lead on style. Although other firms may use only valley grapes, and different varieties at that, the essential notion of smooth, off-dry red pervades their efforts. The prime examples are United Vintners with Italian Swiss Colony and Petri as labels, Guild, Franzia, and Bear Mountain. Bear Mountain's current M. LaMont Burgundy is more than half ruby cabernet (an anomaly that the Bear Mountain people will have to explain for themselves), and appears headed toward a drier, more austere style than the valley has offered before under a widely available label.

The White Wines

Almost everywhere in the world's vineyards, man and nature push together for sprightly, dry whites, the primary role of white wine being a light, cleansing accompaniment to light meals, or the light parts of heavy meals.

In cooler, cloudier places than California, grapes naturally preserve a high percentage of acidity when they ripen; wine from them does its cleansing job as a lemon might. Sunny California tends to drop the natural acidity of grapes to gentler levels. As a result, nearly all California whites ferment in closed, temperature-controlled stainless steel tanks to retain every potentially fresh flavor through that tumultuous process. More than half by numbers and much more by volume go from there to stainless or glass-lined steel tanks for aging, so that no cellarish, or old, or earthy flavors creep in to diminish the carefully sustained taste of the grapes. A handful of exceptions proves the rule, providing some noble drinking as part of the bargain. Most California Chardonnays, to cite the most evident example, age in new puncheons or barrels precisely to lose the sharp edge of freshness in favor of bouquets from wood and time.

Sometimes the primitive creature rouses up in one of us, and someone complains that nature has been put too far to one side in the making of white wines. First, it does not do to forget that the less skillfully made whites of an earlier California were some of nature's duller achievements. Second, it should be admitted that the enthusiasm for technology may have overreached its bounds in the mid-1960s. Finally, it is evident that a certain amount of recent jostling has led back to older roots of winemaking in those kinds of wines in which earthy flavors are admirable. With everybody having been out to the frontier, the decisions to retreat tend to be intelligent, and doubly welcome for that. Most of them affect the richly flavored, durable whites, the costly ones that demand close scrutiny rather than carefree use with the ordinary meals in a week.

Even the retrograde decisions to ferment in redwood tanks and age in small cooperage belong to people who otherwise cling to technological wisdom as a means of amplifying diversity rather than snuffing it out.

The obvious example of diversity in whites is sweet. Old books talk of wines as dry or sweet. They were. The whole middle ground was nearly impossible to hold. Nobody understood yeast, let alone enzymes. Now cultured yeasts, controlled fermenting temperatures, and infinitely controllable filtering allow the gradations in white wine to go from bone dry to overpoweringly sweet by the smallest of steps.

Even though the choices in style among whites are broader than among reds, largely at the sweet end of the spectrum, the choice of grape varieties and where to grow them provide the fundamental variations within the field of California whites. In region of origin the varieties grown in California span the European continent from Germany down to the south of France, but no farther. For whatever curious reason, the white varieties of Italy, Spain, and Portugal have refused to make good wine no matter where tested.

The Germanic varieties are dominated by white riesling (usually labeled Johannisberg Riesling as a varietal wine), and sylvaner. Gewürztraminer, the joyous contribution of Alsace, is the other north European variety with substantial acreage.

Of Burgundian white grapes, chardonnay and pinot blanc are the lone representatives with usable acreages, and pinot blanc is fading away.

The great white grapes of Bordeaux, sauvignon blanc and semillon, grow more widely than almost any of the others, being adapted to a wide range of climate.

Chenin blanc, a principal grape in the Loire, also is widely planted, and rounds out the list of major varieties with definite ancestry in Europe.

The list of varietal-producing varieties also includes several that are, in one degree or another, peculiarly Californian. Folle blanche and french colombard, both brandy grapes in France, make white table wine and sparkling wine in California. Green hungarian and grey riesling are varieties that sported in California, so have no direct counterpart in Europe. The grapes called emerald riesling and flora are purely Californian, hybridized from European ancestors at the University of California at Davis by Dr. H. P. Olmo.

Some useful grape varieties do not have their names out front on labels because they are only useful for blending in generic wines. In the Coast counties, burger and sauvignon vert (along with french colombard) can be had in abundance for making Chablis, Rhine, and Sauternes. In the San Joaquin Valley these same varieties, plus chenin blanc and semillon, began to be planted increasingly in the early 1970s to replace the ubiquitous thompson seedless in generic wines, and also to make varietals in the big valley.

More and more California whites carry vintage dates. Most of the time the year is a mere index number to remind the buyer to drink up soon. But on Chardonnays and Sauvignon Blancs vintages carry information about age-worthiness of the wine in the bottle. Too, the youthful quality of Gewürztraminers and Johannisberg Rieslings varies enough to make the vintage a point for attention.

 CHARDONNAY

(Alias Pinot Chardonnay)

In France Burgundians drink Burgundies, white and red. Similarly, Bordelais prefer all of their wines from vineyards of the region. In the rest of the wine-drinking world, however, skillful bibbers persistently link as favorites red wines from the Bordeaux grape called cabernet sauvignon and white wines from Burgundy's chardonnay.

There is reason for the linking. Wherever it grows cabernet sauvignon produces notably austere reds. Chardonnay makes near counterparts, the only dry white wines likely to cause one to think of wine first and fruit flavors later.

In the U.C.-Davis flavor association lists the primary characteristic of chardonnay is likened to apple. The sharply cleansing taste of an apple is a useful starting point for thinking about this most complex of white wines, but apples never become as richly flavored as sun-warmed peaches, or as smooth as cream. Chardonnays often do.

The differences do not come from blending, or leaving a trace of grape sugar unfermented. Chardonnay is one of the few white grapes in the world complete and balanced enough in flavor to make blending an act of folly. Sweet is all out of place in this wine. Rather, the distinctions between light apple-ish and creamy peaches come from more subtle corners of the winemaster's mind. In effect, they come because he has the option to treat his Chardonnay much as other whites, or to age it right along with his reds.

The Californian who makes his Chardonnay purely as a white will pick his grapes just as they are ripe, ferment them to minimize color, then age the wine for six to eight months in large and neutral cooperage. The apple-ish tastes of the fresh grape will dominate the wine ever after, making it companionable with oysters, white fish, or poultry in its less ornamented forms.

The more willful soul who would embellish chardonnay grape flavors with some of his own choosing will wait a few extra days before picking, ferment to get some golds from the grape into the new wine, then give it a year and more in new oak barrels so it may acquire a subtle hint of oxidation and either a subtle or broad hint of wood in its complex of aromatics. In adding complexities these techniques soften the fundamental austerity of apple flavors in the direction of peaches and cream. Because such Chardonnays mix iron fist with velvet glove they cannot be surpassed as wines for inspired gluttony.

Once, for a mildly sad reason, a meal designed for two became a meal for one. The meal was a pair of butter-soaked Maine lobster tails and a bottle of six-year-old Heitz Cellars Chardonnay. The one was me. I left neither bite nor sip, never regretted a single moment, and gladly would repeat the performance except that the originally outrageous capital investment since has multiplied itself by a factor of two.

Even when portions are wiser, lobsters, Monterey prawns, or whatever other crustaceans can be soaked in drawn butter come to mind and table as superior accompaniments to rich Chardonnays, mainly because the lingering shades of austerity make a useful foil to fats and butters.

Yet, contrarily, these same Chardonnays mate well with stuffed turkey, or even peahen baked with rosemary, because dry meats and pungent herbs bring out the buttery side of the wines as a reverse contrast to the one posed by lobster.

Buttery and creamy continually surface as descriptives for oak-aged Chardonnays. A few years ago an Australian researcher concluded that butyrics—the compounds that make butter taste like butter—are somehow an index to greatness in wine. Butyrics are natural in wine grapes, although the concentrations are minute. In proper proportion, the researcher says, they produce the smooth harmonics of flavor that separate great from not-so-great wines. If there is a dry white wine in the world that can be called buttery smooth it is a six- to ten-year-old Chardonnay that grew up in new European oak barrels.

Other aspects of style and substance aside, age in a bottle of Chardonnay is an acquired taste. Any wine of mature years has darks and deeps of flavor that cannot be found in anything else worth eating or drinking, so there is only one place to learn. Whites show age more than reds, so Chardonnay becomes the particular case.

A rich, firm Chardonnay needs at least three years after the vintage just to round itself into harmonious shape. Four would be better. A truly age-worthy bottle will begin to taste mature and bouquetish when it is five, then will hold a fine edge for another four or five years. Several of the 1968s from the Napa Valley, for example, were just coming into their own in 1973, when several of the 1965s had just begun to rely on wiles in place of main strength. A few of the 1962s, meanwhile, were aging about the way Lena Horne is.

Because Chardonnay is age-worthy, vintages count. The 1969s, to make the point emphatically, were going downhill at an alarming rate in late 1972.

To this juncture only the Napa Valley yields enough Chardonnays in any one vintage to establish a measuring stick, so the department of amplification follows in that subsection.

Among the Burgundians geographic appellations of origin help sort out shadings of style and substance for the person who wishes to pair wine with food. Chablis, Montrachet, and Pouilly Fuissé all use chardonnay grapes, but climate imposes certain limits, and, on top of them, time has produced consensus thinking about style in each commune.

In California varietal labeling disguises whatever differences may exist in style. Although some wines are labeled Chardonnay and other Pinot Chardonnay, no distinction is implied. It is just that chardonnay once was suspected of being a member of the pinot family by botanists, and still is by some vintners. Both wines come from the identical grape variety. For the sake of simplicity all wines are referred to simply as Chardonnay here.

California geography is not yet as complete a clue to the basic character of a wine as the French is because Californians do not yet accept a consensus style based on vineyard locations. After all, Hanzell only opened the door to perceptibly oaky

A simple but appropriate air-lock allows the last few bubbles of CO_2 to escape from a Stony Hill Chardonnay as it finishes fermenting. (HAROLYN THOMPSON)

The Rhine House at Beringer Vineyards.　(HAROLYN THOMPSON)

Preceding page: The vines of independent grower Jerome Draper roll across Spring Mountain.　(WINE INSTITUTE)

Sterling Vineyards on its lofty knoll near Calistoga.   (HAROLYN THOMPSON)

The Joseph Phelps winery nestles in a fold in the hills just above the
main floor of the Napa Valley.   (HAROLYN THOMPSON)

wines with its vintage of 1957, the first winery in post-Prohibition California to make full use of Burgundian oak barrels as a source of flavor and strength. Only a handful of earlier California Chardonnays had been aged in barrels of any kind, most being of American White oak. A great many Californian cellarmasters have yet to make a final decision about oak and age. Until they do, regional styles will remain an open question.

As for substance, the Napa Valley has dominated California Chardonnay since the day most of its winemakers gravitated toward the buttery riches of the Côte d'Or—especially Montrachet—as their essential model, and began expanding plantings around the most successful of their older vineyards.

The earlier developments at Hanzell, combined with later ones in the Alexander Valley in Sonoma County, suggest that the regions north of San Francisco Bay will continue their current dominance for years to come, and perhaps expand on it. The regions south of San Francisco, with so many new vineyards and so few new wineries, cannot help but default. A good many more vintages will have to come and go before the wines of Monterey, San Benito, and Santa Barbara can be talked about as anything but potentially fine. Surviving Alameda and Santa Clara Chardonnays cannot pose a challenge for lack of numbers.

Although growers admired the grape as early as the 1880s, chardonnay got off to a relatively slow start in California. Very little of it was planted anywhere in the state before 1918. After Prohibition the grape did not chase away any other variety because most plantings had been enfeebled by viruses. Acreage remained insignificant into the 1960s, when virus-free nursery stocks finally began to be available.

Americans did not buy what Chardonnay wines were available. Even a roving scout for the French Guide Michelin who gave unstinting praise to Wente Bros. Chardonnays of the 1950s could not stir the American public much, or for long. It was only after European oak barrels came into general use that all styles of California Chardonnay became glamorous enough to seek out.

Napa Valley Chardonnays

The Napa Valley damages generalities about chardonnay as well as any region in California. In theory, chardonnay's best wines should come from old vines rooted in poor soil on slopes of climate Region I, as in Europe. Some excellent ones do. Others as good or better come from young vines in rich valley bottom where Region II begins to shade into III.

It seems that California growers have found that big, healthy vines fare better in the California sun, and that these must be planted in rich soil so they might prosper. However, an infinity of questions remains to be answered.

While the search for a local wisdom goes forward, some outlines have emerged. Most of the valley's chardonnay acreage runs along the floor from Zinfandel Lane, south of St. Helena, on south to Yountville. A handful of venerated vines are up in the Mayacamas Mountains, especially on slopes tipped toward the morning light. The Carneros district in the extreme south end of the valley is young, but becoming a major factor.

From these plantings Napa's wineries produce a remarkable variety of Chardonnays, the qualities of which cannot be linked to any unshakable factor of sun or soil because all of the plusses and minuses seem to run at crosscurrents with vineyard locations. The practitioners with track records as of 1975 were, in alphabetic order: Beaulieu Vineyard, Beringer, Burgess Cellars, Chappellet, Chateau Montelena, The Christian Brothers, Freemark Abbey, Heitz Cellars, Inglenook Vineyards, Charles Krug, Louis M. Martini, Mayacamas, Robert Mondavi, Souverain of Rutherford, Spring Mountain Vineyards, Sterling Vineyards, and Stony Hill. All but The Christian Brothers vintage date their Chardonnays. All save Louis M. Martini and Chateau Montelena use Napa Valley as their appellation of origin.

Heitz Cellars must bear much of the responsibility for the current rage for California Chardonnay, although with a vital boost from Hanzell early in the going.

Joe Heitz acquired Hanzell-made Chardonnays of 1961 and 1962 in cask from the estate of J. D. Zellerbach. Finishing and bottling these wines under his own label, Heitz sold them to a broader audience than Zellerbach had attempted to reach and at prices higher than people were accustomed to paying for any California wine. The audacity paid off. Critics forthwith reevaluated Chardonnay from the western wilds. Connoisseurs paid the price.

Beginning with the vintage of 1965, Heitz has gone on to enhance his original reputation with Napa Valley wines of his own making from two distinct and distinctive vineyards. Lots labeled UCV came from a U.C.-Davis experimental vineyard at Oakville, since uprooted. Lots labeled "Z" are from new vines flanking Zinfandel Lane, just a few hundred yards from the Heitz winery.

In both cases the Heitz Cellars style is, if anything, more sharply drawn than Hanzell's was. Zellerbach's model always was Chassagne-Montrachet. Heitz tries to make a wine that will outrank a fine Montrachet in a blind tasting.

The UCV, always slightly the lighter and more elegant of the two, had its last vintage in 1971. The stronger, earthier wine from the vineyard on Zinfandel Lane had its first crop in 1968, still viewed by Heitz as the finest Chardonnay he has made to date.

One Napa wine closely approaches the Heitz in strength and style each year. It comes from Freemark Abbey. There is no mystery behind the similarities. Bradford Webb, one of seven partners in Freemark Abbey, was Zellerbach's winemaker at Hanzell through all the experiments as well as the final successes. The first Freemark Abbey Chardonnay was from the vintage of 1968. That wine and its successors come from vineyards near Rutherford, in which sun and soil come together very much as they do at Zinfandel Lane.

These two wineries, between them, have scored impressively consistent wins over all comers in double-blind tastings of the best of California Chardonnays and Côte d'Or white Burgundies, even with French vintners on the panels.

Chardonnay is one of the few California wines that might be compared so directly with its European counterparts. In both places the wines tend to be wholly from chardonnay grapes, made and aged in almost identical ways. Even so, the overlaps are tiny. California has no Chablis or Pouilly, while France has no direct echo to several Napa Chardonnays let alone those of other districts.

The first leaves of spring wreathe an old chardonnay vine at Stony Hill. (HAROLYN THOMPSON)

Stony Hill, even though it is not to be bought at any store, has been a strong, long-term influence on Napa Valley Chardonnay. Proprietor Fred McCrea planted chardonnay on his tumultuous slopes northwest of St. Helena in 1948, long before the variety began to attract general attention. The cuttings came from Wente family vineyards in Livermore, almost the only source in the state then. As his wines became more and more polished, other growers in the valley followed McCrea's lead both in planting chardonnay and in acquiring their cuttings from Herman Wente, or from McCrea.

McCrea, although he ferments and ages his tiny annual production of Chardonnay in barrels, is a good deal more reticent then either Heitz or Freemark Abbey about letting the flavor of oak begin to impose itself on the flavor of his grapes. His particularity on the point is legendary, and explains a curious notation on the old Department of State list of American wines fine enough to be served at U.S. embassies around the world. Stony Hill Chardonnay (except 1963) was one of the accredited wines. The proprietor had been obliged to put his 1963 into new barrels rather than seasoned ones, causing it to become too oaky for his taste. It was, he always has agreed, an extraordinarily fine wine, but it was not representative of Stony Hill and he did not want anybody to think so, so he caused it to be exorcised from the list.

Beyond the matter of oak, McCrea prefers the grapes to strike an elegantly understated note. The implication is light wines, but that is not correct. They are pale in color and a bit subdued for nose in their youthful years. But they gain grace with age and gain age with grace. At five and six years they are rich and complex, and not to be mistaken for any other California Chardonnay. A bottle of Stony Hill and a piece of fresh-caught Pacific Salmon bring inimitable pleasures.

Chappellet, Chateau Montelena, Mayacamas, Souverain, Spring Mountain, and Sterling fit themselves into the Napa cosmonology slightly behind Heitz and Freemark Abbey for sheer riches, and somewhat closer to Stony Hill than the other two for style.

Although the Mayacamas vineyards go back to the early 1950s, Bob Travers made his first Chardonnay there in 1969, and should not be held accountable for the curiosity pieces that went before him. His 1972 is superbly rich. Sterling, too, made its first Chardonnay in 1969, using winery-owned vineyards at Calistoga. Winemaker Rick Forman had worked two vintages for Fred McCrea at Stony Hill as a prelude. His Sterling wines are softer than the Stony Hills, but a similarity of style links them. The Sterling 1971 has won critical applause everywhere it goes. Spring Mountain, after a slow start, began to resemble these others very closely with its 1972.

Only Souverain among these kindred wines goes back further than 1969, and then unwillingly. When Lee Stewart owned the original Souverain winery on Howell Mountain east of St. Helena, he would tell any visitor anytime that it would be far better to make the best possible wine out of thompson seedless and call that Chardonnay than to make any wine at all out of chardonnay. Although he made some good ones, using chardonnay, he still professes to hold the opinion, leaving it to the new owners of the transplanted winery to speak in kindlier tones of the grapes they buy from a scattering of independent growers, and to lavish the care chardonnay must have to prosper as a wine.

Only Chateau Montelena came later. Its inaugural Chardonnay, from an assemblage of Napa Valley and Alexander Valley grapes, was the 1972. Of all this lot it comes closest to the Stony Hill for tart delicacy of fruit flavors, but has a more forceful note of oak.

Any of the wines in this cluster of small cellars can come home a winner in any blind tastings. All almost certainly will finish with high marks. They are rich wines and worth seeking out in their rarity to show how many possibilities the Napa Valley offers the grape variety. They also are enough gentler in character than the titans to appeal more readily to people who do not wish to be overwhelmed by what they taste.

Among the larger cellars in the valley, the Chardonnays of Beaulieu Vineyard, Charles Krug, and Robert Mondavi have shown remarkably similar character in recent vintages. The Beaulieu, typically, shades a step deeper in color than the others, tastes somewhat more of oak, and goes past its peak a year or two sooner. Otherwise, all three share an agreeable pungency that in some faint way brings the taste of asparagus to mind. This pungent quality sets these wines apart from all the others. In fact the characteristic is, in my experience, uniquely Californian.

The Charles Krug Chardonnays in particular have challenged for the top rung in preference tastings since the mid-1960s. The asparagus, to summon back that image, has been well buttered.

The older, established vineyards of Charles Krug and Beaulieu are in the mid-valley, from Rutherford south to Oakville. More recently both wineries have added large acreages of chardonnay in the Carneros district without radically changing the wines. Robert Mondavi's chardonnay vines run southward from Oakville on both sides of the valley floor.

Beringer and Inglenook Vineyards have only recently turned toward small oak aging of their Chardonnays, which are lighter than the lightest of the other three sizable wineries in every respect. Beringer uses 150-gallon puncheons to hold down the wood-aged flavors in a soft, light, but pleasantly balanced wine. Inglenook uses regular barrels for a wine that has been coarser than the Beringer, a bit less adroitly balanced, but still a great improvement over earlier eras.

The Christian Brothers and Louis M. Martini have opted thus far to forgo small wood aging of their Chardonnays, which puts them into the category of conservationist Californians, throwbacks to an earlier, more direct style. The resulting wines are pale, rather lightly rigged, and quick to age. The Christian Brothers blend vintages to have bouquet as soon as a bottling is released. They are skillful about it. The wines give consistent pleasure along with a fair lesson in varietal character. Martini vintage dates his Chardonnays, but Louis P. himself views them as modest accomplishments and charges only modest prices. Except that they start out fresher, they are much like The Christian Brothers' Chardonnays.

Because the fine Chardonnays often but not always are durable, a quick summary of recent vintages in the valley is of some use:

1965—A vintage of great durability and considerable strength. Heitz, Charles Krug, and Stony Hill remained eminently drinkable in 1975, though they were past their peaks.

1966—A solid vintage. Several wines from it continue in robust good health, especially Heitz and Stony Hill.

1967—Except for Stony Hill, which unaccountably remains in good form, it was a weak year.

1968—A superior vintage for all hands, perhaps the best balance of elegance and durability of its decade. The smaller wines just began to fade in 1975. The strong ones appear able to go another three to five years in proper cellars.

1969—A weak and disappointing vintage. Many wines already have browned and started sliding downhill. Heitz Cellars is holding up fairly well.

1970—A solid vintage much like 1966, in which all hands fared well but none truly excelled.

1971—A vintage of charms rather than power. All of the wines have been pleasing. Some, such as Sterling, have been at the top of their form to date. Some, such as Heitz, are just beginning to round into drinking form.

1972—Although the vintage was extremely quirky taken overall, the early-ripening chardonnay had all the best of a cool year. The big wines, especially Heitz Cellars, Freemark Abbey, and Mayacamas, seem destined to age to greatness. Already it is an aromatic vintage.

1973—In the early going, the wines seem to be somewhat lighter in fruit character than the 1972s, but strong enough to be called a fine vintage. All are showing well. The Château Montelena won a huge vote of confidence from a panel of French experts, and has been pressed closely by all the rest.

1974—The probabilities are for another strong vintage in the mold of 1966 and 1970.

Sonoma and Mendocino Chardonnays

Once James D. Zellerbach demonstrated with his 1957 Hanzell that California Chardonnays could approach the Burgundian model in depth of flavor and character, the rest of Sonoma County's winemakers stood around for a decade in what was, presumably, a state of shock.

Nothing outstanding from any other Sonoma County vineyard followed the Hanzell example until the 1968 of J. Pedroncelli arrived. Since then the track has grown faster with each passing year. A majority of the genuinely impressive bottlings have come from Alexander Valley grapes rather than the Valley of the Moon. The rules of reason go against that. The Alexander Valley falls in the wavering gap between climate Regions II and III while much of the Valley of the Moon is a cool I, a closer kin to the Côte d'Or.

In 1975 the roster of wineries making Chardonnays from Sonoma grapes remained short: Buena Vista, Dry Creek Vineyard, Hacienda Vineyard, Hanzell Vineyard, F. Korbel & Bros., J. Pedroncelli, Sebastiani Vineyards, Simi Winery, Sonoma Vineyards, and Souverain of Alexander Valley. Z-D makes a Chardonnay in Sonoma, though using grapes from the Napa half of the Carneros district. Chateau St. Jean joined the company early in 1976.

In Mendocino County, Parducci Wine Cellars and Husch Vineyards have grown Chardonnays locally. Cresta Blanca makes Chardonnay at Ukiah, though not all of the grapes come from the home county.

Hanzell, to begin at the beginning, put very little Chardonnay into the world under its own label while Zellerbach was its proprietor. The famous one was the 1957. It also was the last. After Douglas and Mary Day bought the winery and vineyards in 1965 they enhanced the history of the place with a series of excellent wines, especially their 1965 and 1969. Under the Days, Hanzell Chardonnays consistently subdued the grape character, leaving the tastes of oak and age somewhat more in the forefront than Zellerbach had done. It is tempting to say they aimed for Montrachet and hit Meursault instead, but that misleads. Even though there was a softly Meursaultish quality to begin, the taste of the grape finally would win out. By 1972 the 1965 had become easy to identify as a Chardonnay in blind tastings after a long career of being mistaken for a wine made from the comparatively neutral pinot blanc, the softening agent in many Meursaults.

The production, even smaller than Stony Hill's, never went into general circulation, but did travel surprising distances from home in the hands of earnest hobbyists.

Hanzell's neighbors in the Valley of the Moon have stayed with less vigorous styles, less distinctive wines. A tiny cellar, Hacienda, produces a delicately fruity wine with a light kiss of oak aging. It is harmonious in its pale way. Sebastiani's Chardonnay, cleanly made, is pale and rather light, a Sonoma counterpart to Louis M. Martini Chardonnay in the Napa Valley. Buena Vista is just getting into production with new vineyards that straddle the Sonoma-Napa County line in Carneros, and is planning a new winery there. The Chardonnays that result from the new place will want judging rather than the present models.

Z-D, as small or smaller than Hacienda, makes a distinctively dry Chardonnay from Napa grapes. It is one of the best bottlings in the state for seeking out the apple-ish flavors of the grape in a strong, cleanly made wine. Fanciers of white Burgundies will find the wine a bit plain, perhaps coarse, but may be moved to admire its earthy vigor even so.

The Russian River district grows steadily more attractive as a source of Chardonnays.

J. Pedroncelli, beginning with the vintage of 1968, began making Chardonnays that allowed no doubt as to variety. Using Alexander Valley grapes, the brothers James and John Pedroncelli made then and continue to make deeply colored, austerely apple-ish wines. There is a hint of flavor from oak, but in the main the color comes from the fermentation period, for these are Chardonnays made for all chardonnay grapes are worth. The wines are at their best young, even when they bite back a bit, because that is when they teach their best lessons of varietal characteristic.

Simi Winery uses chardonnay grapes from the same part of the Alexander Valley as J. Pedroncelli does, but keeps generalists off balance by making from them a lightly colored, carefully polished wine with some of the faint asparagus-like pungency that marks the Napa Valley Chardonnays of Charles Krug and Beaulieu Vineyard. The first vintage, 1970, was the palest in color, the most Krugian. The 1972 and 1973 have shifted toward a slightly darker, slightly fuller style, more kindred to Beaulieu. Perhaps I am overly suggestible. The 1970 was made by Robert Stemmler, once a winemaker at Krug. The later ones have had André Tchelistcheff in attendance as an adviser. However, I stand by the perceptions.

Sonoma Vineyards produced a fine Chardonnay in 1970, a deeply colored one with strong varietal character, close to the Pedroncellis in those respects, but slightly more polished. Subsequent vintages have not lived up to the original promise, although the attempt has been there. The 1974 shows more promise than the interim vintages.

Souverain of Alexander Valley, a newcomer in 1975, showed a first wine that was light in character, but aimed in the generally clean, firm style of Charles Krug.

Now and again one wine will call up a flood of thoughts, not so much for what it is, but for somehow summing up an idea. F. Korbel & Bros. offered an estate Chardonnay 1974 as its first attempt with the varietal. It made me think of a Port-maker in the Douro wincing over a table wine because it struck him as acidic, the one quality in a healthy wine that is not welcome in a Port. And it made me think of a French Champagne-maker who found far too much fruit flavor in California chardonnay for his taste. So here it was, an atypically light, tart Chardonnay, made by somebody who is far more used to getting chardonnay grapes fermented into something that will grace a cuvée for a Korbel sparkling wine. The wine is easy, agreeable, but all out of character.

Through the vintage of 1974 the one Chardonnay from a small, estate-like cellar in the Russian River region comes from Dry Creek Vineyards. In every way it is the opposite of the Korbel: a big, oaky, full-flavored wine. Proprietor-winemaker David Stare opts for strength ahead of finesse. He draws upon vineyards which reward the notion.

Across the line in Mendocino County, Parducci Wine Cellars makes a vintage-dated Chardonnay of full body and soft finish, a beautifully clean wine, closer in style to Pedroncelli than any other.

Cresta Blanca Chardonnay is a lighter wine in all respects, sound, but indistinct as a varietal.

Central Coast Chardonnays

Up to 1974, all four wineries of size south of San Francisco Bay had been opting for Chardonnays of light and youthful charms, ignoring any Burgundian notions in favor of the traditional California emphasis on grape characteristics. In 1975 a newcomer went them one better, eliminating every hint of wood, age, or other sources of bouquet, but one old-timer, Almadén, turned toward a French style.

The endless shifting of vineyards in face of urban pressure has caused most of the wines by Almadén, Paul Masson, Mirassou, and Wente Bros. to come from a revolving set of sources in recent years. Only a few bottles have been eligible to bear a county name as appellation of origin. The newcomer, from The Monterey Vineyard, was one of the first that could.

Wente Bros., with its virtual monopoly on Chardonnay between repeal of Prohibition and the 1950s, set much of the style not only for the regions south of San Francisco, but for all California Chardonnays up to Hanzell. That style was and still is to emphasize the apple-ish flavors of the grape by picking ripe, then diminishing all other sources of aromatics, especially wood. Advances in technology have aided the Wentes in their search for fresh flavors. The advent of European oak barrels elsewhere in California did nothing to change Karl Wente's mind. Quite the opposite, he began with the vintage of 1971 to bottle just seven months after the harvest instead of the nine or ten he had allowed previously.

On a relative scale, this puts the Wente Bros. Chardonnay at the Chablis end of the scale rather than the Montrachet, but no comparison is quite apt. Wente Bros. provides a bit of pure Californiana because it uses riper grapes than any other region favoring a light fresh wine from the variety.

The great proportion of Wente's chardonnay vineyards are at Livermore, the traditional site, and will continue to be so because Karl Wente prefers the riper fruit he gets in warm Livermore to that grown in a smaller vineyard in cool Monterey County.

With the vintage of 1971 the old family firm of Mirassou began to go Wente one better in producing a light, fresh Chardonnay. The machine-harvested, field-crushed wine of that year was so light and fresh, in fact, that it already was bottled and in the market by June of 1972, ready to be compared to Mirassou's rich, austere vintage of 1969 the way the girl next door might be compared to Marlene Dietrich. Both wines came from the same Monterey County vineyards, which suggests once again that one patch of ground does not govern a wine's character so absolutely as some empirical critics would have us believe. The Mirassous have elected to stay with the girl-next-door style thus far. The wine is affable, but so uncharacteristic of Chardonnay as to defy criticism.

If the Mirassou is uncharacteristic, the 1974 Early Bottled Chardonnay of The Monterey Vineyard is much more so. The Early Bottled was fermented in stainless steel, allowed to soften for a few months still in steel, then bottled as a pure expression of the grape. Nobody has known quite what to think of it. The winery intends producing an orthodox, oak-aged bottling from 1974.

The two abundantly available Chardonnays from Central Coast wineries come from Almadén and Paul Masson, which wines differ from each other as much as styles can differ. The Paul Massons follow the Wente approach. The Almadéns lean now in the oak-aged direction of white Burgundies. The Almadén vines, in San Benito County, seem naturally to yield lusher fruit than do Monterey County chardonnays from the Salinas Valley. Almadén gives the wine a slight boost in the direction of full body with the merest hint of residual sugar.

And then there is the Chardonnay of Chalone Vineyards. The vines grow in scrawny soil beneath one rocky wall of The Pinnacles National Monument, as noted in describing the winery, and, somehow, yield a richly flavored crop which winemaker Dick Graff ferments and ages in European oak barrels. The resulting wine is dark-hued, powerfully aromatic, and powerfully bouquetish. Early vintages have not aged well. But, then, they have not had to do so, because they have been in harmony with themselves from their earliest days. They make a fascinating counterpoint to the similarly rich but far more stable Chardonnays of such Napa Valley producers as Heitz Cellars and Freemark Abbey.

Several of the tiny wineries in the Santa Cruz Mountains, on the west side of the Santa Clara Valley, have made Chardonnays of intense character, following the lead of Martin Ray, who years ago made his wines in American oak barrels and, as a result, redoubled the natural character with bouquets from the wood and from oxidation. Ridge and David Bruce are most likely to appear in a market outside of the Santa Clara Valley. They both are strong wines, with the Bruce being almost as melodramatic as some of Ray's old efforts. The Ridge tends to be coarsely styled but cleanly made. The Bruce wines have been inconsistent from vintage to vintage, but always a fascinating gamble for anybody who will pay $12 or more to see what happened this time.

 CHENIN BLANC

(Alias Pineau de la Loire and White Pinot)

Chenin Blanc, by its primary name or one of the alternates, belongs to the benighted league of small wines, the ones without enough character to age well, or bite back.

Small wine or no, it serves as a kind of backbone among whites. The grape grows rather well in a wide range of climates, yielding a gently flavored wine that can be made dry or modestly sweet. Dry, it makes versatile if unobtrusive company to almost any lightly flavored food. Sweeter, it is California's most successful hammock wine to date.

The grape variety originated in the Loire Valley in France. There, especially at Vouvray, the disarming simplicity of its slightly sweet wine makes people forget the alcoholic content.

Chenin blanc vines were imported to California early in the state's vinous history. While Vouvray always could charm in carafe on the terraces of riverside inns in the Loire, this country did not have the custom of roadside wine drinking, nor did early California have the technology to bottle wines for fresh sweetness so they could be sent to drinkers who wanted some. The grape variety was held in low regard until cold fermentation and more skillful filtering techniques made youthful charms durable enough to survive bottling and shipment. Its reputation began to soar in the mid-1950s when Bob Mondavi coined Chenin Blanc as a varietal name for wine made in the Vouvray style. Up to that point chenin blanc had made a dry white of limited appeal. Improved technology has tuned up the dry ones as much as the sweets.

When Mondavi launched Chenin Blanc as a name and a style in California the Napa Valley had a virtual monopoly on plantings of the grape variety. It since has become one of the most widely planted white grapes in the state, mainly because it has become the base for white table wines and Charmat sparkling wines from the San Joaquin Valley.

Although people on the enology faculty at the University of California at Davis grumble at the popularity of Chenin Blanc on grounds that Semillon has superior character, they do so against their own discovery that most people prefer to begin drinking wine with relatively neutral, definitely sweet whites. We are a nation of beginners, and Chenin Blanc adheres to the profile with unshakable fidelity. Its characteristics are so wispy, in fact, that the scholars never have been able to identify them more closely than by the phrase "pleasantly fruity."

In the mid-1970s most of the commercially available Chenin Blancs from coastal producers come too sweet to fit easily into meals. They serve better as picnic or sipping wines.

A substantial number of the newer, smaller cellars make the wine dry, frequently labeling it Dry Chenin Blanc. Some of the larger wineries follow the same practice, or call the dry wine White Pinot.

The San Joaquin producers occupy a middle ground, offering Chenin Blanc as a softer, milder wine than the drier bottlings from the coastal producers, but a less flowery, less sweet one than the sweeter Chenin Blancs from the coast.

By any name the drier Chenin Blancs do a proper job with chicken in all its guises, and, mayhap, veal or sole meunière. Sweet Chenin Blancs, no matter how called, should follow their true callings as wines to sip ice cold while somebody shows off his folio volume of Norman Rockwell, or summer takes a nice turn while you are in a comfortable posture. All should be drunk young and without second thoughts.

Incidentally, Chenin Blanc has a legitimate alias in Pineau de la Loire, or just Pineau, and an illegitimate one in White Pinot. The latter cropped up in the 1880s as a missed translation of Pineau, and endured because it was easier for Yankee tongues than either of the French originals. (A textbook example of nomenclature problems arose out of Lee Stewart's attempts to sell his wine from this variety at Souverain. The same wine was labeled Chenin Blanc for the San Francisco market and White Pinot for Los Angeles because it would not sell under the alternate name in either city. When Stewart sold Souverain his successors solved the problem by renaming the wine Pineau Souverain, which sells equally well in both places.) I suppose it is a tribute to our linguistic progress that nearly all wines from the variety are known now as Chenin Blanc or Pineau de la Loire. Only three White Pinots linger.

Napa Valley Chenin Blancs

The Napa Valley, traditional home to the chenin blanc grape, has ebbed and flowed on style. For all the years up to the early 1950s all of the wine from the variety was made dry. After Bob Mondavi coined Chenin Blanc, the trend went almost entirely in the direction of sweet. With the coming of the new wave of small cellars after 1967, the field has divided itself half and half. The dividing line, while not rigid, is sharp enough to separate the wines for dinner from the ones for sipping.

The dinner table candidates form a long list. However, the volumes are small in nearly every case. The roster includes Burgess Cellars Chenin Blanc, Chappellet Chenin Blanc, Cuvaison Chenin Blanc, Inglenook White Pinot, Charles Krug White Pinot, Louis M. Martini Dry Chenin Blanc, Mayacamas Chenin Blanc, Souverain of Rutherford Pineau Souverain, Sterling Vineyards Chenin Blanc, and Stonegate Chenin Blanc.

Of these, the Charles Krug White Pinot has been a curiously pleasing wine for many years. Essentially light of body and delicate of flavor, with a year of bottle age it develops subtle overtones of earth, or maybe apple. No light, casual meal deserves a brighter, more polished companion than this wine once it has acquired its distinctive mark of bottle bouquet.

Louis M. Martini Dry Chenin Blanc is darker-hued, rounder, more lush in its fruit flavors. It has enough substance to mate with chicken in cream sauce as easily as with chicken plain, partly because it ages long enough in wood to acquire some bouquet. The wine carries a vintage date.

The others in the roster of dry wines tend to fall between these two, paler in color and fruit flavor than the Martini, but fuller than the Krug. All tend to finish a shade sharper on the palate then either the Martini or the Krug, bearing out the academic warning from the U.C.-Davis that truly dry Chenin Blancs may say good-bye to the palate with just a hint of bitterness.

Sterling Vineyards played a bit of a trick on the world with its 1972 Chenin Blanc by adding a small but forcible presence of Chardonnay to the blend. It was a nerve-shattering precedent for the other producers to think about, a rather better than average white wine to drink with dinner, but unclassifiable as Chenin Blanc.

The picnics-only list includes Beringer Chenin Blanc, Charles Krug Chenin Blanc, The Christian Brothers Pineau de la Loire and Chenin Blanc, Inglenook Vineyards Chenin Blanc, Robert Mondavi Chenin Blanc, and Oakville Vineyards Chenin Blanc. The choice between them is mainly a matter of personal preference.

Robert Mondavi Chenin Blanc is a good reference point for deciding. Mondavi, the father of all Chenin Blancs when he was at Charles Krug, now makes his wine as fresh as techniques and equipment permit. The small degree of residual sugar is elegantly offset by the curiously crisp taste that apparently comes from very cold fermentation in stainless steel and also by a delicate touch of spritz that comes, I have been told, from slightly pressurized bottling tanks.

Another useful reference wine is The Christian Brothers Pineau de la Loire, entirely from grapes grown at Mont La Salle in the cool hills above Napa city. It is much like the Mondavi, but without the hint of spritz.

Sonoma and Mendocino Chenin Blancs

Although the roster of producers is a long one, Sonoma has only recently begun to show some promise as a source of Chenin Blancs. It still cannot compete with the Napa Valley for distinctiveness, but several labels are at the very least price-worthy. Mendocino, curiously, is at least the equal and perhaps the superior of Sonoma as a source of wines from chenin blanc.

Most of the truly promising Chenin Blancs of Sonoma come from the Russian River watershed. Souverain of Alexander promises a clean, richly fruity sweet Chenin Blanc in the style to which winemaker Bill Bonetti became accustomed during his decade at Charles Krug. Simi has a similar wine under the name of Chenin Blanc, and a drier model under the name of Chenin Blanc Sec. The drier one is a well-made, agreeable wine for casual dinners, but only an average wine in the whole field of dry wines from the variety. F. Korbel & Bros. entered the lists of off-dry Chenin Blanc producers in 1974 with a soundly made example at a fair price. Sonoma Vineyards had yet to find a steady stride as of mid-1975, but tends to search in the sweeter end of the realm.

Among the smaller vineyards both Dry Creek and Trentadue work the dry end of the scale, so far with disappointingly sharp results, but with promise of finer bottlings to come.

Cambiaso Winery crushed a Chenin Blanc in 1974. It had yet to reach the market in mid-1975, but the promise was for another dry style.

Over in the Sonoma Valley, Sebastiani Vineyards makes an uncommonly soft, sweet, and very clean Chenin Blanc for picnickers. Nearby a small winery, Kenwood, offers a pale, delicate, rather dry Chenin Blanc suited to light meals in much the same way that Charles Krug White Pinot is, though the Kenwood is not quite so finely polished.

Parducci Wine Cellars, the venerable label in Mendocino County, makes a husky, almost earthy wine from chenin blanc grapes. The merest hint of residual sugar remains to soften the effect, but in the main the wine is a straightforward, tartly fresh accompaniment to easy eating, a savory introduction to the character of the variety.

Cresta Blanca makes a clean, fresh, perceptibly sweet Chenin Blanc that relies more on affability than any other quality to charm its drinkers.

Central Coast Chenin Blancs

The scattered vineyards of chenin blanc in the counties south of San Francisco Bay produce the contradictions of style that familiars of the region expect, and, perhaps, some revolutionary characters.

The cool, misty north end of the Salinas Valley in Monterey County has no respect at all for conventional styles of Chenin Blanc.

Paul Masson nonvintage Chenin Blanc has a more than faintly Germanic cast. The evident smack of sweet balances against a Rhein-like acidity well enough for the wine to finish almost dry. Along with that, the alcohol is an atypically low 11.5 percent. Once the shock of discovery wears off, the wine is pleasant to drink with fresh fruit in a summer garden, but always in lieu of a Sylvaner or a modest Johannisberg Riesling rather than some other Chenin Blanc. The appellation is only California, but it seems rather certain that all or nearly all of the grapes come from Masson's Monterey County vineyards.

The Monterey Vineyard, using only local grapes, makes a paler wine in a kindred style.

Mirassou Vineyards makes its Chenin Blanc along similar, but coarser, less Germanic lines. The first two vintages were not so full-flavored, but the Mirassous say they prefer the newer, heavier style, and intend to pursue it. Even in the revamped form it is a more piquant wine than most Chenin Blancs from north of San Francisco.

Meanwhile, up on the flanks of Mount Chalone several hundred feet above the main Masson vineyards and the valley mists, Richard Graff makes his Chalone Chenin Blanc after the fashion of white Burgundies. He waits for high sugars, then ferments and ages his wines in new French oak barrels. Now and again a fermentation will stick, but Graff tries to make the wine bone dry. In a favorable vintage, after a full fermentation, the wine becomes deep-hued, rich and complex, fit for Burgundian duties. When things go less well, the result is ungainly. In either case the first year in the bottle is the best one. As with other Chalone wines, there are but a few hundred bottles a year, all of them bought by familiars.

The rest of the Central Coast is a good deal more orthodox.

The Novitiate of Los Gatos has a Chenin Blanc which is at once faintly sweet and firmly bouquetish. The sweet part is straightforward enough. The bouquet comes principally from the ancient oak casks at the Novitiate. It is an earthy kind of smell, and not unpleasant. In fact, European-oriented people who think of California wines as relentlessly overclean are likely to find this wine an agreeable one.

Concannon Vineyards joined the list of Chenin Blanc producers in 1975 with a well-produced, typically soft example that stressed fresh flavors and a gentle hint of sweet.

Almadén Vineyards, relying principally on its San Benito County vines, produces one of the sweetest Chenin Blancs in the state, and one of the softest, or, if you will, flabbiest. It is, for my taste, the sweetest of the too-sweet. However, the nonvintage wine is soundly made, and may be just the thing to get a maiden aunt off of Lydia Pinkham's or one of its successors and onto the more versatile charms of table wine.

The remaining two widely distributed Chenin Blancs from wineries with Central Coast headquarters belong to San Martin and Weibel. Both have been sound, and conventionally Vouvrayish in style. Because of new vineyards in Monterey County, the San Martin may shift at least somewhat toward the tarter style of Paul Masson.

In addition to these there are locally available wines from Bargetto in Santa Cruz, Bertero in Gilroy, and Woodside in the town of that name. Except for the Woodside, which is an elegantly dry but infinitesimal production, they are merely white wines.

San Joaquin Valley Chenin Blancs

As the acreage chart makes obvious, chenin blanc has escaped from the old Napa Valley monopoly to become established in staggering quantities in the San Joaquin Valley, where it serves three purposes. It is a base for generic chablis. (Gallo Chablis Blanc is as close to being Chenin Blanc as the name sounds.) Wine from the variety is a major element in Charmat sparkling wines. Finally, and most encouraging of all, it is a pioneer valley varietal along with Emerald Riesling, French Colombard, and Semillon. Already Chenin Blancs from the San Joaquin offer sound, reliable wines competitive with all of the modestly priced Chenin Blancs from coastal producers.

Barengo Cellars near Lodi has had a soft, perceptibly sweet Chenin Blanc for several years as a pleasant picnic or sipping wine. So, too, has the East-Side winery in Lodi under its Royal Host label. Neither has had the luxury of cold fermentation or glass-lined steel for aging, and still the wines have been clean and agreeable.

The first cold-fermented, steel-aged Chenin Blancs from valley producers began to be released in 1972. The roster almost immediately included the M. LaMont label of Bear Mountain, the Setrakian label from California Growers, the Ambassador label of California Wine Association, E. & J. Gallo, Giumarra, and Winemasters Guild. The Gallo and Guild bottlings include some coastal grapes in their blends. The rest are purely valley-grown wines.

Theoretically the valley vineyards are in regions one shade too hot for chenin blanc grapes. However, the proprietors have been convinced by trial efforts that overhead mist irrigation and new pruning techniques in the vineyards and cold fermentation in the winery will more than overcome any excess sunshine. The early signs point to their being right enough to make these wines good values for everyday drinking. The styles consistently are muted in varietal character compared to the most fragrant of the coastal wines. They are less crisp, and, in compensation, a shade less sweet than the sipping-style bottlings such as Charles Krug or Robert Mondavi. In sum, they hover in the middle ground between being dinner and sipping wines.

Southern California Chenin Blancs

To this point the measure of Chenin Blanc in the regions south of the Tehachapi Mountains has been taken by Callaway Vineyards and Winery in two bottlings which are at once alike and not alike.

The Callaway Chenin Blancs are not alike because the 1974 was conventionally dry, even a bit bitter on the finish, while the 1973—subtitled Sweet Nancy—was richly sweet after the grapes for it were heavily botrytised. They were alike in sharing a pungently vegetative aftertaste that kept them from being fruity in the typical way of Chenin Blancs from other parts of the state.

More vintages are required to know what is going on with the varietal wine in the new growing region called Temecula, or Rancho California.

❧ FRENCH COLOMBARD ❧

After a long and most honorable career as a blend grape french colombard began in the early 1970s to gain an identity of its own for making by far the finest white varietal now to be had from the warmer valleys of California.

In its generic days french colombard went into bottles labeled Chablis or Dry Sauternes, where it was valued not so much for its own distinctive flavor as for its brisk acidity. Flavor is easy to get in California; acidity is not.

Some winemasters persist with the dry wine of old, the style that wages successful wars with both fat and herbs in Italianate chicken dishes, or tartly sauced veal. Several of the more adventurous producers prefer to flirt with the flowery, almost perfumey aroma and taste of french colombard fermented not quite dry. The touch of sweet need not be out of place in so tart a wine as colombard can make, especially when cold fermentation has kept its flowery character intact.

Although technical assumptions by nontechnical people are risky, I think this is a case of a good grape having had to wait for temperature-controlled stainless steel fermentors. A normal fermentation gets warm enough to cook some of the delicate aromatics out, leaving a wine both more neutral and more coarse. French colombard demonstrates almost perfectly the role of cold fermenting. Before, the wine tended to be made dry, in the loose role called Chablis in California. Since cold fermentation, the tendency has been to balance sweet and tart, in a style generally identified as Rhine. The latter is more appropriate to the varietal flavor.

In the end French Colombard balks comparison with anything European, although head-to-head tastings can be informative. The 1972 Parducci French Colombard from Mendocino County, for example, put a plausibly good Mainzer Spätlese to rout because it had similar balances of sweet and tart, but embodied them in a wine of richer, cleaner fruit flavors and thus made a happier whole. A drier, less flowery French Colombard from Wittwer (not generally available, alas) suggested itself as an alternative to either a Muscadet or Mâcon Blanc with seafood, again without tasting like the Europeans. In short, it shows all the signs of being a versatile original.

French Colombard is not one of the titans. The comparisons hint at that. But it comes close enough to fuddle the line between wines of the first class and those of the second because, well made, it satisfies one more ably than routine wines from nobler grape varieties.

Curious as the fact may seem, this is the same grape that produces the disagreeably sharp Charentes wines destined not for drinking but for distillation into Cognac. As in the cases of all other French varieties, removal to North America led to less acidity in ripe grapes than was normal in the ancestral home. In the case of colombard, the change was from too much to just enough.

In spite of being well suited to the warmths of interior California french colombard has struggled to survive. It lost its name en route, and was established in the San Joaquin Valley in the 1880s as west's white prolific. (Sauvignon vert already had been mistakenly identified as colombard.) Because west's white prolific would not ship successfully to home winemakers, the variety was uprooted from most of its known acreage during Prohibition. In the 1930s a legendary California winemaker named L. K. Marshall discovered a few vines in mixed plantings in Lodi, recognized quality when he saw it, and propagated the variety as Winkler, in honor of A. J. Winkler at U.C.-Davis. Some years later Winkler's colleagues at the university positively identified french colombard as itself.

The grape is the kind winemakers design when they are having happy dreams. It produces huge crops of healthy fruit in a wide range of climates, and makes sound, balanced table wines almost everywhere it will grow. The wine ferments readily, ages without ailment, and is durable in the bottle.

Now that the country has shown some signs of thirst for table wine, the acreage has begun to attain the volume it should have.

Coast Counties French Colombards

The Russian River Valley above Healdsburg, and most especially the Ukiah district, seems to be a blessed natural home for french colombard and its varietal wine. Although the region is graded down as a source of many whites, it is responsible for the richest, most harmonious bottlings of French Colombard yet made in these exploratory times.

The Parducci French Colombards have blossomed from year to year. The 1969 was good, but not rich. The 1971 had more of the fermentor-fresh quality. The 1972 had that and rich fruit flavor in a fine sweet-tart balance. The 1973 was a wine to make a lifelong believer out of a person. The vineyard from which it comes is a small one, lean soil clinging to an east-facing ridge just above and behind the winery. The vines bear shyly, one of the difficult achievements with this overwilling variety, but a necessity before the wine can have much depth of flavor.

Cresta Blanca's French Colombard, from a scattering of Mendocino vineyards, has not been consistent. Some bottlings have closely approached the Parducci in style and substance. Others have been less fresh, more bouquetish.

Souverain of Alexander Valley appears on the way to a finely fresh style, akin to the Parducci, with the wine it calls Colombard Blanc. Vintage-dated, from vineyards in both Sonoma and Mendocino, the early bottlings tended to be more delicately floral than the Parduccis, but a similarly tart balance made them more than mildly appealing. (Some appeared under the since-abandoned Ville Fontaine and Chateau Souverain labels, but the wines have been as steady as the names have not.) Sonoma Vineyards has a French Colombard of similar style and character.

The Napa Valley's ample acreage of french colombard has gone to make only two varietal wines. Oakville Vineyards made a soft, perhaps too soft wine from the vintage of 1972. But the vinification was clean and the promise of firmer character was there. One Napa vineyardist ships his crop to a little winery in grapeless Humboldt County where it becomes Wittwer French Colombard. The wine is less intensely flavorful than the Parducci, drier, and thus seemingly more tart. This is the limited edition that somehow seems appropriate as an alternative to a young Muscadet or Mâcon Blanc. The day could come when more growers in Calistoga and other warm parts of Napa County will admire french colombard for itself and not as fodder to lose in generics, but no additional bottles loom on the immediate horizon.

San Joaquin Valley French Colombards

The awesome increases of french colombard plantings in the San Joaquin Valley in recent years have become part of the great blossoming of varietal wines from that sunny vastness.

Years ago University of California at Davis experimental wines gave more than mild hints that French Colombards from the big valley could be excellent if the grapes were harvested early enough and the wines made to be fresh. The first commercial bottlings of the 1970s are bearing out the promise.

French Colombards from the San Joaquin do not have quite the savory flavor of their Mendocino counterparts, nor can they be quite as tart. For all of that, several large wineries have succeeded in making French Colombard in a more or less Rhenish style. Several others have been content to go a shade drier, more in the direction of a traditional chablis-type from California.

The first and still the most successful of those seeking to balance sweet with tart is Bear Mountain Winery under its M. LaMont label. The grapes come from the vineyards of member growers of the cooperative, all of them located on a tilting plain just east of Bakersfield, in Kern County.

The French Colombard of E. & J. Gallo attempts a similar style. The wine, although very clean and fresh, does not have as much strength of varietal character, nor does it have quite so crisp a finish. The Gallos use both coast and valley grapes.

Both teeter on the borderline between being afternoon sipping wines and mealtime bottles. If they do go with meals, they go better with chicken than fish.

Of the French Colombards made a shade drier for easier use with food, the one labeled Ambassador has a more generous flavor of its grape than the others, and perhaps a more subtle balance of that flavor with a full body. The wine is made from southern San Joaquin grapes at the A. Perelli-Minetti & Sons winery at Delano, north and west of Bakersfield.

Giumarra French Colombard, made at the family winery east of Bakersfield, and Setrakian French Colombard, made from local grapes at the California Growers Winery near Fresno, both compete favorably.

Other French Colombards

Three French Colombards remain, one hugely available from undefinable sources, the second less widely available from vineyards almost as hard to pinpoint, the third an intensely local wine.

The hugely available one is the Inglenook Navalle French Colombard, probably a blend of coastal and interior grapes much like the counterpart wine of E. & J. Gallo. On its introduction the wine had a lovely perfume of its grape and a brisk finish. Subsequently it has grown blander on both counts until it now ranks about even with the Gallo and a shade behind M. LaMont in distinctiveness of character. It remains perfectly sound, and a good value for money.

Under the Winemasters Guild label, Guild Wineries and Distilleries offers a wine similar in style to the Inglenook, and as deep or deeper in flavor than the original. Some of it comes, undoubtedly, from the same Mendocino County vineyards that yield Cresta Blanca French Colombard. A considerable share must come from valley grapes.

Up in the slowly reawakening Sacramento Valley, the north half of the great central valley of California, a small winery called Butte Creek is making vintage-dated French Colombards in the tart, off-dry style that begins to dominate coast counties bottlings. In its finest vintage to date, 1972, it had a true varietal aroma and a surprisingly tart finish, considering that the grapes grow at Viña, one of the warmest vineyard sites in the state.

❧ GEWÜRZTRAMINER ❧

One of the thoughts about *Vitis vinifera* is that the whole family tree goes back to some ancestral muscat in Persia. If this is so, most north European descendants have changed their profiles enough to hide the fact, but not gewürztraminer.

Muscat remains tangible in the wine after all the years as a haunting shadow of a flavor, a faint touch of bitter at the end of a sip. The quality makes any whole-hearted Gewürztraminer one of the easiest varietal wines in the world to identify and one of the hardest to fit into dinner.

Look past muscat and the essence of the varietal is spice without being any specific spice, and still a flavor too pungent to be called either fruity or flowery. Temper gewürztraminer somehow, and the spice does indeed fade into a softer, more flowery flavor.

In Alsace winemakers unanimously emphasize the pungencies, I think because such a wine makes an effective antidote to the buttery riches of Alsatian cookery. Californians do not have to take into account a national diet based on pâté de foie gras, and anyway all but a few of their vineyards yield a softer wine as a matter of nature. Only Louis M. Martini has a long record of aiming toward an Alsatian style, but, then, only Louis M. Martini has a long record of doing anything at all with gewürztraminer in California. New plantings since 1966 and newcomers to the roster keep making the track faster for Martini as well as those who seek less spice and more flower.

Both spicy and flowery Gewürztraminers have a reputation for tasting better while the sun is up. The spicy ones make superb apéritifs in lieu of light sherry-types. Softer, sweeter bottlings add light to the lazy hours of summer afternoons.

The grape variety emerged from one of the Gothic vaults of European time, but did not catch hold as an important element in its prime Alsatian vineyards until 1920, when the wine industry there reformed itself.

California's experience has been even more laggard. The grape migrated from Alsace before the turn of the century with only a slight loss of acidity, but did not emerge as a variety of any importance until a few years ago. As late as 1959 the total plantings were only 131 acres. The varietal wine did not really catch the public fancy until the early 1970s.

The newer plantings include some of the finest ones, though gewürztraminer of all grapes teaches humility to vineyardists. In the wrong places it retains no character whatever, or else becomes a gross caricature of itself. Thus far Sonoma and Monterey counties appear to be its most compatible environments.

Napa Valley Gewürztraminers

In spite of Louis M. Martini, Gewürztraminers from grapes grown in the Napa Valley thus far have tended to mute spice as a quality.

Martini is the old, reliable source of Gewürztraminer in the valley, but the grapes come from his Monte Rosso vineyards in Sonoma County. Ignoring that fact for the moment, the Martini Gewürz ranks at the head of the list among all Californians in matters of dryness, spice, and inherited traits from muscat. The latter are so pronounced, in fact, that people occasionally accuse Louis P. of mixing a dollop of moscato canelli into the fermentors while the gewürz is in them. Louis, who is big, says no, and that he has begun to think of landing a short right on the ear of the next person who raises the point.

For a good many vintages this has been an elegant accompaniment to cold meats at lunch, but fine enough to be drunk alone. An overlay of bottle bouquet rounds off a wine that can start out sharp. Three years will bring a good bottle to a peak, and it will last as long again without fading. The longer a bottle lasts, the more it deserves to be opened for itself.

Of all the born-and-bred Napa Valley Gewürztraminers, the ones from Stony Hill have the greatest potential kinship to an Alsatian. However, proprietor Fred McCrea has found a style of his own. Somehow he mutes the spice to the point of understatement without losing the essence of it. Perhaps it is because he ferments and ages the wine in small oak cooperage. Perhaps it is because the mountainside vineyards produce a delicacy of flavor in any grape. Whatever the cause, McCrea achieves a dry wine of remarkable richness and balance, one most welcome at a dinner heavy with cream sauces even after sundown, and not a typically rowdy Gewürztraminer.

Alas, it is a lesson in style still waiting to be learned by the world at large. McCrea makes only 160 cases of this wine in a favorable vintage. Nobody else on his mountain grows the variety.

Joe Heitz, at Heitz Cellars, does not make a Gewürztraminer very often. His 1965, from McCrea grapes, pleased both Heitz and a visiting Alsatian vineyardist. His 1971, from an old, perhaps too old vineyard near Oakville, was a disappointment to him for lack of varietal character even though it drank very well.

Oakville Vineyards has a block of young gewürztraminers near the old ones noted above. The first wine, from the weather-beset vintage of 1972, came up light, clean, but of only dimly spicy character. As this vineyard matures through happier growing seasons it may yield wines of the dry, tart quality that marks a good Stony Hill, and with the same subdued spiciness.

The one other Napa Gewürztraminer of real merit over a great span of years, in addition to the Stony Hill, is from Charles Krug. Always without a vintage date, it offers itself as a different wine from all the others. The frank aim is for fresh flavors and a flowery softness. The Mondavi family ferments its gewürztraminers cold, leaves a faint hint of sweet in the wine and may even soften the blend with a gentler grape if the gewürztraminer comes in too strong. It is a wine to take on a spring afternoon of kite flying.

Five other Gewürztraminers, all of recent origin, carry Napa appellations. One comes from Inglenook, and a second from Sterling Vineyards. Both approach the softness of style of the Krug, but lack its delicacy. The Inglenook through its early career has tended to finish slightly sweeter, to be heavier. The vineyards from which it comes are scattered throughout the valley. The Sterling Gewürztraminers from 1972 onward have been dry, but a shade too heavy, or coarse, to match the Krug. The vineyards are at Calistoga. Souverain of Rutherford bowed into the field late in 1974 with an attractive though slightly sweet bottling. In 1976 Villa Mt. Eden and Joseph Phelps introduced Gewürztraminers, both of them light in all respects, and soft.

Sonoma and Mendocino Gewürztraminers

Once Louis M. Martini got across the Napa County line with his gewürztraminers from Monte Rosso, spice used to go out of the rest of the Sonoma crop. Since the emergence of the Alexander Valley the bet is not so sure.

Simi Vineyards offered its first nonvintage Gewürztraminer in 1972. The wine hovered between soft and spicy. That wine was followed by the vintage 1972, which was better, and the 1973, which was well nigh perfect. Somehow it has a great depth of spice without the tinge of bitter in the aftertaste, a rare accomplishment in California, and one not to be predicted from the warmish, rich soils of the Alexander Valley where its grapes grow. A greatly skilled taster might note the softer finish from lower acidity, but this is another wine (with the Louis M. Martini) to serve to people who learned their sense of style from an Alsatian.

J. Pedroncelli launched its Gewürztraminer with the vintage of 1973. The first try was not quite so finely polished as the Simi, but the essentials seemed to be all in place. The label bears close watching. The vines are principally in Dry Creek Valley. Dry Creek Vineyards introduced Gewürztraminer under its label with a vintage 1974. Like the Pedroncelli, it had enough pungent varietal character to be full of promise. The other new Gewürztraminer from the region belongs to F. Korbel & Bros., and it is a wee, wispy thing in comparison, but finely polished and easy to drink.

Sebastiani Vineyards, after several years of impeccably made, overtly sweet nonvintage Gewürztraminers, turned to a vintage date with its 1974. The vintaged wine was fresher than its predecessors, but still as appropriate with dessert as with appetizers.

The small winery called Grand Cru made its first Gewürztraminer in the vintage of 1974, a deft wine but one with subdued spice. The proprietors wish to make a pungent wine, and expect to do so as their vineyard in the Alexander Valley matures.

The one remaining Sonoma Gewürztraminer regularly offered comes from Buena Vista. The effort is toward an Alsatian style, but the results have been woefully browned by oxidation vintage after vintage since the mid-1960s. In spite of the past record, wines from 1975 and later may be worth exploration. The proper varietal character always lurked in the depths of old bottles. New equipment and a new winemaker may bring out that potential.

Mendocino County has two Gewürztraminers, both hard to assess. Husch Vineyards has offered the varietal annually since the vintage of 1972, but only a few bottles each year. The vineyard is in the cool, cloudy Anderson Valley just thirteen miles from the Pacific. It has yielded intensely aromatic fruit. Tony Husch has used the early wines to learn on. Cresta Blanca offered its first Gewürztraminer, from a scattering of Mendocino growers, late in 1975. The first try was appealing in a gentle, almost wispy way.

Central Coast Gewürztraminers

The surge into Monterey and San Benito counties accounts for a large share of the increased acreage of gewürztraminer in California since 1965. It also accounts for two wines that help make the field classier.

Mirassou Vineyards has an obviously blessed block of gewürz on benchland above the town of Soledad in Monterey County. The vines, planted in 1963, yielded a promising wine in 1968, a first-rate one in 1969, and a direct challenger to the most intense of Martini Gewürztraminers in 1971. The 1973 went past the Martini to become a heavy, almost coarse wine, suggesting that the proprietors might need to temper their cellar work in the direction of finesse rather than raw power.

The close resemblance of these grapes to Martini's poses another one of those cheerful little dilemmas that keep experts from becoming cocksure about what is going on in California vineyards. How is it that a wine from young benchland grapes in Monterey County can resemble in close detail a wine from old hilltop vineyards in Sonoma County, in fact do so more closely than any other Sonoma wine?

Time shows one major difference in the wines. They start out alike, sharp and refreshing. However the Mirassou does not hold its years as well as the Martini. It sort of crumples instead of getting rounder.

To amplify the dilemma, Wente Bros. produced its first Gewürztraminer from the vintage of 1972, with grapes from its vineyards near the Salinas Valley town of Greenfield. All of the spice was there, but embodied in a deft, almost delicate wine. The 1974 pushed even further in the direction of ethereal charms. It is not the restrained power of a Stony Hill, but a naturally light-hearted gentleness.

It is hard to imagine two unmistakable Gewürztraminers being more different than the Wente and Mirassou, and yet the vineyards are only a couple of miles apart.

Almadén's Gewürztraminer, primarily from the company's San Benito County vineyards near Paicines, is soft, with a slightly sweet finish, close kin to the Inglenook Vineyards Gewürztraminer in style and character. Cleanly made, always sound, it is one of the most appreciable Almadén whites.

 GREY RIESLING

There is only one thing to want from Grey Riesling: A straightforward, fresh taste to make agreeable company for buckets of steamed clams, or platters of chicken wings, or, at the fanciest, crab Louis.

In use the wine is interchangeable with Sylvaner, Traminer, and Emerald Riesling, all made in the same slightly off-dry, drink-now style.

Style aside, Grey Riesling's varietal character is at some odds with the others. The others share the north European flavor characteristic of tart fruit even though the wines themselves seldom are tart in the technical sense. Grey Riesling, in spite of the name, is bland, a fat Anjou pear rather than a Rhenish berry.

The difference is rooted in the origins of the grape. Grey riesling is not a riesling at all, but rather a Californian offshoot of trousseau, a common grape in the south of France, especially the Jura. Until recently grey riesling was thought to be the *chauche gris* of the Loire, but cannot claim even that small dignity. It is only the surprisingly bright child of altogether witless parentage, trousseau being universally scorned as a producer of poor table wine. Even as a variety of much improved flavor grey riesling wins no planting recommendation from U.C.-Davis, mainly because the fruit is difficult to crush and ferment.

Grey Riesling persists as a varietal wine, I suspect, because a good example is more interesting to taste than the best of Chenin Blancs.

Some producers make Grey Riesling light and as crisp as they are able, presumably in an effort to make the wine live up to its inappropriate name. Others strive more in the direction of a fuller, more flowery style, harking back to the idea that it might make a good, Loire-ish bridge between the Burgundian varieties on the one hand and a faceless generic on the other. Both schools of thought have benefited greatly by temperature-controlled steel fermentors, an easy source of freshness that otherwise is difficult to achieve.

Napa Valley Grey Rieslings

By volume the Napa Valley produces a considerable proportion of California Grey Riesling, though the roster of producers is relatively short.

Beringer, The Christian Brothers, Charles Krug, and Inglenook all make enough of the wine to distribute nationally. A fifth cellar, Cuvaison, produces a tiny amount for local sale in California. Beringer and Charles Krug tend toward soft, fleshy wines. The Christian Brothers and Inglenook favor the leaner, more Germanic approach, as does Cuvaison.

All use Napa Valley as the appellation of origin. Beringer, Inglenook, and Cuvaison vintage date the wines as an advisory to drink them young.

All five are adroit, well made. None is supreme in the modest field of the state at large.

Sonoma and Mendocino Grey Rieslings

Sonoma is the basic source of an imbalance between numbers of producers and numbers of acres of grey riesling. The county has the second smallest acreage of grey riesling on the coast and, with only minor help from Mendocino vines, far the longest list of producers.

Seven Sonoma wineries offer Grey Rieslings. Mendocino has two. The region consistently produces the most engrossing examples of the varietal in all California.

F. Korbel & Bros. makes its Grey Riesling as a modestly tart, surprisingly distinctive wine. The University of California at Davis flavor association lists refer to Grey Riesling as faintly spicy. The Korbel bottling lives up to that advance billing as closely as any. It goes well not only with chicken wings, but with meatier fowl in cream sauces, always a fair test of depth of character in a white.

On its good days, Sonoma Vineyards Grey Riesling is, on my palate, indistinguishable from the Korbel.

Souverain of Alexander Valley has headed toward a softer, rounder style, closer to a dry Chenin Blanc in character. The first attempt, a 1972 bottled under the now defunct Ville Fontaine label, set the pace. It and subsequent vintages have borne the freshness of a cold-fermented wine with just enough residual sweet to avoid any sense of tart, or sharp.

Kenwood Vineyard has worked a similar but not quite so fermentor-fresh vein.

Tiny Trentadue Vineyard reaches for all the strength inherent in the variety. The first two tries were surprisingly rich, suggesting that Grey Riesling can indeed provide a pale but plausible alternative to Chardonnay for those who have the fancy but not the price, somewhat as Aligote is a dimly kindred cousin to a fine white Burgundy in France. Made as dry and full-bodied as Trentadue makes it, Grey Riesling tends to develop a bitter note in the aftertaste. That problem would need curing to make the style consistently admirable.

The remaining producers in the north bay region have been less successful than the others. Both Buena Vista and Cresta Blanca have allowed their wines to wait too long to be fresh in the bottle. A weary Grey Riesling does not have much to recommend it.

Central Coast Grey Rieslings

Only two Grey Rieslings come from the Central Coast counties. One is Almadén's. The other is Wente Bros., the original and still the champion of them all.

Wente Bros. Grey Riesling, light, crisp, usually dried by a faint whiff of sulfur, is the closest wine to a Germanic style in the field. A dollop of sylvaner in the blend helps. The preserving touch of SO_2 (sulfur dioxide) allows the wine to age in the bottle long enough to pick up a faint but agreeable bouquet, as a small German wine will. With that quality it is a wine to impress people who get snooty about second-line varietals. Faculty members at the U.C.-Davis have used it for that purpose with regular success, usually with a shrimp salad designed to enhance its fragile charms.

In the old days the appellation was Livermore Valley. With the advent of the Monterey County vineyards, the appellation is now California, though at no loss of character.

Almadén follows the soft, almost perceptibly sweet style. Weibel has a Grey Riesling, mostly from Mendocino grapes, which is a shade leaner than the Almadén, but essentially in the same style.

JOHANNISBERG RIESLING

(Alias White Riesling)

A few years ago, Dr. Maynard Amerine and his colleagues at the University of California at Davis established some learning curves for wine. A majority of novices, they found, took instant pleasure from faintly sweet whites. A similar majority needed time and experience to grow fond of dry, tannic reds.

That being the case, a typical California Johannisberg Riesling is one of the great learner's wines of the world. However, there is more to this wine than simple likability for learners. Its charms do not fade with experience. Neither do they dwindle before a good bottle is empty, because the character of white riesling grapes is complicated enough to sustain a lifetime of exploration.

Good though it is, California Johannisberg Riesling must be liked on its own terms or not at all. No other grape variety transmogrified itself so thoroughly in the emigration from Europe and still retained recognizable traits. Occasionally there is a haunting kinship between a California Johannisberg and an Alsatian Riesling, though this is unpredictable. A vaster gulf separates Californians from their Rhenish relatives. And a still vaster separation lies between Californian and Mosel wines.

Rhines and Mosels grow with less heat and less sunshine than the coolest, cloudiest districts of California afford. In favorable years the German wines come home at 10 to 11 percent alcohol. Californians run 12 to 13 percent as a matter of course. Well, not always. Now and again a sunny German and a cloudy Californian approach each other closely enough to recognize one another as cousins, dimly, but to the great pleasure of all.

In spite of their alcoholic strength the California Johannisberg Rieslings may be the more delicate and certainly are the more fragile of these wines.

German wines, habitual description aside, are not delicate. Rather they are precariously balanced among a complex series of strengths. An Ockfener, for example, provokes tangled impressions of grapefruit juice on the one hand, and some berryish nectar on the other, with odds and ends of barrels, Botrytis and sulfur thrown in to enhance the confusion. A poor example soon tips irretrievably toward the grapefruit juice, or toward simple syrup, or merely toward SO_2. On the other hand, a really fine bottle never loses its balance. There are German wines in their original cellars that are much older than the oldest living member of the producing firm, and in far better shape. Their durability is as great as it is inexplicable, but not any more delicate than grapefruit juice or sulfur.

California wine from the true riesling grape has more delicate, less contradictory flavors than the great Germans. There is nothing of grapefruit and very little of nectar about a typical California Johannisberg. The dry ones have much of the gentle freshness of a ripe melon, especially a Crenshaw. Sweeter, they somehow remind one of the thick, tart juices of a ripe, sun-warmed apricot.

At its dry best, a new California Johannisberg is an irreplaceable companion to fresh Pacific crab, or another sweet meat of shellfish. When the wine is sweet, it, like the Germans, serves best with light fingerfoods in the morning elevenses, or with a bit of plain cake or some nuts in the evening elevenses.

Dry or sweet, at its best means when it is older than a year but less than three. The freshness of the wine is truly evanescent, and seems more so since cold fermentation has bridged much of the gap between wine in the bottle and wine newly fermenting. The Johannisbergs do ferment cold, most of them in the 40° range.

To cite the classic example of youthful charms, the memory of Souverain Cellars Johannisberg Riesling 1968 still lights the eyes of all kinds of people, me included. I saved a few bottles to see what would happen. The act was sacrificial. By 1971 the wine was a pale ghost of something perfect. I still have two bottles. Damn.

On occasion winemakers grumble about the shortcoming of short life and threaten to abandon the variety and its wine, but the acreage devoted to white riesling grows each year. Except for a handful of new vines at Rancho California, in southern California, white riesling belongs to wineries in the ring of districts around San Francisco Bay. Monterey County has shot up to an enormous acreage in just a few years. The Napa Valley has the greatest diversity of styles in the wine, and the longest legacy of development.

The names, Johannisberg Ricsling and white riesling, require some explanation. The proper botanical name for the grape in California is white riesling. Only one fact lies between the existence of the proper name and its acceptance as a label designation, and that is that people do not buy wine labeled White Riesling half so readily as they buy the same wine labeled Johannisberg Riesling. A round dozen vintners have proven the point with practical experiments. A handful continues to wage the battle.

If the blame for an inappropriate modifier word lies with the American public, the source of the trouble goes back to the Germans who emigrated to California to make wine in the late 1800s. "Riesling" was the first prized white wine from the Napa Valley in an era when that district was dominated by Charles Krug, Jacob Schram, the Beringer Brothers, and a good many other Teutons. That they made their Riesling from the grape variety called sylvaner did not bother them. Later, when the true riesling came to be planted in California, varietal wines from it needed to be distinguished from the existing type. Schloss Johannisberg, the best-known source of true Rieslings, suffered the flattery of imitation.

Napa Valley Johannisberg Rieslings

With the vintages of 1968 and 1969 Heitz Cellars and Souverain Cellars established and epitomized two poles of style in Napa Valley Johannisberg Rieslings. Both wines were impeccably clean, fresh, meant for youthful service. Both came from the same vineyard high on the west hills of the valley. The consistent difference was in degree of sweet and so in all the qualities that hinge on that difference.

The Heitz was bone dry, and consequently rather high in alcohol, an almost austere wine, the one Californian that most readily suggested kinship with an

Newly harvested white rieslings in the Napa Valley. (WINE INSTITUTE)

Alsatian Riesling. The Souverain, on the other hand, was perceptibly but not grossly sweet, marked by the first California appearance of a balance between sugar and acidity that could be called Rhenish in character. All the others since have fallen between these two in style, and rather behind them in intensity of character. The drier Johannisbergs in addition to Heitz have been from Burgess Cellars, Chappellet Vineyard, The Christian Brothers, Freemark Abbey, Louis M. Martini, and Stag's Leap Wine Cellars. The sweeter ones, with Souverain, have been Beaulieu Vineyard, Beringer, Chateau Montelena, Inglenook Vineyard, Charles Krug, Robert Mondavi, Joseph Phelps, and, latterly, Stony Hill, which has gone over from the other camp.

All of these wines save the Louis M. Martini and the Chateau Montelena carry Napa Valley as their appellation of origin. All but The Christian Brothers and Charles Krug are vintage dated.

Year in and year out Heitz Cellars Johannisberg Riesling is a burly, assertive wine by any measure, but especially among Johannisbergs. The vintage of 1972 set what appeared to be an imperishable standard for intensity of character until the 1973 appeared. The Heitz produces, alone among all Californians of the variety, an immediate impression that the beverage is wine, and only secondarily turns on its fruity charms. Somehow, a complicating hint of bouquet sneaks in right at the outset, possible from the wine's doing a short turn in oak tanks. In any case it is elegantly balanced and the quintessential companion is either cold cracked crab or crawdads boiled Louisiana style. I am not sure which, but it is one of those.

Since 1970 the grapes for it come in part from the same Martha's Vineyard that yields the legendary Heitz Cabernet Sauvignons, and in part from the Rutherford vineyard of Dr. Robert Adamson and Dr. Jack Tupper.

In typical years the Johannisberg Riesling of Freemark Abbey approaches the Heitz very closely in both style and substance. Occasionally the Rutherford vineyards from which it comes develop Botrytis, causing a very different wine. Of that, more later.

The Stag's Leap Wine Cellars of Warren Winiarski entered the list of dry Johannisberg producers with a pair of 1972s, one from the Birkmyer Vineyard in Napa County, the other from Mendocino. Both wines were more straightforwardly varietal in character than the Heitz and Freemark Abbey, or, if you will, less bouquetish. Although made in much the same way, they show Winiarski's preference for a gentler character.

Two other small cellars follow the same general approach with slightly less success. Chappellet Vineyards' Johannisberg Riesling has shown a steady tendency to be somewhat sharp, or hot on the finish. Burgess Cellars' Johannisbergs starting with the 1972 have been a shade duller, or heavier. These are small quibbles. Both wines are much more than passably good.

The Louis M. Martini Johannisberg is an ongoing enigma. Each year's vintage seems dry and very light at times, and dry and intensely perfumey at others. A sort of olfactory chameleon, it is hard to recommend and hard not to. Catch it on one of its good days, and it will be a favorite. At the very least it always goes well with food.

The Christian Brothers' Johannisberg is a reliably sound, agreeable white wine, dry, but not strongly aromatic with its varietal character. Frequently it has a pleasant bouquet from its time in wood and bottle. Like the Martini, it is companionable with food.

Souverain Johannisbergs of 1968 and 1969 pushed the idea of a wine balanced between sweet and tart farther than any Californian predecessor of the variety. They did not contrast sweet and sour so intensely as the great German wines, leaving no room for eating between sips, but they were gloriously rich, so well made and so effortlessly balanced that they could be drunk for themselves as readily as they could be mated with fish, fowl, or almost anything that would endure a cream sauce. They and the several nonvintage bottlings that led up to them came from two vineyards, Fred McCrea's Stony Hill and the nearby Spring Mountain vineyard of Jerome Draper.

From 1970 onward, Souverain Johannisbergs have had the familiar style, but not quite the same substance. In the shuffle that accompanied the sale of Souverain by founder Lee Stewart, the original vineyards went out of the blend, to be replaced by several in scattered parts of the valley. Since then the mother has been outshone by several of her children in each vintage since 1972, even though she remains glamorous in her own right.

Joseph Phelps, with its inaugural vintage, 1973, came very close to the rich fruit flavors and sweet-tart balance of the old Souverains. The 1974, just as it was going to bottle, promised to equal, perhaps even surpass those legendary efforts. (In California Johannisbergs, legends tend to grow very fast.) The grapes for both came from a vineyard between Rutherford and Oakville.

Chateau Montelena, beginning with 1972, also flirted with the style, although the balance came at slightly softer, gentler levels. That is to say, the wine had rich fruit flavors, but both its acidity and residual sugar were a shade lower than the other wines of the sort. Winemaker Mike Grgich roused up some strong reactions by labeling both the 1972 and 1973 as *auslese* in spite of their being drier and lighter than German requirements. The 1974 and later vintages are to be identified as Late Harvest, or a similar device, as an indicator of the slightly sweet, slightly botrytised style. The vineyards are in the Alexander Valley of Sonoma County, not far north of Calistoga and the winery, but yield white riesling of astonishingly similar character to that of the mid-Napa Valley.

In 1973 Stony Hill shifted over from a dry style that showed better than any other the inherent melon-like fruitiness of the variety to a sweet one that shows as well as any the berry or apricot-like flavors that come with a bit of residual sugar. Only a few familiars are privileged to taste Stony Hill, but in both styles it has contributed to the literature of Johannisberg in California.

Beaulieu Vineyard, Charles Krug, and Robert Mondavi Johannisbergs combine some of the melon-like softness of the dry but fresh style with more than a faint hint of the sharply berryish qualities of the sweet and fresh approach. If the idea sounds contradictory, that is the essence of its charm. The Krug, nonvintage, extremely consistent, perhaps does it best. The softest of the three, it is a clean, lilting wine that goes only slightly better as an afternoon sipper than a dinner wine of some substance.

Inglenook Vineyards for years brought up the rear as a dry wine of thin, rather sharp character. In recent vintages it has softened and rounded itself, to pull up closer to the pack but not quite enough to catch up. Beringer Winery Johannisbergs lagged behind the Inglenooks for years as a dry wine blended to indistinction. It has now gone past Inglenook, and begins to challenge the Beaulieu as a wine of some character.

Both Beaulieu and Beringer, incidentally, have made special bottlings of Johannisberg in recent vintages in which Botrytis became a tasteable factor in the wines. The Beaulieu, a 1972, was soft and faded early. The Beringer, a 1973 from Knights Valley, in Sonoma County just north of Calistoga, had more stuffings to begin; in 1975 it was just beginning to hit an elegant stride as a wine with more than superficial resemblances to a German of fair quality.

And then there is Freemark Abbey Edelwein, perhaps a freak, perhaps the start of a new tradition, but in any case one of the most astonishingly rich white wines California has produced since I have been old enough to take legal notice. It is a 1973 Johannisberg Riesling from vineyards near Rutherford, owned by partners in the winery. A rare but not unprecedented attack of the Noble Mold brought the berries to that degree of sweet the Germans identify as Beerenauslese. However, in all the other cases of sweet Johannisbergs there is enough of the tartly berryish quality of white riesling to tempt a comparison with Rhenish styles, and in Edelwein there is instead a riper taste that brings the Napa Valley to mind immediately, and does not allow thoughts of the Rhine to creep in at all.

Edelwein is one of those rarities that has to be admired irrationally, for there is no explaining it. It exists as a pure original but, it is devoutly to be wished, not an irreproducible. One has room to hope. *Botrytis cinerea* is not at all an uncommon visitor to California vineyards. The difficulty is that a vineyardist has to be a little bit crazy to encourage the mold. The season must progress within very narrow climatic limits to produce nectarish wines. If matters go awry, the grower ends up with nothing but a field of spoiled fruit. The recent harvest seasons have had the proper sequence of a cool, moist spell, then a warm, dry one. Along with this, both growers and winemakers have been acquiring some experience in dealing with Botrytis.

Sonoma and Mendocino Johannisberg Rieslings

In Sonoma there exist two very different schools of thought about Johannisberg Riesling. The old-timers make it the old way. The newcomers tend toward the fresher, more Rhenish approach.

August Sebastiani makes his Johannisberg Riesling as a throwback to an earlier style in California, a bone dry wine held in cask long enough to acquire a prominent taste of age, then bottled just before the wine shows a first hint of browning.

People familiar with Soaves from Italy will have some notion of what to expect. In fact, this wine can be drunk as a general replacement for Soave with Italian cookery, which, I suspect, is what August does with it. His wife Sylvia is one of the great Italian cooks in the new world or the old.

The appellation of origin is North Coast Counties, the region north of San Francisco Bay. The wine has carried a vintage date since the 1967, and generally goes to market a year or two behind the rest of the field.

Buena Vista, the Sebastiani neighbor to the east, also has preferred dry, wood-aged wines, sometimes to dark-hued, bitter excess. With a new winemaker, a new fermenting facility and new vineyards at Carneros to supplement those at the old winery, all of this may change with the mid-1970s.

The Johannisbergs of J. Pedroncelli in the Russian River region at Healdsburg and those of Parducci Wine Cellars farther upstream at Ukiah have tended to follow along in the old dry, wood-aged style, but less and less with the passing years. They continue as dry wines, but much fresher ones. Korbel, the sparkling wine specialists, offered a vintage 1974 as their first Johannisberg Riesling. It was a pale, light cousin to the Pedroncelli. Kenwood Vineyards in the Valley of the Moon follows along much the same lines.

Sonoma's sweeter, more or less Rhenish-style Johannisbergs have tended to come from a region close around Healdsburg.

Simi Winery Johannisberg Rieslings carry Alexander Valley as their appellation of origin. The first vintage-dated one, from 1971, won a gold medal at the Los Angeles fair judgings and otherwise gave evidence that the new vineyards in the Alexander Valley could produce wines of similar character to those of the Napa

Valley. Subsequent vintages have been much like the first. The style is soft and faintly sweet, very much along the lines of Charles Krug.

Souverain of Alexander Valley had similar success with a very similar wine. It, like the Simi, placed ahead of some prestigious counterparts from the Napa Valley in competition. It also is styled much like the Krug. In its case there is no mystery at all. The Souverain winemaker is Bill Bonetti, who did much to develop that style during his dozen years at Krug.

Sonoma Vineyards fell into a well-botrytised crop of white riesling from vineyards near the little town of Windsor in 1972, and made a wine styled as *spätlese*. Although surprisingly short-lived, that Johannisberg Riesling did deftly balance sweet and tart for a year and more. Its longer-range value is that it led several growers to work harder at cultivating Botrytis in low-lying vineyards along the Russian River.

One of the beneficiaries of broadened grower awareness of Botrytis is Chateau St. Jean, which had a rich, ripe Johannisberg Riesling 1973 as its debut wine. The label bears watching as a source of sipping-sweet Johannisberg.

The remaining two Johannisbergs from the region are perceptibly sweet, commercially sound wines that give good value for money. One is the Voltaire Johannisberg Riesling of Geyser Peak. The other is from Cresta Blanca.

Central Coast Johannisberg Rieslings

Except for Monterey County, where some definite patterns seem to be emerging already, the future of Johannisberg Riesling south of San Francisco Bay is an enigma for lack of a past, or even a present.

There have been but two consistent bottlings, from Concannon Vineyard and Almadén Vineyards, in the whole diverse region. The rest do not go back more than two or three years, or, if so, they have greatly changed their spots during the 1970s. The list includes Paul Masson, Mirassou Vineyard, The Monterey Vineyard, San Martin, and Wente Bros., plus tiny lots from David Bruce and Ridge.

Monterey County had forty-nine acres of white riesling planted in 1969, which is to say it had forty-nine acres worth harvesting in 1972. As of 1973 the figure had reached 1,942 acres, precisely a thousand acres more than the Napa Valley had at the same time. Lord knows where all of it is. Lord knows how all of it will do. But some of the older plantings close to the Arroyo Seco, and in the misty stretches north of Soledad year in and year out yield intensely aromatic fruit, much of it well marked by the withering beneficence of *Botrytis cinerea* Pers., the Noble Mold.

Wente Bros. made the winery's first Johannisberg Riesling in the vintage of 1969. It was styled as a *spätlese* from the vineyards at Arroyo Seco. After skipping 1970 and 1971, Karl Wente came back with another *spätlese* in 1972, then both a *spätlese* and *auslese* in 1973. The German terms were not used lightly, but in conformance with the legal standards of Germany. The 1969 was very good if a bit rough at the outset, and lasted astonishingly well into 1975. The 1972 was better. The 1973 *auslese* moved Frank Schoonmaker, a lifelong observer of German wine, to say that California never had done any better, and that Germany could not make a better *auslese*. In contrast to the Edelwein of Freemark Abbey, in the Napa Valley, the Wente is tarter, airier, not so richly heavy with warmth from the sun. In contrast to the German wines of similar technical balance, it has a more restrained, a less perfumey aroma. I could even be led to call it delicate. The 1974 promises to be much the same kind of wine.

The 1974 inaugural Johannisberg Riesling from The Monterey Vineyard has many of the same notions of style as the Wente, but the fruit did not have the same depth of flavor in its first crop.

Paul Masson has a nonvintage Johannisberg Riesling with a California appellation, but a strong majority of Monterey grapes in each bottling. It is a shade lighter in character than The Monterey Vineyards, but, again, very close in its sweet-tart style. The taste of Botrytis, faint in the others, does not make its presence felt at all here.

Mirassou Vineyard has a Harvest Selection Johannisberg Riesling, vintage-dated and carrying a Monterey appellation, which stands slightly to one side of these others. Somehow it is less tart, more flowery, perhaps even a shade coarser in its fruit flavors than the others. It is very well made, but not so strikingly Germanic. The same winery's regular bottling, a hybrid of Monterey and Santa Clara grapes, goes still further away from any Teutonic qualities.

No pattern unites the rest. Each must be considered for its own merits.

Concannon Vineyards Johannisberg Riesling comes close to being the antithesis of a German white, for being soft, truly delicate, and so cleanly made that it does not require—or prosper for—more than a faint cooling. In a less forcible way it may also be an antithesis of other California Johannisbergs. Because it is soft and a bit bouquetish its closest living relative is the Sebastiani Johannisberg, but even that is blunter, more piquant. And still the Concannon tastes and smells of white riesling.

Whatever it is an example of, it provides the one and only correct accompaniment to charcoal-grilled sea bass at Tadich's Grill in San Francisco.

The appellation has been California because of a small proportion of grapes from the old Hallcrest vineyard in Santa Cruz county. With the 1974 it is to be a Livermore wine from vines at the winery.

Almadén Vineyards Johannisberg Riesling, the other old-timer, is a sweeter wine than the Concannon, and broader in character. In my experience it has been the best of the Big Three Johannisbergs, ahead of both the Paul Masson and The Christian Brothers. Most of the grapes for it come from Almadén vineyards in San Benito County.

In the past the Santa Clara-based Johannisbergs of San Martin have been off-dry and otherwise pedestrian. However, a trial bottling of 1974 from the new vineyards near King City in Monterey County promised finer wines to come. Some hint was in the wine that King City is a sunnier place than Soledad or Greenfield, where the other Monterey Johannisbergs have their origins. The comparisons should fascinate for some years to come, particularly because San Martin winemaker Ed Friedrich is the truest German of all the local cellarmasters.

Weibel tags along after the rest, dry, recognizably varietal, but light in character and without great style or charm.

David Bruce and Ridge Vineyards, in their Johannisbergs as in their other varietals, prefer the primitive style, the unfined, unfiltered earthy stuff that comes out heavy-bodied every time, and usually coarsely fruity as well. When nature does smile without reserve the results can be astonishingly good. When nature holds back, cider is better. In the case of Johannisbergs there is no profit in waiting for age to bring finesse.

PINOT BLANC

The immediate future of Pinot Blanc in California is not grand. Old plantings are not extensive. New ones are rare indeed, except in Monterey County. What is worse, Heitz Cellars, the most adroit vinifier of Pinot Blanc, abandoned the variety after the vintage of 1971.

Back in the 1880s, when the University of California was pessimistic about all Burgundian varieties, a viticultural report said, balefully, "The wine is not very robust, and, in general seems to have no good qualities in which it is not surpassed by the Chardonay [sic]."

It is more kindly to say that Pinot Blanc is to Chardonnay what *Carmen* is to *Tosca*. A good wine of the variety is similar to, though not so formidably specific as a first-rate Chardonnay. People who care little for austere wines find Pinot Blanc easy to like, and yet it has enough character to satisfy an unreconstructable Chardonnay person. It is not unlike a lean, hawkish disciple of Montrachet finding charm in a softly round Meursault when one comes as a change of pace. In fact, the university scholars of recent times have softened the old judgment in the face of several genuinely fine Pinot Blancs, contenting themselves with the admonition that the variety should be planted "only by those who want to produce a very special type of white wine to which they will pay considerable attention."

In that admonition is the seed of Pinot Blanc's destruction. The wine is harder to make than Chardonnay. The vines do not yield more per acre than productive clones of chardonnay, and yet the wine will not fetch more than half the price. As the roster of producers and the coterie of admirers help each other shrink in numbers, more and more of the production goes into sparkling wines, or into other varietals that profit by pinot blanc's gentle nature.

A similarly lamentable fate must have befallen pinot blanc in France. The variety no longer is mentioned in Burgundian planting statistics, although at least two grower-shippers have insisted that *pinot blanc vrai* underlies the gentle nature of their Meursaults in recent years.

In any case, two wines have given Pinot Blanc its dimensions in California. Heitz Cellars was the foremost label. Chalone was a close challenger, and now leads the field. The rest give various degrees of pleasure without adding distinctively to the spectrum of California dry white wine.

North Coast Pinot Blancs

Sonoma County, led by Chateau St. Jean, holds most of the hopes for Pinot Blanc north of San Francisco Bay.

Although Napa is the place where a large part of the definition of Pinot Blanc was written for California, none was made there after the vintage of 1972, and none sold after summer 1973. As the acreage shrinks, there is little reason to hope for a comeback.

Using grapes from a small block of Fred McCrea's Stony Hill vineyard, Joe Heitz produced from 1964 through 1971 a consistent string of Pinot Blancs that often were mistaken for good Chardonnays from California, and for some reputable white Burgundies. The secret of success was that Heitz treated the wines as if they were distinguished, aging them in new European oak barrels, and otherwise lavishing as much care on them as on his Chardonnays.

In two vintages Heitz experimented with grapes from a second vineyard, but was not satisfied. When McCrea uprooted his pinot blanc vines Heitz opted out of the varietal altogether.

Lyncrest Vineyard became a bonded winery in 1972 and planned to carry on with Pinot Blanc, but went out of business before it could get a bottle on the market. No other Napan came forward.

Chateau St. Jean has sold only one Pinot Blanc thus far, using purchased grapes in the vintage of 1974. Richard Arrowood's fidelity to Burgundian ideals made the first effort a fine wine to drink. The winery will have its own vineyards bearing by 1977.

F. Korbel & Bros. makes a light, pleasant wine with the variety.

Central Coast Pinot Blancs

The Central Coast from Alameda down to Monterey County has become the great home and, mayhap, the last bastion of pinot blanc in California. Much of it goes to sparkling wine, but some stays still.

Chalone Vineyard, from its vines on a bench just below the craggy basalt columns of Pinnacles National Monument, now makes the most considerable Pinot Blanc in the state. Unlike the roundly balanced, almost creamy Pinot Blanc of Heitz, this one has edges almost as rugged as the rocks that overlook its vineyard. It is made in the same, Burgundian style using European oak barrels and long aging, but something in its background leaves it sharper. Something else does not allow it to age with grace for so many years as the Heitz, so drinkers must be ready to take pleasure in the flinty character of youth rather than waiting for time to work its velvety tricks on the wine in the bottle.

Alas for Pinot Blanc and the people who like it: Chalone's annual production of the wine fills little more than the back seat of a Volkswagen bug.

The next best bet comes from Almadén, which has far more generous supplies of a somewhat less generous wine. Almadén Pinot Blanc, principally if not exclusively from vineyards around Paicines in San Benito County, has some Burgundian character without being quite rich. All Chardonnays and a few truly dry Chenin Blancs exceed it, but the wine still has enough stuffings and a modest enough price to have a place in the world.

Paul Masson and Wente Bros. offer light, somewhat sharp wines under the name of Pinot Blanc. The wines resemble each other closely even though the vineyards for the Masson are principally in Monterey County while those of Wente are divided between there and the Livermore Valley. Both wines, well made, have their uses as accompaniments to white fish and other bland foods, but neither is distinctive or distinguished, for lack of aging in small wood, I believe.

The Novitiate of Los Gatos makes a Pinot Blanc with a broad hint of sweet, a technique that enhances the variety's fruity character. The wine is affable with cold chicken on a picnic, an alternative to a Chenin Blanc rather than a wine of Burgundian dimensions.

A Pinot Blanc under the gilded label of Villa Armando is a throwback to country winemaking. It has a hint of sweet on the finish, and an infinity of bouquet from old cooperage and oxidation. It is, to adapt an immortal line from a lady who used to review books for a small newspaper in the Pacific Northwest, the kind of a wine you will like if you like that kind of a wine.

SAUVIGNON BLANC

(Alias Fumé Blanc and other variations)

First-rate vineyards of sauvignon blanc have been growing since the early days of wine in California, admired in a lonely kind of way by a few growers and winemakers.

Sauvignon Blanc was one of the early varietal wines, but unheralded. More than that it was eminently ignored by the public even after Dr. Maynard Amerine of the U.C.-Davis went on record saying this wine is fine in California even more consistently than is Chardonnay.

Only in 1971 when the uncanny Robert Mondavi rechristened a dry wine from the grape as Fumé Blanc did the variety begin to command real attention. As others followed his lead it became obvious that there is something in a name. There also may be something in the shape of a bottle. The Fumé Blancs that go to market in Burgundy-style bottles seem to move more quickly than sauvignon blanc by that or any other name in a Bordeaux-style bottle.

Even as the Mondavi coinage rescued sauvignon blanc from a sagging fate, it also led to a confusion in wine names as great or greater than the one surrounding chenin blanc, the other grape Mondavi rescued from oblivion with an inspired choice of name. In addition to Sauvignon Blanc and Fumé Blanc, the recent roster of varietal wines from the one grape includes Blanc de Sauvignon, Fleur de Sauvignon, Blanc Fumé, Pouilly Fumé, Sonoma Blanc and Château Beaulieu (subtitled Sauvignon Blanc).

Sauvignon blanc as a variety deserves at least two names for its wines. The dry ones are more austere than Chardonnays, but sweet ones turn all soft and fruity in a remarkably complete metamorphosis. Further, the two basic names have legitimate origins in French wines of vastly different characters and styles.

Most if not all of California's sauvignon blanc vines are descended from cuttings made in Sauternes and Graves during the last two decades of the nineteenth century. A considerable number of them came from Château d'Yquem to a Livermore Valley grower named Louis Mel, who had family ties to Yquem's proprietors. Sauvignon blanc is the minority grape in Sauternes, where it adds some resolve to the supple character of semillon. It is the majority partner in the blends of Graves, especially dry ones.

The use of Blanc Fumé and assorted variations arises because the wines of Pouilly-sur-Loire and Sancerre are made from a grape known there as blanc fumé, sauvignon blanc, and savignin de jura. The U.C.-Davis says that Pouilly Fumés and Sancerres are indeed from savignin, but that savignin is not the sauvignon of Graves and Sauternes. Be the botanic specifics what they may, enough similarity links a Pouilly Fumé made from savignin to a California Fumé Blanc made dry from sauvignon blanc to explain Robert Mondavi's adaptation of the name.

When Maynard Amerine and Vernon Singleton drew up their cosmonology of flavor associations to help pinpoint varietal characteristics they found in sauvignon blanc reminders of the taste of olives. They also thought the wines herbaceous, as the red cabernet sauvignon also is. (Most back labels say "spicy," but that is a cop-out on herbaceous.) Others have added to the list green grass—not lawn grass, but the tall, jointed kind that is so fresh and juicy to chew in wet, early spring. The French think of smoky as a flavor association. Fumé, the word, translates as smoky.

Hardly neutral flavors, those, and a dry wine of sauvignon blanc can offer them in abundance. In an old technical bulletin for winemakers, the university observed that the distinctive flavor of the grape is carried over "and even increased in the wine." The bulletin goes on to say, "The distinct aromatic flavor is so strong that in some regions and years it may have to be blended with a more neutral-flavored variety to achieve consumer acceptance."

As much as all of the flavor associations suggest dry wine, sauvignon blanc has the curious capacity to change its stripes the more sugar is left unfermented. Made sweet the wine develops a soft, round character well suited to the role. If a mitigating dollop of semillon or some such slips into the blend, the transformation is even greater.

At this point the names are not reliable guides to dry versus sweet. Most wines with names that turn on the word Fumé are bone dry, or just off-dry. Those called Sauvignon Blanc cover the gamut, though with a greater tendency to be sweet. For purposes of keeping the generalities straight, the following paragraphs say only dry Sauvignon Blanc and sweet Sauvignon Blanc. The individual descriptions untangle which wines are dry and which are sweet label by label.

An old recipe of Jim Beard's called Chicken Forty Cloves of Garlic provides a gastronomer's measure of the herbacity or smokiness of a dry Sauvignon Blanc. The dish destroys any wine that vacillates, but is companionable to an uncompromised varietal wine from this grape. The weakness of the test is that it can be made only when no important engagements are scheduled for the next day or two. Forty cloves of garlic *will* linger on a body (though not as much as you might think; the manner of cooking tames it surprisingly).

Under mortal circumstances dry Sauvignon Blancs are recommended by their makers to go with fowl, shellfish, light meats, cold cuts, and dishes covered in cream sauces.

The sweet Sauvignon Blancs, in the conventional wisdom, go with ham or poultry, or, better, chilled fresh fruit. Sweet, in their case, means the degree of sweetness typically found in a Chenin Blanc, a Vouvray, or perhaps a Graves, but not the unctuous riches of a true Sauterne. Botrytis is not a part of their making, nor are they left to grow overripe on the vine.

Dry Sauvignon Blanc does not demand deep chilling. Most are cool enough after forty minutes in the refrigerator, especially if they have five or six years of age. Sweet ones are far better colder when young. In this case, too, bouquetish oldsters do not deserve to be diminished by deep chilling.

As befits a botanic cousin of cabernet sauvignon, sauvignon blanc yields wines that will age handsomely for four, five, a dozen years, depending on how sturdily the winemaker rigged them to start. The Wente Bros., to cite one example, made a sturdy 1937 that still is in good form. There should be vintage charts but, alas, the obscurity of its fame has kept the wine from being made in vintages by enough wineries to give a clear picture.

Napa Valley Sauvignon Blancs

Until Robert Mondavi brought Fumé Blanc into being with the vintage of 1967 the Napa Valley had been little known for its production of wines from sauvignon blanc. In spite of that, Napa offered then and still does offer the greatest number of any district, in the widest range of styles.

The dry ones, in the mid-1970s, were Beringer Fumé Blanc, The Christian Brothers Napa Fumé, Cuvaison Sauvignon Blanc, Charles Krug Pouilly Fumé, Robert Mondavi Fumé Blanc, Oakville's van Löben Sels Sauvignon Blanc, Spring Mountain Sauvignon Blanc, and Sterling Blanc de Sauvignon. The roster of wines is as uniformly fine as the names are wildly erratic.

The dessert-sweet roster includes Chateau Beaulieu, The Christian Brothers' Sauvignon Blanc, Charles Krug Sauvignon Blanc, Robert Mondavi Sauvignon Blanc, and Oakville Vineyards Sauvignon Fleur.

Going back to Jim Beard's garlicky chicken as an index for the dry ones, the candidates for a full forty cloves are Beringer, Charles Krug, and The Christian Brothers. The Beringer, first made in the vintage of 1970, is consistently just a shade off-dry, but has an earthy, pungent varietal character. On balance, it is the strongest wine of the lot, and likely to age well in all of the vintages released to date. Charles Krug introduced its nonvintage Pouilly Fumé * during 1973, and immediately

---

* The government regulatory agency, Bureau of Alcohol, Tobacco and Tax of the IRS, has ruled that Krug may not continue using Pouilly Fumé, a controlled appellation in France. The winery has renamed the wine Blanc Fumé.

elected itself to the top of the forty cloves list. In 1974 the wine appeared slightly less intense in its herbaceous varietal character, but remained very dry and harmonious enough to age well. Still, thirty-five cloves is as far as the wine could reach. The Christian Brothers Napa Fumé is another thirty-five-clove wine, though a faintly sweeter one than the Krug. That is to say, it has a slightly softer aftertaste than the others, not that it can truly be called sweet.

Sterling Vineyards made its first Blanc de Sauvignon from the vintage of 1969. That wine was and still is noticeably less herbaceous than any of the foregoing trio, but was bone dry and forcible enough to go at least thirty cloves. Subsequent vintages have held to the original style and character. Cuvaison made a 1972 Sauvignon Blanc as its first, coming very close to the Sterling on all counts.

Robert Mondavi, having coined the name Fumé Blanc as a hint that his wine would resemble a Pouilly Fumé or Sancerre more than a dry Graves, has drifted away from both notions in favor of a fresh, deft, soft wine rather than a pungent one. The true taste of sauvignon blanc grapes is there, but cloaked in silk. The wine is of a delicacy that calls for sole meunière, or cream sauces, but not garlic, or at least no more than half a dozen cloves on the Beardian scale of forty.

Oakville Vineyards went in a different direction from all of these with the 1972 wine it labeled as van Löben Sels Sauvignon Blanc. The wine had a full body and ample varietal character, but had been made creamy rich somehow. I think the secret was in using a discreet few weeks worth of new oak barrels, or some such source of both softening and a complicating bouquet. In any case, the wine was superbly balanced and richly complex at three years, and gave promise of lasting well for another half dozen years at least.

It is a style that wants a great many more followers.

All of these dry wines of sauvignon blanc carry Napa Valley as their appellation of origin. Save for the winery-owned vineyards of Sterling at Calistoga, most of the vines grow south of St. Helena, and most of the wines draw upon scattered blocks.

The trio of sweet wines from Napa sauvignon blanc resemble each other greatly. All subdue the herbaceous qualities of the variety in favor of its fruity ones. The Chateau Beaulieu is perhaps the most muted of the three in varietal character, and also the least sweet by a narrow shading. The 1967 of Robert Mondavi is delicate, but finely balanced and was remarkably fresh in 1975, apparently ready to endure in good health for another decade or more. The Christian Brothers and Charles Krug Sauvignon Blancs have tended to be more frankly herbaceous than the other two, but still amiable enough to call for a bowl of chilled fruit on a warm afternoon.

Sonoma and Mendocino Sauvignon Blancs

Only one Sauvignon Blanc has come out of Sonoma County regularly. It belongs to Sonoma Vineyards. Dry Creek Vineyards and Cresta Blanca have joined it in recent years.

The dry one belongs, appropriately enough, to Dry Creek Vineyards, which offers it as a vintage-dated Fumé Blanc. The inaugural vintage was 1971. Proprietor David Stare has stayed with his initial notion, a strongly herbaceous varietal character embodied in a full-bodied, slightly rough-hewn wine. With or without some additional polish, it can stand up to a full forty cloves of garlic if served with that Jim Beard chicken dish.

The Sonoma Vineyards Sauvignon Blanc has been consistently sweet. In recent releases it has been fruity enough in character to be balanced and agreeable.

Cresta Blanca falls between the other two in all respects, more polished and less dry than the Dry Creek, not so sweet and a shade lighter or leaner than the Sonoma Vineyards.

Central Coast Sauvignon Blancs

As usual, the wineries south of San Francisco Bay contrive to offer an amazing lack of unanimity within a small group. Livermore, for historical and contemporary reasons, is a focal point, but the variety seems to perform well in many parts of this sprawling area. Almadén, Concannon Vineyard, and Wente Bros. produce dry wines from sauvignon blanc. Almadén also has a sweet one. The Monterey Vineyard will have both a dry and a sweet in 1976.

During the 1930s and 1940s Herman Wente wrote the book on the kind of dry, austere Sauvignon Blanc that caused U.C.-Davis to praise the grape and also to give small warnings about the pure article being too much for faint hearts. Herman's nephew, Karl, is carrying on in the family tradition, though sometimes in a gentler vein.

One day when the last residual sugar was fermenting out of the Wente Bros. Sauvignon Blanc 1970, Karl summed up the family experience: "When we first started making Sauvignon Blanc in the 1930s, nobody cared for it . . . except the Wentes. We thought the situation over and decided to wait for the public to come around. It did."

For a long time this was the only Sauvignon Blanc that could go against a full forty cloves of garlic, to resort once again to the Beardian scale. In those days it was a Livermore appellation wine. In some vintages since vineyards in Monterey County began to contribute to the wine, it has been a shade less deep in flavor, a bit less austere. By and large, however, it has changed very little, and sometimes not at all.

Just across Tesla Road from the Wente vineyards in Livermore, Concannon Vineyard makes a wine extraordinarily at odds with its neighbor, but consistent with other Concannon whites. It is soft, almost wispy at times, a white so gentle it hardly needs chilling.

The differences cannot be attributed to vineyards, which are adjacent in an old arroyo and thus equally rocky. It is tempting to think that the basic differences come from the old redwood fermentors at Concannon as opposed to the steel ones at Wente, a theory that will be tested when the steel-fermented Concannon 1974 comes to market. On the other hand, Wente fermented in redwood for years before it turned to steel. Ah well, it does not matter how the Concannons do it. It does matter that they achieve a gentle wine for gentle meals of sole, or unadorned chicken, or such. Contrasted with the Wente, it is an uncanny demonstration that the winemaker's will can overcome enormous proportions of whatever sun and soil bring to grapes.

Almadén Vineyards offers a dry Blanc Fumé and a slightly sweet Sauvignon Blanc. Both rank high on my list of Almadén whites, and the Blanc Fumé ranks high on my list of wines made from sauvignon blanc grapes. The Blanc Fumé came along in 1972, cast substantially in the earthy, pungent style of the Wente Bros. Sauvignon Blanc. In effect, it was only a change of name for Almadén's older Sauvignon Blanc, which always had hewn to that line. When Blanc Fumé appeared, Almadén developed Sauvignon Blanc into a fruity, perceptibly sweet wine. Neither is vintage dated. Both carry California as their appellation. A fair proportion of the grapes come from Almadén vines in the Livermore Valley, some from San Benito.

The Monterey Vineyard wine, when it comes, is not likely to taste as it did in cask shortly after the vintage of 1974. The varietal characteristic was so strong that it went past being herbaceous, or grassy, to call up reminiscences of the juices of fresh green peppers. The proprietors were intrigued, but a bit overwhelmed, and planned to scale it down to more mortal strengths.

Other Sauvignon Blancs

Callaway Vineyards and Winery began with the vintage of 1974 to offer a Sauvignon Blanc much like those from coastal counties around San Francisco Bay, a great surprise in view of the Temecula region's tendency to produce Chenin Blancs and Johannisberg Rieslings unlike any others. The Callaway Sauvignon Blanc, with a relatively light body and gentle character, is finished dry to go well with food.

Two San Joaquin Valley wineries offer wine made from sauvignon blanc.

A. Perelli-Minetti & Sons has both a Fumé Blanc dry and a Sauvignon Blanc sweet, usually purchased in the Napa Valley as bulk wine and aged and bottled at Delano. Both are modest in character. The label is Eleven Cellars.

E. & J. Gallo Sauvignon Blanc, possibly dominated by grapes from Monterey County, is so self-effacing that no description comes to mind.

SEMILLON

The recent history of Semillon has become contradictory. The wine is fading in numbers among coast counties producers at the same time that it is gaining popularity among wineries in the San Joaquin Valley. There is less contradiction here than meets the eye. Semillon from coastal vineyards has an almost overwhelming fruity character. In the interior valley a warmer sun bakes some of the stronger flavors out, leaving a blander wine for a wider audience to accept.

An unblended Semillon from thoroughly ripe coast counties grapes has an unmistakable character, a cedary pungency, as if someone allowed the wine to rest overlong in brand new redwood tanks. The University of California at Davis flavor associations—cigar-like and figgy—run along kindred lines. Sweet or dry, the problem is to achieve balance, although the problem is greater with a sweet wine than a dry one. With a judicious tempering through early harvesting or blending with something meek, a coastal Dry Semillon can become as delicately fresh as cold well water. The best of Dry Semillons even have some of the smell of damp, cool stone in their bouquets. (Privately I suspect that Dry Semillons were at their best back in the days when more people relied on more SO$_2$; the desiccating whiff of SO$_2$ does wonders to diminish excessive perfume in a wine.)

Even at best it seems as if some universal demographer issues just so many sets of tastebuds per generation with a fondness for a well-tempered California Semillon, let alone a full-blown one.

Karl Wente got on the subject of Semillon one summer day in 1972 and said sadly that Wente Bros. sells x-thousand cases of Dry Semillon a year in prosperous times and poor ones. No more than a week later, in another place, Louis P. Martini lamented that his family's winery had finally given up on its Dry Semillon after selling the same y-thousand cases each year since the early 1950s. The two of them made the Semillons that evoked the refreshing taste of well water.

Although Semillons from the rapidly expanding acreage in the San Joaquin Valley cannot equal the refreshing qualities of the finest ones from the coast, they never suffer of the overdeveloped character that plagues the average example. The steady-handed cellarmasters in Lodi, Bakersfield, and points between, can achieve a reliable supply of soft, gentle wines with enough fruit flavor to make them welcome company to chicken or other such homely fare.

Even the finest of Dry Semillons seem inescapably mired in the realm of second-line companions to modest family meals. The grape has produced treasurable wines only when they are sweet. In fact, the only growers in the world who genuinely treasure semillon are in the Sauternes district of France,* where the variety's thin skin yields easily to the sweetening attacks of the Noble Mold. The Noble Mold, *Botrytis cinerea* Pers. to the cold eye of science, concentrates the juice of semillon into nectar even before fermentation turns it into Château d'Yquem, or Château Suduiraut.

Several experiments intended to concentrate the juices of semillon into a balance with its pungent flavor have done well in California.

The most famous one was at the old Cresta Blanca winery in Livermore where Myron Nightingale induced Botrytis on semillon by picking the fruit and holding it in a controlled environment for a time before beginning the fermentation. The result, called Premier Semillon, appeared only once, from the vintage of 1964. It was a success with critics, but not the Schenley accounting department.

On another plane, Fred McCrea has been exploring the possibilities of a variation on the straw wines of the Jura. Each year McCrea spreads a few raisin trays of semillon to dry in the harvest sun for a few days, thereby attracting several million bees to Stony Hill while the juices concentrate enough for him to make one barrel of a very sweet wine he calls Semillon de Soleil. The wine is astonishingly pale because of meticulous fermentation and aging. The oldest vintage, 1969, continues to develop complexities. Later, stronger vintages show greater promise. Rich elegance is a real possibility in the 1971 especially. Unfortunately these are not commercial wines. They can be bought only at one merchant's in Sacramento.

For the nonce the available Semillons, dry or sweet, are merely good wine. The

---

* Australians, especially in the Hunter River, almost treasure it made dry or sweet.

dry ones may never be any more than that. The sweet ones already have more character than Chenin Blanc's bland charms can offer, but, with few exceptions, are not as balanced or as complex as they need to be.

Napa Valley Semillons

Only Charles Krug sustains a Dry Semillon that goes by the name. Beaulieu Vineyards has a varietal from the grape, although the name is subordinated to Dry Sauterne on the label. In recent years the two other producers, Inglenook Vineyards and Sutter Home Winery, have abandoned semillon entirely.

Charles Krug Dry Semillon steadily gives the impression of being the driest of them all, with the possible exception of Wente Bros. Not vintage dated, the wine is consistently clean and fresh, a laudable companion to poultry. Beaulieu's Dry Sauterne (Semillon) emphasizes the aromatic quality of the grape somewhat more.

Neither wine has the cool, subtle charms that used to mark Louis M. Martini Dry Semillon back in the good old days before it expired for lack of lovers. That one could pick up anything smothered in cream sauce. Some vintages were surprisingly durable. The Sonoma County vineyards whence it came still exist. Maybe the old flower will bloom again.

The lone sweet wine from semillon in the valley comes from Charles Krug. Called Sweet Sauternes, with Semillon as a subtitle, it is redolent of the cedary perfume of Semillon. For some it cloys. For some it charms. Either way, it is a textbook lesson in the varietal character of the grape as it grows in coastal vineyards.

Sonoma and Mendocino Semillons

Although the qualities of Dry Semillons from Louis M. Martini vineyards in Sonoma County should have encouraged others in the region to go forth and do good works with the grape, they did not. In the whole of Sonoma County only the tiny cellar of Leo Trentadue offers a Dry Semillon. A husky, earthy wine, the proprietor likes to serve it with breaded, fried pieces of leopard shark. It goes well, one of the few Semillons that will take to fish.

Only one Sonoma winery has made a Sweet Semillon in recent years. Sonoma Vineyards Haut Semillon, like that of Charles Krug, hovers at the balance point between agreeable and cloying. The problem, as always, is to develop a concentrated bouquet from wood or bottle aging as a counter to the straightforward aromas of the grape.

Cresta Blanca issues a Semillon from its headquarters in Mendocino County, but the appellation of origin is only California because some of the grapes come from the ancient vineyards of the original Cresta Blanca in Livermore. To this point, the wine has been off-dry, a tolerable wine but not specific enough to compete with others of more pronounced character on one side or the other.

Fetzer Vineyards produces a Mendocino County Dry Semillon of strong, earthy qualities much along the lines of the Trentadue, but not quite as clean on the finish. It is a wine of strengths rather than weaknesses, and has a legion of loyal followers.

Central Coast Semillons

For the same reasons that it is the real California home of sauvignon blanc the Livermore Valley is the historic focal point for semillon in the state. A pioneer grower named Louis Mel had ties to Château d'Yquem through his wife, and prevailed upon the Marquis de Lur Saluces to sell cuttings of Yquem vines to another Livermore grower during the 1880s.

The choice of Bordeaux white varieties was not entirely whimsical; Mel was only one of many French emigrants attracted to grape-growing in Livermore by its rocky soils. Years later scientists at U.C.-Davis vindicated the empirical choice, observing that "the reputation of the Semillon from the rocky soils of the Livermore Valley is . . . probably based on a real difference in quality: these wines are said to be more aromatic than those produced at similar temperatures in the Napa Valley." Since the poor and rocky soils of Livermore do not support such a large vegetation and cropping as the rich mid-valley alluvial soils of the Napa Valley, ". . . Livermore produces smaller berries with more aromatic substances because of the narrower ratio of skin to flesh." Also, as its good performance in the San Joaquin Valley indicates, the variety performs well in warm districts.

Wente Bros. makes both a Dry Semillon and a sweet one, the latter called Chateau Semillon. Concannon Vineyard calls its wine from semillon Dry Sauterne, having given up on the varietal name after years of trying.

The two dry wines are, as the university promised long ago, superior. The Wente always is a bit the drier and leaner of the two, the one that can evoke fleeting thoughts of cool water from a stone well. The Concannon wine is, typically, softer, rounder, a shade deeper in perfume. Both were Livermore appellation wines until the Wente began to use some grapes from that company's vineyards in Monterey County. The Wente carries a vintage date. Both profit for being drunk young.

Chateau Semillon is the place to learn the taste of semillon for once and for all, even more than the Charles Krug sweet wine from semillon. It is all there, pure and deep, and not overpoweringly sweet. The first bottle is not as likely to please as the third or fourth one.

Almadén and Paul Masson round out the roster of coast counties producers of Semillon. Almadén makes a solid, irreproachable Dry Semillon with California as the appellation. Paul Masson makes a sweet one under the name of Chateau Masson.

San Joaquin Valley Semillons

As the San Joaquin Valley begins its ponderous turn toward varietal table wines, semillon is a surprisingly important variety. The acreage planted in the valley far outstrips the current need for varietal Semillon because the variety, even though subdued by the climate, still is intensely flavorful enough to enhance neutral grapes in the blending of generic whites.

To date four Semillons are well established, and more wait in the wings.

Lodi has two pioneers. One is Royal Host Semillon from East-Side. The other

Semillon clusters concentrate their sugars on shallow drying trays before being fermented into Stony Hill Semillon du Soleil. (HAROLYN THOMPSON)

is Barengo. Both are dry, or just off-dry. They are, predictably, softer than any of the coast counties wines from the variety. What surprises is the tempered character of the grape. The wines are aromatic Semillons all right, but not so overpowering as coastal cousins from similar Region III climates. Perhaps the vines are trained to bear heavier crops.

The Winemasters Guild, headquartered in Lodi, has a Dry Semillon assembled from coastal and interior vineyards. Just off-dry, it is in much the same soft, round style as the Royal Host or Barengo bottlings.

The real surprise of all the big valley Semillons comes from the Bear Mountain Winery in Bakersfield. Bottled under that winery's M. LaMont label, recent lots of Dry Semillon from vineyards near the winery have been not only dry and clean, but crisply refreshing on the aftertaste, the closest challenger of all the interior wines from semillon to the finest ones from the coast.

SYLVANER

(Alias Riesling and Franken Riesling)

Sylvaner is another of the second-line varietal whites that do heavy duty around the family table or at picnics but do not come out often for stately dinners.

The California style is consistent: just off-dry and fresh, to be drunk in the bloom of the wine's youth without second thoughts. The flavor is agreeably fruity, though often sharpened by the merest hint of a taste like hops. The hops quality is hard to pin down except by comparison with the pale taste of pale American beers. Anyway, the effect is to give the wine a tart edge that makes it a useful penny-saver in place of Johannisberg Riesling.

The grape has its origins somewhere in the ancient lands of the Hapsburg Empire. It is now a secondary variety in the Rhine and The Palatinate and in Alsace.

In California Sylvaner is suffering of second banana-ism of the sort that has made Pinot Blanc almost extinct as a varietal wine, though Sylvaner's case is not so advanced. The vine does not bear much more heavily than white riesling, and the wine is difficult to ferment and age. Pinot Blanc suffers parallel disadvantages compared to Chardonnay. As wine a first-rate Sylvaner can compete with any ordinary Johannisberg Riesling just as Pinot Blanc can surpass mediocre Chardonnay. Sylvaner's healthier survival probably owes to the fact that it is one of the instantly likable off-dry whites rather than a dry, even austere Burgundian white.

California labeling of Riesling is, incidentally, a trifle inexact. A wine made of Sylvaner can be labeled Sylvaner, Franken Riesling, or just plain Riesling. However, wine labeled just plain Riesling also can be used to cover any blend encompassing sylvaner, emerald riesling, johannisberg, traminer, and even grey riesling. Label regulations aside, current economics almost guarantee that anything labeled Riesling is, in fact, also qualified to call itself Sylvaner.

Napa Valley Sylvaners

From the 1860s until Prohibition the innumerable Hocks, Mosels, and Rieslings offered by German winemakers in Napa were made from sylvaner if old acreage surveys are as much as half right. The variety easily dominated white grape vineyards and was, by most accounts, the basis for much of Napa's early reputation as a fine vineyard district.

Now sylvaner is a minor and ebbing factor in the valley, but it still makes its wine as well there as anywhere in California.

Surviving cellar records leave no doubt that the pioneer stuff was bone dry, and kept in small wood for at least two years so it could develop depths of flavor. It must have tasted a good deal like a contemporary pale sherry-type.

Present-day Napa Sylvaners go in opposite directions from the pioneer model. All are at least one shade off-dry. Some are two shades off. All are as youthfully fresh as technology can make them. Cold fermentation and bottling under slight pressure give them a crisp, almost *pétillant* lilt. At the top of their form these Sylvaners are close to unbeatable as distinct but inexpensive companions to steamed clams (plain or bordelais), crab or shrimp Louis, or cold ham or chicken. A breezy summer afternoon is the right time, and a seascape is the quintessential backdrop, although a courtside picnic after a leisurely afternoon of mixed doubles is no bad idea either. It must be the faintly beery taste that shapes the contexts.

Beaulieu Vineyard, The Christian Brothers, Charles Krug, and Robert Mondavi all make Sylvaner at the top of its form with remarkable consistency. All four use Napa Valley as the appellation. BV and Robert Mondavi use vintage dates, mostly to encourage early drinking. Only Charles Krug uses Sylvaner as the main name; the rest of the labels read Riesling, with Sylvaner tucked away in small type.

Souverain Cellars makes a rounder, richer Riesling which is a frank blend of sylvaner, flora and, mayhap, a touch of white riesling. Somehow the effect makes it an inland rather than a seaside wine.

Louis M. Martini Sylvaner is very much kindred in character to the winery's Johannisberg Riesling. That is, the wine initially seems restrained, even neutral, then blossoms with an almost floral aroma at the aftertaste. Atypical, even a mild enigma, it is agreeably dry, a versatile company to food beyond these others.

The locally distributed Nichelini has a Sylvaner of somewhat older style, not the overaged character of the pioneers, but rather the drier, more bouquetish qualities so familiar to people who grew up in the 1940s when everything fermented and aged in redwood or well-seasoned oak.

Sonoma and Mendocino Sylvaners

Sonoma produces only two Sylvaners, both of them good ones. Sebastiani Riesling is, like all Sebastiani whites, very cleanly made and rather soft. It does not have the distinct freshness of cold fermentation, nor does it have the hoplike pungency that marks many Sylvaners. Buena Vista Sylvaner is much like the

Sebastiani, save that it does have the faint kinship with lager. Sebastiani Rieslings are nonvintage, with North Coast Counties as their appellation of origin. Buena Vista varies, but usually shows Sonoma as the appellation with no vintage.

In Mendocino County, Parducci and Cresta Blanca offer Sylvaners of sound quality but inordinately modest character. Ukiah and surrounding territories appear to be too warm for the grape variety to retain more than a minimum of aromatics.

Central Coast Sylvaners

The Central Coast, especially Monterey County, seems to have adopted the sylvaner grape as something of a specialty. The Salinas Valley does appear to offer a beneficent environment. At least the Monterey-appellation Sylvaners to date have been brisk, refreshing, surprisingly aromatic.

Mirassou Vineyards has led the way in Monterey County with a wine faintly disguised under the name Monterey Riesling. As the Mirassou family explains the name, the first wines of the type from their Monterey County vines were as fresh and bracing as sea air, and thus perfect choices to establish a name for the sea-girt county as a viticultural region. The wines are uncannily fresh, as all field-crushed whites tend to be, but they do not brace. The examples to date finish sweet, not dry, soft as lakeshore zephyrs rather than refreshing as a salt air breeze. They are, in fact, less tart than Mirassou Chenin Blancs from the same vineyard near Soledad. For all of that they have enough force to make good company with clams in one of the plain-faced restaurants on fisherman's wharf in Monterey town.

The Monterey Vineyard calls its vintage-dated wine of the type Grüner Sylvaner. (The translation is Green Sylvaner, which somehow lacks romance, or even an appetizing connotation of flavor. The German adjective is there to indicate that winemaker Dr. Richard Peterson has followed an Austrian model, in its original language to keep the sound of the wine tempting.) The first vintage, 1974, yielded an astonishingly perfumey wine, light in body but stout in flavor. It is as fresh as cold fermentation and quick bottling could make it, and just a shade off-dry to keep the finish from being too tart.

Paul Masson makes a nonvintage California Sylvaner as a light wine with enough crisp qualities to qualify as dry. Most of the grapes come from the company's Monterey County vineyards. It is one of the finest values among the Masson whites. Almadén's California Sylvaner is, typically, affable in a shapeless sort of way. A Sylvaner by San Martin is close kin to the Almadén, or has been. New vineyards in Monterey County may reshape it.

Several small local producers also offer Sylvaners. Ridge Vineyards makes Sylvaner in the same heavy, earthy, almost countrified style as its other whites. Bargetto and Fortino also make the wine full and dry, but even more countrified in style than Ridge.

MISCELLANEOUS WHITE VARIETALS

A few little-known, seldom-made varietal whites cling to frail existence in California. Flora, Folle Blanche, Green Hungarian, and Sauvignon Vert bear no particular relationship to one another except for being curiosity pieces. Rkatsiteli is an even greater oddity than the others.

Two of the company, Emerald Riesling and light muscat, have been gaining ground in recent years.

Emerald Riesling

Emerald riesling is the white counterpart to ruby cabernet, which is to say it was an early success from the hybridizing program of Dr. H. P. Olmo at the University of California at Davis.

Somehow the varietal wine has not quite caught on as well as its red cousin, perhaps because of an abundance of off-dry, reasonably tart whites from other sources. However, several producers continue to make Emerald Rieslings. The roster has even grown by a name or two.

The wine gives some hint of its family tie to white riesling, but its essential nature is closer to sylvaner for being light-bodied, and not intensely aromatic. The finest Emerald Rieslings to date have been the tiny annual bottlings from Ficklin Vineyards, the port-type specialists at Madera, in the San Joaquin Valley. Of the commercially available ones, M. LaMont and Ambassador have consistently been fresh, pleasant wines suited to informal, perhaps even homely chicken dinners. Royal Host, the veteran in the field, has tended to be a very soft, even flaccid wine, although cleanly made and acceptable as an everyday white.

Flora

The grape variety flora is another of Dr. H. P. Olmo's U.C.-Davis hybrids. Based in gewürztraminer, it is a moderate artistic success but an economic failure.

Like emerald riesling it was cultivated to grow in the warmth of the San Joaquin Valley. Unlike emerald riesling, it retained the ancestral preference for cool climates where it has not the strength of character to dislodge gewürztraminer, or the prolific production to compete with chenin blanc.

Souverain made an affable medium-dry Flora for several years under Lee Stewart, but could not develop an audience. The grape now is a minority partner in Souverain Riesling. (Schramsberg takes a part of the Napa flora crop for its Demi Sec Cremant, described in the sparkling wine section.)

Parducci, at Ukiah, made a dry Flora which proved that heat does indeed diminish the flowery character that led to the grape's name. The wine was competent, but neutral in flavor. The winery now experiments with a frankly sweet Flora. It shows some promise of becoming a wine of character.

The tiny Z-D winery in Sonoma made one Flora of strikingly full, fruity character, but only one.

The variety may deserve a better fate, but its prospects show no signs of improving. The cumulative acreage is only 417. Nearly half of that is in hottest Kern County and not likely to become varietal wine.

Folle Blanche

Louis M. Martini, the man, developed Folle Blanche as a varietal largely for himself, so he could have a lightly flavored, cleansingly crisp dry wine to go with the delicate poached fish he liked for lunch. It was and is an act of generosity that the winery shares his wine with the world at large.

Folle blanche (it translates from the French as Crazy White) was a principal grape of Cognac before Phylloxera. Now it largely has disappeared from the world. In California most of the crop from 254 acres goes into sparkling wines as a sort of spine stiffener for less acidic but more flavorful varieties. In fact Louis M. Martini first met folle blanche at Almadén in the 1940s where it already was in use as one element in the sparkling wine cuvées. Almadén today owns a great share of the state's total acreage of the variety. Martini's patch at his Monte Rosso vineyard near Sonoma town is the only famous one.

The lack of public favor for Folle Blanche is a modest disappointment for viticulturists at the University of California at Davis, who recommend the grape variety heartily on all counts except its tendency to suffer in damp vintages.

Green Hungarian

Green Hungarian has few friends in this world, except for the small army of people who drink it with relish.

Back in the mid-1940s, the U.C.-Davis consigned the variety to oblivion, noting that the wines were thin, flat, lacking in flavor or character, and poor to ordinary in quality. Even in blending, the researchers said, wines of green hungarian could only dilute the possible good properties of other wines in a blend. There has been no further comment from scholarly quarters.

Producers of Green Hungarian are seldom kinder, except toward their own. I can recall three different winemakers grumbling that none of the competition knew how to make Green Hungarian.

And still Souverain in the Napa Valley, Buena Vista and Sebastiani in Sonoma, Cresta Blanca in Mendocino, and Weibel in Alameda County make Green Hungarians and sell all they make to a clamoring public. All are dry or just off-dry except for the sweet one from Weibel. All are fresh and light, except for Cresta Blanca's, which has a curious, cabbage-like bouquet.

Most Green Hungarian is hard to distinguish from routine chablis, a wine content to lurk in the shadow of the plainest chicken. Its charm, according to cynics, comes from its curious name. However, just often enough to sustain the faith, Green Hungarian makes a satisfying wine close in character and flavor to a good Grey Riesling.

Only 367 acres of the vine are in California, two thirds of that total in the counties north of San Francisco Bay. Once thought to be an obscure German variety, the *weisse heunisch,* the green hungarian's origins are uncertain except for one point. It did not come from Hungary. When you're down and out . . .

Light Muscats

Muscats are much pilloried by snoots who think the wines are vulgar, like women who slap their knees when they laugh. There is no doubt. Muscats are a bit broad of flavor, but it is a good flavor. One of the great tributes to it was spoken by a youngish girl of my acquaintance who took a delicate sip, and said, "Mmmmm. Just like big green grapes."

Muscats, like French Colombard, are another triumph of cold fermentation, which has transformed their formerly coarse flavor into a delicate one without losing the rich, flowery perfume of the variety.

They are sipping wines for people who find even Gewürztraminer a shade too vinous for their taste. The Christian Brothers Chateau LaSalle is the pioneer, though it hides its varietal ancestry. More recently have come Charles Krug and Robert Mondavi Moscato di Canellis, Sutter Home Moscato Amabile, Cresta Blanc Moscato di Canelli, San Martin Moscato di Canelli, The Novitiate of Los Gatos Dry Malvasia (which has the perfume, but is indeed dry), Concannon Vineyards Muscat Blanc and Angelo Papagni Moscato d'Angelo.

The quality of them all is highly consistent. Styles do not differ much, with the exception of the Novitiate's dry bottling. Think of them in the warmth of summer as big green Muscat grapes without all the bothersome skins and seeds.

One light muscat stands out from all the others in style and character. It is the Louis M. Martini Moscato Amabile, a sort of underground legend. The wine is fermented very cold over a period of several months rather than several weeks. It emerges pale, strikingly delicate in its muscat flavors, almost viscous in body, and lazily *pétillant.* It can be bought at the winery only occasionally, for a few months after a lot succeeds. What you do is save up enough money to get a big bag of cashews or a can of Macadamia nuts, and a bottle of Moscato, then you put them away until somebody you like has an anniversary, because Moscato has the romantic taste of a honeysuckle nectar, just right for recalling honeymoons.

Rkatsiteli

The restless capacity for experimentation that marks California winemaking has resulted in tiny lots of a vintage-dated Rkatsiteli from Concannon Vineyard in Livermore. The first came from 1973, a lot of 2,472 bottles from the first harvestable crop of a single acre of test plantings.

The grape, loosely known as Russian Riesling to help identify its tart-fruity character, grows well in the Georgian provinces of the U.S.S.R. Cuttings were brought to California to see if they would yield a distinctive wine with high acidity in a warm, sunny climate. Thus far the tart qualities have been apparent, but the Concannons have only begun to experiment with distinctive varietal flavors. Because the vines tend to overproduce, Jim Concannon pruned them more severely in 1974 than 1973, and more severely still for 1975.

The bottled wines are sold mainly to California's relentlessly curious home audience.

Sauvignon Vert

Sauvignon vert, the black sheep of the sauvignon family, produces a wine incurably low in acid, yet sharp in flavor with the grassy or herbaceous character of the family. Balance is lacking.

The variety has had a long career in California as a prolific blend grape in sherry- and sauterne-types, but now is waning. Its acreage in 1974 was 832, less than half the peak figure.

Two small wineries make Sauvignon Vert as a varietal table wine for old hands who grew up on old-fashioned, common whites with edges to spare. They are Nichelini in Napa and Trentadue in Sonoma County. A third, Sutter Home, recently gave it up.

 # GENERIC WHITE WINES

As in the cases of their red counterparts, generic whites are blended from several grape varieties to achieve balanced, agreeable wines. However, there is less effort to accomplish something special in a generic white for the simple fact that only a rare white wine can profit from aging, and no generic is made as a rarity.

Three principal names shelter the products of California's lesser white wines. Chablis as a name indicates a fresh wine that is dry or just off-dry. Rhine as a name announces perceptible sweet. Sauterne has almost no limits, though many carry a modifying adjective as a hint about style. Dry Sauterne will live up to its promise. Wines called Sweet Sauterne, Haut Sauterne, or Château Nameyourwinery will be very sweet indeed.

By and large, distinguishing among regions is more difficult with whites than reds. A few relatively distinctive white generics come from coastal cellars, to be identified by a close appellation of origin. Nearly all are Chablis. However, many of the coast wineries use neutral valley grapes to temper outrageously flavorful fruit from french colombard grown close to home while interior wineries reverse that process.

To find a suitable white generic for regular table use poses no great problem in spite of the blurred outlines of the field. All one need do is choose a Chablis from a winery whose dry varietals appeal in style, or a Rhine from a cellar which does properly by the Germanic varietals.

A few outstanding examples of each type are catalogued below.

Chablis

From the North Coast counties, several assuredly dry, distinctively styled Chablis are to be had at prices rather higher than the average. Joe Heitz, at Heitz Cellars, makes a white blend to season new barrels each year. The resulting wine is both good and a good place to learn the characteristic imparted to fine whites by aging in new wood. The Beaulieu Vineyards vintage-dated Chablis blends chenin blanc and french colombard into a wine of rich flavor and good balance. The BV carries a Napa Valley appellation. Among less expensive wines, the Los Hermanos Chablis from Beringer shows well what a thoughtful blend of coastal and valley grapes can do to fill a jug at a modest price. In Mendocino County, Parducci Wine Cellars Chablis, of purely local grapes, is a classic old-style California white in the sense that it is dry and slightly austere in its fruit flavors, and yet up-to-date for being fermented cleanly to preserve all the fresh qualities one might wish.

In the Central Coast, Mirassou Vineyards makes a wine they call White Burgundy although Chablis would do just as well. A blend of pinot blanc and sauvignon blanc, it reflects the character of the latter grape and a kiss of new oak as well. The Monterey Vineyard, working to get away from generic name borrowing, calls its blend of chenin blanc and pinot blanc by the name of Del Mar Ranch after the vineyard in which the vines grow. The style is light, barely off-dry, and impeccably clean. It is easily the most tart of all these wines.

A few of the old country wineries in the southern half of Santa Clara County make jug Chablis of distinctive character. One that regularly wins the blind tastings put on by San Francisco underground newspapers is Emile's, from the Emilio Guglielmo winery at Morgan Hill, but theirs is not a country cellar. The Guglielmos have a modern winery operation presided over by George Guglielmo, who was trained in enology at Fresno State.

In the San Joaquin Valley, one always does well to have a look at E. & J. Gallo Chablis Blanc and M. LaMont Chablis as reference points. The Gallo is the softer, less flavorful wine of the two. The M. LaMont, rich with the aromatic french colombard, strikes a huskier balance.

Rhines

Rhines have dwindled in numbers in the past few seasons, especially in the North Coast counties. Too sweet for versatile use with meals, they have found increasing competition from modestly priced varietals of greater character. The light muscats are one example, Chenin Blancs another. However, a few pleasing ones are to be had at very modest cost. In the Central Coast San Martin has blossomed with a finely made, fragrant Rhine since Ed Friedrich assumed the post as winemaker there in 1973. Paul Masson has a Rhine of agreeable quality at a lesser price. The Rhines from the Central Valley tend to be a bit too soft for my taste. Gallo or Guild, the latter under its Winemasters Guild label, have representative choices.

Sauterne

Sauterne was the all-purpose name for all generic white wine directly after repeal of Prohibition. For whatever reason, that was the name that appealed to the unlettered thirsts of the era. As a need for some variety arose, the wineries tacked modifiers onto the front of the name much as Chablis is now becoming Chablis Blanc, Gold Chablis, and even Pink Chablis.

Subsequently, the diffusions defeated the name. People quit buying any and all shades of Sauterne because they could not figure out what they might get out of the bottle.

In spite of the gloomy history, some good wine is available under the name these days, mostly because several coastal wineries use it as a shelter for their excess stocks from semillon and sauvignon blanc. Of this sort, Louis M. Martini in the Napa Valley and Concannon Vineyard in Livermore are particularly characterful. Both are Dry Sauterne. Over on the sweet side Concannon and Wente Bros. are the benchmarks.

The Pink Wines

Every now and again a curmudgeon will write that rosés are too trifling to be noted by serious wine people. Humbug. Rosés are as important as new asparagus, or rhubarb, or any other fine flavor of a fleeting season.

Granted there is no reason to take these wines seriously, but there are ample reasons to take them frivolously at picnics, with barbecued steaks on scaring summer nights, or in lieu of some gummy punch. After all, even serious wine people get thirsty when it is hot, but should not be foolish enough either to give up wine or to waste a fine one.

Rosés are under-done reds because they are made that way. Skins and seeds stay in contact with the juice just long enough to begin coloring the latter, a few hours rather than the several days required to make a red. This early separation of solids leaves wines of no longevity at all, because durability comes from tannins in the skins. Typically rosés then ferment cold, as whites do, to keep the fruit flavors fresh in wines that charm when they are very young.

This does not mean that all rosés are the same thing. Every aspect of character is open to choice. Rosés range from bone dry to overwhelmingly sweet, from fermentor fresh to wearily bouquetish. The varietal ones clearly reflect the characteristic flavors of the grapes that go into them. The generic rosés are blended to a character chosen by the proprietor.

The distinctive varietals come almost inevitably from the coastal counties, Grenache being the lone exception. There are not very many of them, although the recent wave of vineyard plantings may lead to more if some varieties show persistent surpluses as reds.

Nearly every winery in the state offers a generic rosé, an astonishing development considering that California made no rosés at all until Frank Schoonmaker encouraged Almadén to make one based on the model of Tavel. The first one was released only in 1941 or 1942.

☙ VARIETAL PINK WINES ❧

Two varieties of *Vitis vinifera* go regularly into the making of varietal rosés in California. Another five are used at least episodically. They are a divergent lot by geographic origin and by characteristic, though the differences in characteristic are muted somewhat by the inherent delicacy of pink as opposed to red winemaking. The one generality covering them all is that they offer the driest possibilities to go with meals.

Rosé of Cabernet Sauvignon

Cabernet sauvignon makes a curious kind of rosé most times. The characteristic flavor of the variety—tealike, herbaceous, or whichever green leaf strikes a chord—makes an odd note in a pale, fresh wine and above all in a pale, fresh wine with a hint of sweet. On the other hand, any effort to build strength or the bouquets of age into a Rosé of Cabernet is doomed beforehand because the result is only a weak-kneed imitation of the red wine. The handful of people who make pink wine from this grape regularly find themselves impaled on one horn of the dilemma or the other.

André Tchelistcheff long has harbored the thought that Rosé of Cabernet could be a most useful bridge for newcomers to wine. The thought remained an abstract ideal while he was at Beaulieu Vineyards. Now, working with Mary Ann Graf at Simi Vineyards in the Alexander Valley, he is developing a wine that may prove him right.

The 1974 is the first example that shows some signs of satisfying Tchelistcheff. The grapes for it were harvested well ahead of those for the same winery's red, and fermented almost dry. The finished wine has a distinctive flavor, but not an herbaceous one, to go with a clean, refreshingly acidic aftertaste. Earlier vintages, sweeter and more herbaceous, left the impression of Chinese tea with a lot of sugar in it, which is to say they somehow seemed incorrect.

Buena Vista's Vine Brook Cabernet Rosé goes back to the 1950s, consistently a dry, dark, bouquetish rosé. Vintage after vintage the wine has been marked by a slight bitter finish from cabernet sauvignon's abundant tannins, and also by browning. (Technically the one flaw might be expected to inhibit the other's developing, but the wine overcomes probability.) Vine Brook has fans, especially among people who like darkish old flavors in whatever wine, but it is not my cup of tea.

A small but growing Sonoma winery, Davis Bynum, has had an occasional fling at Cabernet Rosé with similar results to those of Buena Vista. Llords and

Elwood has a Cabernet Rosé of no precise pedigree in much the same vein as these others, though somewhat less marked by browning.

With the new abundance of cabernet sauvignon grapes Sterling Vineyards, Dry Creek, Geyser Peak and Firestone vineyards have all joined the rosé parade.

Gamay Rosé

Gamay, the premier grape of the Beaujolais district in France, seems naturally endowed as a source for rosés. It is delicately fruity by nature, and the smack of residual sweet is familiar in some red wines made from it.

In spite of its apparent aptitude for the work only a few producers make a rosé of the variety. Nearly all of the history is in the Napa Valley.

Louis M. Martini consistently produces a pale, light rosé marked with the taste of its aging in big redwood tanks. (A faint tawny tint in the color reliably announces this presence.) In favorable vintages the wine has some of the same forceful character as a Tavel. In lesser seasons it fades toward neutrality. On balance it is one of the most recommendable of rosés. The appellation, as usual, is California. There is a vintage date.

Both Robert Mondavi and Oakville Vineyards make Gamay Rosés darker in color, and detectably sweet on the finish. Fresh in the bottle they bear more than a passing resemblance to Beaujolais Nouveau. Both are best taken in that spirit. Both carry Napa Valley appellations and vintage dates.

Korbel, in Sonoma County, introduced a rosé of gamay under the name of Chateau Rosé late in 1975. The word Chateau guarantees the wine to be a sweet one. Otherwise it is fresh and aromatic, as it should be.

Grenache Rosé

California rosé was invented at Almadén in the early 1940s. The original was a Grenache Rosé, which has been a roaring success since its debut. Grenache Rosés are now made by more producers than any other varietal pink wine by a factor of five. Some twenty Grenache Rosés are available.

Grenache is by nature a grape for rosés. Its color is paler than those of most other red grapes, and tinted with orange. The intensely perfumey flavor of the grape profits for being thinned from red wine to rosé, and is appropriately cloaked with a bit of residual sweet. (The grape's other role in California, in tawny port-types, is consistent.)

Ironically grenache is the grape variety that goes into Tavels in France, but must produce an entirely different style of wine in California. Grenache almost makes itself into a dry, bouquetish pink wine in France. In California that style will not come harmoniously no matter how much effort, but the fresh, sweet one is easy.

Just as curiously, the grape ripens very well in the Rhône districts of France, but in California does not perform well in any of the coastal districts. Nearly all of the acreage devoted to grenache is in the San Joaquin Valley, where the warmer climate suits it exactly.

Almadén has been and continues to be the measuring stick for the rest. Nearly all of them—Sebastiani, Mirassou, San Martin, Weibel, M. Lamont, and East-Side/Royal Host—will run very close to form, which means fermentor-fresh and perceptibly sweet. The purpose is to have a chillable wine of simple, affable character.

A few producers have independent thoughts. Beaulieu Vineyard, drawing grapes from the San Joaquin Valley, makes a Grenache Rosé considerably darker and drier than the Almadén style. The Novitiate of Los Gatos keeps its pale, sweet Grenache Rosé in ancient oak casks long enough for them to impart a distinctive bouquet of old wood to a wine that serves better as a summertime cold replacement for port than as a carefree thirst quencher. Sonoma Vineyards has made its Grenache Rosé pale, with just enough spritz to liven it. The exact model for this bottling is not Almadén, but E. & J. Gallo Pink Chablis, the original for all lightly flavored, sweet, faintly fizzy California pink wines.

In addition to these wines of commercial size, a few small ones offer bottlings for local consumption. The roster includes Gemello, Thomas Kruse, and Davis Bynum.

Grignolino Rosé

California has but one commercially available Grignolino Rosé. It comes from Heitz Cellars in the Napa Valley.

The tart, richly fruity flavor of Joe Heitz's particular clone of Grignolino lends itself to a dry, remarkably refreshing rosé. The fruit taste is so specific that newcomers refuse to believe the wine is dry in the technical sense of having no residual sugar, or at least so little that no mortal palate could perceive it.

This is my own choice to the absurd point that three cases cannot get me through a middling warm summer. It has character enough to replace red wine with barbecued steak when the temperature does not go down with the sun, and is crisp enough to slake the thirsts of such work as digging cockles or hunting *Boletus* mushrooms.

The wine is vintage-dated, from Heitz's own vineyards.

One other Grignolino Rosé exists. Thomas Kruse makes one barrel or so each year from vines near Gilroy in southern Santa Clara County. Kruse opts for a wine much paler in color and lighter in both flavor and body. The taste of the variety is unmistakable in a wine that slakes thirst as well as the Heitz, but does not have equal powers to restore.

Rosé of Petite Sirah

Mirassou Vineyards made its first rosé from petite sirah as an accident of fermentation in 1970. Like a good many other vinous accidents this one turned out well. The wine is a pale but true pink, delicate of flavor, crisp, and effectively dry. It will do the same kind of versatile service as the Heitz Grignolino Rosé although its fruit flavors are less specific, and it does not have quite as much strength to revive a body chilled by Pacific winds.

The label says the wine is Petite Rosé. It carries a vintage date and a Monterey County appellation of origin.

Pinot Noir Rosé

Rosé from pinot noir has been almost nonexistent in recent years because the grape has been in short supply for reds. If the crop does begin to outrun demand for red Pinot Noir, rosé Pinot Noir could be welcome. The varietal characteristic is roundly fruity. The color of the juice is a true red, which remains a joy to see even in its paler forms. Not least, the wine is balanced and agreeable when fermented bone dry.

At the moment one tiny annual lot is to be had, from Husch Vineyards, in the cool Anderson Valley of Mendocino County. It lives up to all of the above descriptions, and thus is a versatile rosé for summer barbecues and other places where the wine wants to stand up to a meal of substance. And still it is lighthearted enough that drinking it chilled causes no pangs of remorse about doing the wrong thing to a bottle of lofty pedigree.

Zinfandel Rosé

Zinfandel grapes make tartly berryish reds. Rosés follow the red footsteps with fidelity. A properly made Zinfandel Rosé accomplishes with ease what the makers of Cabernet Rosés look for: a dry wine of character. A forceful example can even bear two or three years of age with no more than slight fading, which means that zinfandel rather than grenache produces California's closest counterparts to lusty Tavels.

There are not as many Zinfandel Rosés as there ought to be. The class of the field year after year is J. Pedroncelli, where Jim Pedroncelli makes the wine slightly darker than average, dry, and with a faint hint of wood from time in casks. Once the apple-ish taste of bottle bouquet sets in, the resemblance to a woody Tavel is remarkable considering the great differences of varietal character separating zinfandel from grenache. The Pedroncelli comes from Sonoma County grapes.

Concannon Vineyards makes a kindred Zinfandel Rosé, although the 1973 bottling had a fresher quality about it than earlier ones owing to the Concannon's change from wood to steel fermentors. Their grapes once came from Mendocino County for the rosé. With the 1973, the source shifted to the Sierra Nevada foothills in Placer County.

It is a tribute to their vinosity that both go better with meals than alone. Even the garlicky pungency of aïoli cannot overwhelm them.

In occasional years Mayacamas Vineyard in Napa County will make a Zinfandel Rosé lighter in character and a shade paler than the Pedroncelli or Concannon, but still dry enough to want drinking with a meal. Tiny Thomas Kruse winery in Santa Clara County has made a Zinfandel Rosé much akin to the Mayacamas, suggesting to a lamentably small audience that the region around Gilroy could make such a wine well.

The Sparkling Wines

The tradition of sparkling wine in California is long and honorable, but tuned even in its finest moments to affability more than Olympian grandeur.

Because of this the critical reputation of California sparkling wines has been more mixed than that of the still wines. Favorable estimation depends upon a judge who will accept that the ripening sun of California imposes generosity of character while the pale sun of the Champagne region of France demands a somber Gothic elegance.

During the past few years improved vineyard management and the technique of cold fermentation have opened up new avenues of style in the more classical producers in the coastal counties, especially in the Napa Valley. The welcome diversification of styles and characters has included a few examples that came very close to greatness, but no definitive bridging of the old gap between the Champagnes of France and those of California.

By volume, much of the wine labeled as Champagne in California comes from large producer-marketers who use the Charmat process to produce sound, but undistinctive bubbly for sale at bargain prices. These wines are counterparts to the inexpensive generics from the same sources.

The field also encompasses Pink Champagnes, Sparkling Burgundies, and a handful of dessert sparklers in the muscat-ish vein of Asti Spumantes. These latter are minor factors.

Declaring that California sparkling wines are distinctly different in style from those produced in and around Reims invites the question: Why call the Californians "Champagne"? There are, after all, Sparkling Vouvrays and other models.

The fundamental reason is that the word, champagne, describes a process as well as a region. The technique of getting bubbles into a wine by conducting a secondary fermentation in a sealed bottle is called *méthode champenoise* because old Dom Perignon was posted by the Catholic Church to the Abbaye of Hautvillers rather than elsewhere. Presuming that the Dom was fated to make the discovery, the process could just as well be known now as *méthode alsatienne.*

Beyond the conjectural, the word Champagne will sell enough wine to allow a proprietor to stay in business while known alternatives will not. Several have tried. Buena Vista, for example, tried for years to make waves with a wine called Sparkling Sonoma, but the public paid it no heed.

The remedy, if one is needed, lies with us, the buyers. If we support a name other than Champagne for California sparkling wines the producers will hurry to oblige our whim. Even now several of the costliest sparkling wines in California use the word "Champagne" on their labels in the smallest letters allowed by law, relying on other descriptive words to convey the message that the wine is bubbly. The French-owned M & H sparkling wine cellar in the Napa Valley has announced a plan to coin a word, but has not announced the new word thus far. So, some choice already exists, and a clearer one will be available soon for those who would put an end to calling Californian wines Champagne.

Meantime, the wines so called go on being good to excellent in a distinctively Californian way.

The Language of the Labels

Two sets of legal terms cover the wine inside a champagne-style bottle. One set deals with the method of production. The other set describes degree of sweetness or other characteristics of the wine.

The label descriptions of technique for fine bottles are *"méthode champenoise,"* "bottle-fermented," and "fermented in this bottle." The terms overlap, but are not necessarily synonymous.

The *méthode champenoise* of ancient verity includes these specific steps:

• A young, sharp wine of relatively low alcohol is bottled, with the addition to each bottle of a mixture of yeast and sugar.

• This bottle is closed tightly, and a secondary fermentation within it produces slight amounts of alcohol and carbon dioxide (the bubbles). The bottles of each batch, called a cuvée, all are stacked together while this takes place.

• At some point after the fermentation is complete the bottles are riddled, which is to say they are placed in racks, necks downward, and systematically jostled so that the spent yeasts gather on the inside of the sealed cap.

• When the yeasts are satisfactorily gathered, the bottle is opened; the CO_2 pressure ejects the yeast in a spray of wine; the lost liquid is replaced, and the bottle quickly resealed with its final cork closure. At this point the degree of sweetness in the finished wine is established by the replacement liquid, which may be the same dry wine, or a syrup of greater or lesser sweetness, or a mixture of the two.

In recent years the term *méthode champenoise* has been diffused to encompass sparkling wines made with one shortcut in the process. Rather than spending four or more weeks at the laborious task of riddling, some producers use what is called a transfer process. In this method the bottles of a cuvée are opened without the yeasts being gathered in the necks, and emptied into a pressurized filtering system. The wine is filtered clear of spent yeast then rebottled in a matter of hours.

The ancient method, with riddling, is quirkier, more craftsmanlike. The transfer technique is economical and improves reliability. Since quality can be defined to favor either technique, the judgment has to be with the individual drinker.

As best I have been able to taste the evidence, the quality of the original cuvée is more important than the technique. It also is true that quirky craftsmen have assembled nearly all of the truly fine cuvées. In any case, sparkling wines that say "Fermented in this bottle" are made to the ancient standard. Those that say only "Fermented in the bottle" or "Bottle fermented" may be made either in the ancient manner or by a transfer method, but most likely by the latter.

The name Champagne also can be used in California to describe wines that undergo their secondary fermentations not in individual bottles but in glass-lined steel tanks of 500 to 5,000 gallons capacity. Once the fermentation is completed the wine is filtered and bottled under pressure. Wines made in this way must say on their labels "Bulk Process" or "Charmat Process," the latter after the French inventor of the technique, Eugène Charmat.

Because Bulk Process was designed as a penny saver its use is restricted to inexpensive cuvées.

The degrees of sweet in white sparkling wines called California Champagne are noted by the traditional French descriptives. As in France, regulations do not specify precise degrees of sweetness because perception of sugar is linked to other factors including total acidity and intensity of fruit flavors. The usages:

· Natur (or Naturel or Natural) indicates a bone dry wine, one with no dosage (syrup) added after removal of the yeasts.
· Brut is the designation for an effectively dry wine, although practice allows enough dosage to be added so that a faintly perceptible softening takes place. House style dictates the point.
· Extra Dry announces a perceptibly sweet wine, but one still dry enough to be taken with a meal as easily as it might go with hors d'oeuvres.
· Sec ranges from the same general level of sweetness as Extra Dry on into dessert-sweet qualities.

In California any wine labeled Natur, or one of the variations, is almost guaranteed to be made in the classic way of old Champagne. Brut is offered primarily as a wine made in the classical way, but may have been finished by the transfer process. Extra Dry and Sec may be classical, transfer method, or bulk process.

The handful of outright dessert sparkling wines do not use any designation for degree of sweetness. Most go by particular names, especially as varietals from muscats. Neither do pink sparkling wines or red sparkling wines use designations of sweet or dry. Most of the pinks are called Pink Champagne, most of the reds Sparkling Burgundy. A few of the latter go by the name of Champagne Rouge.

Varietal designations are legal under the same regulation that governs still wines, except that the varietal name must be accompanied by a legally defined term showing that the wine is a sparkling one. As examples, there have been Beaulieu Vineyards Champagne de Chardonnay; Schramsberg Champagne Rosé-Cuvée de Gamay, and Mirassou Vineyards Sparkling Gamay Beaujolais.

Appellations of origin and vintage dating are governed by the same regulations that apply to table wines.

There is another side to the sparkling coin. Neither "Champagne" nor "Sparkling" may appear on labels of wines made bubbly by any process other than the ones noted above. Anything labeled Crackling or Carbonated has not been produced by any of those processes.

∽ CHAMPAGNES ∽

As it applies to California sparkling wines, the word "Champagne" covers, to repeat a point, almost as much ground as the word "dog." There are big ones and little ones, soft ones and sharp ones, and purebreds and mutts. This is not to put down California Champagnes in general, or the mutts in particular. I would much rather have a mutt than a Doberman Pinscher any day of the week. Still, there is difficulty in dividing up the field sensibly.

For lack of any better way, the basic divisions are by technique of production from classical champagne method to Charmat. This tends to range the wines from most distinctive to least, and also most expensive to least.

Classical Method Champagnes

California began making estimable Champagnes early in its vinous history. Pietro Rossi at Italian Swiss Colony produced some that fared very well in competition at international expositions in Europe. Paul Masson managed to torment some of his French peers with Champagnes from his hilltop estate in Santa Clara County. Jan Hanuska at F. Korbel & Bros. added luster to the early image.

Post-Prohibition heroes came harder, partly because the Great Depression was no environment for the luxuries of costly sparkling wine. Hanuska made the comeback for F. Korbel & Bros. A gentle man named Oliver Goulet made a name at Almadén beginning in the 1940s. However, it has been only since the 1960s that sparkling wine in California has blossomed with new labels and new ideas of style, with the Napa Valley as a newer partner of the old bastions of excellence, Sonoma and Santa Clara.

Napa Valley Champagnes

Although interest blossomed late, the Napa Valley has come to eminence as a source of California sparkling wines produced in the classical manner. Beaulieu Vineyards, Hanns Kornell, and Schramsberg can provide, in three bottles, an amazing variety of choices, all of them fine.

Steam-driven conveyors lifted grapes to crushers at the old Stanford winery at Warm Springs in the 1880s. The property is now part of Weibel Champagne Cellars. (WINE INSTITUTE)

Beaulieu Vineyards, after several years of fitful interest, has launched a concerted effort to make a sparkling wine with a strong varietal character of chardonnay. Beginning with the vintage of 1972, the label even identifies the wine as Cuvée de Chardonnay. Small lots from earlier harvests, especially 1968, had convinced the proprietors that the rich flavor of ripe Napa Valley Chardonnay has individual merit made into Champagne by the traditional handcrafted method. The 1972 was finished very dry, as Brut.

Jack Davies at Schramsberg makes his Napa Valley Blanc de Blancs and Blanc de Blancs Reserve with a huge proportion of chardonnay grapes, but, in searching for a style closer to the traditional one of France, disguises the varietal character to a great degree. As noted in the Napa Valley chapter, Davies achieves this in part by picking the grapes early, before their flavors bloom to the fullest, and also by discreet blending with pinot blanc and other muted varieties. What he seeks in a Blanc de Blanc is a light, pointed enough set of grape flavors to allow some of the yeasty flavor to shine through. The Blanc de Blancs Reserve goes further in the same direction by staying in tirage for an extra one to two years, so the yeasts have extra time in which to impart their curiously earthy note to the wine.

The rounder, more richly fruity wine of Schramsberg is the Blanc de Noir, made principally from pinot noir grapes. Marked by the unmistakable perfume of the variety, the wine also acquires a fuller body, a more velvety texture on the palate than the brisker, more refreshing Blanc de Blancs.

Both Beaulieu and Schramsberg vintage date, and both use the Napa Valley as their appellation of origin.

Hanns Kornell opposes the French ancestral idiom with Sehr Trocken and Brut, but agrees with it when he makes Extra Dry and Sec.

Sehr Trocken is the ultimate expression of Kornell's sense of style, which was formed during his training in France and Germany. In the end he came away with a preference for dry, sharp, strongly bouquetish wines made of riesling. California growing conditions have intensified his feelings, especially about grape varieties. Sehr Trocken uses a riesling-based cuvée. The bouquet comes from leaving the wine on the yeasts for five to seven years rather than the two years customary in California. The yeasty flavors grow much more pronounced as one consequence. More striking is the flavor of old riesling. The flavor association, as in the case of still wines, is petroleum to many, wizening apples to others. Petroleum sounds terrible in the abstract, but the fact is better because the aroma is not of concentrated fumes, but rather the faint, clean smell of gasoline that comes as a wind-borne gift from some distant source. Because of that and because of all the other qualities of age in a white wine, this is a Champagne for those who have developed a fondness for strengths of character.

Kornell Brut makes a bow in the same direction. Riesling is the base, but the wine remains on the yeast only for the typical two years, so this is a much sprightlier wine than Sehr Trocken. Also, it is not bone dry as Sehr Trocken is, another source of affability.

Kornell Extra Dry and Sec are made from cuvées with considerable amounts of chenin blanc, balanced with colombard or chardonnay, or similar grape varieties. They are soft, roundly fruity wines, and impeccably clean.

Hanns Kornell does not use vintage dates, except on the back labels of Sehr Trocken. The appellation always is California, though many cuvées are entitled to Napa Valley.

M & H, the subsidiary of the French firm that owns Moët et Chandon, has yet to market its first sparkling wine, made from the vintage of 1973. However, some hints have emerged from the cellars. Edmund Maudière, the French cellarmaster in charge of production, has said that California chardonnay seems to him too rich in fruit flavor to make a fine sparkling wine. The first cuvées have, as a result, leaned toward pinot noir, pinot blanc, and ugni blanc. The cuvées were made dry. That fact plus the effort to diminish fruity flavors suggests that M & H will offer wines as close to Champagne from the homeland as California will produce.

M & H has vineyards in the Napa Valley, but all too young to bear fruit. The early wines will come partly from a vineyard near Napa city and partly from outside purchases, including some from Rancho California, south and east of Los Angeles.

Sonoma Champagnes

Sonoma County is in great degree the ancestral home of true *méthode champenoise* sparkling wine in California. Arpad Haraszthy made one of the first attempts on the old Buena Vista estate in the 1860s. Pietro Rossi had one of the first celebrated successes at Asti in the 1880s. F. Korbel & Bros. has been a standard bearer on either side of Prohibition. For all of that, only Korbel and Sonoma Vineyards were actively making fermented-in-this-bottle sparkling wines through the first half of the 1970s. They are soon to be joined by Chateau St. Jean.

Korbel offers the range of degrees of sweet in its nonvintage, California appellation Champagnes. Natural has a classically austere character. No gentle grapey flavors mitigate the fact that the wine is bone dry. It is the oyster man's choice every time for being lean of flavor and sharply clean on the finish. Brut all by itself makes a modestly austere impression. Side by side with the natural its softer qualities become readily apparent. It is the most versatile style to carry straight through a meal. Extra Dry makes no gesture at all in the direction of austerity. The hint of sweet is broad, and the fruit flavors are companionably round. Sec is sweetly pneumatic, without a complication. The style in all cases is direct, fresh, and youthful rather than bouquetish from yeast or age.

If these descriptions ring hauntingly of the generalized ones on style in California Champagne it is because F. Korbel & Bros. has done much to define that style.

The early day Champagne master Jan Hanuska is given much of the credit for establishing french colombard and chenin blanc as the basic grape varieties for California white sparkling wine. He and most others used first-year wines to form their cuvées, and left the wines on the yeasts for an average two years. His successors at Korbel continue within that framework. Infusions of chardonnay, sauvignon blanc, and other varieties help distinguish the cuvées one from another as much as sweetness does.

The long, steady track record makes Korbel sparkling wines useful measuring points for all others as well as satisfying drinks, for they are as good or better than when they were preeminent. They have one other advantage. They are more widely available by far than any other sparkling wine made in California with the ancient methods.

Sonoma Vineyards made its debut as a "serious" sparkling wine producer in 1974 with wines it identified as Cuvée 102 and Cuvée 104. The notion behind them is a revolutionary one in California.

Nearly all sparkling wine cuvées are very young when they go into the bottle for secondary fermentation. These were not. Both blanc de blancs, almost purely of chardonnay grapes, they aged a year or more each in new oak barrels before being bottled for their secondary fermentations. As a result they were curiously thick, strongly flavored wines bearing only a fleeting resemblance to other sparkling wines, French or Californian.

The first two bottlings were not the top of the form. Two years was not enough time for any yeasty flavors to make themselves felt against the powerful aromatics of ripe chardonnay and new oak. Neither were the latter two flavors in harmony with each other. However, as pioneers of a new style, the two cuvées, both finished as Bruts, promised much. If further blends smooth out some of the rough patches without losing the essential richness of the wine they could be the start of a new legend.

Further efforts in this direction may come from Chateau St. Jean, a new cellar in the Valley of the Moon at the town of Kenwood. Richard Arrowood, who was the Champagne master responsible for Cuvées 102 and 104, now has the same responsibility for Chateau St. Jean. The first sparkling wines under that label will not appear before 1977.

Central Coast Champagnes

An overwhelming percentage of California's bottle-fermented Champagne comes from cellars headquartered in the Central Coast region, but it is left to Mirassou Vineyards to produce the only distinctly regional wines, and the only classical *méthode champenoise* ones in the general market.

Mirassou makes Monterey County sparkling wines bone dry under the label Champagne Au Naturel, and barely off-dry under the designation of Champagne Brut. The wines are vintage dated, appearing on the market about three years after the harvest with the producer's recommendation that they be drunk within a year of purchase, or two at most. The style is lean, crisply acidic, and very clean, and owes itself to Champagne-master Max Huebner.

Thus far the Mirassous have resisted any temptation to flirt with the austere bouquets that come from long aging of the wine with its yeasts, probably wisely. Although the style is lean in the sense of being tart and dry, Monterey grapes tend to have highly developed varietal characters. The fruit aromas in Mirassou sparkling wines are intense enough so that the earthy tastes of the yeasts would have a great deal to overcome before they were easy to find on the palate.

In addition to the Mirassou wines, some of the tiniest cellars in the region devote small fractions of their production to fermented-in-this-bottle sparkling wines. The roster includes Thomas Kruse in Gilroy, plus a pair of still smaller places. Anybody who does not know the proprietors by name and sight has no chance of finding the wines.

Careful observers will think of several more labels which say that the sparkling wine within the bottle was fermented in that bottle. They will be correct, but it is a matter that some of the sparkling-wine specialists bottle lots for friends and neighbors who do not specialize in Champagne.

Transfer-Method Champagnes

A few paragraphs ago I said that producers located in the Central Coast counties were responsible for an overwhelming percentage of California Champagnes fermented in the bottle, but finished by the transfer process.

Almadén Vineyards, Paul Masson Vineyards, San Martin Vineyards, and Weibel Champagne Cellars are the responsible parties.

The only other producers of transfer-method Champagnes are Cresta Blanca and United Vintners for the Inglenook label. The trade magazine, *Wines & Vines,* produces an annual roster of sparkling wine producers that showed in its 1975 edition some maximum and minimum sales figures for each company. Taking Cresta Blanca, Inglenook, and all of the classical producers at their maximums would yield

The fermenting winery of Weibel Champagne Cellars is flanked by vineyards even newer than the buildings. (HAROLYN THOMPSON)

360,000 cases. Taking the Central Coast transfer process producers at their minimums would yield 850,000 cases.

For the most part the transfer-process Champagnes have no clear geographic source. Almadén, Masson, and the others buy base wines for their cuvées to fit taste and technical profiles, and make their blends accordingly. The results are steady, sound, reliable, and all those other modest virtues. The prices are fair. The choices among them are personal preferences, not variations in quality. Paul Masson, for example, favors a leaner, sharper style than Almadén or the others. San Martin and Weibel Vineyards tend to occupy the softest, grapiest end of the stylistic pole.

In spite of the overall modesty of pedigree among these wines, some cuvées have particular character.

Almadén's most prestigious Champagne is its vintage-dated Blanc de Blancs, which appears in a squat bottle with a long neck. It is, true to the Almadén style, a soft, even fatly fruity wine. Styled as Brut, it is nonetheless perceptibly off-dry. The hint of yeast is fugitive, as usual in California sparkling wines.

Paul Masson has as its premier Champagne one called Blanc de Pinot. As the name suggests the cuvée is a blend of chardonnay and pinot blanc grapes. It is as much a Masson wine as the Almadén that typifies its label. The general approach of lean, sharp flavors calls to mind that Masson's Champagne masters for years were

Germans who may well have thought that Sekt was a better idea than Champagne, that riesling was a better idea than chardonnay, even though the cuvée uses the classic varieties of France.

Charmat Champagnes

For the most part Charmat Champagnes come from wineries with headquarters in the San Joaquin Valley, or in the Los Angeles region. Failing that, a majority of the grapes used in them are likely to come from those regions.

If there is an exception it is The Christian Brothers, whose Charmat Champagne seems to be dominated by grapes from coastal vineyards. The San Joaquin producers include California Growers under the Growers and Setrakian labels, California Wine Association under the Ambassador and L&J labels, Franzia under its own and a host of private labels, E. & J. Gallo under its own name and as André, Guild Wineries and Distilleries under the Roma, Winemasters Guild, and Cribari labels, United Vintners under the Lejon and Jacques Bonet labels, and the new Filice Winery under the labels Monet and Chateau Chambord. Bronco, another San Joaquin winery, has Charmat Champagnes under private labels as does Weibel from its winery in Alameda County.

The point was made earlier that the transfer-process Champagnes outweighed the classical champagne method ones by almost three bottles to one. Charmat Champagnes have a far greater edge, almost ten to one.

Every last one of the Charmat sparkling wines is soft, roundly fruit, fresh wine. Quite a few have a kiss of muscat in the blend to assure that they are fat and happy. No reasonable producer expects connoisseurs to take these wines seriously, but, on the other side of the coin, no producer expects a reasoning connoisseur to serve a serious Champagne to a thirsty mob at a wedding reception.

Blends and styles do vary from one producer to another enough to make personal preferences valid. The best yardstick is the rest of the producer's list of wines, especially white table wines. If Chablis *G* tastes better than Chablis *F,* then Champagne *G* is likely to prevail for all the same reasons.

Dessert Sparkling Wines

A slim handful of sweet sparkling wines other than Sec-style Champagnes are to be had. Nearly all are varietal muscats patterned after Asti Spumante. The roster reliably includes San Martin Sparkling Malvasia Bianca, Weibel Sparkling Malvasia, and sometimes includes Hanns Kornell Sparkling Muscadelle de Bordelais. Schramsberg has experimented recently with a Cremant made from the grape called flora, a hybrid based in gewürztraminer. Cremant in practice means a wine with rather less CO_2 pressure than a normal Champagne, but one made by the same process.

PINK SPARKLING WINES

Pink Champagne has a mixed history in California, but only for diligent students. Very nearly all of the wine that goes by the name is simple, sweet, devised to lubricate bridal showers, afternoon teas and other such.

Once in a great while, though, someone aims at the loftier challenge posed by the best of French pink sparkling wines. The classicists classic was the 1958 Champagne Rosé de Pinot Noir by André Tchelistcheff at Beaulieu, long since gone everywhere except in memory.

Jack Davies at Schramsberg makes a pale, bone-dry Cuvée de Gamay each year. The wine is released after a year to eighteen months on the yeasts, at which point it is crisp and fruity. For those who wish something more than a deft rosé with bubbles, time is an answer. The Schramsberg quickly acquires bouquet. By the time it is four or five years beyond the vintage it is an intriguing complex of young and old flavors.

The closest challengers for dry distinctiveness are bottle-fermented Pink Champagnes from Korbel and Hanns Kornell.

RED SPARKLING WINES

Most red sparkling wine from California has gone by the name of Sparkling Burgundy. In the mid-1970s a move was afoot to opt instead for Champagne Rouge as a gesture toward standardizing nomenclature. One company, Mirassou Vineyards, has introduced a varietal Sparkling Gamay Beaujolais.

It has been hard for me to think about sparkling red wine since Hugh Johnson evoked the unbearable image of such a wine being as inappropriate as a fat old man in a fairy suit.

However, let us suppose for the moment that you are trying to stay on the good side of a rich old uncle with an unquenchable thirst for the stuff, or that you in fact like it.

Hanns Kornell has a Sparkling Burgundy based in a nicely mature, quite dry red. The result is a bouquetish wine of enough complexity for a purist to pursue while ignoring the bubbles, and enough amiability to indulge a palate seeking only whimsy.

The Mirassou Sparkling Gamay Beaujolais is a dry, surprisingly tart red, vintage-dated, and carrying a Monterey County appellation of origin. One would say it is berryish. Fat man in a fairy suit or no, it can have a place at a summery beef barbecue where a cold wine is the only kind to have.

The rest of the field tends to be unabashedly sweet, fresh, frivolous, no matter what the technique of its making.

I do not believe I ever have heard anyone speak of Cold Duck.

1974 GRAPE ACREAGES—KEY VARIETIES IN KEY COUNTIES

RED WINE VARIETIES

	Barbera	Cabernet Sauvignon	Gamay	Gamay Beaujolais	Grignolino	Petit Sirah	Pinot Noir	Ruby Cabernet	Zinfandel
Mendocino	9	1,148	140	589	–	454	300	24	1,042
Napa	36	5,209	1,006	603	72	1,137	2,526	43	1,315
Sonoma	53	4,164	328	471	–	1,194	2,523	27	3,721
Alameda	12	18	53	56	–	58	76	–	135
Monterey	202	5,634	1,218	1,233	–	2,234	2,590	530	3,194
San Benito	–	549	–	518	–	–	746	–	206
San Luis O.	58	1,045	126	97	–	129	103	–	1,176
Santa Barbara	–	1,889	37	426	–	–	862	–	46
Santa Clara	10	169	26	38	135	126	89	59	227
Fresno	5,694	47	62	–	–	1,358	37	4,014	239
Kern	4,313	1,246	425	94	–	1,887	9	4,802	268
Madera	3,751	52	10	–	–	753	–	2,525	132
Merced	1,363	300	–	163	–	402	–	1,206	495
San Joaquin	601	291	90	–	–	1,081	76	277	10,927
Stanislaus	1,729	85	138	–	–	536	–	2,169	572
Tulare	2,320	43	–	43	17	555	–	1,462	15
Riverside	–	182	–	33	–	204	5	–	213
San Bernardino	–	–	–	–	17	–	18	47	3,303
STATE TOTALS	20,576	24,539	4,760	4,490	241	13,074	10,098	17,583	29,616

These acreage figures can be used to make rough estimates of potential volumes of pure varietal wines. For the coast counties, one acre of mature vineyard yields 250 to 320 cases of finished wine, depending upon variety, soil, and the vintage. In the San Joaquin a typical acre yields 580 to 710 cases, depending mainly upon grape variety. The basic formula: 1 ton of grapes yields 170 gallons of bottled wine. Coastal yields average 3.5 to 5 tons per acre; San Joaquin yields average 8 to 10 tons. A case equals 2.4 gallons.

Tables from the 1974 Grape Acreage Survey, by California Crop and Livestock Reporting Service

1974 GRAPE ACREAGES—KEY VARIETIES IN KEY COUNTIES
(continued)
WHITE WINE VARIETIES

Chardonnay	Chenin Blanc	Emerald Riesling	French Colombard	Gewürztraminer	Grey Riesling	Pinot Blanc	Sauvignon Blanc	Semillon	Sylvaner	White Riesling
355	156	2	970	63	90	32	81	17	26	230
2,249	1,134	–	641	300	348	64	534	197	194	1,141
1,808	299	–	1,149	473	74	74	261	180	93	814
165	103	–	100	–	226	68	98	338	59	24
2,929	2,092	331	474	795	482	670	1,027	519	531	2,374
871	104	–	–	263	61	180	25	34	127	395
291	86	–	13	88	51	–	186	53	27	148
843	45	–	–	159	–	30	67	–	152	1,009
41	33	12	123	–	–	73	9	74	151	55
39	2,373	464	5,835	–	–	8	–	325	11	–
47	4,844	1,529	4,995	17	138	–	–	670	108	57
63	1,266	147	3,365	–	15	–	–	107	144	–
20	2,377	155	2,509	–	–	–	390	21	–	–
8	930	78	1,185	1	104	–	–	44	24	–
–	1,702	–	2,184	–	–	36	90	504	–	64
43	1,162	42	2,882	–	–	–	–	269	–	–
140	132	57	17	–	1	20	184	3	–	549
–	6	–	–	–	–	–	–	–	–	–
10,037	19,826	2,846	26,666	2,175	1,698	1,296	3,193	3,356	1,668	7,194

Index

INDEX

INDEX

Sylvaner, 286-288

Talmage Ranch, 95
Tavel, 297, 299
Taylor, Jack, 47
Tchelistcheff, André, 25-26, 37, 39, 61, 72,
    172-175, 182, 200-202, 207, 225, 248,
    296, 310
temperature-controlled stainless steel fer-
    mentors, 36, 43, 45, 46, 51-52, 94,
    95, 109-110, 237, 256-257
Thée, Etienne, 100
Thomann, J., 54
Thomas Kruse Winery, 98-99, 115-116,
    195, 225, 228, 298, 299, 307
Thomas Vineyards, 147, 152
thompson seedless, 137-140
Tiburon Vintners, 73
Timothy, Brother, 29
Togni, Philip, 41, 44
ToKalon Vineyards, 62, 174
Travers, Bob, 47, 178, 245
Trefethen family, 60
Trefethen Vineyards, 22, 57, 60
Trentadue, Leo, 80, 183, 222, 283
Trentadue Winery and Vineyards, 80, 192,
    198, 230, 253, 265, 283, 292
Trinchero family, 54, 220
Tubbs, Alfred, 41
Tupper, Dr. Jack, 269

Uhlinger, Adam, 143
Ukiah Valley, 89, 184, 222-223
United Vintners, 16, 25, 30-32, 75-76, 96,
    124-130, 136, 137, 142, 227, 236

Vai family 152
Valley of the Moon, see Sonoma Valley
Van Löben Sels, Jean, 48
Van Löben Sels, Wilfred E., 33, 48-49,
    278, 279
Vandervoort, Henry, 79

Varietal Vintners, 116
varietal wines, 159-160
Veedercrest Vineyards, 60, 180
Venge, Nils, 60
Viano, Conrad, 193, 225, 235
Vignes, Jean Louis, 84, 149
Villa Armando Winery, 98-99, 116-117,
    168, 188, 193, 225, 235
Villa Mt. Eden Winery, 22, 60, 98-99, 114,
    123, 262
Viña Monterey, 107-108
Vineburg Winery, 82

Wagner, Charles, 58
Warm Springs Vineyard, 107
Webb, Bradford, 45, 87, 197, 243
Weibel Champagne Cellars, 92, 93, 96-99,
    107, 108, 188, 210, 224, 236, 255,
    265, 273, 290, 298, 304, 307-309
Weibel family, 108
Wente Brothers, 97-99, 108-110, 119, 121,
    193, 200, 208, 209, 223, 224, 236,
    242, 249-250, 263, 265, 272-273, 276,
    278-284, 294
Wente family, 53, 108-110, 201, 209, 244,
    249-250, 272, 280
Werner, Karl, 146
Wetmore, Charles, 93
White Pinot, see Chenin Blanc
white riesling, 112, 119, 121, 146, 148,
    163, 238, 266
    Napa Valley, 53, 61-63
    Sonoma County, 65, 73, 81
    statistics, 312
White Riesling, see Johannisberg Riesling
Williams, Brother, 116
Windsor Vineyards, 73
Wine Institute, 8, 30, 32, 55, 77, 88, 105,
    107, 149, 157, 173, 175, 218, 268,
    304
Winemasters Guild, 188, 255, 286, 293
Winiarski, Warren, 51-52, 60, 180, 269

Winkler, A. J., 257
Winkler-Scheid Vineyards, Inc., 134
Wittwer Winery, 257, 258
Wood, Laurie, 45
Woodside Winery, 98-99, 114, 255
work-core designs, 40-41, 74

York Mountain Winery, 117
Young, George, 21
Young's Market Company, 84
Yverdon Vineyards, 22, 54-55, 180, 191

Z-D Wines, 82, 90-91, 205-208, 247, 248,
    290
Zellerbach, Hannah, 87
Zellerbach, James D., 45, 57, 87, 88, 166,
    201, 205, 243, 247
Zepponi, Gino, 90, 206
zinfandel, 146, 148, 152, 165, 167, 170,
    177, 215
    Central Coast, 106, 112, 119, 122, 123
    Mendocino County, 94, 96, 222
    Napa Valley, 39, 40, 43, 52, 55, 62, 63
    San Joaquin Valley, 136, 143, 226
    Sonoma County, 79, 81, 86, 89, 220
    statistics, 311
Zinfandel, 15, 151, 167, 188, 195, 215-228
    Central Coast, 106, 112-116, 121, 223-
    225
    Late Harvest, 228
    Mendocino County, 92-94, 216, 222-
    223
    Napa Valley, 30, 37, 40-44, 47, 50, 54,
    216-220, 228
    Rosé, 299
    San Joaquin Valley, 133-135, 143, 226-
    227
    Sonoma County, 75, 78, 79, 84, 86, 91,
    216, 220-222
    white, 228